Second Edition

Speed Reading Naturally

LILLIAN P. WENICK
Cerritos College

D1568391

Prentice Hall, Englewood Cliffs, New Jersey 07632

Library of Congress Cataloging-in-Publication Data

WENICK, LILLIAN P.
   Speed reading naturally / Lillian P. Wenick.—2nd ed.
     p. cm.
   ISBN 0-13-833955-4
   1. Rapid reading. I. Title.
LB1050.54.W46   1990
428.4′3—dc20   89-48342

Editorial production/supervision: *Edith Riker/Sylvia Pafenyk*
Cover design: *Patricia Deevy*
Manufacturing buyer: *Ray Keating*

To
SYLVIA POMERANTZ
my mother

©1990, 1983 by Lillian P. Wenick

Printed in the United States of America

10 9 8 7 6 5 4 3 2 1

ISBN   0-13-833955-4

PRENTICE-HALL INTERNATIONAL (UK) LIMITED, LONDON
PRENTICE-HALL OF AUSTRALIA PTY. LIMITED, SYDNEY
PRENTICE-HALL CANADA INC., TORONTO
PRENTICE-HALL HISPANOAMERICANA, S.A., MEXICO
PRENTICE-HALL OF INDIA PRIVATE LIMITED, NEW DELHI
PRENTICE-HALL OF JAPAN, INC., TOKYO
SIMON & SCHUSTER ASIA PTE. LTD., SINGAPORE
EDITORA PRENTICE-HALL DO BRASIL, LTDA., RIO DE JANEIRO

Contents

Preface

The speed reading method presented in this book has now been used with exceptional success for over twenty years. It is based on established scientific information on how the brain and eyes function and on tested principles of learning. But this book goes beyond teaching an effective speed-reading method; it develops skills needed to become a more intelligent reader and a more accomplished student. These skills include speed-studying, speed researching, recognition of writing structures of fiction, and various types of non-fiction and critical reading.

This speed-reading method works because it follows a process that is natural for you, the way you were intended to read. It applies to reading abilities you already possess and use in doing other things. The process begins with teaching the eyes to make fewer eye stops and shortening the duration of each eye stop—changing an outmoded, lazy habit you acquired when you first learned to read. It gradually progresses to enlarging your focus of attention from one word to many words, to decreasing the amount of subvocalization you do while reading and increasing your visualization ability, to using flexibility in speed to adjust to the difficulty of the material and your purpose for reading it, to using knowledge of the way things are written to improve comprehension, to applying study techniques, research techniques and critical reading skills.

This edition makes significant changes. Because all the basic speed-reading techniques are so interdependent, they are here presented earlier and more clustered, rather than separately, so that you experience success quickly. The order in which the lessons are presented is improved; for instance, speed researching, which depends heavily on using skimming techniques, now directly follows the lesson on skimming. Critical reading skills and a method for using them with speed reading commands an entirely new and important chapter. The emphasis in the practice readings has been shifted to current non-fiction, and most of their topics deal with useful information that should help you improve yourself and your chances for success in school and in life.

Anyone who conscientiously applies the skills as given in this book, whether in a classroom or individually, will learn to read rapidly, efficiently, and intelligently.

Lillian P. Wenick

Acknowledgments

The author would like to express her thanks for kind permission to use the following materials:

Junius Adams, "Money: Our Most Intimate Relationship." Reprinted with permission of the author. Copyright © 1987 by the Hearst Corporation.

Kendra R. Bonnett, "Robots and Beyond: The Age of Intelligent Machines." Reprinted by permission of the author.

David Burner, Robert Marcus, and Emily Rosenberg, *America: A Portrait in History.* Vol. 2, Many Americans, © 1974, pp. 496–508. Reprinted by permission of Prentice Hall, Inc., Englewood Cliffs, New Jersey.

Michael Korda, "The Will to Win: How to Get It and Use It," *Glamour,* December, 1977. Reprinted with the author's permission.

Michael Murphy, "The Mysterious Powers of Body and Mind," *ESQUIRE,* May, 1986. Reprinted with permission of Esquire Associates.

Roy Rowan, "That Filing System Inside Your Head." Reprinted from the August 28 issue of *Fortune* magazine by special permission; © 1978 Time, Inc.

Sally Squires, "Visions to Boost Immunity," *American Health,* July/August, 1987. Reprinted with permission of American Health Partners.

Nancie B. Wenick, "The Anniversary." Printed with the author's permission.

Kim Wright Wiley, "Going for the Goal." Reprinted with permission from Weight Watchers ® Magazine, © 1988.

Kenneth L. Woodward, "You Know More Than You Think," *McCall's,* January, 1977. Reprinted with the author's permission.

Introduction to Speed-Reading Techniques

SOME ANSWERS TO QUESTIONS ABOUT SPEED READING

So you want to read faster! You've heard about some high-priced speed-reading courses that will teach you how to "read" a 500-page book in ten minutes. You are filled with the anticipation that some miracle will transform your 250 words per minute into an astronomical rate, but you secretly harbor doubts. You feel that you may not be "smart" enough or may not have whatever it takes to do it right—that somehow you will fail.

Let's set you straight now. You can learn to read faster. Whatever you can now understand reading at your present rate, you can read faster and still understand. If you can't understand it by reading slowly, reading faster won't help. But you have been reading something, and that something can be read faster. However, no miracles will occur. What will happen is that you will be instructed in how to acquire a new reading habit of moving your eyes faster and seeing more with each eye stop. You will have to practice this skill until you can do it well. Nothing will be done to you; you will have to work hard and be willing to try new ways of reading that will be unfamiliar and perhaps awkward at first. But if you are willing to go through these initial stages, you will definitely learn to read faster than you are now reading. That's a promise!

Do you have to be a genius or have some special abilities? No. The way you move your eyes in reading is a habit that has nothing to do with intelligence. You need no unusual abilities to learn to read faster. You will learn any skills you need through instruction and practice. The only abilities required are that you know how to read and that you have an average number of words in your reading vocabulary that you know by sight, without having to look them up, because rapid reading depends on rapid recognition of most of the words used. Many of the unfamiliar words you do encounter will not trouble you because their meanings will become clear to you by the way they are used in the writing. Since you have been reading for many years, you undoubtedly have an adequate sight vocabulary for the purpose of rapid reading. And the more you read, the more new words you will learn, and the larger your sight vocabulary will become.

How fast will you read when you have finished this book? I don't know. I do know that you will be reading faster, and more importantly, in a different manner. Now you probably are reading between 200 and 350 words per minute, and you probably read the comics and difficult scientific books all at the same habitual rate. When you have finished this book, you will read different materials at different rates, depending on the difficulty of the material and your purpose for reading. If you are reading an article in *Reader's Digest* just to get the main idea, you will read at your fastest rate. If you are reading a history textbook on which you will be tested, you will use a different, slower rate. You will also read it in a different manner, because you will have learned that history is organized in a particular way, and you will use that organization as an aid to reading it. In other words, you will have many rates for many purposes and uses. I cannot even tell you what your highest rate or your lowest rate will be. Each person is different, and people are constantly amazing me with what they can do. You *will* be reading considerably faster, but you'll have to wait to find out just how fast. I expect that you, too, will be amazed at your progress and your final rates.

What will happen to your comprehension? When your reading rate has increased remarkably, will you understand and retain the material? When you first begin to practice reading faster, your comprehension will temporarily drop significantly. In fact, during drills when you are training your eyes to move faster than they have ever moved before, you will probably understand very little of what you are reading. Luckily, this phase passes after a few weeks. Then, gradually, as your eyes become accustomed to seeing the print more rapidly, you will begin to understand more and more of what you are reading, as well as to remember what you have read. By the end of the book, your comprehension and retention of the written material should be equal to, or better than, the *level* at which you started, but with a much higher reading rate. You will also have an extra benefit: In the amount of time it used to take to read a chapter of a book once, you will be able to read it several times; and reading the same material several times will result in your getting more out of it than if you had read it only once.

So there you have it. You *can* read much faster. Your comprehension will be at least as good as it is now. You now possess all the abilities necessary to learn this method of rapid reading. All you have to do is follow the instructions, be willing to try a new way of reading, and practice, practice, practice until you can do it.

PREVIEW OF THIS SPEED-READING METHOD

Since most people feel more comfortable knowing what to expect, I will briefly explain the plan of study as it will be presented. At first, you will be given a short reading test to reveal your present rate of reading and level of comprehension. Then, the new training in speed reading will begin. This will consist of frequent eye-pacing drills to teach your eyes to move faster and see more with each movement. You will also begin to use a unique eye pacer, your hand, to help your eyes move in new patterns. Since you are unaccustomed to seeing your hand on the printed page, you may find it distracting at first; but with practice, in a short time the difficulty will be overcome, and this manner of reading will seem natural to you. During the extent of your study in this book, you will read many and varied materials as practice exercises. You will begin practicing on easy short stories and articles. As you improve in this method, the materials will increase in difficulty until you are reading college-level novels, articles, textbook excerpts, and informational materials of different types. Instructions on how to read these various types of materials will be presented as you need them. After each practice reading, you will answer a few questions on the material to assess your comprehension level for that exercise. On a special sheet called a Course Data Sheet, you will record your reading rate and comprehension score. In this way, you will be able to see your progress easily.

Since daily practice is needed for maximum improvement, and the number of selections that can be included in this book is limited, additional practice readings from outside sources will be required. The purpose is to provide reading material for practicing regularly the new rapid-reading skills you are learning. However, these outside readings should not burden you unduly because in a very short time you will be spending much less time on any reading that you normally do in the course of your work and pleasure, and this saved time will be greater than the time spent on your speed-reading practice.

The first part of your study will concentrate on learning this new speed-reading method until it becomes automatic, and your objective should be to use the techniques, always trying for greater speeds in reading and not worrying about comprehension. Learn the techniques first.

The second portion of your study will deal extensively with methods to improve your comprehension while retaining high reading rates, especially in studying, researching, and other high-level reading. Difficult college-level materials will provide abundant practice and reinforcement until you can read and comprehend virtually everything rapidly and effectively.

You will need certain materials. The Course Data Sheet, questions on reading selections, and all short reading selections are included in this book. You will need certain paperback books for practice reading, which may be obtained from any library or may be purchased (see Appendix page 251 for list). You will also need a book for drilling. It is not necessary to buy the drill book, as all libraries have books suitable for this purpose. Choose one that has large print, without too many pictures, and a fairly simply story to follow. A novel intended for junior high school students is ideal. If you don't know which books fall into that category, ask the librarian to point them out.

Specific detailed drills begin each instructional chapter. You should start each session with a drill, even if it is only a short warm-up drill; and once a week, your rate of drilling should be recorded on your Course Data Sheet. All the drills used, plus some additional ones, are printed in the Appendix for easy reference.

The instructions are presented in a sequence that experience has shown to be the most natural progression for most people. I recommend that you follow the order presented for optimum results.

The major techniques you will need to learn to read rapidly are set forth in this book, and with conscientious application, you can learn speed reading on your own. However, if you are fortunate enough to be using this book in a speed reading class, you should take advantage of the bonuses it offers by attending regularly. An instructor will be especially valuable to check that you are using the techniques correctly, to explain any aspects of the method that may not be perfectly clear, to answer questions, to provide additional information to help you overcome any special problems, and most of all, to provide the encouragement and motivation essential to your progress. In fact, you will undoubtedly find that your most significant improvement will be made in class; what you do on your own will primarily reinforce your in-class accomplishments.

Basically, that's the method. You move from easy to difficult materials. You constantly chart your progress. You work on the speed-reading techniques first and then on comprehension improvement. You do eye-pacing drills and some additional practice. You follow the instructions in sequence. No miracles are necessary; only a few short weeks of modest conscientious effort and you will achieve the prize of being able to read rapidly for the rest of your life.

Go to it!

RATE AND COMPREHENSION PRETEST

Directions: *In the space provided, record the times that you start and finish reading this article in hours, minutes, and seconds. Subtract your starting time from your finishing time to find your total.*

	Hours	*Minutes*	*Seconds*
Your finishing time:			
Your starting time:			*(subtract)*
Your total time:			

GETTING YOUR HEAD TOGETHER

Lillian P. Wenick

When the phrase "getting your head together" first came into popular usage by a generation fond of inventing its own language, some of us shrugged and passed it off as sloppy communication. How wrong we were! Lately scientists have been telling us about the split-brain theory, which does in fact show that we have a separated head, and that "getting it together" puts us in better harmony and peace with ourselves. For what some people intuitively felt was a pulling apart by two conflicting mental processes, science now gives logical reasons.

Just as we have two arms, legs, eyes, and ears, we have two brains. Recent scientific evidence reports that each side of the brain is like a separate brain, each having certain functions, and that they can work independently of each other or they can work together. When each side is going in a different thought direction we feel disjointed, out of sync, not "with it." Learning how to get both sides to go in the same thought direction really *is* "getting your head together."

Although the total average brain weighs only about three pounds, it is many times more complex than the most advanced computer. It has an electrical system and a chemical system. It contains billions of neurons. The right brain controls the motor and sensory operations of the left side of the body. The left brain controls the motor and sensory operations of the right side of the body. In addition, each side has specialized functions, and each operates on a different level of consciousness. The left brain is what we recognize as conscious thought; the right, unconscious thought. The two sides are two separate organs that are connected by a large mass of nerves capable of integrating the functions of the two brains.

The left brain is believed to be the dominant side and usually specializes in functions that require logical, sequential thought, such as reading, writing, and calculating. It proceeds in a step by-step manner. It is the rational brain. It probably gained the dominance it now possesses because early man needed these skills to search for clothing, shelter, safety, and food. The left brain is used primarily in the basic subjects taught in school. It is more readily measured by traditional intelligence tests. It is the more conscious part of the mind. We can tell someone what we are thinking in the left brain.

Left-brain problem solving moves in a systematic way: size up the situation, decide what the main problem is, organize a method of solution, devise step-by-step procedures to carry it out. Highly organized methodical solutions are left-brain solutions.

The right brain is believed to be less dominant and to specialize in functions that use intuition and spatial relationships such as in art, music, and meditation. It processes information all at once instead of step-by-step. It is more unconscious, more visual, and more creative. It is difficult to measure by traditional tests. Ordinary school subjects do not readily develop its functions.

Right-brain problem solving is intuitive and unsystematic, trying out one idea after another in a process of free association, or brainstorming. The thought process used usually cannot be explained in words—the solution just suddenly comes to mind. When we "sleep on a problem" and get up in the morning with new solutions, the right brain has been at work during the night.

What would "getting it together" entail and how would it be beneficial? All problems cannot be solved in a logical, sequential left-brain manner. The "creative leap" that seems to come from nowhere is the right-brain unconscious thinking. Reason (left brain) and intuition (right brain) working together express the whole self more accurately, widen the limits of self-experience, increase creativity and implementation of the creative impulses, put us in touch with our subconscious, and decrease inner conflicts.

Creative block results from conflict between the two brains. It is solved when both brains cooperate. Albert is an artist. Lately when he tries to paint he has difficulty; he just can't get it right and is not able to do much painting. He knows precisely what he wants to put on the canvas, but the painting is not turning out as he planned. He feels like he has lost control of the painting, as if the painting has a mind of its own. What is happening to Albert is that the creative, intuitive side of himself (right brain) is expressing itself and overriding the precise preconceived idea (left brain) of the painting. Albert is in conflict, which is shown by his "creative block." To unblock, Albert must listen to and accept both sides of his brain.

Outstanding creative thinking is possible when both sides of the brain work together. Einstein's famous theories of relativity came to him as a creative leap over what scientists "knew" to be true about the world. His ideas seem to violate common sense and what we can see and verify with our senses. Einstein's left-brain calculations working with his right-brain ability to process information as a whole resulted in his fantastic results, which logical tests have still not been able to prove definitively.

But how can we get these two brains "together" and reap these harmonious benefits for ourselves? Schooling and society stress reasoning and left-brain development. Both brains would work together more easily if the right, creative brain were equally as well-developed, and the pathways of communication between both brains got regular use. Certain activities strengthen the communication between the brains and improve our awareness of right-brain thoughts. A conscious effort to get a mental picture of ideas presented in written or spoken language uses both sides of the brain. Regular meditation, fantasies, verbal descriptions—these activities help to develop the communication.

Once the pathways of communication between the two brains are open and free and your intuitive brain messages pop into your mind regularly, you have to listen to them. You have to accept them and use them along with the logical, reasonable brain messages. When both are really a part of your conscious thinking and acting, you will have your head together!

Directions: *In the space provided at the beginning of this article, write the time you finished reading. Subtract your starting time from your finishing time to find how long it took you to read it. Then, look at the rate table (7) to find your reading rate.*
Your reading rate is_____

COMPREHENSION QUESTIONS

From memory, answer the following comprehension questions for this article.

_____ 1. In this article "getting your head together" refers to
  a. always relying on intuition.
  b. always relying on logic and reason.
  c. being part of the "in" culture.
  d. communication between the two sides of the brain.

_____ 2. Each side of the brain has
  a. identical functions.
  b. totally different functions.
  c. some similar functions and some specialized functions.
  d. a different shape.

_____ 3. Scientists believe that
  a. one side of the brain is dominant.
  b. neither side of the brain has dominance.
  c. brain dominance plays no part in the thought process.
  d. traditional schools develop dominance of both sides of the brain.

_____ 4. Which of the following groups describe brain functions that normally go together
  a. unconscious, logical, reasoning, creative?
  b. visual, conscious, systematic, free association?
  c. highly organized methodical, conscious, rational, systematic?
  d. brainstorming, highly organized, methodical, systematic?

_____ 5. For "creative block"
  a. there is no solution.
  b. the solution lies in better systematic planning.
  c. the best way to handle it is to ignore it.
  d. the best solution is to get both sides of the brain to cooperate.

_____ 6. This article proposes that
  a. all problems can be solved through reasoning.
  b. all problems can be solved through intuition.
  c. problem solving has nothing to do with either reasoning or intuition.
  d. sometimes reasoning is needed to solve a problem and sometimes intuition.

_____ 7. When the right and left brain work together
   a. the whole self is expressed more accurately.
   b. the mind is confused.
   c. inner conflicts result.
   d. creativity is decreased.

_____ 8. The phrase "getting your head together"
   a. is a translation of an old Greek saying.
   b. was coined by the young, modern generation.
   c. is part of an old proverb.
   d. was first used by scientists.

_____ 9. Some things you can do to get your head together are
   a. take courses in logic.
   b. study Einstein and other creative thinkers.
   c. practice visualizing ideas presented in words.
   d. practice taking I.Q. tests.

_____ 10. The main idea of this article could be stated as follows:
   a. Essentially, we have two brains that should be equally developed and the communication between them strengthened to express ourselves accurately and totally.
   b. Our two brains are separate for good reasons and integration would destroy creativity.
   c. The concept of two brains has been proven false and there is no need to do anything.
   d. Intuition is better than logic, and the part of the brain that governs intuition should be developed so that it is more dominant.

Directions: *Correct your answers by using the answer key on page 271. Allow 10 points for each correct answer.*

Your comprehension test score _____ %
Your reading rate (find on the Rate Table for Pretest) _____

Rate Table for Pretest

TIME Min.:Sec.	Rate	TIME Min.:Sec.	Rate	TIME Min.:Sec	Rate
1:00	—1200	4:30	—267	8:00	—150
1:10	—1000	4:40	—255	8:15	—146
1:20	— 923	4:50	—250	8:30	—141
1:30	— 800	5:00	—240	8:45	—138
1:40	— 706	5:10	—231	9:00	—133
1:50	— 667	5:20	—226	9:15	—130
2:00	— 600	5:30	—218	9:30	—126
2:10	— 545	5:40	—210	9:45	—124
2:20	— 522	5:50	—206	10:00	—120
2:30	— 480	6:00	—200	10:30	—114
2:40	— 444	6:10	—194	11:00	—109
2:50	— 428	6:20	—190	11:30	—104
3:00	— 400	6:30	—185	12:00	—100
3:10	— 375	6:40	—179	12:30	— 96
3:20	— 364	6:50	—176	13:00	— 92
3:30	— 343	7:00	—171	13:30	— 89
3:40	— 324	7:10	—167	14:00	— 86
3:50	— 316	7:20	—164	14:30	— 83
4:00	— 300	7:30	—160	15:00	— 80
4:10	— 286	7:40	—156	15:30	— 77
4:20	— 279	7:50	—154		

COURSE DATA SHEET 1

Cut out Course Data Sheet 1 in the Appendix, page 267. Fill in the information on the top line. On the second line write your beginning pretest reading rate for this article and your beginning pretest comprehension score.

Now that you know your present reading rate, what improvement would you like to make? What reading rate would make you happy or satisfied? Write this desired reading rate on the second line of your Course Data Sheet next to *Goal*. It is important that this goal is one you choose for yourself. It makes no difference what the "average" speed-reading rate may be or what goals others are choosing, or even whether or not your goal appears to be realistic. You must have a consciously chosen level of achievement toward which you strive; it says to you, "This may be possible for me." You will make it possible by choosing it. You may change your goal later if you make another choice of a level of achievement.

1

The Start toward a New Reading Method

Materials:
- Drill book
- Paper, pencil

Objectives:
- To teach your eyes to follow your hand-pacer
- To learn to move your eyes more rapidly
- To learn how to compute your reading and drill rates

In order to read rapidly, your eyes must move more rapidly over the printed material. Wanting your eyes to increase the speed of their movements, or even willing it, is just not enough. You have formed a strong habit of slow eye movements that you have been practicing for too many years to give up easily. Therefore, you need an aid, a moving object, that your eyes can follow, increasing in speed as the object is moved more rapidly. This moving object is called a pacer. You already own the ideal pacer—your hand. It is always with you; its speed can be varied instantaneously at your will (no machine settings to adjust); its pattern of movement can be changed and varied; it allows you to have your very own pacer so that you can proceed at your individual rate; and it's yours forever to use whenever you choose, at no cost to you whatsoever.

For the eye-pacing drills that follow, you will use your hand-pacer. You will also need a drill book (the junior high school novel described in the introduction). You may use the same drill book until you have finished it. Then you should get a new one of a similar level. In addition, you should have some scratch paper, a pencil or pen, and your Course Data Sheet 1, which you should have cut out of the Appendix after taking the pretest. (The Course Data Sheet 1 is on page 267.)

EYE-PACING DRILLS

You will have two objectives in this chapter. The first is to begin to teach your eyes to follow your hand, which will be used as a pacer. The second is to try to move your eyes more rapidly across the printed line. Although you must always try to read during all the eye exercises or you will teach your eyes nothing, you should not be concerned about your poor comprehension. You will work on comprehension later. At the beginning, getting your eyes to move more rapidly is the primary goal.

Now, open to the first page of the story in your drill book. Using your whole hand in a relaxed position, move your hand from left to right under each line as you try to read the line. Move your hand steadily without slowing down on any part. If you are right-handed, use your right hand. If you are left-handed, use your left hand. Remember, your objective is to move your eyes along the print, trying to keep up with your hand. You may not be able actually to read very much, if anything, when your eyes are moving faster than you are used to; but the only way to teach them to move faster is to practice moving fast until you can do it.

Move your hand under each line and try to read the line faster than you ever have before, continuing this drill for one minute. Begin to read (1 minute).

The minute is up. (If you are timing yourself at home, it is helpful to use a timer with a bell, such as a cooking timer.) Write down on a piece of paper anything you can remember from the reading. Write in key words and phrases, not sentences. Write names, places, what happened, what was described, and so on. This part of the method is intended to help you concentrate and retain what you've read—skills essential to rapid reading.

Naturally, you felt it awkward to use your hand. You probably found yourself looking at your hand more than at the print. You are not used to seeing your hand on the page, so it was distracting. With time, it will seem natural, and you will later marvel at how you ever read without your hand.

Were you able to read anything? If you were, be sure to go even faster next time. Did you remember anything to write down on your recall sheet? If you can't remember anything, guess. First of all, when you think you are guessing, you may not really be guessing, because you did see the material but just can't recall it. Second, if you guess, you will be looking to see if you were right when you go over the material the next time; and if you're looking for something, you're more apt to see it than if you're not looking.

Let's go back to the drill. You will do the same thing, using your hand as a pacer under each line, trying to read the line; but you will go faster and attempt to cover one-half page more than you did the last time in the same amount of time, one minute. Start at the beginning of the story. Begin to read (1 minute).

One minute is up. Add whatever you can to your recall sheet. Do not look back into the book for information. Guess if you have to.

In your anxiety to follow your hand with your eyes, some of you may be moving your whole head back and forth. This movement is understandable, but unfortunately the movement makes it more difficult to read. As an experiment, without using your hand, try to read while you move your head back and forth. It is difficult to read, isn't it? So try to keep your head still. Move only your eyes and your hand.

You will do the same thing again with a slight modification. This time start your hand and eyes one-half inch in from the beginning of the line of print, and end one-half inch before the end of the line. Look at this example:

Between us there was the bond of the sea.

(½″) (hand follows this line) (½″)

You can do this because your eyes have marvelous abilities. When you look at a letter or word, your eyes actually see all the area surrounding it. In the example above, if you look at the *en* at the end of the word *between*, you see the whole word; and when you look at the last *the*, you also see the word *sea*. So you won't be missing anything by excluding the edges of the printed page. In fact, the empty space of the margins often takes up as much as one-third of the printed page. By keeping your eyes well into the print at all times and off the blank margins, you will automatically increase your reading speed by one-third—your eyes will have that much less to cover.

Go back to the beginning of the story you are using for drill. This time, starting one-half inch in, use your hand under each line; end each line one-half inch from the end of the print; keep your head still; move your eyes and hand only. Go over all the material you read the first time plus the half-page you added, but this time add another half-page—all in the same one minute. You must move your eyes and hand faster than the previous times. If you guessed in writing your recall information last time, this time particularly look to see if you were right. Begin to read (1 minute).

Your minute is up. Again, add what you can to your recall sheet. Guess if you can't remember.

Before taking a drill rate, you may wish to repeat the last one-minute drill for more practice. If you do, add another half-page and follow the preceding instructions.

TAKING A DRILL RATE

It is important to keep track of how fast you are drilling. This information will tell you whether or not you are actually pacing your eyes to move faster. It will also show if you have reached the point of letting go of your old word-by-word reading and started to read for ideas instead of words. This drill rate should be taken and recorded on your Course Data Sheet weekly. Later, after you have had an opportunity to read, not drill, a comparison of your drill rates with your reading rates will reveal certain problems that you may have, which can be corrected easily. This topic will be discussed more thoroughly in a later chapter.

Turn to new material in the same drill book. Either begin on a new page or a new chapter. Write down the page number on which you are starting so that you can find it later. You are going to take a drill rate. That is, you will move your eyes and your hand as rapidly and in the same manner as you have been practicing; after one minute, you will tell someone what you remember or what you think the story is about. Then you will figure out how fast you drilled and record this rate on your Course Data Sheet as your drill rate for this week. Remember to move along the printed line smoothly, following your hand, and without going back, no matter how poor your comprehension is. Begin one-half inch from the left edge of the print, and end one-half inch before the right edge. This is still a drill, the object of which is to learn how to teach your eyes to move faster and to follow your hand. This is not really reading for comprehension. Begin (1 minute).

The minute is up. Write down the page number where you finished. Find a partner and tell each other what you think you read, or speak aloud to yourself. Guess if you don't remember.

Before you compute your rates, you will have an opportunity to verify the story you just told your partner or yourself. That is, you will reread that part of the story that you just drilled. This time, still using your hand, you will slow down as much as you have to in order to understand what you are reading. The purpose of this step is to see how much of the actual story you understood when you drilled rapidly.

Now go back to the beginning of the part of the story you just read (you should have written down the page number). You will have two minutes to read this same section more slowly. You may not finish, but you will have time to read enough to determine whether or not you understood it the first time. Begin to read (2 minutes).

Time is up. Are you surprised to find that you did understand more than you thought you had? However, if this slower reading revealed a totally different story from the previous rapid reading, don't be discouraged. It will all come in time and with more practice.

How to Compute Reading and Drill Rates

Whenever you need to figure out your rate of reading—the number of words you read per minute—in material that does not inform you of the total number of words in the selection, you will want to use the following instructions.

To compute your drill rate, the very rapid rate at which you went over this last section in your book, follow the steps listed here.

To figure the number of words on a page:

1. Choose any full page in the book. That is, it should have print from the top margin to the bottom margin, with no pictures.
2. On this page, choose three full lines, lines that begin at the left margin and end at the right margin.
3. Count all the words in these lines, including the tiny words like *I* and *the*.
4. Divide the total number of words in these lines by three to get the average number of words in one line.
5. Count all the lines on the full page. Include every line even if it only contains one word.
6. Multiply the total number of lines on the page (number 5) by the average number of words in a line (number 4) to get the approximate number of words on a page in that book.

To figure your number of words per minute:

1. Count the number of pages you drilled. If you ended somewhere other than at the bottom of a page, approximate how much of the page you read, one-half, one-third, and so on.
2. Multiply the number of pages you read by the number of words on a page to get the number of words you read. Since you read all these words in one minute, that figure is your rate, or words per minute. For example, if your book has 162 words on each page and you covered 2½ pages, your drill rate would be 405 words per minute:

162 (words) $\times$ 2½ (pages) = 405 words per minute

Write this computed drill rate on your Course Data Sheet in the column headed *Drill Rate*.

This drill rate should be considerably higher than your reading rate for the pretest. If it isn't, consciously decide to allow yourself to let go of your old reading habit and to move your eyes faster in the next drills. You can do it if you just let it happen.

Here's an example of the technique:

Count words in
3 full lines (26
words)

Divide by 3. (26
÷ 3 = approxi-
mately 9)

There are 9
words per line
on this page

Count all lines
on this page
(18 lines)

> sir. Tod, rush these things through, and send them
> to the gentleman's address without any waste of
> time. Let the minor customers wait. Set down the
> gentlemen's address and—"
>   "I'm changing my quarters. I will drop in and
> leave the new address."
>   "Quite right, sir, quite right. One moment—let
> me show you out, sir. There—good day, sir, good
> day."
>   Well, don't you see what was bound to happen?
> I drifted naturally into buying whatever I wanted,
> and asking for change. Within a week I was sump-
> tuously equipped with all needful comforts and
> luxuries, and was housed in an expensive private
> hotel in Hanover Square. I took my dinners there,
> but for breakfast I stuck by Harris's humble
> feeding-house, where I had got my first meal on
> my mil

9(words per line) × 18(lines per page) = 162 words per page. There are approximately 162 words on each page of this sample book.

SUMMARY

The first step in this new rapid-reading method is to use your hand as a pacer under each line of print. You start your hand and eyes one-half inch in from the left margin and end one-half inch before the right margin. Your eyes should follow your hand-pacer and speed up as you move your hand more rapidly.

The eye-pacing drills, which you will do at each session, will teach your eyes to move faster and to see more with each movement.

Your drill rate should be taken each week as a measure of your progress in learning to pace your eyes.

2

More Rapid-Reading Techniques

Materials:
- Drill book
- Readings:
  "The Anniversary"
  "To Build a Fire"

Objectives:
- To reinforce your skill of using your hand as a pacer
- To learn how to change the eye-pacing speed from a drill rate to a reading rate without slowing down to your old habitual slow rate
- To begin the habit of previewing
- To learn a method for computing your reading rate
- To learn to turn the pages properly for increased ease and speed
- To learn a simple modification of the hand movement

EYE-PACING DRILLS

Since improvement in eye-pacing is a continuous process, each session must start with an eye-pacing drill.

Open your drill book to where you finished last time. (The drill book is the easy junior high school-level novel.) You will go as rapidly as you can for one minute, moving your hand under each line smoothly and at a constant speed. As you do this, you will move your eyes along the print at the same rate as your hand and try to read. Your eyes and hand will start each line one-half inch in from the beginning of the line and end one-half inch in from the end of the line. Your head will remain still. Begin to read (1 minute). Stop. Write down what you can remember, using key words and phrases only. Guess if you can't remember.

MODIFICATION OF THE HAND MOVEMENT

This modification is very slight but important to your progress. Still going under each line, excluding one-half inch at the beginning and end of each line, you will not take your hand off the page at the end of the line but rather curve it around, keeping it on the page, bringing it way over to the left to be ready to go under the next line:

The next two hours flew by quickly. She was busy looking everywhere in the stores.

Practice this movement for a few minutes until you feel that you have it right.

This time use the modification of the hand movement that you just learned through the drill practice. Keep your hand on the page and curve it around under each line. Add one-half page, or one whole page if you feel you can, to what you just read. This time, push yourself to go faster so that you will finish all the material. Remember not to move your head. If you are in a class, the instructor will tell you when you have only ten seconds left before time is called. If you are not close to the end, speed up so that you will finish.

Back to the beginning. Begin to read (10 seconds . . . 1 minute). Stop. Add what you can to your recall sheet.

PAGE TURNING

As you increase your drilling and reading speeds, the way that you move your hand and turn pages becomes more important. Now you will learn how to turn pages so that your hand movement is not disturbed or slowed down by this necessary operation.

If you are using your right hand for reading, curve your left arm over the top of the book with your arm resting on the book, but in such a way that you do not cover any of the print. With your left hand reaching to the top right edge of the book, separate the pages between your left thumb and index finger in preparation for turning (Figure 2-1). Turn the page. Immediately reposition your arm and hand and begin to separate the next page so that you will be ready to turn it when you need to. Practice this movement for a few pages. Adjust your position and the book for comfort.

Figure 2-1   Page turning with the left hand

If you are using your left hand for reading, use your right hand to separate and turn pages, still at the upper right corner of the book. Experiment to find the best position for you.

Did you finish all the material in this last drill? If you did, add another whole page this time. If you didn't, add only one-half page (in addition to the half page you added before). Decide that you are going to reach this new goal no matter how fast you have to go, even if you understand absolutely nothing. The objective is just to get your eyes moving. Use the new modified curved hand movement. Turn the pages properly.

Once more, go back to the beginning. Begin to read (10 seconds . . . 1 minute). Stop, and add to your recall sheet.

If you have not taken a drill rate this week, do so now. Refer to "Taking a Drill Rate" instructions given in Chapter 1.

PREVIEWING A SHORT STORY

It is important to preview all reading material before you begin to read. There are many methods of how to study; but no matter how varied they may be, they all agree that previewing is essential, whether you are reading at your old slow rate or your new faster rate. However, in rapid reading, previewing is even more important because you must be able to get into the material right at the beginning or you will find yourself halfway through before you have any idea of what it is about.

Previewing is a fast, simple way to find out certain important information about the material you are going to read, to help you channel your thoughts and focus your attention and enable you to get an idea of what type of information you need to retain.

At this time we will discuss a simple form of previewing a short story. In other chapters you will be instructed in more thorough methods of previewing short stories and other types of materials.

You will use these instructions to preview the short story "The Anniversary" on page 17.

1. Look at the title of the story. What is the story going to be about? Titles are usually chosen by the author to point up an important idea that the story illustrates. "The Anniversary" tells you that some event that occurred on the same date in an earlier year is important. Anniversaries are often celebrated. Will this be a celebration? If so, of what event? Why is this anniversary special enough for a story to be written about it?

2. If there is a picture, look at it. What does it tell you about the story? This story has no picture. However, when there is an accompanying picture, ask yourself questions about the people and things illustrated. What are the people doing? How do they look? What are they wearing? Can you get a hint of the relationship between them? What do their financial circumstances seem to be?

    So far, you haven't read a word of the story, yet you know a great deal about it and are probably curious to know more. You are beginning to channel your thoughts and focus on the story.

3. Now, as a preview, you will go through the story at a very rapid rate, a rate almost as fast as you have been drilling. You will look for the names of the main characters (you can tell

who they are because their names will be seen more frequently than the names of the minor characters), where the story takes place, when the story takes place, and the general sequence of events. Since this will be your first experience with rapid previewing, you will only be expected to see the names of the major characters. Gradually, with more practice, you will be able to see the where, when, and what of the story, too.

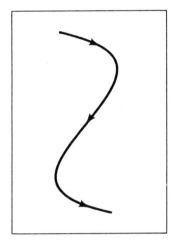

Figure 2-2

For this rapid preview, use your whole hand in a relaxed position and swoop down each page, trying to have your eyes follow your hand (as shown in Figure 2-2). If you are in a class, as your instructor says "page," you will swoop down the next page, and so on until you have completed previewing the entire story.

Start on the first page of the story and begin swooping when your instructor tells you to begin. Go to the next page when "page" is called. If you are doing this at home by yourself, allow about three seconds per page. Begin. Page (three seconds). Page (three seconds). Page (three seconds) and so on.

Stop. Can you name the main characters? Take a guess at where you think the story takes place. Guess when you think the story takes place.

SPEED READING A SHORT STORY

You are now ready to speed-read "The Anniversary." Remember that the purpose for reading it is to practice what you have been learning. The story chosen for this practice is not difficult because, until you are better at using your new skills, it is

wise to practice on material that you may be able to understand easily. However, you may still be distracted by your hand on the page and the pressure of trying to move your eyes rapidly. Get what you can out of the story, and don't worry if you don't get all the details. Practicing the technique is still the most important goal.

In this story, move your hand under each line, curving around between the lines, turning the pages with your free hand. Move rapidly and smoothly as you did in the drills, but do not go as fast. Try to pace yourself at about one-half to three-fourths the speed of your drill rate. Before you begin, read all the instructions, and then follow each instruction in the order given.

1. Record your starting time in hours, minutes, and seconds. If you are reading a story at home, plan to start about forty-five seconds later than the time you look at the clock. Write down your planned starting time; when the clock reaches the time you have written down, begin.
2. While you are waiting for the clock to reach the starting time, clear your mind of any outside thoughts.
3. Focus your attention on the story. Think about the information you learned in your preview and any questions that may have arisen.
4. Read the story through to the end. Do not go back over anything you think you missed. Keep moving ahead. Use your hand as a pacer, as you have been practicing.
5. As soon as you have finished, write down your finishing time in hours, minutes, and seconds.
6. Answer the questions at the end of the story immediately, while the story is fresh in your mind. Guess any answers you don't know. Use your first guess; it is likely to be the most accurate.
7. Turn to the answer key on page 271. Correct your answers. Each answer is worth ten points. Score your answer sheet. (Answer keys are provided in the Appendix for all comprehension questions in this book.)
8. Compute your reading rate. Detailed instructions are given below.
9. On your Course Data Sheet next to the title of the story, record your reading rate, and your comprehension score.
10. Discuss the story in class or verify your knowledge of the story by rereading it more slowly, but still use your hand.

Computing Your Reading Rate

1. To find how long it took you to read the story, subtract the starting time from the finishing time. For example:

	Hour	*Minutes*	*Seconds*
		60	
	12:	~~0~~	80(60 + 20)
Finishing time	~~1~~	~~01~~:	~~20~~
Starting time	12:	59:	50
Your time		1:	30

Notice that when you have to borrow, you must borrow 60 because there are 60 seconds in a minute and 60 minutes in an hour.

2. Since you cannot use two different kinds of units (minutes and seconds) in mathematical computations, you must convert the seconds to minutes by using the table on the back of your Course Data Sheet or in the Appendix on page 269. In the table, look at the *Seconds* column to find the number of seconds in your time (round off seconds to fit the table). Then look across to the next column to find out how many tenths of a minute your figure equals.

   Example: If your time was 1 minute and 30 seconds, the converted time in minutes would be 1 minute and 0.5 (five-tenths) of a minute or 1.5 minutes.

3. Divide your converted time into the total number of words in the story. This number is found at the end of the questions. For example:

$$
\begin{array}{r}
573 \text{ your rate (WPM)} \\
\text{your time } 1.5 \overline{)\, 860.0 \text{ words in the story}} \\
75 \\
\hline
110 \\
105 \\
\hline
50 \\
45 \\
\hline
5 \\
\end{array}
$$

Notice that in the preceding example you have to get rid of the decimal by moving it one place to the right, making your time 15. Whatever you do on one side of the division, you must also do on the other side. Since every whole number really has a decimal point at the end, you move it one place to the right by adding a zero: 860 becomes 8600. If you have a remainder, forget about it.

Now that you know your reading rate and comprehension score, record them on your Course Data Sheet.

Evaluation

After each reading, it is a good idea to evaluate what you are doing and to set a goal for your next reading or drill exercise. To do this, compare this reading rate with your drill rate. If it is approximately one-half to three-fourths of the drill rate, you did very well. If it is as great or greater than your drill rate, you need to drill faster. If your comprehension score is 90 percent or 100 percent, you could have read the story more rapidly. If your reading rate is very high but your comprehension score is less than 50 percent, you need to speed up in your drills but slow down slightly in reading the short stories. Take a minute to do this evaluation and consciously decide what you will strive for next time. Will you drill faster? Will you read faster? More slowly? What will be your goal next time?

Now repeat the entire speed-reading process for additional practice when you read the story, "To Build a Fire" on page 20. First, review the instruction sections in this chapter: "Speed Reading a Short Story," "Computing Your Reading Rate," and "Evaluation." Follow all of the instructions as you read "To Build a Fire." (Before you begin, recall what you decided you needed to do in the next story reading after you evaluated the last reading. Do you need to speed up or slow down?)

SUMMARY

In this chapter you learned how to turn the pages with the hand you are not using for pacing your reading, to keep your pacing hand on the print at all times by curving around after each line, and to evaluate your reading and drilling rates so that you will know what to work toward in your practice drilling and reading.

In using the basic rapid-reading method for short stories, you should

1. Preview the story by finding out as much as you can from the title and the picture; then go over each page very rapidly for the names of the characters, where and when the story takes place, and a sense of the general sequence of events.
2. Read by slowing down from your drill rate so that you can follow the story, but do not slow down any more than is absolutely necessary.

THE ANNIVERSARY

Nancie Wenick

"Good morning, Jennifer," Jason Maxwell whispered as he dutifully kissed his wife lightly on the forehead.

"Darling! How lovely; you've brought breakfast in. Where's Emily this morning?"

"I've given the servants the day off so that we could spend our anniversary alone." Jason exited to the terrace and set down the culinary delight he had prepared for the pleasure of his bride of two years. Pleasing Jennifer had become a habit he had grown to resent.

Jennifer eyed him lovingly, appreciating how happy she had become since her marriage to Jason. Three years ago, when Jennifer Macy's father died, the problems confronting her seemed insurmountable. She had always been helplessly frail and dependent upon her father's care. At 42, she had never done a day's work in her life, and suddenly she had the monumental responsibility of managing the family's nationwide chain of department stores. Thanks to the bright, capable young psychiatrist who counseled her through those difficult times, the business was doing better than ever.

Many of Jennifer's friends were skeptical when she announced her marriage to that bewitching chestnut-haired Adonis of New York's psychiatric circles, eleven years her junior; but now they could see that Jason seemed indeed the model husband. Jennifer had never been happier and could not imagine her life without Jason.

"I've made your favorite breakfast, Jen. Blueberry waffles with fresh blueberries and whipped cream," Jason boasted as he poured them each a glass of Dom Perignon.

"Oh, Jason," Jennifer whined. "That's not enough champagne. Please, darling. Fill my glass." Jennifer always wanted the most and best of everything, and she had become accustomed to getting it. Jason, in turn, had become accustomed to satisfying her whims.

As he handed Jennifer her glass, Jason settled next to her on the bed and masked his contemptuous thoughts with an adoring gaze. He had become quite adept at feigning adoration in the two years he had been tied to the pitiful creature he called his wife. He supposed that some men might find her stately manner and sleek lines moderately attractive, but all he could see was the fading remnant of a woman, declining with each passing year. It had become increasingly difficult for him to camouflage the revulsion he felt whenever he saw this drab, meagerly endowed woman, completely insubstantial and deficient when compared with the youthful beauty and vitality of Rachel, the lover with whom he sought refuge from the charade he called his marriage.

Jason had grown to despise Jennifer's childlike dependency and the energy he had to expend toward a relationship which meant nothing to him. The only thing which had any meaning for Jason was the Macy fortune, a fortune that was no longer worth the sacrifices it entailed. Jason had merely been biding his time until he could arrange for Jennifer's premature demise.

After months of careful preparation, he was finally ready to execute his plan as part of this anniversary celebration. It had not been easy to come up with the proper weapon for Jennifer's elimination from Jason's life, but after repeated experimentation in his basement laboratory, Jason had finally concocted the perfect poison: Artre-pomine. This chemical mixture could easily be concealed in Jennifer's food, would cause her to have an apparently natural heart attack, and would remain undetectable in her body after death. The plan was so brilliantly conceived that Jason smiled with self-satisfaction. His extensive medical training was not in vain.

"What are you smiling about, darling?" Jennifer inquired.

"I'm just happy about the prospect of being alone with you all day," was Jason's obligatory response. "Let's go out on the terrace and have breakfast," he remarked anxiously.

As they enjoyed another glass of champagne, Jason lavished blueberries and whipped cream on the waffles, being careful to place the waffle with the extra ingredient in front of Jennifer.

"This looks scrumptuous." Jennifer was brimming with delight at the sight and smell of her favorite breakfast. "Oh Jason. This is all so perfect. You're such a wonderful husband and I'm such a lucky woman."

This touching scene was abruptly interrupted

when the phone rang. "I'll get it, Jen. You sit and enjoy your waffle."

Jason hurried to answer the telephone, annoyed that Rachel was calling so early. When he returned he found Jennifer savoring the last bite of her waffle. He poured her another glass of champagne and sat back in his chair with a sigh of relief as he ate his waffle and awaited the inevitable. As he finished his breakfast, he watched Jennifer impatiently. Jennifer looked back at him with the face of a mischievous child and said, "I have a confession to make, Jason. You know how much I love whipped cream; and since your waffle had more whipped cream than mine, I traded. I hope you don't mind, darling."

COMPREHENSION QUESTIONS

_____ 1. Jason's profession was that of a
    a. banker.
    b. psychiatrist.
    c. stock broker.
    d. lawyer.

_____ 2. The relationship between Jennifer and Jason was one of
    a. mutual love.
    b. mutual hate.
    c. Jennifer loving, Jason hating.
    d. Jason loving, Jennifer hating.

_____ 3. Jason planned to kill Jennifer by
    a. poison.
    b. shooting.
    c. strangulation.
    d. pushing her off the balcony.

_____ 4. The story takes place in the
    a. morning.
    b. afternoon.
    c. evening.
    d. night.

_____ 5. Jason had married Jennifer because she was:
    a. beautiful.
    b. rich.
    c. intelligent.
    d. popular in high social circles.

_____ 6. As a person, Jennifer was
    a. independent.
    b. used to hardships.
    c. ill-tempered.
    d. dependent.

_____ 7. The breakfast consisted of
   a. bacon and eggs.
   b. pancakes and syrup.
   c. waffles, whipped cream, and blueberries.
   d. French toast, whipped cream, and strawberries.

_____ 8. The anniversary was their
   a. first.
   b. second.
   c. third.
   d. fifth.

_____ 9. Jason is described as being
   a. average-looking
   b. ugly.
   c. very handsome.
   d. very old.

_____ 10. We can infer* that in the end
   a. Jennifer would die.
   b. Jason would die.
   c. neither would die.
   d. both would die.

Allow 10 points per correct answer.   Your score _____ %
Number of words: 860   Your rate _____
Answer key is on page 271.
Record your rate and your comprehension score on your Course Data Sheet.

Infer means to come to a logical conclusion, decision, or opinion through reasoning and by using the facts and information available (in this case, those given in the story).

TO BUILD A FIRE

Jack London

For land travel or seafaring, the world over, a companion is usually considered desirable. In the Klondike, as Tom Vincent found out, such a companion is absolutely essential. But he found it out, not by precept, but through bitter experience.

"Never travel alone," is a precept of the north. He had heard it many times and laughed; for he was a strapping young fellow, big-boned and big-muscled, with faith in himself and in the strength of his head and hands.

It was on a bleak January day when the experience came that taught him respect for the frost, and for the wisdom of the men who had battled with it.

He had left Calumet Camp on the Yukon with

a light pack on his back, to go up Paul Creek to the divide between it and Cherry Creek, where his party was prospecting and hunting moose.

The frost was sixty degrees below zero, and he had thirty miles of lonely trail to cover, but he did not mind. In fact, he enjoyed it, swinging along through the silence, his blood pounding warmly through veins, and his mind carefree and happy. For he and his comrades were certain they had struck "pay" up there on the Cherry Creek Divide; and, further, he was returning to them from Dawson with cheery home letters from the States.

At seven o'clock, when he turned the heels of his moccasins toward Calumet Camp, it was still black night. And when day broke at half past nine he had made the four-mile cut-off across the flats and was six miles up Paul Creek. The trail, which had seen little travel, followed the bed of the creek, and there was no possibility of his getting lost. He had gone to Dawson by way of Cherry Creek and Indian River, so Paul Creek was new and strange. By half past eleven he was at the forks, which had been described to him, and he knew he had covered fifteen miles, half the distance. He knew that in the nature of things the trail was bound to grow worse from there on, and thought that, considering the good time he had made, he merited lunch. Casting off his pack and taking a seat on a fallen tree, he unmittened his right hand, reached inside his shirt next to the skin, and fished out a couple of biscuits sandwiched with sliced bacon and wrapped in a handkerchief—the only way they could be carried without freezing solid.

He had barely chewed the first mouthful when numbing fingers warned him to put his mittens on again. This he did, not without surprise at the bitter swiftness with which the frost bit in. Undoubtedly it was the coldest snap he had ever experienced, he thought.

He spat upon the snow—a favorite northland trick—and the sharp crackle of the instantly congealed spittle startled him. The spirit thermometer at Calumet had registered sixty below when he left, but he was certain it had grown much colder, how much colder he could not imagine.

Half of the first biscuit was yet untouched, but he could feel himself beginning to chill—a thing most unusual for him. This would never do, he decided, and slipping the packstraps across his shoulders, he leaped to his feet and ran briskly up the trail.

A few minutes of this made him warm again, and he settled down to a steady stride, munching the biscuits as he went along. The moisture that exhaled with his breath crusted his lips and mustache with pendent ice and formed a miniature glacier on his chin. Now and again sensation forsook his nose and cheeks, and he rubbed them till they burned with the returning blood.

Most men wore nose-straps; his partners did, but he had scorned such "feminine contraptions," and till now had never felt the need of them. Now he did feel the need, for he was rubbing constantly.

Nevertheless he was aware of a thrill of joy, of exultation. He was doing something, achieving something, mastering the elements. Once he laughed aloud in sheer strength of life, and with his clenched fist defied the frost. He was its master. What he did he did in spite of it. It could not stop him. He was going to the Cherry Creek Divide.

Strong as were the elements, he was stronger. At such times animals crawled away into their holes and remained in hiding. But he did not hide. He was out in it, facing it, fighting it. He was a man, a master of things.

In such fashion, rejoicing proudly, he tramped on. After an hour he rounded a bend, where the creek ran close to the mountainside, and came upon one of the most insignificant-appearing but most formidable dangers in northern travel.

The creek itself was frozen solid to its rocky bottom, but from the mountain came the outflow of several springs. These springs never froze, and the only effect of the severest cold snaps was to lessen their discharge. Protected from the frost by the blanket of snow, the water of these springs seeped down into the creek and, on top of the creek ice, formed shallow pools.

The surface of these pools, in turn, took on a skin of ice which grew thicker and thicker, until the water overran, and so formed a second ice-skinned pool above the first.

Thus at the bottom was the solid creek ice, then probably six to eight inches of water, then the thin ice-skin, then another six inches of water and another ice-skin. And on top of this last skin was about an inch of recent snow to make the trap complete.

To Tom Vincent's eye the unbroken snow surface gave no warning of the lurking danger. As the crust was thicker at the edge, he was well toward the middle before he broke through.

In itself it was a very insignificant mishap—a man does not drown in twelve inches of water—but in its consequences as serious an accident as could possibly befall him.

At the instant he broke through he felt the cold water strike his feet and ankles, and with half a dozen lunges he made the bank. He was quite cool and collected. The thing to do, and the only thing to do, was to build a fire. For another precept of the north runs: Travel with wet socks down to twenty below zero; after that build a fire. And it was three times twenty below and colder, and he knew it.

He knew further, that great care must be exercised; that with failure at the first attempt, the chance was made greater for failure at the second attempt. In short, he knew that there must be no failure. The moment before a strong, exulting man, boastful of his mastery of the elements, he was now fighting for his life against those same elements—such was the difference caused by the injection of a quart of water into a northland traveller's calculations.

In a clump of pines on the rim of the bank the spring high-water had lodged many twigs and small branches. Thoroughly dried by the summer sun, they now waited the match.

It is impossible to build a fire with heavy Alaskan mittens on one's hands, so Vincent bared his, gathered a sufficient number of twigs, and knocking the snow from them, knelt down to kindle his fire. From an inside pocket he drew out his matches and a strip of thin birch bark. The matches were of the Klondike kind, sulphur matches, one hundred in a bunch.

He noticed how quickly his fingers had chilled as he separated one match from the bunch and scratched it on his trousers. The birch bark, like the dryest of paper, burst into bright flame. This he carefully fed with the smallest twigs and finest debris, cherishing the flame with the utmost care. It did not do to hurry things, as he well knew, and although his fingers were now quite stiff, he did not hurry.

After the first quick, biting sensation of cold, his feet had ached with a heavy, dull ache and were rapidly growing numb. But the fire, although a very young one, was now a success; he knew that a little snow, briskly rubbed, would speedily cure his feet.

But the moment he was adding the first thick twigs to the fire a grievous thing happened. The pine boughs above his head were burdened with a four months' snowfall, and so finely adjusted were the burdens that his slight movement in collecting the twigs had been sufficient to disturb the balance.

The snow from the topmost bough was the first to fall, striking and dislodging the snow on the boughs beneath. And all the snow, accumulating as it fell, smote Tom Vincent's head and shoulders and blotted out his fire.

He still kept his presence of mind, for he knew how great his danger was. He started at once to rebuild the fire, but his fingers were now so numb that he could not bend them, and he was forced to pick up each twig and splinter between the tips of the fingers of either hand.

When he came to the match he encountered great difficulty in separating one from the bunch. This he succeeded in managing, however, and also, by great effort, in clutching the match between this thumb and forefinger. But in scratching it, he dropped it in the snow and could not pick it up again.

He stood up, desperate. He could not feel even his weight on his feet, although the ankles were aching painfully. Putting on his mittens, he stepped to one side, so that the snow would not fall upon the new fire he was to build, and beat his hands violently against the tree-trunk.

This enabled him to separate and strike a second match and to set fire to the remaining fragment of birch bark. But his body had now begun to chill and he was shivering, so that when he tried to add the first twigs his hand shook and the tiny flame was put out.

The frost had beaten him. His hands were worthless. But he had the foresight to drop the bunch of matches into his wide-mouthed outside pocket before he slipped on his mittens in despair, and started to run up the trail. One cannot run the frost out of wet feet at sixty below and colder, however, as he quickly discovered.

He came round a sharp turn of the creek to where he could look ahead for a mile. But there was no help, no sign of help, only the white trees and the white hills, and the quiet cold and the brazen silence! If only he had a comrade whose feet were not freezing, he thought, only such a comrade to start the fire that could save him!

Then his eyes chanced upon another high-water lodgment of twigs and branches. If he could strike a match, all might yet be well. With stiff fingers which he could not bend, he got out a bunch of matches, but found it impossible to separate them.

He sat down and awkwardly shuffled the bunch about on his knees, until he got it resting on his palm with the sulphur ends projecting, somewhat in the manner of the blade of a hunting-knife would project when clutched in the fist.

But his fingers stood straight out. They could not clutch. This he overcame by pressing the wrist of the other hand against them, and so forcing them down upon the bunch. Time and again, holding thus by both hands, he scratched the bunch on his leg and finally ignited it. But the flame burned into the flesh of his hand, and he involuntarily relaxed his hold. The bunch fell into the snow, and while he tried vainly to pick it up, sizzled and went out.

Again he ran, by this time badly frightened. His feet were utterly without sensation. He stubbed his toes once on a buried log, but beyond pitching him into the snow and wrenching his back, it gave him no feelings.

His fingers were helpless and his wrists were beginning to grow numb. His nose and cheeks he knew were frozen, but they did not count. It was his feet and hands that were to save him, if he was to be saved.

He recollected being told of a camp of moose-hunters somewhere above the forks of Paul Creek. He must be somewhere near it, he thought, and if he could find it he yet might be saved. Five minutes later he came upon it, lone and deserted, with drifter snow sprinkled inside the pine-bough shelter in which the hunters had slept. He sank down, sobbing. All was over, and in an hour at the best, in that terrific temperature, he would be an icy corpse.

But the love of life was strong in him, and he sprang again to his feet. He was thinking quickly. What if the matches did burn his hands? Burned hands were better than dead hands. No hands at all were better than death. He stumbled along the trail until he came upon another high-water lodgment. There were twigs and branches, leaves and grasses, all dry and waiting the fire.

Again he sat down and shuffled the bunch of matches on his knees, got it into place on his palm, with the wrist of his other hand forced the nerveless fingers down against the bunch, and with the wrist kept them there. At the second scratch the bunch caught fire, and he knew that if he could stand the pain he was saved. He choked with the sulphur fumes, and the blue flame licked the flesh of his hands.

At first he could not feel it, but it burned quickly in through the frosted surface. The odor of the burning flesh—his flesh— was strong in his nostrils. He twisted about in his torment, yet held on. He set his teeth and swayed back and forth, until the clear white flame of the burning match shot up, and he had applied that flame to the leaves and grasses.

An anxious five minutes followed, but the fire gained steadily. Then he set to work to save himself. Heroic measures were necessary, such was his extreme danger, and he took them.

Alternately rubbing his hands with snow and thrusting them into the flames, and now and again beating them against the hard trees, he restored their circulation sufficiently for them to be of use to him. With his hunting knife he slashed the straps from his pack, unrolled his blanket, and got out dry socks and footgear.

Then he cut away his moccasins and bared his feet. But while had had taken liberties with his hands, he kept his feet fairly away from the fire and rubbed them with snow. He rubbed till his hands grew numb, when he would cover his feet with the blanket, warm his hands by the fire, and return to the rubbing.

For three hours he worked, till the worst effects of the freezing had been counteracted. All that night he stayed by the fire, and it was late the next day when he limped pitifully into the camp on the Cherry Creek Divide.

In a month's time he was able to be about on his feet, although the toes were destined always after that to be very sensitive to frost. But the scars on his hands he knows he will carry to the grave. And—"NEVER TRAVEL ALONE!"—he now lays down the rule of the North.

COMPREHENSION QUESTIONS

_____ 1. Tom Vincent traveled
  a. alone.
  b. with a dog.
  c. with a friend.
  d. with a small group.

_____ 2. The temperature was
  a. 75 degrees below zero.
  b. 60 degrees below zero.
  c. 25 degrees below zero.
  d. 90 degrees below zero.

_____ 3. Tom's serious problems began when
  a. the dog fell through the ice into the water.
  b. the sun didn't come out.
  c. he lost his way.
  d. he wet his feet by falling through the ice.

_____ 4. The first fire he built went out because
  a. the snow from the tree above fell on it.
  b. there were not enough twigs to keep it going.
  c. the wind blew it out.
  d. it was too cold even for a fire to burn.

_____ 5. The second time he tried to build a fire he failed because
  a. there were not enought twigs.
  b. the match burned his hand, forcing him to drop the burning match into the snow.
  c. he could not light the match.
  d. the snow from the tree above fell on it.

_____ 6. The third time he tried to build a fire he
  a. severely burned his hand.
  b. couldn't light a match.
  c. was too frozen to gather twigs.
  d. burned his whole body.

_____ 7. At the end of the story, Tom
  a. was rescued by his friends from a nearby camp.
  b. finally succeeded in building a fire.
  c. died.
  d. and the dog both died.

_____ 8. Each time Tom thought he was going to freeze completely, he
  a. covered himself with snow.
  b. jumped up and down.
  c. prayed.
  d. ran rapidly.

_____ 9. Another appropriate title for this story would be
  a. "The Cold of the Klondike."
  b. "Frostbite."
  c. "Nature Will Have Its Way."
  d. "Never Travel Alone."

_____ 10. A main point of this story illustrates

    a. how cold the Klondike can get.

    b. that man may conquer cruel nature by the strength of his love of life.

    c. young men are often foolish.

    d. below the surface of life lies hidden dangers.

Allow 10 points per correct answer.   *Your score* _____ %

Number of words: 2,700.   *Your rate* _____

Answer key is on page 271.

Record your rate and comprehension score on your Course Data Sheet.

3

Using Rapid-Reading Skills on Informational Material

Materials:
- Additional reading report sheets (in the Appendix)
- Reading:
    "Dream Your Way to a Better You"
- Drill book

Objectives:
- To become aware of the structure or organizational pattern the author used
- To learn how to preview and read this type of material
- To understand how to use the additional reading assignments as practice in rapid reading

EYE-PACING DRILLS

Always begin each lesson with eye-pacing drills, and each time try to pace your eyes faster than any previous time.

Open your drill book to where you left off the last time, but start at the top of a page. Go as rapidly as you can, beginning one-half inch in from the left margin and ending one-half inch from the right margin, curving your hand around between the lines so that your hand stays on the print and does not go off the page. Turn the page properly with the non-pacing hand. Keep your head still; move your eyes rapidly. Begin. (1 minute). Stop. Write down what you can remember. Guess if you can't remember!

Add one page to what you read last time. Do the same thing. Go back to the beginning. Begin (10 seconds . . . 1 minute). Stop. Write down what you can, guessing if necessary.

Add another page. Do the same thing. Begin. (10 seconds . . . 1 minute). Stop. Add to your recall sheet.

Did you finish all the material? Really try this

time. Add another page. Begin (10 seconds . . . 1 minute). Stop. Add to your recall sheet.

Turn to a new secion in your drill book. Either turn the page or begin a new chapter. You will take your weekly drill rate. For this drill you will go as fast as you have been going and use the modified curved hand movement. When you have finished, you will tell your story aloud to yourself or someone else, compute your rate, write it on your Course Data Sheet under *Drill Rate*. Write down the page number where you are starting. Begin (1 minute). Stop. Write down the page number. Tell your story aloud. Again, guess if you don't remember. Compute your rate (refer to instructions in Chapter 1) and write down your drill rate on your Course Data Sheet.

Did you remember to turn the pages with your free hand? Was your rate faster than the one you recorded last week? If it wasn't, you need to let yourself go. Stop worrying! If you want to read rapidly, you have to practice reading rapidly until you can do it. The drill is the place to get the best practice. It doesn't matter if you don't understand much of what you are reading. The purpose is to break old, slow word-reading habits. As long as you are trying to read at a fast rate, you will be moving toward new, faster reading habits.

CHARACTERISTICS OF INFORMATIONAL MATERIAL

The term *informational material* encompasses a large range of different kinds of writing, including textbooks, articles, essays and nonfiction books. All forms of informational material have certain qualities in common.

Informational material deals with ideas that the author believes to be true. These ideas are presented as fact or opinion, and each main idea is generally substantiated with evidence of some type in order to convince the reader of its validity. The author's ideas are usually stated directly, that is, put into words. It is this directness of stating ideas and evidence that gives informational material such entirely different writing structures, and it is these structures that determine the method to be used in reading them.

STRUCTURE OF INFORMATIONAL MATERIAL

Most types of informational materials, regardless of their length, have three major parts: introduction, body and conclusion.

The introduction in a short work generally consists of the first one or two paragraphs and usually contains the main idea of the whole work, called the thesis statement. This is the first and most important information that the reader must understand, because all the other ideas presented in the work will relate to and develop this thesis statement in some way. The meanings of these other supporting ideas are incomplete when considered by themselves; their relationships to the thesis statement complete their meanings. Although the thesis statement may appear anywhere in the work, it appears in the introductory paragraphs so frequently that the reader should always watch for it at the beginning.

The body is the longest part of the work and contains many paragraphs. No matter how long and complex these paragraphs seem, each paragraph contains only one main idea, called the topic sentence. All the other sentences in the paragraph relate to and develop this topic sentence, and they depend upon the topic sentence for their complete meaning. Therefore, for good comprehension of the details in the paragraph, the reader must first be aware of the information in the topic sentence to which the details will relate in some way. Again, although the topic sentence may appear anywhere in the paragraph, it appears at the beginning so frequently that the reader should be especially alert to sight the topic sentence immediately upon beginning each paragraph.

The conclusion in a short work generally consists of one or two final paragraphs that reinforce the major ideas presented in the work. It often contains a restatement of the thesis statement and/or a summary of the major details that support and develop the thesis statement. It gives the reader a chance to reaffirm the information obtained and to fill in any missed important details.

ORGANIZATIONAL PATTERNS

An organizational pattern is a writing blueprint, the basic form that the author has chosen in which to present his ideas and substantiating evidence. When readers are aware of the form the author has chosen, they are in a better position to recognize the main ideas, follow the progression of the writing, and distinguish the important information from the unimportant details. Thus, the reader's comprehension, recall, and retention of the material are greatly improved. When ideas are seen in an organized manner, they can be remembered easily through association: One idea follows the next in a logical manner. Isolated facts with no apparent association are difficult to remember.

In the introduction, thesis statement, or conclusion, the author may let the reader know the organizational pattern he or she is using, but it is the body of the work that is actually organized according to the chosen pattern. So, in looking for clues to the organization, try to recognize the relationships between the thesis statement and the main ideas and details given in the paragraphs of the body of the work.

Since recognition of writing patterns is a complex skill, you may not be able to identify the pattern of the organization accurately. However, just being aware that there is a pattern being used and perhaps getting a sense of what that pattern might be will improve comprehension. Then, your organizing the information you get out of the reading into some pattern will enhance your understanding and recall even more.

The following is a list of the most commonly used organizational patterns and some distinguishing characteristics of each to aid you in your attempt to recognize these patterns as you read.

List: ideas placed in any order. Ideas may be examples that prove thesis statement.

Time order sequence: ideas placed in chronological order, what happened first, second, third, and so on. Narration of a story gives events in time order. Describing a process tells how something happens or works in time order.

Importance order sequence: ideas placed in order of importance, most important to least important, or least to most.

Spatial order sequence: ideas arranged as they appear in space. Sequence may progress from front to back, back to front, top to bottom, bottom to top, side to side, near to far, etc. Descriptions that tell what it looks like use this pattern.

Comparison or contrast: ideas to show how two or more subjects are similar (comparison) or different (contrast) in respect to certain qualities. Ideas may be arranged as lists or in order of importance, but their purpose is to point out the similarities or differences of the subjects discussed.

Cause and effect: ideas to show why something occurred (cause) and what happens because of it (effect), usually shown in a time relationship.

PREVIEWING INFORMATIONAL MATERIAL

Since informational material deals primarily with the presentation of ideas, finding the main ideas of the total work and of each paragraph is your important first task. Although the main idea may appear anywhere in a paragraph, it most frequently appears at the beginning. Therefore, in previewing, quickly go under each line of the first paragraph, trying to catch the main idea of the work (thesis statement). Then go under the first line only of each paragraph in the body to catch the main idea of each paragraph, since it will most likely be right at the beginning. The last paragraph may contain a summary that will fill in any main ideas you missed, so go under each line of this final paragraph.

First paragraph: Use hand under each line, rapidly. Look for main idea of the whole work.

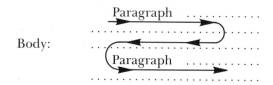

Last paragraph: Use hand under each line, rapidly.

Perform each of these previewing steps on the article, "Dream Your Way to a Better You," on page 32.

1. Read the title. What does it tell you about what you can expect in the article?
2. Read the short blurb, if there is one. What does this tell you?
3. Using your hand in a relaxed manner, go through the first paragraph very rapidly. In each succeeding paragraph, go under the first line, curve it around over the entire paragraph so that you are in a position to begin the first line of the next paragraph at the left margin.
4. Pay special attention to all titles and subtitles.
5. Go through the entire last paragraph rapidly to read the summary, if there is one.
6. If there are any questions at the end, go over them rapidly to get an idea of what the author thinks is important enough to ask questions about.
7. When you have finished, you should have a sense of the organizational pattern the author used. Write down what you think it is. See the answer key on page 271 to check what you wrote down.

Read the article now.

READING INFORMATIONAL MATERIAL

In reading "Dream Your Way to a Better You," you use the same hand movement that you have been using for the short stories, but you should pay special attention to the first and last paragraphs, the beginning of each paragraph, and any titles and subtitles.

After finishing the article, consider its pattern of organization. Did you write the correct pattern after the preview? Change it if necessary. This time, place this pattern and the information from the article that fits this pattern into an organized form so that it can be remembered easily. If the pattern was a list, write out the items of the list. If it was a sequence, write out what came first, second, third, and so on. If it was a comparison or contrast, make a column for each of the qualities of comparison. Then in each column write what the author said about each that made them the same as or different from each other, as shown in this example:

	Apartment Living	House Living
Outside area	patio only	yard, patio
Inside area	usually smaller	usually larger
Neighbors	in same building	at least 10 feet away
Maintenance	by landlord	by homeowner

Whenever you can organize the information in a graphic or picture form, do so; it is the easiest way to remember it because all you have to do to recall it is flash the picture in your mind.

At the end of the article you will find an outline that organizes the information in this article according to its correct pattern. Fill in this outline before answering the questions.

Additional Reading Assignments

In the Appendix you will find five Additional Reading Reports (p. 253). Pull out the first one (along the perforated line). Read the instructions given on this report. You should complete one Additional Reading Report each week for five weeks or until you begin the Speed-studying techniques in Chapter 13.

In doing this assignment, always use the most recent hand movement that you have learned. Preview and read the articles according to the instructions given in this chapter. Your purpose in doing the assignment is to practice what you are learning in each chapter. Always keep this in mind.

In the first portion of this assignment you are asked to read as rapidly as you can for fifteen minutes in a drill type book. This exercise is extremely important. It is similar to a drill except that it is longer. You may find that one day while doing this exercise in a quiet place at home with no distractions that you will suddenly know for certain what the story is about, and you will then know what it is really like to read rapidly with understanding.

SUMMARY

Informational material is read for the main ideas and important details, which are generally stated directly. It is previewed and read by paying special attention to the first and last paragraphs, the beginnings of paragraphs, and titles and subtitles. It is remembered most easily by recognizing the pattern of organization the author has used and writing out in a summary form the pattern and the basic information that fits it.

DREAM YOUR WAY TO A BETTER YOU

Lillian P. Wenick

Dreaming plays an important role in our lives. By understanding the three major types of dreaming and their purposes, you may be able to use your states of dreaming to improve various aspects of your life, such as your ability to cope with the problems of life, having more creative insights, learning more effectively, and maintaining mental health.

Dreams may occur while awake, in the period of semiwakefulness, or when asleep. Each has special characteristics and purposes, but they have certain aspects in common. All three are products of the imaginative nonverbal right side of the brain. During any state of dreaming, whether awake or asleep, external stimuli are shut out to varying degrees. All dreaming uses knowledge of the outside world; usually events that occurred recently triggers dreams; but the actual dream consists of events from the imagination and, to varying degrees, the unconscious part of the mind.

In the daydreaming state, the dreamer has the most conscious control of the dream. Daydreams or fantasies are stories we tell ourselves, usually about ourselves. Daydreaming includes our memories and our private inner commentaries on what is happening around us. They can serve many constructive purposes. They allow us to try out threatening situations—to rehearse how we will handle them. But in daydreams, no matter how we deal with these situations, we don't pay any consequences. And if we don't like how they turn out, we can fantasize them again and again and keep changing the script until we are satisfied with the outcome.

For instance, you want to ask your boss for a raise but are afraid of what his reaction might be. In fantasy, you can try out many different approaches. This not only gives you a chance to select which approach you think will work best but also makes you feel more comfortable in the situation because you have experienced it several times in your mind. Experience tends to make a situation less threatening. And, in fantasy, no matter what you say or do, you don't face the boss' anger or rejection—no consequences to pay!

Children use daydreams to help them accept the social and moral values of the adults. They role-play being "father," "mother," "president," "nurse," "teacher." In this fantasy-play they try out the complex and relatively self-controlled behavior of adults. Through imagining themselves in adult roles over and over again, children gradually adopt the adult attitudes with their accompanying values. Research indicates that children who are unimaginative and who do little role-playing are more apt to become delinquent than those who are actively imaginative.

Role-playing in daydreams also allows us to get rid of aggressive and antisocial feelings. By pretending in fantasy to do these destructive acts, we get them out of our systems and are less likely to feel the need to do them in actuality. Being aggressive in fantasy appears to help control real aggression. This saves us unpleasant consequences and guilt: there is no need to feel guilty for thinking or imagining bad things; only when we actually do them do we have realisitic guilt.

Fantasy and daydreaming develop the imagination. The more we daydream, the easier it becomes. Since daydreaming is all imaginative, we develop this facility by using it.

Daydreaming enriches the environment. Active daydreamers change their inner environment, which leads to a change in their reaction to the outer environment. They are rarely bored. Whenever you have to wait, at the doctor's office, at the airport, at a restaurant, if you can entertain yourself with mental pictures or stories or commentary that you choose, you will enjoy having this "time out" for fantasy and will react to the situation pleasantly. If you just sit there blankly, you will probably feel bored and will react with hostility to being kept waiting.

While daydreaming is a state over which we can have complete control, in other states of dreaming the conscious mind has less control. In another state called "twilight" dreaming, we are not fully awake nor yet asleep. It happens spontaneously while the conscious mind is relaxing its hold upon us but has not yet given up complete control. During this in-between state, more primitive mental processes may be brought into activity. It is a time when the conscious mind may be more in touch with the unconscious than either in fantasy or in sleep dreaming. It is a state in which the analytical and logical part of the brain is giving up its control.

In this semisleep state a unique aspect of the unconscious is available to the conscious part of the mind. Creative insights coming from the unconscious may be grasped by the conscious. These are insights that logic and analysis have not been able to form. They seem to appear from nowhere but are frequently solutions to "unsolvable" problems in life.

"Twilight" dreaming can sometimes help us eliminate mental blocks that keep us from using certain types of information. During this state, the mind is hypersuggestible. Through autosuggestion fat people are able to absorb the idea of not overeating, smokers can instill the idea of not smoking, or a difficult subject can be learned. However, this type of learning and change may not take place automatically. Special circumstances must exist for the mind to grasp the information. Tapes, containing the suggestions, played to the dreamer, or programmed thoughts at this time may need to be used to start the "twilight" state of dreaming to accomplish these purposes.

However, the "twilight" state for most people lasts only a short time, perhaps ten minutes. Then, deep sleep sets in. To make use of "twilight" dreaming, it would be an advantage to purposely remain in that state a longer period of time, especially if you wish to do programmed or taped learning. And it would also be helpful to "set your mind" to remember any creative insights that occur during this state of dreaming.

Nighttime dreaming, which occurs when we are in deep sleep, is not under our conscious control but still has necessary functions which take place automatically. Night dreaming preserves the efficiency of our brains during the day. Experiments suggest that dream sleep restores a chemical, which we use up during the day, essential to thinking logically and to focusing our attention. Maybe, if you can't concentrate you aren't dreaming enough!

Another purpose of sleep dreaming is to separate the two realities which we experience. We have an outer reality comprised of the sensory stimulation of the outside world and an inner reality which arises from the brain itself. The brain has no way of telling the difference between ordinary reality and waking dreams. Sleep dreams hold back the inner images from sneaking in upon the outer waking reality and keep us from experiencing a confusing and sometimes frightening jumble of perceptions. Hallucinations occur when the brain is experiencing the inner reality while awake. Sleep dreams keep us sane!

Experiments show that people deprived of the opportunity to sleep and dream for a long time lose their ability to act in common-sense ways. They have hallucinations and appear to be mentally ill. Sleep dreaming is essential to healthy functioning during the day. Luckily, unless you are taking drugs that inhibit dreaming, you will dream during sleep, even if you don't remember the dreams.

Daydreaming, "twilight" dreaming and sleep dreaming are three states of dreaming, with the dreamer having the most control in daydreaming and the least control in sleep dreaming. Each has distinct purposes. In daydreams you can try out difficult situations, learn to internalize social and moral standards, dissipate antisocial feelings through role-playing, develop your imagination, change your reaction to the environment, and keep from being bored. In "twilight" dreaming you can get in touch with your creative insights, eliminate mental blocks, and learn new modes of behavior. In sleep dreaming you preserve the efficiency of your brain, keep the inner reality from disturbing your waking time, and keep sane. By recognizing the importance of each state of dreaming and by indulging your dreaming capabilities, you will improve your physical and mental well-being.

Directions: *This outline is one possible way of organizing your information. Fill in the outline before answering the questions.*

States of dreaming:

1. _____

   Purposes

   1. _____

   2. _____

   3. _____

   4. _____

   5. _____

2. _____

   Purposes

   1. _____

   2. _____

   3. _____

3. _____

   Purposes

   1. _____

   2. _____

   3. _____

Turn to the answer key on page 271 to check your completed outline.

COMPREHENSION QUESTIONS

_____ 1. The number of states of dreaming discussed in this article are (is)
   a. one.
   b. two.
   c. three.
   d. four.
   e. five.

_____ 2. According to this article, dreaming may do all of the following *except*
   a. use up important brain chemicals.
   b. increase creative insights.
   c. help cope with problems.
   d. improve learning.

_____ 3. The constructive purposes for daydreaming mentioned in this article include all of the following *except*
   a. trying out threatening situations.
   b. accepting adult social and moral values.
   c. keeping the inner and outer realities separate.
   d. lessening aggressive feelings.

_____ 4. The constructive purposes of "twilight" dreaming include all of the following *except*
   a. learning difficult material.
   b. restoring brain chemicals.
   c. getting in touch with the unconscious part of the mind.
   d. getting in touch with creative insights.

_____ 5. The constructive purposes of night dreaming include all of the following *except*
   a. preserving the efficiency of the brain.
   b. restoring necessary chemicals to the brain.
   c. keeping the inner and outer realities separate.
   d. developing the imagination.

_____ 6. The main idea of this article could be stated as follows:
   a. There are several states of dreaming.
   b. By understanding the three major types of dreaming and their purposes, you may be able to use dreaming for constructive purposes.
   c. Daydreaming can be used to try out situations, internalize values, dissipate aggressive feelings and improve imagination.
   d. "Twilight" dreaming aids in grasping creative insights, eliminating mental blocks, and learning; whereas night dreaming preserves the efficiency of the brain, restores important chemicals, and keeps the inner and outer realities separate.

_____ 7. According to this article, if you wanted to stop excessive drinking, listening to a taped message would be helpful during
   a. daydreaming.
   b. "twilight" dreaming.
   c. night dreaming.
   d. hypnosis.

_____ 8. The conscious mind exerts the most control during
   a. daydreaming.
   b. "twilight" dreaming.
   c. night dreaming.
   d. hypnosis.

_____ 9. From the information given, you could infer that people with highly developed imaginations have more _____ than people with underdeveloped imaginations.
   a. daydreams.
   b. "twilight" dreams.
   c. night dreams.
   d. problems coping with life.

_____ 10. The overall organizational pattern used in this article could be described as
   a. comparison of the states of dreaming.
   b. definition of the states of dreaming.
   c. description of the state of dreaming and examples.
   d. list of states of dreaming and purposes.

Allow 10 points per correct answer.   *Your score* _____ %
Number of words: 1,700.   *Your rate* _____
Answer key is on page 271.
Record rate and comprehension score on your Course Data Sheet.

4

A New Way of Thinking and a Shift in Focus

Materials: • Drill book
• Readings:
"The Lady, or the Tiger?"
"Going for the Goal"

Objectives: • To begin thinking in ideas and images instead of words while reading
• To understand the difference between sharp focus and soft focus
• To begin to use soft focus in reading

Why do you need a new way of thinking when you speed read? Most of you now think each word in your mind as you read. When you do that, you severely limit your reading speed. This is a serious obstacle that must be overcome before you can increase your reading rate significantly.

Happily, you all have the ability to think in ways that do not require saying each word. You can think in ideas and in images or pictures. You have been using these alternate ways of thinking in other areas of your life, but you may never have applied them to reading. That is what you will be doing now.

The transition from thinking words while reading to thinking ideas and images may not occur right away, but you must begin your awareness of it. As you read more rapidly in succeeding chapters, you may find that at first you can only do it occasionally; but as with all skills, with practice you will soon be able to think this way while reading all or most of the time.

END SUBVOCALIZATION

Subvocalization means saying the words to yourself either aloud or half aloud, with lip movements only, or just hearing them in your head. As long as you must say each word, you cannot read any

faster than you can speak. If you want your reading rate to be faster than your speaking rate, you must change your manner of reading so that you are not dependent on saying the words. This is not an easy thing to do. Trying not to say the words doesn't seem to work very well. The best way to conquer subvocalization is to allow yourself to go over the print faster than you can speak so that there isn't time to say each word. Thus, as you go faster and faster, you will gradually lessen the amount of your subvocalization; and soon you may be saying every other word, then every fourth word, then only the key words, and eventually none of the words. Some people can overcome this habit completely, but others may always say some of the words to themselves, even when they are reading very rapidly. However, the aim is not to be dependent on saying the words.

A NEW WAY OF THINKING

If you don't say the words, how then can you still get the thought in your mind? There are alternate, better ways. One is to think the thought or idea of what is happening in the story. When you watch someone walking across the room, you don't say to yourself, "He is walking." You just know the idea. You can do the same thing in reading. Another alternate way is to picture what is happening. When you recall a past experience or a dream, you are able to see pictures of it in your mind. Why, then, shouldn't you be able to translate the events of a story into pictures also? Picturing what is happening is particularly well-suited to stories. People who have learned how to do it say that when they are reading a story it is as if they are watching television, where they see the story acted out. Some people do this easily, and others have to practice a great deal before they can accomplish it.

When you think in images and ideas rather than words while reading, you are using both the left and right hemispheres of your brain. The left hemisphere is decoding the language, and the right hemisphere is changing the message into pictures or ideas. For this to occur naturally, you only have to go over the print fast enought to give your brain all the information quickly; then, you only need to keep your mind clear so that the thought or picture can enter it. When it does, accept it without questioning it. Don't have a dialogue going on in your head about whether you're doing it right or whether the thought or picture is accurate because when your mind is occupied with other thoughts, those from the print will be blocked out.

SHIFTING FROM SHARP TO SOFT FOCUS

Shifting your attention from a small area of print (sharp focus) to a larger area of print (soft focus) is a technique that will allow you to go fast enough to end subvocalization and to substitute thinking in ideas and images.

To aid you in understanding sharp and soft focus, information about how the eyes function will be helpful. Studies indicate that only a small part of the retina of the eye, the fovea, has the ability to focus sharply and that the area of sharpest focus is only the size of a dot. In contrast, the total area that you can see at any one time is quite large. You can see all the area in front of you and a portion of the area on both sides. Within this large total vision field, the clearest view is at the small dot; and as you get farther away from the small area of sharpest focus, your vision becomes less and less clear. Unless you direct your attention to what you are seeing at the outer edges of your total field of vision, you may not be aware of seeing anything in this area at all.

Sharp eye focus occurs when your visual attention is confined to a very small area surrounding your point of sharpest focus. When you read one word at a time, your fovea is focusing sharply on a tiny portion of the word; but since the rest of the word is very close to the most central area of sharp vision and you are paying attention to the entire word, you perceive the whole word distinctly. Whenever you limit your visual attention to a severely restricted space around a single point, you are using sharp focus.

It is possible to increase the area you see clearly from one word to many words by expanding the area to which you consciously pay attention. Soft eye focus occurs when your visual attention is expanded beyond the narrowly restricted area of sharp focus. Since this increased area will be only a relatively small portion of your total field of vision, it will still fall close enough to your point of sharpest focus to be seen clearly. Whenever you extend your visual attention to a larger space, you are using soft focus.

To illustrate the difference between sharp and soft focus, look at Figure 4-1. At first, concentrate only on the dot. You see the dot clearly and are only aware of the circles because they are close to the point of sharpest vision. Now, continuing to concentrate on the dot, focus your attention only on the circles. This time, the circles appear clearer. You could still see the circles even if they covered the entire page.

Another illustration: In any book, look down at a particular word. You see it sharply. Look up. This time, look down, focusing your attention on an entire paragraph of print. Look up. Notice that when your attention was on a large section of print, you were not so aware of any particular word. If you continued to look at the paragraph, however, your attention would focus on a word. If you moved your eyes quickly to another large section of print, the larger awareness would continue. Look down at the book again. This time, become aware of everything you can see without moving your eyes from the book. Pay attention to your arms,

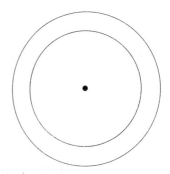

Figure 4-1 Sharp and Soft Focus

your hands, the floor, the people sitting next to you, and so on. Your awareness covers your entire field of vision, which extends far beyond the book.

Now, let's discuss how the foregoing ideas should be used in rapid reading and how they tie in with what you have learned. As you can see, there are advantages to using soft focus in reading. You no longer need to focus sharply on each word and therefore don't need to make seven or eight eye stops on each line. Instead, you can make only one, two, or three eye stops. By extending your visual attention to include the words between the eye stops, you can still perceive all the words. However, your aim is to comprehend the meaning of the words in thoughts and pictures in your mind rather than saying each word to yourself. This is not really difficult. Most of the words in the print you have seen millions of times in the course of your many years of reading, and therefore your mind is able to get meaning from them instantaneously without dwelling on each word. To use this larger field of visual concentration, you need only allow your mind to accept all the printed pictures of the words and to process the information without your interference, without trying to limit it to one word at a time. In fact, it is natural for your brain to translate the meanings of many words into a single thought. It is more difficult for it to send you the message of the meaning of each individual word when you are actually seeing several words at one time.

Another ability that you possess is in operation when you pay attention to a large segment of print with soft focus. This is the ability to derive meaning from words you are not consciously aware of having seen; it is called *subliminal communication*. Advertisers take advantage of this ability to sell their products. Vance Packard in his book, *The Hidden Persuaders* exposed the use of subliminal communication to influence many aspects of our lives without our being aware of it. There is a growing industry of subliminal audio and video tapes that purport to change your behavior through subconscious subliminal suggestions.

In speed reading, you see the words more rapidly than you can consciously recognize each word; but unknowingly the meanings of the words are registered in your mind and the ideas from the meanings pop into your mind, if you don't stop them from entering by blocking them. When you receive subliminal suggestions of which you have no awareness, you don't block them (not knowing they are there) and so they enter your mind. In speed reading, however, you are aware that the print has meaning, a message, and you tend to block it, unless you relax and keep your mind clear to receive the message.

"S" HAND MOVEMENT

In order to use soft focus, you need a hand movement that will pace your eyes more rapidly over a larger segment of the print than you have been using. The "S" hand movement is exactly like the one you have been using but is slightly larger. Instead of curving your hand around between the lines to start at the left of the next line, curve it around under the next line from right to left to the end of the line. Then, curve it around the next line from left to right. So, you go from left to right under the first line, from right to left under the second line, from left to right under the third line, from right to left under the fourth line, and so on down the page. This hand movement cannot be done slowly, because in order to get meaning when going from right to left, you must see the whole line at a time, not just a few words. Keep your hand well below your eyes so you don't cover nearby print. Here's an example:

Now, there were two possessions in which Jim
and Della took great pride. One was Jim's gold
watch, that had previously been his father's
and, before that, his grandfather's.

Figure 4-2 will give you an idea of how your eyes will move across the print by using soft focus. The dot represents your sharpest vision area. The circles represent the larger area of visual concentration in soft focus.

Take a few seconds to practice the new hand movement in your drill book.

Practice Exercise

Reread "The Anniversary" going as fast you as can with the new, enlarged "S" hand movement, using soft focus, and keeping your mind clear to receive the thoughts or images. This will give you the experience of reading rapidly and knowing what you are reading. Since you already know the story, as your eyes go over the print, the ideas or pictures will pop into your mind.

Repeat this exercise with any previously read material.

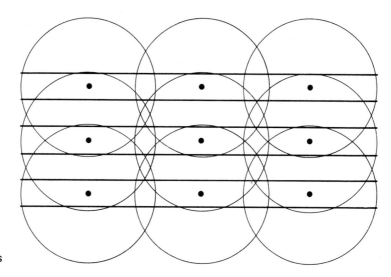

Figure 4-2 Using Soft Focus

Drill Practice

In doing the practice drills and story reading today, clear your mind of any outside thoughts so that you will be prepared to receive the ideas and pictures related to the story. Although you may be fortunate enough to be able to stop subvocalization right away, don't expect a complete sudden change in the way you think while reading. If you can stop subvocalizing even for a few second at first, you are on your way to breaking the habit.

Open your drill book to where you are going to start. Go as rapidly as you can for one minute, using the new "S" hand movement. Direct your attention to a larger area of print than you have done before. Get your hand started like a machine, then forget about it; allow yourself to "think" the ideas or to picture what is being described in print. Just concentrate on the print, and *think something* that you think is what the print says. If you can, allow the pictures of what is happening in the story to appear in your mind. It is essential that you just let it happen. If you are worrying about it, your mind is already filled with thoughts of worry, and there is no room for the thought of the story. Begin (1 minute). Stop. Start your recall sheet.

Add three pages to what you have just read. Try to finish all the pages in the next drill. To do so, if you feel you can, enlarge the hand movement so that you take in more than one line with each curve of your hand. For example, start under the second line from left to right, curve around to the fourth line from right to left, curve around under the sixth line from left to right, and so on down the page. Some of you have already been doing this naturally in your attempt to go faster. Those of you

who have not been doing it, try it, even if you think you can't. You don't know what you can do until you try. If you've already tried this way and found that you could do it, try more than two lines at a time. Always work to expand your hand movement taking advantage of your ability to use soft focus and peripheral vision. Go to the beginning of this section in your drill book. Begin (10 seconds . . . 1 minute). Stop. Write it down.

Did some of you find that you got just as much or more meaning by using this enlarged hand movement as you did by going more slowly? Keep practicing.

Add three more pages, doing the same thing again. Start at the beginning of your section. Begin (10 seconds . . . 1 minute). Stop. Write it down.

This is the last time. Add three more pages, and start at the beginning. Begin (10 seconds). Stop. Add to your recall sheet.

Here are some drills to end subvocalization: Reread "The Anniversary." This time count "one . . . two . . . three . . ." aloud over and over again as you read the story, using the expanded curved hand movement. "Think" the ideas or picture what is happening in the story. Use soft focus.

Turn to the story. Begin ("one, two, three . . .").

In a story that you already know, use your hand in the enlarged curved hand movement; going rapidly, say the story out loud. Do not say each word. Instead, tell the story in your own words as the ideas become known to you. These ideas will be a condensed version of the story. For this drill use the story "To Build a Fire," which you have already read and know.

Your spoken condensed story may go something like this for the first page:

Klondike. Tom Vincent. Never Travel Alone. Laughed. Big. Faith in self. Strong. January. Respect. Sixty below. Thirty miles to go. Carefree. Returning to Cherry Creek.

Reading Practice

Read the story "The Lady, or the Tiger?" on page 42 and the article "Going for the Goal" on page 48. For both, use the enlarged "S" hand movement. Slow down from your drill rate, but remember that you must go reasonably fast to use soft focus. Also remember that if you got 90 or 100 percent on your last reading, you should push to go faster today. If your tendency is to subvocalize, go faster than you can talk. Relax and keep your mind clear so that the ideas or images can enter it. Whatever thoughts come into your mind, accept as being from the story; don't question them. Don't worry if you do say some of the words to yourself.

Follow these directions:

1. Preview: swoop down page for the story. For the article, go over the entire first and last paragraphs and then the first line only of all the other paragraphs.
2. Write the starting time.
3. Read (use Curved "S" hand movement).
4. Write the finishing time.
5. Answer questions at the end.
6. Correct answers (answer key is on page 271), score comprehension.
7. Compute reading rate.
8. Record both on Course Data Sheet.
9. Evaluate what you did.
10. Have a class discussion of the reading or verify it by rereading more slowly, using your hand-pacer.

SUMMARY

Dependence on subvocalization while reading severely limits your reading rate. Practice in reading faster than you can talk while thinking the idea of what is in the print or picturing what is happening will gradually decrease your need to subvocalize and will permit you to increase your reading speed.

You have the ability to see and understand words in a larger section of your total vision field than you have been using in reading. You can develop this ability by changing your visual focus of attention from a small area to a larger one. The new "S" hand movement will help you develop this ability by pacing your eyes more rapidly over a larger section of print. Your success in using these methods is dependent on your willingness to permit your mind to accept the ideas and pictures that enter it.

THE LADY, OR THE TIGER?

Frank R. Stockton

In the very olden time there lived an uncivilized king. He was a man with a rich, fruitful fancy which grew from his strange imagination. He was also a man of an authority so irresistible that, at his will, he turned his varied fancies into facts. He was greatly given to self-discussions. When he and himself agreed upon anything, the thing was done. When every member of his home and kingdom moved smoothly in its planned course, his nature was friendly. But, whenever there was a little hitch, and some of his orbs got out of their orbits, he was even more friendly, for nothing pleased him so much as to make the crooked straight, and crush down uneven places.

He had the idea that everything could be settled in the public arena, and that, by exhibitions of manly and beastly bravery, the minds of his subjects were refined and cultured.

But even here his uncivilized imagination had its way. The arena of the king was built not to give the people an opportunity of hearing the songs of dying gladiators, nor to enable them to view the unavoidable outcome of a conflict between religious opinions and hungry jaws. It was built for purposes far better suited to widen and develop the mental energies of the people. This great outdoor theater, with its balconies on all sides, mysterious underground caves, and its unseen passages, was an agent of poetic justice. Here crime was punished, or virtue rewarded, by the decrees of a just and honest chance.

When a subject was accused of a crime of enough importance to interest the king, public notice was given that on a set day the fate of the accused person would be decided in the king's arena. It was a structure which well deserved its name; for, although its form and plan were borrowed from distant lands, its purpose arose solely from the brain of this man. When all the people had gathered in the balconies, and the king, surrounded by his court, sat high up on his throne of royal state on one side of the arena, he gave a signal. Then, a door beneath him opened, and the accused subject stepped out into the arena. Directly opposite him, on the other side of the enclosed space, were two doors, exactly alike and side by side. It was the duty and privilege of the person on trial to walk directly to these doors and open one of them. He could open either door he pleased. He was subject to no guidance or influence but that of chance. If he opened the one, there came out of it a hungry tiger, the fiercest and most cruel that could be found. The tiger immediately sprang upon him and tore him to pieces, as punishment for his guilt. The moment that the case of the criminal was thus decided, sad iron bells were clanged, great cries went up from the hired mourners posted on the outer rim of the arena. The large audience, with bowed heads and downcast hearts went slowly their homeward way, mourning greatly that one so young and fair, or so old and respected, should have deserved so terrible a fate.

But if the accused person opened the other door, there came forth from it a lady. She was the most suitable lady to his years and station that his Majesty could select among his fair subjects. To this lady he was immediately married, as a reward of his innocence. It mattered not that he might already have a wife and family, or that his affections might be engaged upon an object of his own selection. The king allowed no such arrangements to interfere with his great scheme of punishment and reward. The exercises, as in the other instance, took place immediately, and in the arena. Another door opened beneath the king, and a priest appeared. He was following by a band of singers and dancing maidens blowing joyous airs on golden horns and dancing to wedding music. The wedding ceremony was promptly and cheerily performed. Then the gay brass bells rang forth their merry chimes. The people shouted glad hurrahs. The innocent man, led by children throwing flowers on his path, led his bride to his home.

This was the king's method of administering justice. Its perfect fairness is obvious. The criminal could not know out of which door would come the lady. He opened either he pleased. He did not have the slightest idea whether, in the next instant, he was to be devoured or married. On some occasions the tiger came out of one door. On some the tiger came out of the other door. The decisions of this court of justice were not only fair, they were final and without delay. The accused person was instantly punished if he found himself guilty. And if he found himself innocent, he was rewarded on the spot, whether he liked it or not. There was no escape from the judgments of the king's arena.

The system was a very popular one. When the people gathered together on one of the great trial-days, they never knew whether they were to witness a bloody killing or a happy wedding. This element of uncertainty lent an interest to the occasion which it could not otherwise have had. Thus the masses were entertained and pleased. The thinking part of the group could bring no change of unfairness against this plan. After all, did not the accused person have the whole matter in his own hands?

This king had a daughter as blooming as his most flowering fancies. She also had a soul as passionate and willful as his own. As is usual in such cases, she was the apple of his eye, and was loved by him above all others. Among the people of his court was a young man of that fineness of blood and lowness of station common to the usual heroes of romance who love royal maidens. This royal maiden was well satisfied with her lover. He was handsome and brave to a degree not equaled in all this kingdom. She loved him with a passion. This love affair moved on happily for many months. However, one day the king happened to discover this love affair between his daughter and the lowly young man. He did not hesitate nor waver in regard to his duty in the situation. The youth was immediately thrown into prison, and a day was set for his trial in the king's arena. This, of course was an especially important occasion. His Majesty, as well as all the people, was greatly interested in the workings and progress of this trial. Never before had such a case occurred. Never before had a subject dared to love the daughter of a king. In after years such things became commonplace enough. At that time they were, in no slight degree, new and startling.

The tiger-cages of the kingdown were searched for the most savage and pitiless beasts, from which the fiercest monster might be selected for the arena. The ranks of maiden youth and beauty throughout the land were carefully inspected by able judges. This was done in order that the young man might have a fitting bride in case fate did not decide for him a different fate. Of course everybody knew that the deed with which the accused was charged had been done. He had loved the princess. Neither he, she, nor anyone else thought of denying the fact. But the king would not think of allowing any fact of this kind to interfere with the workings of the court of justice, in which he took such a great delight and satisfaction. No matter how the affair turned out, the youth would be gotten rid of. And the king would take pleasure in watching the course of events, which would determine whether or not the young man had done wrong in allowing himself to love a princess.

The appointed day arrived. From far and near the people gathered. They crowded into the great balconies of the arena. Those people, unable to gain admittance, massed themselves against the outside walls. The king and his court were in their places, opposite the twin doors—those fateful gates, so terrible in their likeness.

All was ready. The signal was given. A door beneath the royal party opened. The lover of the princess walked into the arena. Tall, beautiful, fair, his appearance was greeted with a low hum of admiration and concern. Half the audience had not known so grand a youth had lived among them. No wonder the princess loved him! What a terrible thing for him to be there!

As the youth advanced into the arena, he turned, as the custom was, to bow to the king. As he bowed, he did not think at all of that royal personage. His eyes were fixed upon the princess, who sat to the right of her father. Had it not been for the uncivilized part of her nature it is probable that lady would not have been there. However, her intense and passionate soul would not allow her to be absent on an occasion in which she was so terribly interested. From the moment that the decree had gone forth that her lover should decide his fate in the king's arena, she had thought of nothing, day or night, but this great event and the various subjects connected with it. Possessed of more power, influence, and force of character than any one who had ever before been interested in such a case, she had done what no other person had done. She had learned of the secret of the doors. She knew in which of the two rooms that lay behind those doors stood the cage of the tiger and in which waited the lady. Through these thick doors, it was impossible that any noise or suggestion should come from within to the person who should approach to raise the latch of one of them. But gold, and the power of a woman's will, had brought the secret to the princess.

And not only did she know in which room stood the lady ready to come forth, all blushing and radiant, should her door be opened, but she knew who the lady was. It was one of the fairest and loveliest of the maidens of the court who had been chosen as the reward of the accused, should he be proved innocent of the crime of loving one so far above him. The princess hated her. Often had she seen, or imagined that she had seen, this fair creature throwing glances of admiration upon the person of her lover. Sometimes she thought these glances were noticed and even returned. Now and then she had seen them talking together. It was but for a moment or two, but much can be said in a brief space. It may have been on most unimportant topics, but how could she know that? The girl was lovely. She had dared to raise her eyes to the loved one of the princess. With all the intensity of the savage blood passed along to her through long lines of wholly uncivilized ancestors, she hated the woman who blushed and trembled behind that silent door.

Her lover turned and looked at her, and his eyes met hers as she sat there paler and whiter than any one in the great ocean of anxious faces about her. He saw, by that power of quick insight which is given to those whose souls are one, that she knew behind which door crouched the tiger, and behind which door stood the lady. He had expected her to know it. He understood her nature. His soul was sure that she would never rest until she had made plain to herself this thing, hidden to all other lookers-on, even to the king. The only hope for the youth in which there was any element of certainty was based upon the success of the princess in discovering this mystery. The moment he looked upon her, he saw she had succeeded, as in his soul he knew she would succeed.

Then it was that his quick and anxious glance asked the question, "Which?" It was as plain to her as if he shouted to her from where he stood. There was not an instant to be lost. The question was asked in a flash. It must be answered in another.

Her right arm lay on the cushion before her. She raised her hand, and made a slight, quick movement toward the right. No one but her lover saw her. Every eye was fixed on the man in the arena.

He turned, and with a firm and rapid step he walked across the empty space. Every heart stopped beating. Every breath was held. Every eye was fixed immovably upon that man. Without the slightest hesitation, he went to the door on the right and opened it.

Now, the point of the story is this: Did the tiger come out of that door, or did the lady?

The more we think upon this question the harder it is to answer. It involves a study of the human heart. This leads us through winding pathways of passion, out of which it is difficult to find our way. Think of it, fair reader, not as if the decision of the question depended upon yourself, but upon that hot-blooded princess. Remember that her soul was at a white heat beneath the combined fires of despair and jealousy. She had lost him. Who should have him?

How often, in her waking hours and in her dreams, had she started in horror. How many times had she covered her face with her hands as she thought of her lover opening the door on the other side of which waited the cruel fangs of the tiger!

But how much oftener had she seen him at the other door! How in her sorrowful daydreams had she ground her teeth and torn her hair when she saw his start of wild delight as he opened the door of the lady! How her soul had burned in agony when she had seen him rush to meet that woman, with her flushing cheek and sparkling eye of triumph. When she had seen him lead her forth, his whole frame had seemed to burn with the joy of recovered life. In her dreams she had heard the glad shout of the crowd and the wild ringing of the happy bells. She had seen the priest, with his joyous followers, advance to the couple, and make them man and wife before her very eyes. She had seen them walk away together upon their path of flowers. She had seen them followed by the wild shouts of the happy people, in which her one hopeless cry was lost and drowned!

Would it not be better for him to die once and go to wait for her in the blessed regions of the future?

And yet, that awful tiger, those shrieks, that blood!

Her decision had been shown in an instant, but it had been made after days and nights of painful self-argument. She had known she would be asked. She had decided what she would answer. Without the slightest hesitation, she had moved her hand to the right.

The question of her decision is not one to be lightly considered. It is not for me to take it upon myself to set myself up as the one person able to answer it. And so I leave it with all of you: Which came out of the opened door—the lady, or the tiger?

COMPREHENSION QUESTIONS

——— 1. In this kingdom a criminal's guilt or innocence was decided by
    a. the king alone.
    b. a jury of his peers.
    c. chance.
    d. a special court.

——— 2. The king's arena was used for
    a. gladiator fights.
    b. deciding criminal justice.
    c. sports events.
    d. animal fights.

——— 3. When an accused person was proved innocent, he was
    a. given his complete freedom.
    b. rewarded with money.
    c. given a choice of gifts.
    d. rewarded with a beautiful wife.

——— 4. When an accused person was proved guilty, he was
    a. torn apart by a fierce animal.
    b. hanged until dead.
    c. sent out of the kingdom, never to return.
    d. killed by the king's guards.

——— 5. The young man in this story was accused of the crime of
    a. loving the princess.
    b. stealing the church bells.
    c. working against the king in political matters.
    d. illegally killing a tiger.

——— 6. Regarding the secret of the doors, the princess
    a. was unable to learn the secret.
    b. did not want to know the secret.
    c. learned the total secret.
    d. personally arranged what was to be behind each door.

——— 7. When the princess's lover asked for the secret of the doors, she
    a. signaled to the right.
    b. signaled to the left.
    c. did not signal at all.
    d. signaled that she did not know.

——— 8. The lady chosen for the arena event was
    a. old and plain-looking.
    b. a total stranger to the princess and the young man.
    c. young and lovely.
    d. the princess's closest and most intimate friend.

_____ 5. One helpful strategy to keep you working effectively toward your goal is to reward yourself
  a. only when the final goal is completely met.
  b. once a week whether or not you have stuck to the goal plan.
  c. frequently after specific accomplishments.
  d. whenever you increase the difficulty of the goal.

_____ 6. Another helpful strategy is to
  a. keep a diary of information pertinent to your goal.
  b. try not to think about the behavior you want to change.
  c. go off your goal plan once a week.
  d. talk about your goal at every opportunity.

_____ 7. One caution given is that
  a. unless you work on all the changes at once, you will not succeed.
  b. the changes must be made in a certain order.
  c. it is best to have an expert decide on the needed changes.
  d. you should make only one change at a time.

_____ 8. The author states that
  a. corporate goals bear no relationship to personal goals.
  b. the same goal-setting skills used at work can be used for personal improvement.
  c. some corporate goals can be used for personal improvement, but most cannot.
  d. it is better to keep work ideas separate from personal ones.

_____ 9. Regarding a support group, the author states that it
  a. helps keep motivation high.
  b. can become an unneeded crutch.
  c. can get you off the goal track.
  d. is too difficult to listen to others' problems.

_____ 10. The overall message of this article is that you can reach your goals if you
  a. have willpower.
  b. really want to.
  c. have the emotional support of loved ones.
  d. have a realistic plan.

Allow 10 points per correct answer. *Your score* _____ %
Number of words: 2530   *Your rate* _____
Answer key is on page 271.
Record rate and comprehension score on Course Data Sheet.

5

New Reading Patterns

Materials: • Reading:
            "Superman—An Immigrant Who Really Made It."
          • Drill Book

Objectives: • To learn new hand movements:
            (1) the "L," (2) the Loop, (3) the Open "X", (4) the Closed "X",
            (5) the Straight Down

Many of you may have been aware that your eyes have wanted to move in a different way from the way that the curved hand movement paced you. If so, these new hand movements may feel more comfortable to you. However, even if you felt comfortable with the last hand movement, it is important that everyone be able to use more than one hand movement well. Certain kinds of materials are best read with one hand movement, whereas other kinds require a different one. Also, when you find your attention wandering, changing hand movements will help to bring your concentration back to the print. After you have had practice with all the hand movements, you will probably have a favorite one that you will use most of the time; but you will find that knowing other hand movements will facilitate certain kinds of reading, a fact you will discover when you have had an opportunity to practice on more varied materials later on. Don't decide on a favorite until you have practiced them all.

NEW HAND MOVEMENTS

In the first four of these new hand movements, you should use one finger only, preferably the index finger. They are done smoothly, rhythmically, and rapidly.

1. **The "L"** Starting at the left side of the print, go under the line with the index finger only, moving to the right. At the end of the line, lift the finger and place it directly above about two lines up on the page (at right). Move the finger downward on a slant, going toward the left to finish about six lines down, at the beginning of the line (at left). Lift the finger and place it directly above about two lines up on the page at the beginning of the line (at left). Move the finger straight across to the right under the line. Continue and repeat entire hand movement (see Figure 5-1). Practice the hand movement for a few seconds.

2. **The Loop** This movement is done exactly like the "L" except that the index finger remains on the page. Do *not* lift the finger to place it two lines above. Instead, curve it around upward so that loops are made around the beginnings and ends of the lines that take in about two lines (see Figure 5-2). Practice for a few seconds.

   Now you are ready to try these new hand movements in your drill book. This first time use the "L." Look back and review how it is done. Keep finger under the line when going left to right.

   Using the "L," drill for thirty seconds.

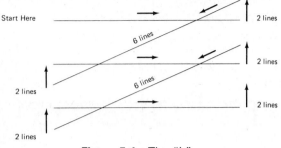

Figure 5-1   The "L"

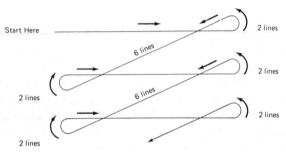

Figure 5-2   The Loop

Begin (30 seconds). Stop. If you had any problems, reread the instructions.

Use the same hand movement and the same material for fifteen seconds. Begin (15 seconds). Stop.

Now practice the Loop. Remember, it is just like the "L," only you must keep your finger on the print at all times. Look back and review if you need to.

Using the Loop, drill for thirty seconds, on the same material. Begin (30 seconds). Stop. Reread the instructions for using the Loop if you had trouble.

Drill for fifteen seconds on the same material. Begin (15 seconds). Stop.

These two hand movements direct your eyes in a specific pattern. They should be used whenever you want to emphasize a particular line, such as in previewing and reading informational material. For use in the preview, go from left to right under the first line of each paragraph, and use the slanted return over the rest of the paragraph. In regular reading, use the finger for emphasis under the first line of each paragraph and a repeat of the hand movement as many times as necessary to complete the paragraph. The number of repeats will depend on the length of the paragraph.

3. **The Open "X"** Still using the index finger only, start at the beginning of a line (at left).

Move the finger to the right in a downward direction on a slant to end at the right about six lines down the page. Lift the finger and place it two lines above, still at the right side of the page. Move the finger in a downward direction to the left on a slant again to end about six lines down the page at the left, at the beginning of a line. Again, lift the finger. Place it two lines above, still at the left. Repeat the hand movement (see Figure 5-3). Practice a few seconds.

4. **The Closed "X"** This hand movement is like the Open "X" except that the index finger remains on the page at all times. It is *not* lifted off the print. Instead, it is curved around upward to form loops at the beginnings and ends of lines (see Figure 5-4). Practice a few seconds.

Let's practice these two hand movements in drills. First try the Open "X." Review instructions above.

The thirty-second drill with Open "X." Begin (30 seconds). Stop. If you had problems, reread the instructions.

The fifteen-second drill: Use the same material. Begin (15 seconds). Stop.

Now try the Closed "X" for thirty seconds, using the same material. Review the instructions. Begin (30 seconds). Stop.

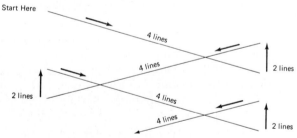

Figure 5-3   The Open "X"

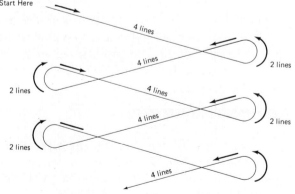

Figure 5-4   The Closed "X"

The fifteen-second drill: Use the same material and same hand movement. Begin (15 seconds). Stop.

5. **The Straight Down** Some of you will find that this is the pacing technique you have been waiting for. However, despite its simplicity, it cannot be used effectively on regular width pages until you have trained your eyes sufficiently to be able to use a wider range of your field of vision.

This is the way it is used: Place your whole hand on the printed page about two lines down from the top of the print, with your fingers spread slightly so that they extend across the entire line of print. Move your hand down the page evenly and smoothly, without stopping under any line. When you go to the next page, your hand again starts about two lines down from the top of the print and then moves straight down the page. Your eyes may either move directly down the center of the page or they may make two stops on each section of print: one stop in the center of the left portion and one in the center of the right portion (see Figure 5-5).

This hand movement cannot be used slowly. If you slow down in your reading, you must change to another hand movement. The most convenient one to use in this case is the Curved "S" (see Figure 5-6).

Now try using the new Straight Down hand movement in your drill book. Turn to any section, and practice for thirty seconds. Begin (30 seconds). Stop. Fifteen seconds: Begin (15 seconds). Stop. Did you find it easy? Were you able to use it well? If not, you may not be quite ready for it yet. Continue to practice it at home, and each week hereafter try using it in the drills until you feel that you can use it well.

Figure 5-5 Straight Down Hand Movement

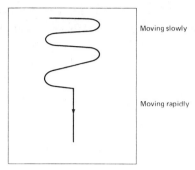

Figure 5-6 The Curved "S"

Drill Practice

In a new section of your drill book, you will practice each new hand movement, going as rapidly as you can for one minute. Use the "L" hand movement this time. Begin (1 minute). Stop. Start your recall sheet.

Add several pages, deciding how many yourself. Now use the Loop. Don't forget the other things you've learned. Turn pages properly. Think ideas or images. Expand your visual attention. Begin (10 seconds . . . 1 minute). Stop. Add to your recall sheet.

Add several more pages. This time use the Open "X." Begin (10 seconds . . . 1 minute). Stop. Write it down.

Add more pages. Use the Closed "X." Begin (10 seconds . . . 1 minute). Stop. Try to add something to your recall sheet.

Add more pages. This time use the Straight Down. Since you always try to move your eyes as rapidly as you can in the drills, do not slow down into the "S" pattern; keep the pace fast, going straight down only. Begin (10 seconds . . . 1 minute). Stop. Write down what you can add to your recall.

Turn to new material for your weekly drill rate. Use one of the new hand movements, whichever is easiest for you. Think images or ideas. Begin (1 minute). Stop. Tell your story aloud to yourself or someone else.

Verify the story you just told (see Chapter 1, page 11 for instructions). You will have two minutes. You may use any hand movement to do this. Begin (2 minutes). Stop.

Figure your drill rate and record it on your Course Data Sheet. You may find that your rate is lower than the one for last week. Whenever you start a new hand movement, your rate may fall temporarily because you are paying attention to the hand movement and therefore are having difficulty reading. However, for those of you who found these hand movements natural, your rate may have increased significantly.

Reading Practice

The practice reading is the article, "Superman—An Immigrant Who Really Made It!" on page 56. Of the new hand movements, the "L" and Loop are best suited for informational material. Use one of these hand movements in the preview and reading of this article.

In the preview, go under the first line of each paragraph and use the slanted return of your index finger to cover the rest of the paragraph so that you are making only one complete "L" or Loop pattern on each paragraph.

In the reading, go under the first line of each paragraph, but this time make the slanted return smaller, taking in about three to four lines. Repeat the pattern several times in each paragraph.

SUMMARY

This lesson presented new hand movements for new reading patterns that utilize overlapping and redirection of eye focus. The "L" and Loop emphasize one line as you use one finger from left to right and skim several lines as you draw your index finger on a slant from right to left. Generally, the "L" and Loop patterns are well-suited to reading informational material. The Open "X," Closed "X," and Straight Down patterns give you additional choices that may suit your individual needs.

SUPERMAN—AN IMMIGRANT WHO REALLY MADE IT!

Dennis Dooley

"If one of the unarguable criteria for literary greatness is universal recognition, consider this: In all of the histroy of literature, there are only five fictional creations known to every man, woman and child on the planet. The urchin in Irkutsk may never have heard of Hamlet; the peon in Pernambuco may not know who Raskolnikov is; the widow in Jakarta may stare blankly at the mention of Don Quixote or Micawber or Jay Gatsby. But every man, woman and child on the planet knows Mickey Mouse, Sherlock Holmes, Tarzan, Robin Hood—and Superman."
Harlan Ellison

Superman celebrates his 50th birthday this year; he first appeared in 1938. But he was actually created four or five years earlier by two Jewish high-school kids from Cleveland, Ohio—Jerry Siegel and Joe Shuster. It took them until 1938 to get Superman into print.

In the Jewish neighborhood on Cleveland's east side where Jerry and Joe lived, they did not exactly cover themselves with academic glory, nor were they worth much as athletes. Perhaps hardest

This article appeared in MOMENT Magazine, Vol. 13, No. 4; excerpted from *Superman at Fifty: The Persistence of a Legend* (Octavia Press: 1987) with permission from the publisher. *Superman at Fifty* is now a Collier paperback. To order a MOMENT Magazine subscription or back copies, call 800 221-4644.

of all to bear, they entertained no ambitions their families could tell friends about.

The precise events that came together to ignite a fantastic idea in a 19-year-old boy's brain are not known. Shuster and Siegel now live in Los Angeles and so far have given no interviews to celebrate Superman's 50th birthday.

In connection with a book I edited (with Gary Engle), entitled *Superman at Fifty*, I went back to old Glenville High School, on Parkwood between St. Clair and Superior Avenues; it is now named Franklin Delano Roosevelt Junior High. The high school library where Jerry and Joe once shared furtive whispers behind history books is now populated by black students from lower middle-class and poor families. But the little room on the first floor where Jerry and his friends put out the weekly student newspaper, *The Glenville Torch,* from 1931 to 1934, is still there.

If you had opened the door of that first-floor room almost any day of the week, back in 1932, you would have come upon one of the most remarkable collections of people ever brought together on the staff of a high school paper anywhere. There, banging away at one or another of those old black upright typewriters, you would have seen the youthful Willie Gilbert, who would subsequently write material for early television shows such as *Howdy Doody* and later wrote a play with the improbable title, *How to Succeed in Business Without Really Trying.* You would also have seen Jerome Lawrence, who would later co-author *Inherit the Wind, Auntie Mame* and other plays. And Seymour Heller, who would wind up out on the West Coast managing a glitzy pianist named Liberace. There was Charlotte Plimmer, who would one day edit *Seventeen* magazine. And Albert Maslow, who was to win national prominence in the field of psychological testing. And finally—a mysterious bespectacled boy named Jerry Siegel, maybe the zaniest of them all.

In those days, Willie Gilbert was still Willie Gomberg; Jerome Lawrence was still Jerry Schwartz; and Charlotte Plimmer was still Charlotte Fingerhut.

Jerry Siegel was a paradox. Outwardly shy, thin, unathletic, bumping about behind glasses that slipped down his nose, he lived almost totally within a boyish imagination teeming with spectacular adventures and tales of outrageous daring.

Here was the soul of a D'Artagnan imprisoned in the body of an undernourished delivery boy. Jerry daydreamed his way through school and went through the motions of his after-school job making deliveries for a printing plant. The four dollars he earned each week helped his family make it through the hard times that afflicted the country. He lived for those precious hours in his room when he did his best to quench his voracious appetite for swashbuckling tales with an all-but-ceaseless intake of dime detective novels and adventure stories by Edgar Rice Burroughs and H. G. Wells and the latest installment of Buck Rogers comics.

He would often arrive late for his first class and tiptoe clumsily to his seat while the annoyed history teacher looked on. His shirt would be hanging out, his rumpled striped pajamas visible below the cuffs of his hastily donned pants—foreshadowing Clark Kent's eccentric habit of wearing his Superman costume underneath his clothes in order to save time in emergencies.

The October 6, 1932 issue of the *Torch* announced with a flourish of nouns and adjectives the publication of a new magazine called *Science Fiction: The Advance Guard of Future Civilization,* J. Siegel—owner, editor, secretary, treasurer and office boy, which will feature "action-adventure stories upon this and other worlds."

The work of "several prominent Glenvillites," writing under pseudonyms, we are informed confidentially, appears in its pages. And among its illustrators is a *Torch* staff cartoonist, one Joe Shuster.

In a sudden outburst of boyish enthusiasm, the writer of the unsigned news piece confides Siegel's excited expectation that the magazine will soon be featuring the work of "well-known" authors as well, then adds, touchingly, that "until a large enough circulation has been reached to warrant printing, the magazine will remain mimeographed."

"Meanwhile," continues the story (which although unsigned bears all the marks of Siegel's prose), "a great deal of capital is being used for advertising which is expected to bring staggering results." For it is the youthful editor's hope, through ads placed in *Amazing Stories* and "practically every other pulp paper magazine on the newsstands," to reach somewhere "in the vicinity of five million magazine readers."

While it never reached a circulation of five million, *Science Fiction: The Advance Guard of Future Civilization* did appear for several issues—and brought Jerry Siegel and Joe Shuster closer together.

The idea for Superman came to Siegel, he once told a reporter for the *Saturday Evening Post,* on a warm summer night in a blinding flash as he lay unable to sleep. Suddenly he saw before him the meek, slope-shouldered figure of Kent, the reporter, banging out at his typewriter the excruciatingly sweet and uninhibited adventures of his other self, who dashed about in a red cape and blue tights leaping buildings, snapping railroad trains like giant whips, knocking gangsters' heads together and rescuing Lois Lane—a hero who could do everything Jerry had ever dreamed of, and do it wonderfully, basking in the admiration of women and the envy of his fellow men.

Even before the sun was all the way up, Siegel dashed, shirt hanging out, several blocks to the house of his friend and sometime collaborator, Joe Shuster.

Like Jerry, Joe was shy with girls and was an insatiable consumer of science fiction and comic strips, especially of the exotic variety, such as *Flash Gordon* and the surrealistic classic *Little Nemo*.

Jerry quickly told Joe about his newest idea and asked Joe to work up the drawings. It was going to take some refinement, but Jerry Siegel and Joe Shuster knew that at last they had their hands on the idea with which they were going to make it—big.

What they didn't know on that mild morning in 1934 was that it was going to take them four exasperating years to get a publisher to give the strip a trial run.

The models for poor Clark Kent were Jerry and Joe themselves. The model for Superman was Douglas Fairbanks, Sr., at least as far as his physical appearance was concerned. As teenagers Jerry and Joe had haunted the local movie houses like addicts, and the swashbuckling Fairbanks' pictures were among their favorites.

Jerry would try to recreate the excitement of those Saturday-afternoon matinees as they worked together, Jerry leaning close in by Joe's shoulder, as he talked him through the story. Though Jerry had never seen a screenplay, he talked instinctively in cinematic terms. "He would describe each scene, and the shot used—long shot, medium, close-up, overhead shot. It was marvelous," Joe recalled years later in an interview with comic book historian Tom Andrae.

For his part, Joe Shuster squinted through thick glasses at the blurry figures of Clark Kent and Lois Lane taking shape beneath his fingers, his nose only a few inches from the drawing board. He had always suffered from poor eyesight; now his creation's powerful X-ray eyes bored through foot-thick walls to expose to the reader the clandestine deeds of dour men.

In the depths of the Depression the Shusters had no heat in their apartment, and during the cold months Joe was sometimes forced to work with gloves on, often wearing two or three sweaters and a jacket or two. One imagines the two friends hunched over the first story boards of *Superman*, trading bursts of frosty breath excitedly, as they shaped the myth and set of characters that would be their ticket out of the poverty and anonymity of their Glenville boyhoods.

But in 1934 the world was not yet ready for Superman. Or at least the adult businessmen who controlled the comics industry were not. It was too far out, the boys were told.

By 1938, Siegel and Shuster had submitted Superman to practically every newspaper syndicate around. Publisher Harry Donenfeld of *Action Com-ics* finally bought the story, but when he was shown the cover drawing for the first comic book—a scene depicting a caped man in tights lifting a car over his head while a stunned gang looks on—Donenfeld is said to have rolled his eyes and pronounced it "ridiculous."

Superman made his first appearance in *Action Comics* in June 1938, but Donenfeld told his editors to choose more sensible cover subjects in the future.

Soon *Action Comics* was selling like hotcakes—as many as half a million copies a month. American youth could not get enough of Superman. And so in 1939, he got his own comic book, which was soon selling an incredible one and a quarter million copies bimonthly—in addition to the *Action Comics* in which he still appeared.

So great was the demand for more adventures of Superman that the McClure Syndicate commissioned Siegel and Shuster to do a daily newspaper strip. In 1940, a 15-minute serial that aired three days a week debuted on the Mutual Radio Network, under the sponsorship of—what else?—Kellogg's Pep, forever emblazoning on the American psyche the immortal words, "Up in the sky, look . . .!" Between 1941 and 1943, 17 lavishly colored animated shorts were turned out for Paramount by Max Fleischer's studios. And in 1942, a full-blown novel by George Lowther was published by Random House.

Superman also spawned a whole new genre of comic books as competitors—even *Action Comics* itself—scrambled to get a piece of the new market. By 1942 more than a dozen other superheroes, all more or less patent imitations, had arrived on the scene. In time this doughty band would include such latter-day Olympians as the Flash, the Torch, Hour-Man, Starman, Hawkman, Plastic Man, the Ultra-Men, Wonder Woman, Wonder Man, Captain Marvel, Captain America, Dr. Fate, Air Wave, the Red Knight, Green Mask and Green Lantern.

But there was no catching him. Superman was an authentic American dream; he simply outclassed all rivals and seemed to thrive on having enemies. The Man of Tomorrow rose unfailingly to the occasion, wrapping girders around bank robbers.

The Nazis took such a whale of a beating at the hands of Siegel and Shuster's hero, both on land and in the air, that Nazi minister of propaganda Joseph Goebbels himself is said to have bounded to his feet in the middle of a Reichstag meeting waving an American comic book and furiously denouncing Superman as a Jew.

For years Siegel and Shuster had been

irritated by all the ripoffs of their famous character. Then National Periodicals itself, the parent company of *Action Comics,* joined the pack and began publishing the adventures of a new character named Superboy, who purported to be the earlier Superman. In 1947, tired of watching others making millions on their character while their own income was declining, Siegel and Shuster went to court. They sought to regain the rights to their creation, cancel their contracts with the McClure Syndicate and Donenfeld, and recover $5 million in what they claimed was lost income. The court, however, denied their claim to ownership of Superman.

Back in 1938, beaten down by years of rejections, the two boys had turned over the first 13 pages of Superman, along with a customary release form relinquishing all rights to their character. For this, they were paid $130, or $10 a page, which they split equally. They had sold Superman.

Soon after Superman had become an overnight sensation, they had complained about the $130 deal. According to Siegel, they were dismissed as "inexperienced" young men with swelled heads who were "grossly exaggerating the importance of Superman." They were told to put their energies into "your work with zest and ambition to improve."

When publisher Harry Donenfeld agreed to let them do a regular newspaper strip for the McClure Syndicate, he stipulated as a condition that they would have to work exclusively for Donenfeld for the next ten years at $35 a page. Donenfeld pointedly reminded them in the negotiations that it was he, Donenfeld, who held all the rights to Superman. If Siegel and Shuster wanted to draw Superman, they had little choice but to sign the agreement.

It was that agreement, confirming the relinquishment of all their rights to Superman, that the Court upheld. Siegel and Shuster are estimated to have earned only about $400,000 from Superman between 1938 and 1947. By 1941, Superman was appearing regularly in 230 newspapers across the country with an estimated total circulation of 25 million, as well as in multiple overseas translations, the marketplace was glutted with Superman toys and other spinoff products.

The year after the court decision, the contract with Donenfeld ran out, and Shuster and Siegel were fired. They could no longer draw Superman.

Long years of bitterness and frustration followed, marked by further legal attempts, also unsuccessful, to regain ownership of Superman. Now outsiders, they watched as others made millions on various Superman deals, and their names no longer appeared on the Superman stories.

In 1963, Siegel went to work as a mailroom clerk at $7,000 a year and Shuster was taken in by his brother Bern. But the two never surrendered their belief that Superman rightfully belonged to them. In 1975, the news that a $20-million *Superman* movie was in the works drew an anguished cry from Siegel in the form of a nine-page, single-spaced press release mailed to a thousand newsrooms around the country. The industry hoopla already surrounding *Superman: The Movie* had been too much for Jerry Siegel to bear, and he asked the public to boycott the film.

Perhaps fearful of the negative publicity, Warner Communications agreed to pay Siegel and Shuster each $20,000 a year for life along with medical coverage for themselves and their families. Warner also promised, in the event of their deaths, to take care of Siegel's wife and Shuster's brother—in exchange for Siegel and Shuster's agreeing to suspend hostilities.

One final gesture was thrown into the bargain: Their names were to be restored to their creation.

Superman is in a way the ultimate immigrant's success story. He came from afar and became *the* greatest American hero.

He was born on the planet Krypton. On the eve of the planet's destruction his parents put him in a tiny rocket ship that hurled him into space. A starchild, he became the only survivor of a wonderful race. After crossing millions of miles of interstellar space, he landed on Earth. There the helpless babe was found—like Moses?—in a cornfield by a gentle couple, the Kents, who raised the lad as their own son. Soon the young Clark Kent discovered his miraculous powers—tremendous strength, X-ray vision, the gift of flight—powers he vowed at his dying foster father's bedside to use only for the good of humankind and the deliverance of the oppressed. For this purpose he hid his true identity behind the bland exterior of timid Kent, the newspaper reporter, emerging from a phone booth or a handy alleyway in his bright red and blue costume with flowing cape and jutting chin whenever evil showed its ugly head or catastrophe endangered the innocent.

Last but not least is his doomed love, as the ineffectual Kent, for his female colleague on the *Daily Planet,* the raven-haired Lois Lane. Lane's ignorance of poor Kent's true identity leaves her continually mooning for yet another glimpse of her manly rescuer, Superman, while Kent increasingly eats his heart out at the third desk from the window.

Here is a peculiarly American myth. And one that could only have been born in the Depression and created by a generation with immigrant traditions seeking to become "real" Americans.

It is impossible to imagine Superman being as popular as he is and speaking as deeply as he does to the American character were he not an immigrant and an orphan. The myth of Superman asserts with total confidence and a childlike innocence the value of the immigrant in American culture. Its theme is cultural assimilation, according to Gary Engle, professor of popular culture at Cleveland State University.

When George Lowther novelized the comic strip in 1942, he revealed that Superman's real, Kryptonic name was Kal-El. *El* in Hebrew is, of course, a name of God, as in *Elohim*. It also appears as an element in a host of names in the Hebrew Bible: Ishma-el, Dani-el, Ezeki-el, Samu-el. *Kal* resembles the Hebrew word for "all." Just as biblical names are compressed sentences—Samuel, for example, means "asked of God"—Kal-El can be read as "all that is God," or perhaps more in the spirit of the myth of Superman, "all that God is."

Superman raises the American immigrant experience to the level of religious myth. He's not just some immigrant from across the waters like all our ancestors, but a real alien, an extraterrestrial, a visitor from heaven if you will.

America has no national religious icons. The idea of a patron saint is ludicrous in a nation whose Founding Fathers wrote into the founding documents the fundamental if not eternal separation of church and state. America, though, is pretty much as religious as other industrialized countries. It's just that our tradition of religious diversity precludes the nation's religious character from being embodied in objects or persons recognizably religious.

In America, cultural icons that manage to tap the national religious spirit are of necessity secular on the surface and sufficiently generalized to incorporate the diversity of American religious traditions. Superman doesn't have to be seen as an angel to be appreciated, says Engle, but in the absence of a tradition of national religious iconography, he can serve as a safe, nonsectarian focus for essentially religious sentiments, particularly among the young. In the last analysis, Superman is an American boy's fantasy of a messiah. He is the heroic male match for the Statue of Liberty, come like an immigrant from heaven to deliver humankind by sacrificing himself in the service of others. He protects the weak and defends truth and justice and all the other moral virtues inherent in the Judeo-Christian tradition, remaining ever vigilant and ever chaste. What purer or stronger vision could there possibly be for a great American folk tale?

COMPREHENSION QUESTIONS

_____ 1. When the character of Superman was first created,
  a. many publishers wanted to put it into print right away.
  b. it took 4 years to get a trial publication.
  c. the creators kept him a secret for fear he would be stolen.
  d. it took 20 years to get publication.

_____ 2. The creators, Joe Shuster and Jerry Siegel, were models for
  a. Superman.
  b. Clark Kent.
  c. Superman's friend.
  d. Clark Kent's boss.

_____ 3. Jerry and Joe's high school, Glenville High, was
  a. the center for many who later become famous.
  b. made famous because of Jerry and Joe.
  c. ordinary in every way and never became famous.
  d. considered substandard academically.

_____ 4. Superman first appeared in a
   a. movie.
   b. novel.
   c. comic strip.
   d. radio series.

_____ 5. The creators sold rights to Superman for
   a. $10 million.
   b. $130.
   c. $50 million.
   d. $50.

_____ 6. Joe and Jerry are
   a. still drawing Superman.
   b. working on the next Superman movie.
   c. no longer allowed to draw Superman.
   d. writing a Superman novel.

_____ 7. The author of this article compares Superman to the biblical character
   a. Jesus, who inspired a new religion.
   b. Abraham, who was chosen by God to father many nations.
   c. David, who fought Goliath.
   d. Moses, who was found as a helpless babe.

_____ 8. Superman was at one time given the biblical-type name
   a. Joshua.
   b. Kal-El.
   c. Samuel.
   d. Adam.

_____ 9. This article says that the reason Superman became so popular is that he is
   a. what each boy dreams of becoming.
   b. the symbol of good.
   c. always involved in new, interesting adventures.
   d. an American boy's fantasy of a messiah.

_____ 10. One conclusion that can be drawn from the information in this article is that
   a. some of the characters copied from Superman will eventually surpass Superman in popularity.
   b. Superman's popularity will continue and may even become greater.
   c. Superman-type characters have outlived their usefulness.
   d. a character greater than Superman is yet to be created.

Allow 10 points per correct answer.   *Your score* _____ %
Number of words: 3170   *Your rate* _____
Answer key is on page 271.
Record rate and comprehension score on Course Data Sheet.

6

Using Rapid-Reading Skills on the Newspaper

Materials: • A few pages of the news part of the newspaper

Objectives: • To become aware of the journalistic style and organizational pattern of writing
• To learn how to use this pattern as an aid in reading the newspaper
• To learn modifications of the basic speed-reading hand movements so that they fit narrow columns of print

Drill Practice

In the drills today, practice the hand movement with which you are having the most difficulty—either the "L," the Loop, the Open "X," or the Closed "X."

Read as rapidly as you can for one minute, using the troublesome hand movement. Begin (1 minute). Stop.

Begin your recall sheet. In addition, write down a question about what you read—something you may have seen but can't remember, or something about which you want more information.

Set a goal for yourself. How many additional pages do you want to cover? Add them. See if you can reach this goal in one minute. Also, specifically look for the answer to the question you wrote down.

Begin (10 seconds . . . 1 minute). Stop. Try to answer your question. Write another question. Did you reach your goal? Set another goal. Try harder this time.

Begin (10 seconds . . . 1 minute). Stop. Answer your question. Did you reach your goal this time?

JOURNALISTIC STYLE AND ORGANIZATION

Newspapers are probably the most important and most readily available source of current information. Television newscasts usually give only highlights of some of the current happenings; for complete coverage with all the details, one must rely on the daily newspaper. However, for the ordinary slow reader, it is a chore to get through an entire newspaper in one day. For the rapid reader, it is a simple task, as you shall see.

Although a news article may appear to be narrating a story in that it relates a sequence of events, may deal with characters, and may have a setting of time and place, it is not a story in the literary sense. There are some important differences. The newspaper reports facts instead of imaginary incidents. It deals with real people rather than made-up characters. The sequence of events is usually told in the order of occurrence, not in an order to suit the author's personal purpose. A literary story has a beginning, a middle, and an end, which together comprise a unified whole; and none of its parts can be omitted or changed without changing the meaning of the total story. A newspaper article has no such unity. If any portion is left out, the story remains basically the same; only some details may be missing. Most literary stories are written to interpret and make a comment on life, as seen by the author. Newspaper articles, by their very nature, are supposed to relay verifiable data to the reader without interpretation or comments by the author. A well-written story does not lose its impact on the reader with a lapse of time, even of many years—even centuries. Newspaper articles, on the other hand, become outdated quickly, often in one day.

In addition, because most important newspapers are published daily, such articles have certain limitations imposed on them. They must be written quickly; they must all fit together within the allotted space with no blank areas left on the page; they must be written on a level that can be read and understood by the majority of the population; and the entire newspaper must be able to be read on the day of publication.

These limitations and the basic requirements of news articles dictate the style of writing and the manner of organization. Events are revealed in a relatively simple language generally as the author observed them, as told to him or her by someone else or as sent over the national news wires. A very brief condensation of the most important idea in the article is placed in the headline. If the article is extremely important, it may have a subheadline, which states the most significant detail in a short form. The first few inches of the article relate all the most notable facts. The remainder of the article restates these facts and adds the details. The end of the article rarely contains any new information, because the journalist knows that readers may not bother to read that far and that if the editor is short of space, the last few inches may be cut off entirely.

HOW TO READ THE NEWS

In reading the newspaper, we make use of our knowledge of its structure. No formal previewing is necessary; the headlines supply all the foreknowledge needed. You read the first few important inches at a good comprehension rate, slowly enough to understand it. You speed up over the rest of the rehash and details. If you read the entire paper, it will be all in one day, and thus it is easier to start on the first page and continue consecutively without turning back and forth to the "continued" sections.

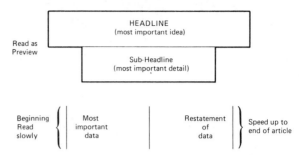

Figure 6-1 How to Read the Newspaper

You will not have forgotten what the article on page one was about when you get to page seven a few minutes later. (See Figure 6-1.)

This information covers articles written in the journalistic manner only, the news part of the newspaper. It does not cover the editorial page or special columns by columnists. These are written in the essay style. They have a beginning, a middle, and an end, and sometimes a punch line at the end for effect. They are not changed or shortened by the editor; they are printed as originally written.

HOW TO READ NARROW COLUMNS

Newspapers are written in narrower columns than ordinary book print. Some adjustments are necessary to fit these narrow columns so that your fingers are only on the print that you are reading. They should not spill over into adjoining columns. These adjustments in hand movements can be used on any narrow column: newspapers, magazines, textbooks, and so on.

When using the Curved "S" hand movement, instead of using your whole hand, use only two fingers. Any two fingers that feel comfortable will do. Use these two fingers exactly as you did the whole hand, curving back and forth down the page. (See Figure 6-2.)

The "L," Loop, Open "X," and Closed "X" require little change. These hand movements will be smaller because of the limited space. All the slanted parts of the movements will, of course, be shorter but will still cover the usual number of lines. (See Figure 6-2.)

The Straight Down hand movement is especially effective for reading narrow columns. Place as many fingers on the column as will fit comfortably. Move them straight down the page smoothly, without stopping under any line. (See Figure 6-2.) This hand movement will not work if you go slowly; it must be fast. If you have to move slowly,

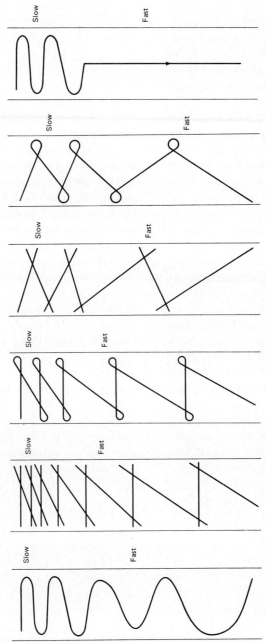

Figure 6-2 Hand movements for reading narrow columns. From left to right: The "S" (use one or two fingers); the "L," Loop, Open "X," and Closed "X" (use one finger); the Straight Down (use one or more fingers).

as you will at the beginning of the article, use the "S" hand movement; then change to The Straight Down hand movement as you speed up for the rest of the article.

Reading Practice

You will now have a chance to try each hand movement on the newspaper. Choose an article. Use the Curved "S" hand movement this time. You will have thirty seconds to read the article. Just read the portion that is on one page; do not turn to the continued part on another page. When time is up, you will recite aloud to yourself or to someone else what you have read. Begin (30 seconds). Stop. Recite aloud.

Choose another article. This time, use the "L." Begin (30 seconds). Stop. Tell what you read to yourself or to a partner.

Read another article, using the Loop hand movement. Begin (30 seconds). Stop. Tell your story aloud.

Read another article, using the Open "X." Begin (30 seconds). Stop. Tell what your article was about.

Use the Closed "X" for another article. Begin (30 seconds). Stop. What was in your article?

For the last time, pick an article. This time use the Straight Down hand movement. Remember, it cannot be done slowly. At the beginning when you must go slowly, use the Curved "S"; go into the Straight Down movement when you can speed up. Begin (30 seconds). Stop. Tell what you read to yourself or a partner.

See how easy it is to be informed? You can read the whole newspaper at breakfast or while you are waiting for dinner.

SUMMARY

Newspaper articles differ from literary stories in their basic requirements, the most notable of which is that the news must relate timely facts of interest to the general population. They also have the specific limitations of immediate time, allotted space, and readers' abilities.

The style and organizational pattern of newspaper articles are used as aids in reading. They are read in the following manner: headline; subheadline, first few inches, containing the main facts, slowly; the rest of the article, containing the details, rapidly.

Narrow columns necessitate modified versions of regular hand movements that require fewer fingers and less space.

7

Flexibility

Materials: • Readings:
      "The Mysterious Powers of Body and Mind"
      "The Tell-Tale Heart"
    • Drill book

Objectives: • To learn how to speed up and slow down according to the difficulty and importance of the material and the purpose for reading it
    • To learn how to change hand movements as needed

Drill Practice

Pretend that your head is a magic movie camera and that your eyes are the lenses of the camera. Starting at the top of the page, move the camera from one large segment of print to the next rapidly and smoothly, photographing the print with soft focus until you have covered the whole page; then, move on to the next page and do the same thing. This magic camera photographs the print, but the print is magically transformed into pictures of the story that you can see on the screen in your head, the tiny screen that is like a third eye in the center of your forehead. However, you must keep this screen empty and available to show the pictures from the story. Whatever appears on this screen you must accept as being from the book without question.

Now in a new section of your drill book, go over the print with your magic camera as rapidly as you can, faster than you have ever gone before. Ready? Begin (1 minute). Stop. Begin recall sheet.

Count the number of pages you covered. Add an equal number so that you will be going twice as fast to finish to your new goal. Back at the beginning. Ready? Begin (10 seconds . . . 1 minute). Stop. Write it down.

This time cover the same amount of material in less time, 45 seconds. Back at the beginning.

Ready? Begin (10 seconds . . . 45 seconds). Stop. Add to your recall.

To take your drill rate, turn to new material, starting at the top of a page. Go at least as fast as you have been doing. Ready? Begin (1 minute). Stop. Figure your rate and record it on your Course Data Sheet.

FLEXIBILITY

All parts of any story, article, or book are not of equal difficulty. Even within one paragraph there may be some portions that are more difficult and other portions that are easier. To read efficiently, you must adjust your speed according to the difficulty of the lines you are reading and your purpose for reading them. On hard parts you slow down, and on easy parts you speed up. If you are reading for study purposes, your general overall rate will be slower, but still you should slow down more on the important parts and speed up on the parts of lesser importance. If you are reading just to get the general idea of what the material is about, your overall speed should be faster; but again, within that higher speed range you will want to slow down slightly to get the main ideas and then speed up on the rest of the material.

It is also important to be able to change from one hand movement to another as you read. If you start the material with the "L" hand movement, and for some reason the print suddenly appears in short sentences only on the left with large open blank spaces at the right, that hand movement would no longer be apropriate because it would lead your eyes into the blank spaces. In such a case, you would be better off to change to the Curved "S" hand movement and only go over the printed section. So you see, you want to suit the hand movement to the layout of the print on the page.

Another reason to change hand movements is to force your attention back to what you are reading if your mind wanders. By doing so, you must think about the mechanics of making the change and your attention will be brought back to reading.

Up to now, you have been using your hand like a little machine pacer that once started at a particular speed, you forgot about and allowed to continue at the same rate throughout the material. It is time to learn to exert more control over that little hand-machine pacer. This chaper will prepare you to gain control and read in a more flexible manner.

Practice in Speed Flexibility

In order to get the feel of slowing down and speeding up, you will do a short exercise. When you are reading, you will, of course, change your speed as necessary for comprehension of the materials. In this exercise, however, you will practice by slowing and speeding on command of the instructor, or every three to seven seconds if you are doing this exercise by yourself.

Open your drill book to any part. Using the "S" hand movement, you will go slower or faster as instructed. To slow down, you move your hand at a slightly slower rate and tighten the curve by taking in fewer lines with each curve (Figure 7-1).

Begin reading at your regular rate for seven seconds. Speed up for three seconds. Speed up more for three seconds. Slow down for three seconds. Slow down more for three seconds. Speed up for three seconds. Slow down for three seconds. Speed up for three seconds. Speed up more for seven seconds. Stop.

Notice that when you slow down it is only for a very short time, only until you have completed the very difficult part or understood the important idea presented. If you stay at a slow rate, you are not using flexibility; you are reading slowly.

Next, try the same thing, using the "L" or the Loop hand movement. Again, slow down by moving your hand slightly slower and by taking in fewer lines when you move your finger on the slant to bring your eyes back to the left. Speed up by moving your hand faster and taking in more lines, making the hand movement larger (Figure 7-2).

Begin at your regular rate for seven seconds. Speed up for seven seconds. Slow down for five seconds. Speed up for five seconds. Speed up more for seven seconds. Slow down for three seconds. Speed up for five seconds. Speed up more for seven seconds. Stop.

With the Open or Closed "X," you slow down by making both slanted movements shorter so that you take in fewer lines while slowing your hand slightly. You speed up by moving more rapidly and by making the slanted movements longer to take in more lines of print (Figure 7-3).

Try using these hand movements. Begin at your regular rate for seven seconds. Speed up for five seconds. Speed up more for seven seconds. Slow down for three seconds. Slow down more for five seconds. Speed up for five seconds. Speed up more for five seconds. Speed up still more for seven seconds. Slow down for three seconds. Speed up for seven seconds. Stop.

The last hand movement, going Straight Down, is different in that you cannot use it when you are going very slowly. You can slow it slightly, but when you must go very slowly, you have to

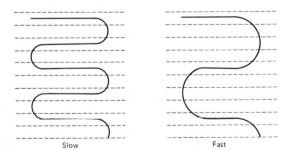

Slow   Fast

Figure 7-1 Speed Flexibility: The "S"

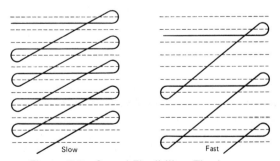

Slow   Fast

Figure 7-2 Speed Flexibility: The Loop

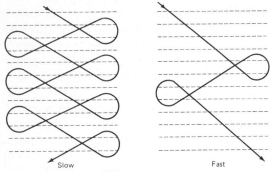

Slow   Fast

Figure 7-3   Speed Flexibility: The "X"

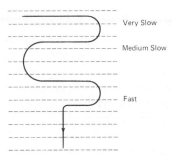

— Very Slow

— Medium Slow

— Fast

Figure 7-4   Speed Flexibility: Straight Down and the "S"

change to the "S" hand movement until you can speed up again (Figure 7-4).

Let's try it. Begin for seven seconds. Speed up for seven seconds. Speed up more for seven seconds. Slow down for five seconds. Slow down more for three seconds. Slow down more for three seconds (use the "S"). Speed up for five seconds. Speed up more for seven seconds. Slow down for three seconds. Slow down more for three seconds. Slow down still more for five seconds (use the "S"). Speed up for seven seconds. Stop.

Now you can see one advantage to using your hand as a pacer—you can control the speed on each line if necessary, and you can change the pacing pattern whenever you wish. You could not do these things if you were using a machine.

In case you are wondering how you will know when to slow down, experience will soon guide you. However, as a rule, the parts that need to be read more slowly are the beginnings of things, where the most important ideas are likely to appear: the beginning of the article or story, the beginning of a chapter, the beginning of a paragraph, the beginning of a new idea. Reading beginnings more thoroughly will improve your overall comprehension, because it will allow you to become absorbed in the material from the start, increase your chances of catching the main ideas, and enable you to follow the sequence of ideas presented.

However, your tendency will be to read the whole thing at your starting rate—don't. Start slowly; speed up as soon as you understand what the material is about; then maintain your speed with only a slight decrease at the outset of each new paragraph and any parts within the paragraph that seem to be especially important or difficult. Always remember to increase your rate again after your have slowed.

Practice in Hand Movement Flexibility

Still using your drill book, you will practice changing from one hand movement to another on command of the instructor, or approximately every ten to fifteen seconds, if you are doing this exercise by yourself. Use all six hand movements in this exercise. Begin with any hand movement, change to another hand movement, change to a third hand movement, change again, change, change, change, and so on.

Drill Practice in Flexibility

Return to the section of your drill book from which you took your drill rate today. Using flexibility, read this section for comprehension to verify what you drilled. You will have two minutes to cover as much as you can with understanding. Remember to slow down on beginnings and any place that you don't understand, but be sure to speed up on all other parts. If you slow down and stay slow, you are just doing slow reading, not using flexibility! You may also wish to try changing hand movements, especially in large places where the print appears on one small portion of the page. Always keep your hand on the print, not on open blank spaces. Change to whichever hand movement will accomplish this. Ready? Begin (2 minutes). Stop.

Reading Practice in Flexibility

In the reading practices, your primary objective will be to use flexibility. Slow down at the beginning of the work, each paragraph, each section and any place that is difficult to understand or where you suspect an important idea or detail is being presented. Speed up where you find it is easy to understand and places of lesser importance. Since the readings are printed in narrow columns, modify your hand movement to fit the column, as instructed in the previous chapter.

As you read the article "The Mysterious Powers of Body and Mind" on page 69, use flexibility so that you understand the main idea and important details, which will most likely appear at beginnings. Preview by going rapidly over the first and last paragraphs and only under the first line of each of the other paragraphs.

As you read the story "The Tell-Tale Heart" on page 72 use flexibility to follow the sequence of events. Preview by swooping down each column.

SUMMARY

You do not progress through material at one rate, nor do you necessarily use only one hand movement. Rather, you speed up and slow down continuously according to your purpose and the difficulty of the material you are reading, and you suit the hand movement to the type of material and to the way it is printed on the page so that your hand and eyes always remain on the print.

The Mysterious Powers of Body and Mind

Michael Murphy

In places as far from you as a Buddhist temple, or as close as the nearby gym, the mental and physical have interacted to bring about extraordinary capabilities

Psychiatrist Robert Moody was probably not surprised when one of his patients began struggling as if he were tightly bound. It's not uncommon for someone undergoing psychotherapy to relive a traumatic experience in a realistic manner, and this man had been tied up with ropes during a trip to India. But then something extraordinary began to happen.

"After a few minutes," Moody wrote, "weals appeared on both forearms; gradually these became indented; finally some . . . hemorrhages appeared along their course. . . . Next morning, the marks were still clearly visible and were photographed."

Moody went on to describe other cathartic episodes he had witnessed during which patients spontaneously developed clear physical marks. A man who had been buried during a bomb explosion, for example, suddenly displayed a swelling on his left ankle and another on his head, where he had been hit in the incident. A woman who relived a riding accident exhibited bleeding and bruising on her right side, where she had fractured some ribs. And another female patient, during a cathartic recall of a terrible beating by her father, spontaneously developed a bruise on her hand that closely resembled the imprint of an elaborately carved walking stick with which her father had struck her.

Moody's accounts, which appeared with photographs in 1946 and 1948 in the British medical journal *The Lancet*, are part of a vast literature that reveals the transformative power of mental events upon the physical body. For centuries, these accounts have come down to us in the form of legends, folktales, religious documents, and stories of warriors and saints. In recent years, however, scientific investigation has added to the evidence that the idea of the separation of mind and body simply will not hold, and that when the mental and physical are jointly cultivated, they give rise to extraordinary human capabilities.

In 1976, with financial help from the Esalen Institute, Laurence Rockefeller, and others, a small group of us organized the Transformation Project to collect and analyze evidence of the human body's supernormal capabilities, to better understand the disciplines and circumstances that evoke them. So far, we have assembled more than ten thousand scientific studies and anecdotal accounts of exceptional human capacities exhibited during such practices as psychotherapy, hypnosis, meditation, spiritual healing, shamanism, the martial arts, sports, and a variety of esoteric disciplines. We have established relations with a number of organizations that have scholarly libraries, among them the Menninger Foundation, the Religious Research Unit at Oxford, the American Society for Psychical Research, and the Medical Bureau at Lourdes.

The work is guided by the idea that our bodies possess the capacity for more effective functioning, and that this capacity can be cultivated through a combination of mental and physical disciplines. This capacity often emerges in the performances of great athletes and dancers and in the charismatic powers of yogis, but also shows up in people under extreme pressure: in pathology, during therapy or hypnosis, and even in the course of everyday life. The pervasiveness of this phenomenon strongly suggests a species-wide endowment waiting to be developed. Indeed, our research has revealed that the power of the mind to change the body can manifest itself in all sorts of people, in all sorts of circumstances:

• In false pregnancy, or pseudocyesis, women can develop a greatly swollen abdomen, cessation of menstruation, breast enlargement, secretion of milk, and apparent fetal movement. *The Journal of Nervous and Mental Disease* recently reported the case of a schizophrenic man who had a great desire for a child. While hospitalized for his mental condition, he said he felt something moving in his stomach, "like a baby." During the next three weeks his abdomen became more and more protuberant and he gained sixteen pounds. Repeated medical tests showed no pathology that could account for the growth.

• The specificity with which mental images can affect the body is revealed dramatically when deeply hypnotized people spontaneously exhibit welts that spell out words the hypnotist has suggested.

• The body's responsiveness to highly specific suggestion is demonstrated by placebos, which deceive patients into activating their own mind-body healing powers. After taking pills made of sugar or some other inert substance, subjects in various studies have experienced relief from asthma, hay fever, headache, high blood pressure, diabetes, peptic ulcer, seasickness, warts, chronic pain, and arthritis. The patient who is told what to expect from a certain drug can produce that exact effect when given a dummy pill, down to creating a surplus of specialized blood cells called eosinophils. Placebos can even produce the *side effects* of the drugs they mimic. Studies of the effectiveness of a surgical procedure designed to relieve the pain of angina pectoris testify to the power of the placebo effect. The procedure involves cutting into the chest and tying off the mammary artery. Two double-blind studies (studies in which neither the subjects nor the experimenters know the makeup of the test and control groups) were performed, in which some of the patients were given the actual surgery, while others, the control group, were given sham surgery—an incision was made in their chests, but the arteries were not tied off. In one of the studies, 100 percent of those receiving the sham surgery reported improvement, compared with only 76 percent of those whose arteries were actually tied.

• Scientific journals have reported at least twenty-six kinds of physio-logical changes caused by transcendental meditation, Zen Buddhist sitting, and other types of contemplative activity. Based on calm concentration, they can produce a complex but integrated set of bodily reactions—termed the relaxation response by Dr. Herbert Benson of Harvard—that include the slowing and synchronization of brain waves, the slowing of heart rate and breathing, the lowering of lactate and adrenal-hormone levels in the blood, and the reduction of sweating. This is the opposite of the fight-or-flight response provoked by threatening situations, and it forms a physiological basis for the exalted states of mind associated with mystical experience.

• Through biofeedback, many people have learned to modify physiological functions once considered inaccessible to conscious will. Such self-control may even be extended to single cells within the body, as researcher John Basmajian showed when he trained people to vary the firing patterns of designated nerve cells and the muscle fibers to which they attached. Biofeedback subjects also learn to control their brain waves, heart rate, blood pressure, muscular tension, gastric activity, and other processes, and there is now a consensus among researchers that any physiological process that can be brought to awareness through biofeedback can be voluntarily modified.

• The Jesuit scholar Herbert Thurston investigated the unusual physical powers of a group of Catholic saints and mystics for some fifty years and made detailed, balanced appraisals of them. His classic work, *The Physical Phenomena of Mysticism*, contains careful studies of "inedia" (the ability to live for long periods without food), levitation, luminosity, and other extraordinary phenomena associated with sanctity. He described, for example, Teresa Neumann, a German peasant who died in 1962, and her spontaneously recurring wounds, or stigmata, that appeared on Fridays and particular holy days. The French physician Antoine Imbert-Gourbeyre, in compiling an exhaustive account of such phenomena, described 321 people with similar marks. Like the welts and bruises that have appeared on the bodies of some psychiatric patients, these wounds dramatize the body's highly specific responsiveness to passionate feelings and their associated imagery.

• A few Western scientists have recently studied Indian yogis, Tibetan lamas, and other contemplation adepts, looking for powers such as those attributed to Catholic stigmatics. Elmer Green of the Menninger Foundation, for example, found that the Indian swami Rama could deliberately produce a difference in temperature between two parts of his hand that exceeded 13 degrees Fahrenheit, and Herbert Benson and his colleagues tested Tibetan meditation masters who could raise the temperature of their feet by as much as 15 degrees.

We need not turn to Catholic stigmatics or Tibetan meditation masters, though, to observe powers akin to those I've just described. The body's marvelous capacities are revealed daily in gymnasiums, on football fields, racetracks, mountainsides, and beaches—in every arena of modern sport.

When Lee Evans set the world record for the 400-meter dash at the 1968 Olympics, for example, his time of 43.86 seconds was so far ahead of its day that it still stands as the record. He prepared for the race using a relaxation method suggested by his coach, Bud Winter, who'd previously trained other national and Olympic champions in the same way. Evans mentally practiced every stride he would make, as well as anticipated the emotions that might arise before and during the race. He'd used this technique for several years prior to his Olympic tryouts, rehearsing the races stride for stride to perfect his form and minimize energy expenditure. At the Mexico City Olympics, he said, his physical talent was more powerful than ever before, lifting him to a level no one has matched in the last eighteen years.

Stunning athletic achievements suggest that all of us possess bodily powers we have only begun to cultivate. And we are learning that transformations of the body tend to be accompanied by transformations of consciousness. Though this fact is rarely reported on the sports pages or in biographies of prominent sports figures, athletic endeavor often triggers feelings of freedom, exaltation, and personal power, of unity with nature and with people. Intense athletic effort is also reported to be accompanied at times by telepathic, precognitive, and other paranormal experiences. According to some athletes, such states of expanded consciousness have improved their performance and enhanced the way their bodies function in general.

Western sport, it seems to me, has become a vast laboratory for personal transformation. The problem is, we haven't yet learned to read the dials. Most coaches, trainers, and reporters are oblivious to such experiences, but many top-flight athletes can be eloquent in their descriptions of transformative experiences.

Take Frank Zane's account of the 1977 Mr. Olympia contest, when he won the first of his three world body-building championships. Zane held a firm belief in the power of the mind, and, while training, he would visualize his muscles just the way he wanted them. During the months preceding this event, his mental practice went even further, into a realm that could be called religious. He started to practice a silent Buddhist mantra with such continuity that it produced a serenity and power he'd never before experienced. His inner state became so concentrated, he said, that it helped his body develop along the lines he desired and also seemed to generate an inner illumination that was reportedly perceived by others.

Such events as this and the other examples that we've collected suggest to me that we have reached a new frontier. And in exploring its possibilities, I believe, we can examine the basic ways in which these phenomena occur. From biofeedback research, for example, we can learn how to modify involuntary processes such as blood pressure and body temperature. From physical-fitness research we can find those training regimens that will best fit our particular physiques. From meditation studies we can discover ways to promote the integration of physiological and psychological processes, thus balancing our mind and body so that together they may realize their greater capacities. And from saints and mystics we gain a vision of the powers of the body transformed by the energies of mind and spirit. We now know that the human body, as wonderful as it is, has even more wonderful secrets to reveal in the years to come.

COMPREHENSION QUESTIONS

_____ 1. The Transformation Project, a group organized to collect and analyze evidence of the human body's supernormal capabilities has assembled
a. 100,000 verified scientific studies.
b. half a million anecdotal accounts only.
c. more than 10,000 scientific studies and story accounts.
d. 20 books full of evidence.

_____ 2. In experiments, when a dummy pill was given, patients
a. did not improve.
b. experienced the same effects, including side effects, of the real medication.
c. always improved more than those taking the real medication.
d. often experienced the opposite effects from what was expected.

_____ 3. Researchers believe that through biofeedback one can voluntarily modify
a. any physiological process that can be brought to awareness.
b. only those processes that are partially voluntarily controlled, such as breathing.
c. all physiological processes.
d. only those dealing with muscular control.

_____ 4. This article states that calm concentration such as relaxation response or transcendental meditation
a. increases one's I.Q.
b. increases the heart rate and breathing.
c. slows and syhnchronizes brain waves.
d. cleanses the body through sweating.

_____ 6. Lee Evans, who set an astonishing Olympic record, reported that he prepared by
a. pushing himself to the limit physically.
b. pushing himself to the limit mentally.
c. paradoxically holding himself back physically and mentally.
d. mentally rehearsing the race over and over.

_____ 7. Frank Zane, winner of three body-building championships, reported that he trained
a. using no traditional weights.
b. by visualizing his muscles the way he wanted them to be.
c. by carefully observing what his competition did.
d. by eating only red meats and fruits.

_____ 8. Regarding the extraordinary control the mind has over the body, illustrated in this article, the author suggests that
a. the capabilities must be trained from early childhood.
b. in the future everyone will possess these capabilities, but not now.
c. all in the species have these capabilities waiting to be developed.
d. a select few are endowed with these extraordinary capabilities.

_____ 9. This author also suggests that
a. transformations of the body, such as in great athletics, tend to be accompanied by transformations of the consciousness.
b. to excel in an athletic endeavor one must experience telepathic episodes regularly.
c. there is no way to consciously develop the mind-body connection.
d. the mind's control over the body works best in athletics, not in other areas.

_____ 10. The author believes that we now know
a. all the wonders of which the body and mind are capable; we only have to accept and use them.
b. the human body has even more wonderful secrets to reveal.
c. how to cure cancer and other so-called incurable diseases.
d. exactly what to do to improve in any area.

Allow 10 points per correct answer. Your score _____ %
Number of words: 2060 Your rate _____
Answer key is on page 271.
Record your rate and comprehension score on Course Data Sheet.

THE TELL-TALE HEART

Edgar Allan Poe

True!—nervous—very, very dreadfully nervous I had been and am. But why will you say that I am mad? The disease had sharpened my senses—not destroyed—not dulled them. Above all the sense of

This story has been adapted by the author for use in this book.

hearing was sharpened. I heard all things in the heaven and in the earth. I heard many things in hell. How, then, am I mad? Listen carefully! and observe how healthily—how calmly I can tell you the whole story!

It is impossible to say how the idea first entered my brain. But

once begun, it haunted me day and night. Object there was none. Passion there was none. I loved the old man. He had never wronged me. He had never insulted me. For his gold I had no desire. I think it was his eye! Yes, it was this! He had the eye of a vulture—a pale blue eye, with a film over it. Whenever it fell upon me, my blood ran cold. And so by degrees—very gradually—I made up my mind to take the life of the old man, and thus rid myself of the eye forever.

Now this is the point. You think me mad. Madmen know nothing. But you should have seen me. You should have seen how wisely I proceeded. With what caution—with what foresight—with what pretense I went to work! I was never kinder to the old man than during the whole week before I killed him. And every night, about midnight, I turned the latch of his door and opened it—oh so gently! And then, when I had made an opening large enough for my head, I put in a dark lantern, all closed, closed, so that no light shone out. And then I pushed in my head. Oh, you would have laughed to see how cleverly I pushed it in! I moved it slowly—very very slowly, so that I might not disturb the old man's sleep. It took me an hour to place my whole head within the opening so far that I could see him as he lay upon his bed. Ha! would a madman have been so wise as this? And then, when my head was well in the room, I undid the lantern carefully—oh, so carefully—carefully (for the hinges creaked), I undid it just enough so that a single thin ray fell upon the vulture eye. And this I did for seven long nights—every night just at midnight. But I found the eye always closed. And so it was impossible to do the work. For it was not the old man who angered me, but his Evil Eye. And every morning, when the day broke, I went boldly into the room, and spoke bravely to him, calling him by name in a hearty tone, and asking how he had slept. So you see he would have been a very smart old man, indeed, to suspect that every night, just at twelve, I looked in upon him while he slept.

Upon the eighth night I was more than usually careful in opening the door. A watch's minute hand moves more quickly than did mine. Never before that night, had I felt the extent of my own powers—of my wisdom. I could scarcely contain my feelings of triumph. To think that there I was, opening the door, little by little, and he not even dreaming of my secret deeds or thoughts. I fairly chuckled at the idea. And perhaps he heard

me. For he moved on the bed suddenly, as if startled. Now you may think that I drew back—but no. His room was as black as pitch with the thick darkness (for the shutters were fastened, through fear of robbers). And so I knew that he could not see the opening of the door, I kept pushing it on steadily, steadily.

I had my head in, and was about to open the lantern, when my thumb slipped upon the tin fastening, and the old man sprang up in bed, crying out—"Who's there?"

I kept quite still and said nothing. For a whole hour I did not move a muscle. In the meantime, I did not hear him lie down. He was still sitting up in the bed listening—just as I have done, night after night, listening to the death sounds in the wall.

Soon I heard a slight groan, and I knew it was the groan of mortal terror. It was not a groan of pain or of grief. Oh, no!—it was the low stifled sound that arises from the bottom of the soul when full with fear. I knew the sound well. Many a night, just at midnight, when all the world slept, it has sprung up from my own bosom, deepening, with its dreadful echo, the terrors that drove me wild. I say I knew it well. I knew what the old man felt, and pitied him, although I chuckled in my heart. I knew that he had been lying awake ever since the first slight noise, when he had turned in the bed. His fears had been growing ever since. He had been trying to believe them causeless, but could not. He had been saying to himself—"It is nothing but the wind in the chimney—it is only a mouse crossing the floor," or "it is just a cricket, which has made a single chirp." Yes, he had been trying to comfort himself with these possibilities. But he had found all in vain, All in vain; because Death, in approaching him, had walked quietly with his black shadow before him, and surrounded the victim. And it was the mournful influence of the unknown shadow that caused him to feel—although he neither saw nor heard—to feel the presence of my head within the room.

When I had waited a long time, very patiently, without hearing him lie down, I decided to open a little—a very, very little crack in the

lantern. So I opened it—you cannot imagine how stealthily, stealthily—until, at length, a single dim ray, like the thread of the spider, shot out from the crack and fell full upon the vulture eye.

It was open—wide, wide open—and I grew furious as I gazed upon it. I saw it with perfect clarity—all a dull blue, with an ugly veil over it that chilled the very marrow of my bones. But I could see nothing else of the old man's face or person. I had directed the ray as if by instinct, exactly upon the damned spot.

And have I not told you that what you mistake for madness is but great sharpness of the senses? Now, I say, there came to my ears a low, dull, quick sound, such as a watch makes when wrapped in cotton. I knew that sound well, too. It was the beating of the old man's heart. It increased my fury, as the beating of a drum increases the courage in the soldier.

But even yet I kept still. I scarcely breathed. I held the lantern motionless. I tried how steadily I could maintain the ray upon the eye. Meantime the hellish beating of the heart increased. It grew quicker and quicker, and louder and louder every instant. The old man's terror must have been extreme! It grew louder, I say, louder every moment! I have told you that I am nervous. So I am. And now at the dead hour of the night, in the middle of the dreadful silence of that old house, so strange a noise as this excited me to uncontrollable terror. Yet, for some minutes longer I stayed back and stood still. But the beating grew louder, louder! I thought the heart must burst. And now a new worry seized me—the sound would be heard by a neighbor! The old man's time had come! With a loud yell, I threw open the lantern and leaped into the room. He shrieked once—once only. In an instant I dragged him to the floor, and pulled the heavy bed over him. I then smiled gaily, to find the deed so far done. But, for many minutes, the heart beat on with a muffled sound. This, however, did not anger me. It would not be heard through the wall. At length it stopped. The old man was dead. I removed the bed and looked carefully at the corpse. Yes, he was

8

Speed Reading an Easy Novel

Materials:
- Reading:
  Lilies of the Field, or a novel of similar length (19,800 words) and difficulty
- Questions on *Lilies of the Field* or general novel questions at the end of this chapter

Objectives:
- To use the rapid-reading techniques you have learned on a longer work
- To attempt to finish a novel within one hour
- To try to visualize the story as you read it

Certainly all of your reading will not be short, simple stories. Thus you will now begin to practice reading longer works more like those you will normally be reading. Reading a novel will give you an opportunity to use the techniques that you have learned in a sustained way over a longer period of time, and it will allow you to become more involved with the story.

Today you will read the short novel, *Lilies of the Field,* or a novel of similar length and level of difficulty. One day each week hereafter, until Chapter 13, you will read one novel in class or within one hour at home. As you progress, the novels will increase in difficulty and length, and the questions will increase in difficulty.

Don't be concerned that you may not be able to do it. I anticipate that not only will you finish in the allotted time, but even that many of you will finish early. However, if you should not finish within the time, just continue reading until you do finish.

PREVIEWING A NOVEL

Look at the title and the front cover. Turn to the back cover and read what is written (with your hand, of course). Turn to the first page of the story.

Using the swooping hand movement that you use for previewing short stories, either pace yourself, or the instructor will pace you at about three seconds per page. Preview the first five pages. Turn at random to another spot farther along and preview five pages. Turn again to another spot farther along and preview five pages. Turn to the last five pages and preview them.

Begin to preview. Swoop down five pages.

Turn to another section approximately one-third into the book. Begin (5 pages).

Turn to another section about two-thirds into the book. Begin (5 pages).

Turn to the last five pages of the book. Begin (5 pages).

Answer the following questions silently to yourself about your story. Who is the main character? Who are some other characters? Where do you think the story takes place? When do you think the story takes place? Can you remember an event in the story? How does the story begin?

READING A NOVEL IN ONE HOUR

Place a bookmark at the approximate halfway point in your novel. In twenty minutes you should be at or near the bookmark, or you will need to speed up in order to finish within the hour. If you are in class, your instructor will notify you when twenty minutes are up. If you are reading the novel at home, set a clock or timer to ring in twenty minutes (the timer on the kitchen stove will do fine).

Record your starting time in hours and minutes (disregard seconds). Read the novel at about the same rate that you have been using for the short stories. Record your finish time in hours and minutes. Answer the questions on *Lilies of the Field* or the general novel questions at the end of the chapter. Correct your answers. (For the general questions there is no answer key. You may wish to correct them by finding the answers in your novel.) Compute your rate by dividing the number of words in your novel by the number of minutes it took you to read it. Since you are not using seconds, no conversion of the time is needed. If you read a different novel, you will need to figure out how many words it contains. First figure out how many words there are on a page in that book (see Chapter 1 for instructions); then multiply the number of words on one page times the number of pages in the book, subtracting pictures and blank pages. Figure your comprehension score. On the general questions if you don't find the answers in the book you may describe your comprehension as "excellent," "good," "poor," and so on. Record your rate and comprehension score for the novel on your Course Data Sheet in the space provided.

If you are reading in class and you do not finish, record the time you stopped reading and the number of the page on which you stopped. At home, complete the reading, continuing to time yourself. Add this time to the time you spent in class to find the time it took you to read this novel.

A word of advice. Your tendency will be to slow down as you get interested in the story. The purpose of this assignment is to give you practice in reading rapidly over a longer period of time, so, don't slow down. Use your interest to speed up. When you are interested and involved in the story, you will understand it just as well if you go faster. Also, you may get tired since you are not accustomed to reading actively for so long a time. If you do, look at the clock and record the time; then close your eyes and relax for one minute. Be sure to subtract this minute from your total reading time when you compute your reading rate.

Use whichever hand movement works best for you.

Now go back to the beginning of the story. Read.

Twenty minutes have passed—you should be at your bookmark.

Summary of procedure for reading the novel:

1. Place a bookmark at the halfway point. You will read the whole book!
2. Look at the front and back covers. What will the novel be about?
3. Preview by swooping down the pages at about three seconds per page. Preview the first five pages, five pages at random in the first half of the book, five pages in the second half of the book, and the last five pages.
4. Answer these questions: Who is the main character? Name some other characters? Where do you think the story takes place? When do you think the story takes place? Can you remember an event in the story? Try to recall how the story begins.
5. Record your starting time in hours and minutes only. (Disregard seconds.)
6. Read the novel, using all the speed reading techniques you have learned.
7. In twenty minutes you should be past the middle of the story where you placed a bookmark, or you will need to speed up.
8. Record your finishing time in hours and minutes only.
9. Answer the questions on the novel at the end of the chapter. If you are reading the novel for which there are specific questions, answer those; otherwise, answer the General Comprehension Questions.
10. Correct your answers with the answer key in the appendix. For the general novel, correct the answers by finding the answers in the book, or estimate your comprehension and write a descriptive term such as "excellent," "good," "poor," and so on.
11. Compute your rate. Since your time will be totally in minutes, no conversion is needed. Just divide the number of words by the number of minutes it took you to read the book.

    Note: If you do not know the number of words your book contains, refer to Chapter 1, "How to Compute Reading and Drill Rates."
12. Compute your comprehension score by giving yourself ten points for each correct answer on the comprehension test.
13. Record your rate and comprehension score on your Course Data Sheet. If you read a general novel, you will also need to record the title.

SUMMARY

As in a short story, you use the swooping hand movement in previewing a novel. However, you only preview the first five pages, five pages at two random places in the book, and the last five pages. You read the novel with all the speed-reading techniques you possess. You use your involvement in the story to sustain your speed, and you try to picture what is happening in the story.

LILIES OF THE FIELD
COMPREHENSION QUESTIONS

_____ 1. Homer Smith was
   a. German.
   b. Oriental.
   C. Black.
   d. Indian.

_____ 2. Homer's first job for the nuns was to
   a. fix a roof.
   b. harvest the wheat.
   c. build a chapel.
   d. build a fence.

_____ 3. Mother Maria Martha treated Homer as if
   a. God had given him to her.
   b. he was very kind and thoughtful to them.
   c. he might leave at any moment.
   d. he was not wanted there.

_____ 4. Mother Maria Martha wanted to build a place where
   a. nuns could study.
   b. people all over the world would visit.
   c. poor Spanish boys who got into trouble could be cared for.
   d. no one could intrude upon their privacy.

_____ 5. Homer had
   a. built a chapel once before and knew how to do it.
   b. never built a chapel before.
   c. no experience in any building skills.
   d. built other large structures, but never a chapel.

_____ 6. When the townspeople wanted to help Homer build the chapel, he
   a. accepted happily.
   b. was indifferent.
   c. was resentful.
   d. refused to continue building.

_____ 7. The chapel that Homer built was
   a. a copy of the church in the city.
   b. a copy of a church he remembered from his childhood.
   c. different from any chapel anywhere.
   d. similar to the famous St. Peter's Cathedral.

_____ 8. Regarding Homer's race,
   a. Homer was constantly aware of others' attitudes toward his race.
   b. Homer paid no attention to how others reacted to his race.
   c. the book is not concerned with the racial aspect at all.
   d. the main purpose of the story was to deal with the racial aspect.

_____ 9. The author uses the notion of the "lilies of the field" to communicate the idea of.
   a. wealth.
   b. freedom.
   c. color.
   d. ability to do things.

_____ 10. When Homer left, he
   a. planned to return one day.
   b. hoped he would be able to return one day.
   c. had no thoughts one way or the other about returning.
   d. knew that he would never come back.

Allow 10 points per correct answer.   *Your score* _____ %
Number of words: 19,800   *Your rate* _____
Answer key is on page 272.
Record your rate and comprehension score on your Course Data Sheet.

GENERAL NOVEL COMPREHENSION QUESTIONS

(To be used only when reading a novel other than *Lilies of the Field.*)

Title _____ Author _____

1. Name the main character(s). _____

   _____

2. Where does the story take place? _____

   _____

3. Approximately when does the story take place? _____

4. Name two other characters. (1) _____

   (2) _____

5. What type of story is it (love story, adventure, science fiction, war story, fantasy, etc.)? _____

6. Briefly summarize the situation at the beginning of the story.

   _____

   _____

   _____

7. List three things that happen to the main character.

   (1) _____

   (2) _____

   (3) _____

8. State the relationship(s) between the main character and at least one other character (husband and wife, father and son, friends, etc). _____

9. How does the story end? _____

_____

_____

10. Write one sentence that tells what this whole story illustrates (author's message). _____

_____

Directions: *You may wish to look back into the story to find out if you wrote the correct answers. If you do, give yourself 10 points for each correct answer.*

If you do not correct your answer sheet, estimate your understanding of the story by writing "excellent," "good," "fair," or "poor" in the place for your score.

Your score _____ %

Total number of words _____   Your rate _____

To find your rate:

1. *Figure out how many words are on one page in the book you read. (Words per page _____.)*
2. *Multiply the number of words on one page by the number of pages in the book to find the total number of words in the book. (Total number of words _____.)*
3. *Divide your time, converted to minutes (disregard seconds) into the total number of words in the book to find your rate.*

Record title, rate, and comprehension score on your Course Data Sheet.

9

Using Key Words

Materials:
  • Readings:
    "Visions to Boost Immunity"
    "The Adventure of the Speckled Band"
    The Old Man and the Sea (or another 29,000-word novel)
  • Drill book (a book you have previously read)

Objective:
  • To learn to think in key words (another way of thinking while speed reading)

DRILL PRACTICE

Using *Lilies of the Field,* or another book that you have read before, do the same drills that you did at the beginning of Chapter 7, page 66. Take a drill rate for this week. Record the drill rate on your Course Data Sheet.

THINKING IN KEY WORDS

This technique is for you *only* if you still find it impossible to understand what you are reading by thinking in ideas or images—if you must say some words to yourself in order to comprehend.

In any written material certain words carry the meaning. These are called key words. If you must say some words to yourself, they should be the key words. The easier the material, the fewer key words there will be. By saying the key words only, you will subvocalize about one-tenth of the words, instead of all of them as you did before you began this speed-reading method. You still see all the words in soft focus, but only say the important ones. In this way you can consciously follow the ideas, because the meanings of the words you do *not* say will be filled in in your mind automatically through association.

Turn back to the story, "To Build a Fire," on page 20. Go through the story, underlining the essential words, the words that you must get to understand and follow the story.

To help you start, the essential words in the first few paragraphs are underlined here. Study the sample and notice why the underlined words are the key words: the name of the main character, the places where the story happened, the precept that the whole story illustrates, and the most important characteristics of the character.

For land travel or seafaring, the world over, a companion is usually considered desirable. In the <u>Klondike</u>, as <u>Tom Vincent</u> found out, such a <u>companion</u> is absolutely <u>essential</u>. But he found it out, not by precept, but through bitter <u>experience</u>.

"<u>Never travel alone</u>," is a precept of the north. He had heard it many times and laughed; for he was a strapping <u>young fellow</u>, big-boned and big-muscled, with <u>faith in himself</u> and in the <u>strength</u> of his head and hands.

It was on a bleak <u>January</u> day when the experience came that taught him respect for the frost, and for the wisdom of the men who had battled with it.

He had left Calumet Camp on the Yukon with a light pack on his back, to go up Paul Creek to the divide between it and Cherry Creek, where his party was prospecting and hunting moose.

Now underline the key words in the rest of the story. Then go back and read the story rapidly. Your eyes should sweep over all the print in soft focus, but the few words you say in your mind (subvocalize) should primarily be the underlined ones. It may not be necessary to subvocalize all the underlined words, and you may find that you are subvocalizing some words that are not underlined. Don't be concerned about that. The goal is to subvocalize as few words as possible and still follow the story; and if they are primarily the key words, your comprehension will improve. Do not subvocalize every word.

It is good practice to try this technique on stories you have previously read and know, stories in which you can locate the key words easily; doing this will help you gain successful experience with this technique.

How will you be able, while reading rapidly, to pick out the key words in materials you have not read, either stories or nonfiction? Until you have had lots of practice, you may not always be able to say just the key words because you will not recognize them instantaneously and you won't have time to figure them out. However, if you follow the suggestions given here, you can still use this technique to improve your comprehension. In places where you should slow down with flexibility, such as at the beginnings of chapters and paragraphs, you will have time to say more words; and where you should go faster, you will have time to say fewer words. This requirement will improve comprehension in the places where the important ideas are most likely to appear. However, try to say the main noun and verb; these are the essential parts of a sentence. Say more words at the beginning of each chapter and paragraph, places where new ideas are introduced and where you have more time because you have slowed down. Say the name of a character the first time he or she is introduced. Say the name of the location the first time it is mentioned.

Although saying the key words only will allow more reading speed and better comprehension, worrying about whether or not the words you are saying are key words will distract you and keep you from understanding anything. So the best way is to say whatever words you have time for, without slowing down too much. Some of these will be key words and some will not, but even the ones that aren't will act as "hooks" to help you recall the ideas in the in-between words you didn't say, but did see. Basically, this technique is a compromise between thinking in images and ideas and your old way of saying words: it allows you consciously to say words so that you feel that you are reading the story; it is not really necessary for reading the story, but it makes you feel secure. That's why any words you say, key words or non-key words, will improve your conscious comprehension.

READING PRACTICE

Preview and read the article, "Visions To Boost Immunity" on page 83 and the story, "The Adventure of the Speckled Band" on page 87. If you can visualize or just know the ideas, most certainly use those preferred methods; but if you cannot, subvocalize some of the words. When you slow down slightly as you use flexibility at beginnings and difficult parts, say as many words as you have time, without doing additional slowing purposely just to say more words. Don't forget to speed up again!

Your purpose is still to continue to increase your speed in reading. You now have permission to say some of the words, but don't allow this to act as an excuse to revert to your old slow habits. You will still be seeing and processing all the unspoken words just the same as a reader who does not subvocalize. This key word technique is primarily used to assist recall and make you feel more comfortable.

SECOND NOVEL READING

Read *The Old Man and the Sea* (questions are at the end of the chapter) or another novel of about 29,000 words (general questions are at the end of the chapter).

Follow the summary of procedure for reading the novel in Chapter 8 on page 77. Visualize, just know the ideas, or use the key word technique presented in this chapter.

SUMMARY

Subvocalizing (saying in your mind) the essential key words is an alternate way of thinking while reading rapidly. It will improve comprehension.

VISIONS TO BOOST IMMUNITY

Sally Squires

The Power of Positive Imagery
This mind technique is medicine's new tool—for everything from headaches to experimental cancer therapy.

In her office in Little Rock, AK, a 39-year-old woman sits deep in meditation. An American convert to Tibetan Buddhism, she has made it a daily ritual for the past nine years. Today, however, her meditation adds a twist: Using a simple visualization technique, she will attempt to control her immune system's response to a foreign invader. It's part of an unusual nine-week experiment by researchers at the University of Arkansas for medical Sciences—and part of a whole new frontier in mind/body research.

Over the past few years, scientists have gathered more and more evidence that thoughts and emotional states can affect your body's immune system—the white blood cells and other substances that together defend against disease. The immune systems of depressed and bereaved people, for example, function below par. There's been talk that certain attitudes may make people more susceptible to cancer, and less able to fight back when it strikes.

But now researchers are studying the flip side of those troubling findings: Some psychological techniques may help keep the immune system on track, perhaps even *enhance* it. Chief among them: guided imagery, which is training your mind to visualize health-promoting images.

In Arkansas, the woman under study is testing the precision with which visualization can affect the immune system. The Arkansas researchers, headed by psychiatrist G. Richard Smith, want to see if she can turn her immune system's response up or down like the volume of a radio. If she can, there's hope that many of us may be able to use positive imagery to strengthen our immune systems and improve our physical health.

Body Control Through Imagery

The Arkansas experiment begins with a simple injection of chicken pox virus on the underside of the woman's arm. Because she has already had chicken pox, the researchers know she can't get it from the injection. But they also know that her immune system will "recognize" the virus and respond to it by causing a small bump to rise at the injection site in 48 hours.

Sure enough, a nickel-sized bump appears and then slowly fades over the next four to five days. Blood samples confirm the skin test: Her white blood cells become larger as they confront the virus.

After the researchers repeat this test twice, the real experiment begins. Can the woman actually "turn down the volume"—*lessen* her white blood cells' reaction to the virus? The virus is injected three more times over the next three weeks. Each time, the woman uses an imagery technique as part of her daily meditation, visualizing the bump from earlier injections growing smaller. Result: All three injections produce a smaller bump. Blood tests confirm the change.

Finally, the woman is instructed to let her immune response return to normal for a few more injections. It does, and the bumps become nickel-sized again. "We were startled by the outcome," says Dr. Smith. But experiments with other experienced meditators gave the same results.

The Arkansas experiments are among a cluster of new studies suggesting that visualization may be an effective way to harness the mind for health's sake. Learning the technique may be a practical way for many people to prevent—and battle—disease.

The Scientists Step In

The idea that the mind and body are engaged in two-way conversation is nothing new. It's been a part of Eastern philosophy for centuries. Even Western doctors have long recognized that sheer willpower pulls some patients through life-threatening illnesses or injuries. But now researchers at major universities are putting visualization and other mental techniques to rigorous scientific testing. At the same time, cutting-edge research is uncovering what seems to be the chemical basis of this communication between brain and body.

Together, these researchers have created a new field of scientific inquiry. It's PNI, short for psychoneuroimmunology—a term coined in 1980 by psychologist Robert Ader at the University of Rochester medical school.

Even before these researchers got to work, visualization had a rich tradition. Imagery has been used by Olympic athletes to enhance performance and by yoga practitioners for spiritual and physical health. But it was the use of visualization by cancer patients trying to boost their immune systems that made researchers take notice.

In the 1970s, Texas-based clinicians Carl and Stephanie Simonton stirred great emotional debate with their claims that cancer patients could live longer if they combined guided imagery with simple relaxation techniques. Since the Simontons did no double-blind controlled trials, however, critics characterized the results as suspect.

Now, at the University of Arkansas, Stephanie Simonton is doing careful research that she hopes will show imagery can boost the immune system. And other PNI researchers are working to prove or disprove work such as the Simontons', and move beyond it.

The Mind's One-Two Punch

PNI researchers often study imagery techniques paired with relaxation exercises. Since Transcendental Meditation and the Relaxation Response became household terms in the 1970s, there's been strong evidence that their calming effects can de-stress the body and perhaps even boost the immune system. Now it seems relaxation and imagery together can promote physical healing. The combined techniques are like a one-two punch.

At the Medical Illness Counseling Center in suburban Maryland, 10 patients with metastatic cancer added relaxation and guided imagery to their conventional treatment with chemotherapy. The goal: Mobilize the body's defenses against the cancer. Under the direction of psychologist Barry Gruber and psychiatrist Stephen Hersh, they learned to "see" the malignant cancer cells in their bodies. Then they would mentally turn the tide by imagining the bad cells were weaklings easily engulfed by the body's stalwart immune cells.

The Maryland researchers took advantage of new technology to test their patients' blood for changes in immune function. After one year of regular imagery sessions, all 10 patients were still alive. Blood tests showed their white blood cells had multiplied to fight the cancer cells, and had accelerated the rate at which they attacked foreign bodies in general.

Now, at the two-year mark, two of the patients have died—one from chemotherapy complications, the other from unknown causes. But the group's overall survival rate offers preliminary evidence of imagery's promise.

Preventing Cancer

Imagery may also help people who are still healthy—particularly the elderly. Immune function often declines with age, which may explain why some old people have a harder time fighting off illnesses like the flu—and have a higher cancer rate.

Recently Ohio State University psychologist Janice Kiecolt-Glaser and her husband and colleague, immunologist Ron Glaser, studied 45 healthy senior citizens in retirement homes in Columbus, OH. They divided them into three groups. Those who were taught relaxation techniques and guided imagery by a visiting medical student showed a significant boost in "natural killer" cells—a special type of white blood cell that helps fight tumors. No such change in the other two groups, who got either social visits without the training or no visits at all.

"Just as distress may be able to decrease immune function, these findings suggest that there may also be ways to enhance it," Dr. Kiecolt-Glaser says. She's quick to point out limitations of her own experiment—high levels of natural killer cells don't necessarily translate into less disease. "But in *theory*," she says, "one would expect that people with more competent immune systems might have better health."

Although much of the new work on imagery focuses on its immune-system benefits, it helps in other ways too. In the short run, imagery seems to mute the body's stress reactions: Visualizers showed lower resting heart rates, slower breathing and less perspiration. And the technique can help psychologically as well. "People report being more relaxed, more confident and less easily upset by minor hassles," says Kiecolt-Glaser. "They feel more in control of their lives and may be able to think more clearly, because they are not distracted."

Chemicals of Emotion

Exactly how imagery and relaxation exert their effects on the body is still not known. But the answers may lie in exciting new discoveries about brain chemicals by such researchers as neuroscientist Candace Pert, section chief of brain biochemistry at the National Institute of Mental Health.

Brain cells, or neurons, have long been known to communicate with each other through chemical signals. But in the past, these signals were thought to move only in preset paths from cell to cell. In recent years, however, Pert and other

scientists have uncovered another communication system: chemicals that work like free-floating telegrams, sending messages between cells in different parts of the brain and other parts of the body. Some of these substances such as insulin, have been known for years. But scientists are now discovering they are produced by the brain, not just by organs like the pancreas.

So far, about 40 to 50 of these chemicals are known to be manufactured by the brain. Technically they're called neuropeptides, though Pert has referred to them as "molecules of emotion" because so many are directly linked to emotional states. Example: "feel-good" opiates such as beta-endorphins that may be produced at an increased rate after exercise.

What's the link with the immune system? Pert and her colleagues now believe some neuropeptides, including the opiates, are also produced in minute amounts by certain white blood cells known as macrophages. These large, Pacman-like cells travel the bloodstream eating up bacteria and viruses. Macrophages not only produce certain emotion-linked neuropeptides, they are also attracted to these same chemicals when they're sent out by the brain. If macrophages "sniff out" these chemicals in the blood, they'll travel to them, make contact and get the brain's message to be more vigilant—or less so. Some researchers think other white blood cells may also communicate through peptides.

Although this work is still highly theoretical, it suggests some fascinating scenarios for the mind's effect on the immune system. It's possible, for example, that relaxation and visualization techniques can cause certain opiates to be released into the blood. They may attract macrophages and perhaps other immune cells, and signal them to turn on. Result: a more vigilant immune system, less disease.

The possibilities are just beginning to be explored, says Maryland researcher Nicholas Hall, a neuroimmunologist at George Washington University School of Medicine. Hall worked his way through college by wrestling alligators in South Dakota, and always mentally rehearsed each physical movement with guided imagery. The use of positive visualization, he believes, may be a natural human response—and an effective one—to challenging situations. "What we have seen was a brief period in history, the last 150 to 200 years, where we departed from a way of treating disease," he says. "Our ancestors showed through intuition what we are showing today through science."

HOW TO USE GUIDED IMAGERY

Guided imagery and relaxation are best learned from experienced health professionals trained to teach these techniques. But some simple exercises—adapted from those used by Borysenko and others—can at least help you learn relaxation.

- First, lie down or sit in a comfortable, back-supporting chair away from distractions. Take your shoes off. Loosen clothing. Dim the lights.
- Close your eyes. Take a deep breath through your nose, one that fills your abdomen—not just your upper chest—as you inhale. Slowly let the air out, concentrating on letting go. Repeat. Then take a slightly deeper breath. Feel yourself relax. Be aware of your breathing. Repeat a simple word, phrase or prayer to yourself—such as "I am calm"—as you exhale. If other thoughts intrude, take another breath and go back to repeating your word or phrase. Says Bory-

senko: "Experienced meditators say that thoughts are like birds that fly back and forth over your head. You can't stop them flying, but you can stop them from making a nest in your hair."

- Slowly tense and then relax the muscles in your body, beginning with your forehead and working down to your toes. Feel the difference between a tensed and relaxed state.
- As you begin the imagery, picture a place where you feel safe, secure, calm and quiet: perhaps a beach setting, the woods, or a cozy bed with the covers pulled over your head. Whatever the setting, try to make yourself a participant in the vision, not just an observer. Try to pay attention to your body's signals. For example, UCLA psychiatrist Bernard Towers asks patients to be aware that the air they breathe in through the nose is slightly cooler than the air they breathe out.
- The next step is to picture the setting you are trying to change or control. First, draw pictures of what you are trying to visualize. If you want to boost your immunity against the common cold, sketch a drawing of how you see your white blood cells and what they're doing to fight the cold virus.

These pictures can be revealing. One cancer patient drew her white blood cells lying on the beach

underneath umbrellas. "She had pictured her white blood cells, but had not activated them," says psychophysiologist Sharlene Weiss of the Medical Illness Counseling Center in Chevy Chase, MD. "When she was able to start them moving, she started getting better."

Don't get caught up in trying to do guided imagery or relaxation "right." The images must be personal. So these suggestions are general guidelines only:

Weight Loss. Imagine yourself at the weight you're trying to reach. Try to "see" this svelte new you.

Quitting cigarettes. Imagine yourself feeling the urge to light up. Then see yourself overcoming the pull—feeling confident about not smoking, and succeeding.

Pregnancy. Imagine a protective, loving white light coming down through you into the womb and bathing your baby. One high-risk expectant mother visualized sending her struggling unborn child more nutrients through the umbilical cord. Sonograms showed that imagery seemed to increase the blood volume to the fetus. The unborn child began to thrive.

Illness. From colds to cancer, some people benefit by imagining the immune system as a cadre of fierce warriors easily defeating the foreign invader. Others find the image too violent. One priest with cancer derived his imagery from his favorite hobby: gardening. He imagined only feeding or "watering" his body's healthy cells. Like weeds, the cancer cells got no water.

COMPREHENSION QUESTIONS

_____ 1. Guided imagery, as used in the article, is
   a. visualizing a predetermined group of specific images.
   b. training your mind to visualize health-promoting images.
   c. recognizing the significances of a set of scientific pictures.
   d. learning a group of pictures and recalling them as requested.

_____ 2. The best way to use guided imagery is
   a. in a classroom setting.
   b. while sleeping.
   c. in a relaxed, meditative state.
   d. while doing strenuous physical activity.

_____ 3. This article tells of imagery's success with
a. sick and healthy people.
b. sick people only.
c. healthy people only.
d. children only.

_____ 4. New discoveries about brain chemicals have led scientists to believe that the brain can
a. only send chemical messages to other parts of the brain.
b. only send chemical messages to parts of the body.
c. only send chemical messages in preset paths.
d. send chemical messages to parts of the brain and parts of the body.

_____ 5. So far, the number of neuropeptides—chemicals—found to be manufactured by the brain are
a. 40 to 50.
b. 5 to 10.
c. 7.
d. 24.

_____ 6. This article suggests that guided imagery may work by
a. self-hypnosis.
b. visualization, causing certain opiates to be released into the blood stream.
c. visualization, causing lessened internal body activity.
d. using will power.

_____ 7. In the instructions on how to use guided imagery, central to relaxation is
a. focusing your eyes upon a moving object.
b. extreme tiredness after physical exercise.
c. a non-stressful life.
d. deep breathing.

_____ 8. According to this article, the following is known to be helped by guided imagery
a. excess weight.
b. nearsightedness.
c. baldness.
d. hallucinations.

_____ 9. From the information in this article you can conclude that guided imagery
a. has limited applications.
b. may prove useful in yet undreamed of ways.
c. may have undiscovered serious side effects.
d. can take the place of prescribed medication and chemotherapy.

_____ 10. This article leads one to believe that
a. it takes special capabilities to use guided imagery.
b. guided imagery gives one a false sense of control.
c. we can exert significant control over the health of our bodies.
d. it is better to doubt and avoid disappointment than to believe and suffer disappointment.

Allow 10 points per correct answer.   *Your score* _____ %
Number of words: 2530   *Your rate* _____
Answer key is on page 272.
Record your rate and comprehension score on Course Data Sheet.

THE ADVENTURE OF THE SPECKLED BAND

Sir Arthur Conan Doyle

Early one morning in April in the year '83, my friend Sherlock Holmes called me into his sitting room to meet a young lady. As I entered I could readily see that she was in a state of agitation. Her face was drawn and gray, with restless, frightened eyes, like those of some haunted animal. Her features and figure were those of a woman of thirty, but her hair was shot with premature gray, and her expression was weary and haggard.

"Sir, I can stand this strain no longer," she said. "I shall go mad if it continues. I have no one to turn to. Oh, sir, do you think that you could help me? At present it is out of my power to reward you for your services, but in a month I shall be married, with the control of my own income, and then you shall not find me ungrateful."

"I beg that you will lay before us everything that may help us in forming an opinion upon the matter," said Holmes.

"My name is Helen Stoner, and I am living with my stepfather who is the last survivor of one of the oldest families in England. At one time they were very rich, but through several generations their fortune has been dissipated. Nothing is left now save a few acres and a two-hundred-year old house. My stepfather did manage, however, to take a medical degree in India where he established a large practice. In a fit of anger, however, he beat his native butler to death and narrowly escaped a capital sentence. As it was, he suffered a long term of imprisonment and afterwards returned to England a gloomy and disappointed man.

"When Dr. Roylott was in India he married my mother, Mrs. Stoner. My sister Julia and I were twins, and we were only two years old at the time of my mother's remarriage. She had a considerable sum of money—not less than 1000 pounds a year—and this she bequeathed to Dr. Roylott entirely while we resided with him, with the provision that a certain annual sum should be allowed to each of us in the event of our marriage. Shortly after our return to England my mother died. Dr. Roylott then abandoned his attempts to establish himself in practice in London and took us to live with him in the old ancestral house at Stoke Moran. The money which my mother had left was enough for all our wants, and there seemed to be no obstacle to our happiness.

"But a terrible change came over our stepfather about this time. Instead of making friends with our neighbors, who at first had been overjoyed to see a Roylott of Stoke Moran back in the old family seat, he shut himself up in his house and seldom came out save to have violent quarrels with whoever might cross his path. Consequently, he had no friends save the wandering gypsies, and he would give these vagabonds leave to encamp upon the few acres of land which represent the family estate. He has a passion also for Indian animals, and he has at this moment a cheetah and a baboon, which wander freely over his grounds.

"You can imagine from what I say that my poor sister Julia and I had no great pleasure in our lives. She was but thirty at the time of her death, and yet her hair had already begun to whiten, even as mine has."

"Your sister is dead, then?"

"She died just two years ago, and it is of her death that I wish to speak to you. We have an aunt, my mother's maiden sister, and we were occasionally allowed to pay short visits at this lady's house. Julia went there at Christmas two years ago, and met there a half-pay major, to whom she became engaged. My stepfather learned of the engagement and offered no objection to the marriage; but within two weeks of the day which had been fixed for the wedding, the terrible event occurred."

"Pray, be precise as to details," said Holmes.

"It is easy for me to be so, for every event of that dreadful time is burned into my memory. The manor-house is very old, and only one wing is now inhabited. The bedrooms in this wing are on the ground floor, the sitting-rooms being in the central block of the buildings. Of these bedrooms the first is Dr. Roylott's, the second my sister's, and the third my own. There is no communication between them, but they all open out into the same hallway. The windows of the three rooms open out upon the lawn. That fatal night Dr. Roylott had gone to his room early, though we knew that he had not retired to rest, for my sister was troubled by the smell of the strong Indian cigars which it was his custom to smoke. She left her room, therefore, and came into mine, where she sat for some time, chatting about her approaching wedding. At eleven o'clock she rose to leave me, but she paused at the door and looked back.

" 'Tell me, Helen,' said she, 'have you ever heard anyone whistle in the dead of the night?'

" 'Never,' said I.

" 'I suppose that you could not possibly whistle, yourself, in your sleep?'

" 'Certainly not, But why?'

" 'Because during the last few nights I have always about three in the morning, heard a low, clear whistle. I am a light sleeper, and it has awakened me. I cannot tell where it came from—perhaps from the next room, perhaps from the lawn.'

" 'I have not heard it. It must be those wretched gypsies on the plantation.'

" 'Very likely. And yet if it were on the lawn, I wonder that you did not hear it also.'

" 'Ah, but I sleep more heavily than you.'

" 'Well, it is of no great consequence.' She smiled back at me, closed my door, and a few moments later I heard her key in the lock."

"Indeed," said Holmes. "Was it your custom always to lock yourselves in at night?"

"Always, because of the cheetah and the baboon. We had no feeling of security unless our doors were locked."

"Quite so. Please proceed with your statement."

"I could not sleep that night. It was a wild night. The wind was howling outside, and the rain was beating and splashing against the windows. Suddenly, in the middle of the hubbub of the gale, there burst forth the wild scream of a terrified woman. I knew that it was my sister's voice. I sprang from my bed and rushed into the hall. As I opened my door I seemed to hear a low whistle, such as my sister described, and a few moments later a clanging sound, as if a mass of metal had fallen. I ran down the passage and opened my sister's door. By the light of the hall-lamp I saw my sister appear at the opening, her face whitened with terror, her hands groping for help, her whole figure swaying to and fro like that of a drunkard. I ran to her and threw my arms around her, but at that moment her knees seemed to give way and she fell to the ground. She twisted and turned as one who is in terrible pain, and her limbs were dreadfully convulsed. At first I thought that she had not recognized me, but as I bent over her she suddenly shrieked out in a voice which I shall never forget, 'Oh, my God! Helen! It was the band! The speckled band!' There was something else which she wanted to say, and she stabbed with her finger in the air in the direction of the doctor's room, but a fresh convulsion seized her and choked her words. I rushed out, calling loudly for my stepfather and I met him hastening from his room in his dressing gown. When he reached my sister's side she was dead. Such was the dreadful end of my beloved sister."

"One moment," said Holmes; "are you sure about this whistle and metallic sound? Could you swear to it?"

"That was what the coroner asked me at the inquiry. It is my strong impression that I heard it, and yet, among the crash of the gale and the creaking of an old house, I may possibly have been mistaken."

"Was your sister dressed?"

"No, she was in her night-dress. In her right hand was found the charred stump of a match, and in her left a match-box."

"Showing that she had struck a light and looked about her. That is important. And what conclusions did the coroner come to?"

"He was unable to find any satisfactory cause of death. My evidence showed that the door had been fastened upon the inner side, and the windows were blocked by old-fashioned shutters with broad iron bars, which were secured every night. The walls were carefully sounded and were shown to be quite solid, and the flooring was also thoroughly examined, with the same result. The chimney is wide, but is barred up by four large staples. It is certain, therefore, that my sister was quite alone when she met her end. Besides, there were no marks of any violence upon her."

"How about poison?"

"The doctors examined her for it, but without success."

"What did you gather from the reference to a band—a speckled band?"

"Sometimes I have thought that it was merely the wild talk of one out of her mind, sometimes that it may have referred to some band of people, perhaps to the gypsies on the plantation. I do not know whether the spotted handkerchiefs which so many of them wear over their heads might have suggested the strange adjective which she used."

"These are very deep waters," said Holmes; "please go on with your story."

"A month ago, a dear friend, whom I have known for many years, has done me the honor to ask my hand in marriage. My stepfather has offered no opposition to the match, and we are to be married in the course of the spring. Two days ago some repairs were started in the west wing of the building, and my bedroom wall has been pierced, so that I have had to move into the room in which my sister died, and to sleep in the very bed in which she slept. Imagine, then, my terror when last night, as I lay awake, I suddenly heard the low whistle. I sprang up and lit the lamp, but nothing was to be seen in the room. I was too shaken to go to bed again, however, so I dressed,

and as soon as it was daylight I came to seek your advice."

"You have done wisely," said my friend. "There are a thousand details which I should desire to know before I decide upon a course of action. If we were to come to Stoke Moran today, would it be possible for us to see over these rooms without the knowledge of your stepfather?"

"As it happens, he spoke of coming into town today upon some important business. It is probable that he will be away all day, and that there would be nothing to disturb you.

"Excellent. You may expect us early in the afternoon."

Miss Stoner nodded and left.

"And what do you think of it all, Watson?" asked Sherlock Holmes, leaning back in his chair.

"It seems to me to be a dark and sinister business."

"Yet if the lady is correct in saying that the flooring and walls are sound, and that the door, window, and chimney are impassable, then her sister must have been undoubtedly alone when she met her mysterious end. When you combine the ideas of the whistles at night, the presence of a band of gypsies who are on intimate terms with this old doctor, the fact that we have every reason to believe that the doctor has an interest in preventing his stepdaughter's marriage, the dying reference to a band, and, finally, the fact that Miss Helen Stoner heard a metallic clang, which might have been caused by one of those metal bars that secured the shutters falling back into its place, I think that there is good ground to think that the mystery may be cleared along those lines. But what in the name of the devil!"

The exclamation had been drawn from my companion by the fact that our door had been suddenly dashed open, and that a huge man had framed himself in the opening. His costume was a peculiar mixture of the professional and of the agricultural, having a black top-hat, a long frock-coat, with a hunting-crop swinging in his hand. So tall was he that his hat actually brushed the cross bar of the doorway, and his breadth seemed to span it across from side to side. A large face, covered with a thousand wrinkles, burned yellow with the sun, and marked with every evil passion, was turned from one to the other of us, while his deepset bile-shot eyes, and his high thin, fleshless nose, gave him somewhat the resemblance to a fierce old bird of prey.

"I am Dr. Grimesby Roylott, of Stoke Moran," said this strange sight.

"Indeed, Doctor," said Holmes smoothly. "Please take a seat."

"I will do nothing of the kind. My stepdaughter has been here, I have traced her. What has she been saying to you?" screamed the old man furiously.

"It is a little cold for the time of year," said Holmes.

"Ha! You put me off, do you?" said our new visitor, taking a step forward and shaking his hunting-crop. "I know you, you scoundrel! I have heard of you before. You are Holmes, the meddler."

Holmes chuckled heartily. "Your conversation is most entertaining," said he. "When you go out close the door, for there is a decided draught."

"I will go when I have said my say. Don't dare to meddle with my affairs. I am a dangerous man to fall foul of!" he said as he strode out of the room.

"He seems a very likable person," said Holmes, laughing. "And now, Watson, we shall order breakfast, and afterwards, I shall walk down to Doctors' Commons, where I hope to get some data which may help us in this matter."

It was nearly one o'clock when Sherlock Holmes returned.

"I have seen the will of the deceased wife," said he. "The total income is now not more than 750 pounds. Each daughter can claim an income of 250 pounds, in case of marriage. It is evident, therefore, that if both girls had married, this beauty would have had a mere pittance, while even one of them would cripple him to a very serious extent. My morning's work has not been wasted, since it has proved that he has the very strongest motives for standing in the way of anything of the sort. Watson, this is too serious for dawdling. I should be very much obliged if you would

slip your revolver into your pocket. That and a toothbrush are, I think, all that we need."

At Waterloo we were fortunate in catching a train for Leatherhead, where we hired a trap at the station inn and drove for four or five miles through the lovely Surrey lanes. My companion sat buried in deepest thought. Suddenly, however, he started, tapped me on the shoulder, and pointed over the meadows.

"Look there!" he said.

A heavily timbered park stretched up in a gentle slope, thickening into a grove at the highest point. From between the branches there jutted out the gray gables and high roof-top of a very old mansion.

"Stoke Moran?" said he.

"Yes, sir, that be the house of Dr. Roylott," remarked the driver. "There's the village," said the driver, pointing to a cluster of roofs some distance to the left; "but if you want to get to the house, you'll find it shorter to get over this stile, and go by foot-path over the fields. There it is, where the lady is walking."

"And the lady, I fancy, is Miss Stoner," observed Holmes. "Yes, I think we had better do as you suggest."

We got off, paid our fare, and the trap rattled back on its way to Leatherhead.

Our client of the morning had hurried forward to meet us with a face which spoke her joy. "I have been waiting so eagerly for you," she cried. "All has turned out splendidly. Dr. Roylott has gone to town, and it is unlikely that he will be back before evening."

"We have had the pleasure of making the doctor's acquaintance," said Holmes, and he sketched out what had occurred. Miss Stoner turned white to the lips as she listened.

"Good heavens!" she cried, "he has followed me, then. He is so cunning that I never know when I am safe from him. What will he say when he returns?"

"You must lock yourself up from him tonight. Now, we must make the best use of our time, so kindly take us at once to the rooms which we are to examine.

The building was of gray

stone with a high central portion and two curving wings, like the claws of a crab, thrown out on each side. In one of these wings the windows were broken and blocked with wooden boards, while the roof was partly caved in, a picture of ruin. The central portion was in a little better repair, but the right-hand block was comparatively modern, and the blinds in the windows, with the blue smoke curling up from the chimneys, showed that this was where the family resided. Some scaffolding had been erected against the end wall, and the stone-work had been broken into, but there were no signs of any workmen at the moment of our visit. Holmes walked slowly up and down the ill-trimmed lawn and examined with deep attention the outsides of the windows.

"This, I take it, belongs to the room in which you used to sleep, the center one to your sister's, and the one next to the main building to Dr. Roylott's room?"

"Exactly so. But I am now sleeping in the middle one."

"Because of the alterations, as I understand. By the way, there does not seem to be any very pressing need for repairs at that end wall."

"There were none. I believe that it was an excuse to move me from my room."

"Ah! that is suggestive. Now, would you have the kindness to go into your room and bar the shutters?"

Miss Stoner did so, and Holmes, after a careful examination through the open window, tried in every way to force the shutters open, but without success. There was no slit through which a knife could be passed to raise the bar. Then with his magnifying glass he tested the hinges, but they were of solid iron, built firmly into the massive masonry. "Hum!" said he, "my theory certainly presents some difficulties. No one could pass these shutters if they were bolted. Well, we shall see if the inside throws any light upon the matter."

We went at once into the chamber in which Miss Stoner was now sleeping, and in which her sister had met with her fate. It was a homely little room, with low ceiling and a gaping fireplace, after the fashion of old country-houses. A brown chest of drawers stood in one corner, a narrow white bed in another, and a dressing-table on the left-hand side of the window. These articles, with two small wicker chairs, made up all the furniture in the room save for a square of carpet in the center. The boards round and the panelling of the walls were of brown, worm-eaten oak, so old that it may have dated from the original building of the house. Holmes drew one of the chairs into a corner and sat silent, while his eyes travelled round and round and up and down, taking in every detail of the apartment.

"Where does that bell communicate with?" he asked at last, pointing to a thick bell-cord which hung down beside the bed, the tassel actually lying upon the pillow.

"It goes to the housekeeper's room."

"It looks newer than the other things?"

"Yes, it was only put there a couple of years ago."

"Your sister asked for it, I suppose?"

"No, I never heard of her using it. We used always to get what we wanted for ourselves.

"Indeed, it seemed unnecessary to put so nice a bell-pull there. You will excuse me for a few minutes while I satisfy myself as to this floor." He threw himself down upon his face with his magnifying glass in his hand and crawled swiftly backward and forward, examining minutely the cracks between the boards. Then he did the same with the wood-work with which the chamber was panelled. Finally he walked over to the bed and spent some time in staring at it and in running his eye up and down the wall. Finally he took the bell-rope in his hand and gave it a brisk tug.

"Why, it's a dummy," said he.

"Won't it ring?"

"No, it is not even attached to a wire. This is very intersting. You can see now that it is fastened to a hook just above where the little opening for the ventilator is."

"How very absurd! I never noticed that before."

"There are one or two very singular points about this room. For example, what a fool a builder must be to open a ventilator into another room, when, with the same trouble, he might have communicated with the outside air!"

"That is also quite modern," said the lady.

"Done about the same time as the bell-rope?" remarked Holmes.

"Yes, there were several little changes carried out about the same time."

"Now with your permission, Miss Stoner, we shall carry our researches into Dr. Roylott's chamber."

The doctor's apartment was larger than that of his stepdaughter, but was plainly furnished. A camp-bed, a small wooden shelf full of books, mostly of a technical character, an armchair beside the bed, a plain wooden chair against the wall, a round table, and a large iron safe were the principal things which met the eye. Holmes walked slowly round and examined each and all of them with the keenest interest.

"What's in here?" he asked, tapping the safe.

"My stepfather's business papers."

"Oh! you have seen inside, then?"

"Only once, some years ago. I remember that it was full of papers."

"There isn't a cat in it, for example?"

"No. What a strange idea!"

"Well, look at this!" He took up a small saucer of milk which stood on the top of it.

"No; we don't keep a cat. But there is a cheetah and a baboon."

"Ah, yes, of course! Well, a cheetah is just a big cat, and yet a saucer of milk does not go very far in satisfying its wants, I daresay. There is one point which I should wish to determine." He squatted down in front of the wooden chair and examined the seat of it with the greatest attention.

"Thank you. That is quite settled," said he, rising. "Hello! Here is something interesting!"

The object which had caught his eye was a small dog whipcord hung on one corner of the bed. The whipcord, however was curled upon itself and tied so as to make a loop.

"What do you make of that, Watson?"

"It's a comon enough whipcord. But I don't know why it should be tied."

"That is not quite so common, is it? I think that I have seen enough now, Miss Stoner. Now, it is very essential that you should absolutely follow my advice in every respect."

"I shall most certainly do so."

"In the first place, both my friend and I must spend the night in your room."

Both Miss Stoner and I gazed at him in astonishment.

"Let me explain. I believe that that is the village inn over there?"

"Yes, that is the Crown."

"Very good. Your windows would be visible from there. You must confine yourself to your room, on pretence of a headache, when your stepfather comes back. Then when you hear him retire for the night, you must open the shutters of your window, put your lamp there as a signal to us, and then withdraw quietly with everything which you are likely to want into the room which you used to occupy. I have no doubt that in spite of the repairs, you could manage there for one night. And now, Miss Stoner, we must leave you, for if Dr. Roylott returned and saw us our journey would be in vain. Good-bye, and be brave."

Sherlock Holmes and I had no difficulty in engaging a bedroom and sitting-room at the Crown Inn. They were on the upper floor, and from our window we could command a view of the avenue gate, and of the inhabited wing of Stoke Moran Manor House. At dusk we saw Dr. Roylott drive past, and a few minutes later we saw a sudden light spring up among the trees as the lamp was lit in one of the sitting-rooms.

While we waited Holmes conversed with me regarding his observations at Stoke Moran. He said, "I knew that we should find a ventilator before ever we came to Stoke Moran. You remember that Miss Stoner said that her sister could smell Dr. Roylott's cigar. Now, of course, that suggested at once that there must be a communication between the two rooms. It could only be a small one, or it would have been remarked upon at the coroner's inquiry. I deduced a ventilator. Also, did you observe anything very peculiar about that bed?"

"No."

"It was clamped to the floor. Did you ever see a bed fastened like that before? The lady could not move her bed. It must always be in the same relative position to the ventilator and to the rope—or so we may call it, since it was clearly never meant for a bell-pull."

"Holmes," I cried, "I seem to see dimly what you are hinting at. We are only just in time to prevent some subtle and horrible crime."

About nine o'clock the light among the trees went out, and all was dark in the direction of the Manor House. Two hours passed slowly, and then, suddenly, just at the stroke of eleven, a single bright light shone out right in front of us.

"That is our signal," said Holmes, springing to his feet; "it comes from the middle window."

A few moments later we were out on the dark road and entering the grounds. Making our way among the trees, we reached the lawn, crossed it, and were about to enter through the window when out from a clump of bushes there darted what seemed to be a hideous and distorted child, who threw itself upon the grass and then ran swiftly across the lawn into the darkness.

"My God!" I whispered; "did you see it?"

Holmes was for the moment as startled as I. Then he broke into a low laugh and put his lips to my ear.

"It is a nice household," he murmured. "That is the baboon."

I confess that I felt easier in my mind when, after following Holmes' example, I found myself inside the bedroom. My companion noiselessly closed the shutters, moved the lamp onto the table, and cast his eyes round the room. Then creeping up to me and making a trumpet of his hand, he whispered into my ear:

"The least sound would be fatal to our plans. We must sit without light. He would see it through the ventilator. Do not go to sleep; your very life may depend upon it. Have your pistol ready in case we should need it. I will sit on the side of the bed, and you in that chair."

I took my revolver out and laid it on the corner of the table.

Holmes had brought up a long thin cane, and this he placed upon the bed beside him. By it he laid the box of matches and the stump of a candle. Then he turned down the lamp, and we were left in darkness.

How shall I ever forget that dreadful vigil? I could not hear a sound, not even the drawing of a breath. The shutters cut off the least ray of light, and we waited in absolute darkness. Far away we could hear the deep tones of the parish clock, which boomed out every quarter of an hour. How long they seemed, those quarters! Twelve struck, and one and two and three, and still we sat waiting silently for whatever might befall.

Suddenly there was the momentary gleam of a light up in the direction of the ventilator, which vanished immediately, but was succeeded by a strong smell of burning oil and heated metal. Someone in the next room had lit a dark-lantern. I heard a gentle sound of movement, and then all was silent once more, though the smell grew stronger. For half an hour I sat with straining ears. Then suddenly another sound was heard—a very gentle, soothing sound, like that of a small jet of steam escaping continually from a kettle. The instant that we heard it, Holmes sprang from the bed, struck a match, and lashed furiously with his cane at the bell-pull.

"You see it, Watson?" he yelled. "You see it?"

But I saw nothing. At the moment when Holmes struck the light I heard a low, clear whistle, but the sudden glare flashing into my weary eyes made it impossible for me to tell what it was at which my friend lashed so savagely. I could, however, see that his face was deadly pale and filled with horror and loathing.

He had ceased to strike and was gazing up at the ventilator when suddenly there broke from the silence of the night the most horrible cry to which I have ever listened. It swelled up louder and louder, a hoarse yell of pain and fear and anger all mingled in the one dreadful shriek. It struck cold to our hearts.

"What can it mean?" I gasped.

"It means that it is all over," Holmes answered. "Take your pistol, and we will enter Dr. Roylott's room."

With a grave face he lit the lamp and led the way down the hall. Twice he struck at the chamber door without any reply from within. Then he turned the handle and entered, I at his heels, with the cocked pistol in my hand.

It was a singular sight which met our eyes. On the table stood a dark-lantern with the shutter half open, throwing a brilliant beam of light upon the iron safe, the door of which was ajar. Beside this table, on the wooden chair, sat Dr. Roylott. Across his lap lay the short stock with the long whipcord which we had noticed during the day. His chin was cocked upward and his eyes were fixed in a dreadful, rigid stare at the corner of the ceiling. Round his brow he had a peculiar yellow band, with brownish speckles, which seemed to be bound tightly round his head. As we entered he made neither sound nor motion.

"The band! The speckled band!" whispered Holmes.

I took a step forward. In an instant his strange headgear began to move, and there reared itself from among his hair the squat diamond-shaped head and puffed neck of a loathsome serpent.

"It is a swamp adder!" cried Holmes; "the deadliest snake in India. He has died within ten seconds of being bitten. Let us thrust this creature back into its den, and we can then remove Miss Stoner to some place of shelter and let the police know what has happened."

As he spoke he drew the dog-whip swiftly from the dead man's lap, and throwing the noose round the reptile's neck he drew it from its horrid perch and, carrying it at arm's length, threw it into the iron safe, which he closed upon it.

Such are the true facts of the death of Dr. Grimesby Roylott, of Stoke Moran. The little which I had yet to learn of the case was told me by Sherlock Holmes as we travelled back next day.

"I had," said he, "come to an entirely incorrect conclusion which shows, my dear Watson, how dangerous it always is to reason from insufficient data. The presence of the gypsies, and the use of the word 'band' which was used by the poor girl, no doubt to explain a hurried glimpse by the light of her match, were sufficient to put me upon an entirely wrong scent. I can only claim the merit that I instantly reconsidered my position when it became clear to me that whatever danger threatened an occupant of the room could not come either from the window or the door. My attention was speedily drawn to this ventilator, and to the bell-rope which hung down to the bed. The discovery that this was a dummy, and that the bed was clamped to the floor, instantly gave rise to the suspicion that the rope was there as a bridge for something passing through the hole and coming to the bed. The idea of a snake instantly occurred to me, and when I coupled it with my knowledge that the doctor was furnished with a supply of creatures from India, I felt that I was probably on the right track. The idea of using a form of poison which could not possibly be discov-

ered by any chemical test was just such a one as could occur to a clever and ruthless man who had an Eastern training. The rapidity with which such a poison would take effect would also, from his point of view, be an advantage. It would be a sharp-eyed coroner who could distinguish the two little dark punctures which would show where the poison fangs had done their work. Then I thought of the whistle. Of course he must recall the snake before the morning light revealed it to the victim. He had trained it, probably by the use of the milk which we saw, to return to him when summoned. He would put it through the ventilator at the hour that he thought best, with the certainty that it would crawl down the rope and land on the bed. It might or might not bite the occupant, perhaps she might escape every night for a week, but sooner or later she must fall a victim.

"I had come to these conclusions before ever I had entered his room. An inspection of his chair showed me that he had been in the

habit of standing on it, which of course would be necessary in order that he should reach the ventilator. The sight of the safe, the saucer of milk, and the loop of whipcord were enough to finally dispel any doubts which may have remained. The metallic clang heard by Miss Stoner was obviously caused by her stepfather hastily closing the door of his safe upon its terrible occupant. Having once made up my mind, you know the steps which I took in order to put the matter to the proof. I heard the creature hiss, and I instantly lit the light and attacked it."

"With the result of driving it through the ventilator."

"And also with the result of causing it to turn upon its master at the other side. Some of the blows of my cane came home and roused its snakish temper, so that it flew upon the first person it saw. In this way I am no doubt indirectly responsible for Dr. Roylott's death, and I cannot say that it is likely to weigh very heavily upon my conscience."

COMPREHENSION QUESTIONS

_____ 1. Miss Stoner and her sister were
  a. 5 years apart in age.
  b. 10 years apart in age.
  c. twins.
  d. stepsisters.

_____ 2. Dr. Roylott's income was derived from
  a. his medical practice.
  b. an inheritance from his father.
  c. leasing land to the gypsies.
  d. an inheritance from his wife.

_____ 3. Dr. Roylott's character was
  a. calm and friendly.
  b. violent and unfriendly.
  c. friendly only on the surface.
  d. violent only when provoked by good cause.

_____ 4. Dr. Roylott's pets were
  a. a baboon and a cheetah.
  b. cats.
  c. three large dogs.
  d. tiger cubs.

_____ 5. At the time of the story, Miss Stoner was
   a. engaged to be married.
   b. planning to enter a convent.
   c. living with her aunt.
   d. planning to kill her stepfather.

_____ 6. The mystery centered around
   a. how Miss Stoner's sister died.
   b. why Dr. Roylott objected to Miss Stoner's marriage.
   c. what the gypsies were doing at Stoke Moran.
   d. what experiments Dr. Roylott was performing.

_____ 7. Holmes and Watson, in trying to solve the mystery, decided to
   a. ask Dr. Roylott to visit them.
   b. watch the gypsies' activities.
   c. break into Dr. Roylott's laboratory.
   d. spend the night in Miss Stoner's sister's former room.

_____ 8. One of the unusual things involved in the mystery was
   a. why Dr. Roylott chose to live at Stoke Moran.
   b. what caused the whistling sound.
   c. what caused Miss Stoner's sister's disappearance.
   d. where the secret passage led to.

_____ 9. The speckled band turned out to be
   a. the spotted scarfs worn by the gypsies.
   b. the dog whipcord used by Dr. Roylott.
   c. a swamp adder snake.
   d. a band of robbers.

_____ 10. Some of the clues that helped Holmes solve the mystery were
   a. a ventilator, rope-pull, clamped bed.
   b. a broken floorboard, loose shutter hinges.
   c. a hole in the wall, teeth marks, animal fur.
   d. a bottle of poison, an unusual odor, footprints.

Allow 10 points per correct answer.   *Your score* _____ %
Number of words: 6,900.   *Your rate* _____
Answer key is on page 272.
Record rate and comprehension score on your Course Data Sheet.

THE OLD MAN AND THE SEA
COMPREHENSION QUESTIONS

_____ 1. The boy's feelings toward the old man were those of
   a. fear, because the old man was so strange.
   b. love and an eagerness to serve him.
   c. jealousy, because the old man owned more than his family.
   d. anger, because the old man would not take him fishing.

_____ 2. When the old man hooked his great fish he
   a. pulled him in by the fishing line, but with difficulty.
   b. had to release the fish because he couldn't pull him in.
   c. was towed out to sea by the fish.
   d. asked a fisherman in a neighboring boat to help him pull in the fish.

_____ 3. On the fishing trip the old man kept wishing that
    a. the boy was with him.
    b. he had something to eat.
    c. it wasn't so cold.
    d. he was a young man again.

_____ 4. While the old man was trying to get the big fish he
    a. was lucky not to have fish bite on the other lines.
    b. had to cut the other lines as fish bit on them, and he lost those fish.
    c. pulled in three fish that bit on the other lines.
    d. caught another big fish.

_____ 5. The old man kept referring to the great fish as his
    a. friend and brother.
    b. enemy.
    c. savior.
    d. test.

_____ 6. The author tells this story in such a way that we
    a. do not know what the old man is thinking.
    b. know what the fish is thinking.
    c. know what the old man is thinking.
    d. only know what the boy is thinking.

_____ 7. The old man kept his strength up by
    a. drinking some whiskey he had brought along.
    b. eating dried food he had brought along.
    c. willing himself to stay strong.
    d. eating raw fish which he had caught.

_____ 8. The great fish was destroyed by
    a. vultures.
    b. tourists.
    c. sharks.
    d. jealous fishermen.

_____ 9. In the end, the old man probably would
    a. never go out to sea again.
    b. go out to sea as soon as he recuperated.
    c. curse the sea.
    d. curse the fish.

_____ 10. In this story, the author has illustrated a conflict between
    a. man and sharks.
    b. man and a noble fish that represents nature.
    c. man and his inner problems.
    d. man and the forces of society.

Allow 10 points per correct answer.   Your score _____ %
Number of words: 29,000.   Your rate _____
Answer key is on page 272.
Record your rate and comprehension score on your Course Data Sheet.

GENERAL NOVEL COMPREHENSION QUESTIONS

(To be used only when reading a novel other than THE OLD MAN AND THE SEA)

Title _____ Author _____

1. Name the main character(s). _____

   _____

2. Where does the story take place? _____

   _____

3. Approximately when does the story take place? _____

4. Name two other characters. (1) _____

   (2) _____

5. What type of story is it (love story, adventure, science fiction, war story,

   fantasy, etc.)? _____

6. Briefly summarize the situation at the beginning of the story.

   _____

   _____

   _____

7. List three things that happen to the main character.

   (1) _____

   (2) _____

   (3) _____

8. State the relationship(s) between the main character and at least one other

   character (husband and wife, father and son, friends, etc). _____

9. How does the story end? _____

   _____

   _____

10. Write one sentence that tells what this whole story illustrates (author's

    message). _____

    _____

Directions: *You may wish to look back into the story to find out if you wrote the correct answers. If you do, give yourself 10 points for each correct answer.*

If you do not correct your answer sheet, estimate your understanding of the story by writing "excellent," "good," "fair," or "poor" in the place for your score

Your score _____ %

Total number of words _____   Your rate _____

To find your rate, refer to directions in Chapter 8, page 80. Record title, rate, and score on your Course Data Sheet.

10

Skimming, Scanning, and Marking a Text

Materials: • Readings:
   "The Ph.D. Degree: What It Is and Where It Takes You"
   The Incredible Journey, or another 33,000-word novel
   • Drill book, a novel previously read

Objectives: • To learn the reading technique of skimming
   • To learn the reading technique of scanning
   • To learn a new system of marking a text

DRILL PRACTICE

Do the same drills that you did at the beginning of Chapter 7, page 66. Take a drill rate for this week. Record the rate on your Course Data Sheet. (A good drill book is *The Old Man and the Sea.*)

SKIMMING

Skimming is a reading technique that involves going over a text at a rate that exceeds your normal reading rate for the limited purpose of understanding only the main idea without the details or of getting the gist of the material. It is of great value in doing research and has two goals when used for this purpose. One is to find out if the text in fact contains information on your research topic. The other is to select portions suitable for note-taking. (Speed Researching is discussed in detail in Chapter 11.) Skimming can also be used as a preview when reading for study. Then the objective is to gain foreknowledge of the total idea so that when you actually read the material, the details will fall into place in a more meaningful and easier to remember manner.

Skimming will be simple for you to master since that is what you have been doing when you drill. You need only learn how to apply it to other uses. In research, you progress through the text at a drill rate; and when you see data of importance to your research topic, you slow down to read that portion, keeping in mind all the material you went over. In previewing, you proceed at a drill rate, noticing the important thoughts and the overall ideas which will prepare you for studying. The primary difference in these two applications, therefore, is that in research the important ideas are those that relate to your topic, whereas in previewing the important ideas are the author's main ideas. In some cases they are the same.

Skimming Practice

Turn to the article, "The Ph.D. Degree: What It Is and Where It Takes You," page 99. You will skim this article as a preview, looking for the main idea, reading it at only slightly lower than a drill rate because your purpose is only to get the main ideas, not the details. When you are finished, write one sentence that states the main idea of what the article is about.

Begin. Write a statement of the main idea. Look at the answer key for chapter 10 at the back of the book to check the accuracy of your statement.

SCANNING

Scanning is a reading technique that also involves going over a text at a rate that exceeds your normal reading rate for the limited purpose of locating specific information in the body of print. In scanning, you progress rapidly but are unconcerned with the main ideas or general thought of the text; your only concern is to find the definite word, phrase, or idea you are seeking. It is a reading technique for locating information. You have used it countless times when you have looked in the telephone book for a specific name. Other uses include finding answers to questions and picking out facts on a single topic that are included in a work on a broader topic. For instance, if you wanted to find all the information on the violin and you scanned a book on musical instruments, you would scan looking for the word *violin;* whenever you saw that word, you would stop to read that portion, but you would disregard all the other portions that did not bear on that particular topic. This technique differs from skimming in that the in-between ideas are not even registered in the brain; it is as if you didn't see them.

Scanning is not more difficult than skimming, just different. To accomplish it, you must have a picture in your mind of the word, phrase, or key words of the ideas for which you are looking. As your eyes proceed rapidly over the print, you watch only for a duplication of the picture you have kept in your mind, and you ignore everything else. When you find a match for the image in your mind, you stop to read that portion. Then you proceed as before, always looking to match your mind's picture.

Scanning Practice

Again using the same article, scan to find out how many times the word "Ph.D." appears. Think of possible synonyms, such as doctor of philosophy. Keep the picture of the words in your mind. Every time you see one of these words, mark it with a pencil. When you have finished, count how many times "Ph.D.", or its synonym appears. Begin scanning.

How many did you find? Write down the number.

The answers can be found in the answer key for chapter 10 at the back of the book.

From now on, scan to find the answers to questions you miss on the readings of short stories, books, or articles.

MARKING A TEXT

The purposes for marking a text are to point up important parts and to indicate aspects that you don't understand or parts that you want to reread for better understanding. It is the base on which an effective study procedure can be built, and it is a valuable tool in doing research. If your present text-marking method is not accomplishing these purposes, you can improve your results by adopting the marking system suggested in this chapter.

The most commonly used method of marking a text is underlining. However, this method has disadvantages. Underlining clutters up the print so that it is more difficult to read. It only points up important parts and is, therefore, not a complete system. It cannot be used in books that you do not own; and as you go further along in your education, you will be using fewer and fewer books of your own and more and more books from the library. Because it takes a lot of time and effort to stop your reading to underline, it is not suited to speed reading.

USING SYMBOLS

There are better ways of marking a text. One is to use dots, small vertical lines, question marks, or some other inconspicuous signs to call your attention to certain parts of the text. These symbols are all placed in the margins and are made in light pencil so that they can be erased in books you do not own. Each symbol has a meaning for you. For example, the dot means that the portion next to it contains an important idea. Small vertical lines tell you that the whole paragraph, or a large portion of it, is important. Checks are placed next to parts of the text that require a rereading later for better understanding. Question marks indicate that you have a question regarding the statement that you may wish to think about or discuss. Here's an example of these markings:

.	single important idea
|	several sentences or whole paragraph important
√	don't understand
?	have question regarding statement
1, 2, 3, 4, etc.	items in a series

It is not necessary for you to use these particular symbols in order to have a complete and effective marking method; they are only suggestions. You may devise your own marks, if you choose, as long as they are simple, do not deface the text, are done in pencil, and you know what they mean.

USING A PENCIL

Before you can use any marking method, you need to find a suitable way of holding a pencil so that it is comfortable, you can use it at will, and it does not interfere with your hand movement. You may hold the pencil in the hand that you use for reading or in the other hand, whichever is more comfortable. The pencil may be placed across the palm of the hand or between any two fingers. I prefer to hold my pencil between the first and second fingers in the normal pencil-holding position with the point facing away from the paper. When I wish to use the pencil, I simply lower the point to the paper and mark, immediately swinging the point up again leaving my hand free to continue the hand movement. No matter which way you choose to hold the pencil, it is best to keep the point out of the way of the hand movement when the pencil is not in use. Practice several different ways of holding the pencil until you find one that seems best for you.

MARKING FOR STUDY

In studying, you do not mark the text during the entire reading procedure, only when you are reading for good comprehension. First, you *preview by skimming* the entire article so that you get an idea of the total work and are in a better position to know what is important. Then you read the material and mark the text as you read. When you read a sentence that seems to contain a main or important idea, you place a dot in whichever margin is closer to your hand at the time. If several sentences or the whole paragraph is important, you place two or three short vertical lines in the margin next to the important part. If you come across a part that you don't understand, you place a check in the margin. When you have a question regarding the material, you make a question mark in the margin. When you have finished all the material, you go back to your checks and reread those parts. Most of the time, after reading the rest of the material, you will understand parts that you didn't understand earlier. Also, when you understand the total idea, the parts fall into place more easily. If you feel that note-taking would be beneficial, you need to read only those portions marked with dots and vertical lines and take notes on them. When you need to

review the material for a test, all you have to do is reread the material quickly, paying special attention to the parts you marked as being important.

Practice in Marking for Study

When marking a text for study, you always preview first by skimming the entire article, slowing down slightly on the whole first paragraph, the beginning of each paragraph, and the whole last paragraph. You pay special attention to the subtitles. You do *not* mark in this preview skim.

For practice in marking a text use the article, "The Ph.D. Degree: What It Is and Where It Takes You." Since you also used this article in the skimming practice, you have already completed the necessary preview.

Begin by reading the article at a good comprehension rate, slower than your skimming rate. In this reading, mark the text with the symbols presented in this chapter. Remember to use flexibility, slowing down on hard parts and speeding up on easy parts. Use any hand movement you wish.

Before answering the questions, go over the article once more, going very rapidly (skimming) but slowing down to reread the parts you marked for reinforcement of the important ideas. If you wish, you may take notes at this point; you will now know what is important enough to be included in your notes.

When you have finished all of these steps, you will have read an article as you should read your textbooks or any material that you must know well. You are now ready to answer the questions at the end of this article. Do so.

Here is an outline of reading procedure to use when marking a text for study purposes:

1. Preview by skimming entire article.
2. Record starting time.
3. Read and mark text. Use flexibility.
4. Record finish time.
5. Skim, slowing down on marked parts.
6. Take notes (optional).
7. Answer questions at the end of the article.
8. Correct answers. (Answer key is in the Appendix.)
9. Compute rate and comprehension score, and record on Course Data Sheet.

Third Novel Reading

Read *The Incredible Journey* (questions are at the end of the chapter) or a novel of about 33,000 words (general questions are at the end of the chapter).

Follow the instructions "Summary of procedure for reading the novel" on page 77, but preview by skimming at your own pace, without anyone calling "page." Skim the usual first and last five pages and five pages in several random places in the book. This time, also skim over the questions to your book as part of the preview. Answer the usual questions to yourself on the characters, time, place, an event, the way it starts. Don't forget your bookmark at the halfway point, which you should reach in twenty minutes.

Read the novel, using flexibility by slowing down slightly on the first chapter, the beginnings of chapters, the last chapter, and any difficult parts. Speed up whenever you can. In this reading, mark the text as instructed in this chapter.

Go over the book again to reinforce the important ideas, skipping from marked part to marked part. Reread these marked parts. *Erase* your marks as you go along.

Answer the questions. This time, do not guess on any answers. Only answer the questions for which you are sure you know the answers; leave the ones about which you are uncertain blank for now. Do not correct your answers yet. First, do the following scanning assignment.

More Scanning Practice

On the test for the novel, find the first question you were unable to answer. Reread the question carefully. Pick out the key words or phrase that state(s) precisely what the question asks for. For instance in question 7 for *The Incredible Journey*, "The animals were traveling to . . . ," the key words are *traveling to*. You would keep these key words or the idea of the key words in your mind and look for them as you scan. Figure out where in the book you are most likely to find the answer. Would it most likely be in the beginning, or do you recall

seeing it somewhere around the middle of the book? Do not scan the whole book looking for one answer. Try to pick out the most likely spots and scan these places only. If your book has a table of contents, the titles of the chapters may give you some clues about where to find the answer.

Repeat the process of recognizing the key words or idea in the question, scanning and finding the answer for each question you couldn't answer before until you have answered all the questions. You may have to scan for each answer separately.

Now correct your answers, using the answer key in the Appendix. For any other novel, scan for the correct answers to the questions you thought you knew to see if you were right.

Your comprehension score should be higher than usual because you will find answers you ordinarily might not know, but your reading rate may be lower than usual because marking takes a little more time.

SUMMARY

Skimming and scanning are additional reading techniques. In skimming you go over the material very rapidly to get an idea of what it covers. In scanning you also go very rapidly but with a picture in your mind of what you are looking for, and you slow down to a reading rate when you have found it.

You should use a complete marking system, rather than underlining, as a part of your study method. The marks should be made in pencil and should point up important ideas and parts you have questions about or don't understand. You use the marks to signal areas you need to reread for complete comprehension and as an aid in reviewing for a test.

THE PH.D. DEGREE: WHAT IT IS AND WHERE IT TAKES YOU

Douglas Braddock

Diane, a college senior majoring in electrical engineering, enjoys studying engineering and does well in school. One of her professors is urging her to get a Doctor of Philosophy (Ph.D.) degree. Although the thought of continuing her studies is appealing, she has many questions about what obtaining a Ph.D. entails. How does it differ from other postgraduate education? Why do people seek Ph.D.'s? How long does it take? How are graduate studies financed? What kind of work do people with a Ph.D. do? And, most importantly for Diane, will appropriate jobs for people with Ph.D.'s in her field be available? This article answers some of these questions.

WHAT IS A PH.D.?

The Ph.D. is the most common doctoral degree. Although Ph.D. stands for doctor of philosophy, the degree is granted in most academic subjects: Engineering, humanities, life sciences, physical sciences, and social sciences. It is primarily designed to develop research skills, unlike the M.D., for example, which is designed to develop the skills needed by a practitioner. Doctoral degrees are the highest given in academic subjects, although further study beyond the Ph.D., called postdoctoral study, is becoming important in some fields.

The total number of Ph.D.'s awarded in recent years has declined. Almost every discipline has experienced a decline, though some—such as the humanities—have been hit harder than others. Among the few disciplines in which the number of degrees rose between 1973 and 1983 are computer science; earth, atmospheric, and marine science; biological sciences; health sciences; agricultural sciences; psychology; anthropology; music; and communications.

People may have a combination of reasons for obtaining a Ph.D. Many obtain a Ph.D. because it is a prerequisite for some careers—college teaching in particular. Also, in some occupations—physics or mathematics, for example—a Ph.D. is needed to reach full professional status. Other people just enjoy learning about a particular subject. Driven by intellectual curiosity, they want to continue studying the subject and perhaps add to the knowledge of the subject through their own research. Others are motivated to be among the best and to be regarded as a member of an elite learned group. These motivations are so strong that some students in recent years continued to pursue a Ph.D. even though they knew that they would have difficulty finding a job in their field.

In general, obtaining a Ph.D. involves taking 20 or more increasingly specialized courses, conducting research on a very narrow subject, and writing a dissertation that describes the research and its results. The coursework usually takes several years to complete even though it is equivalent to 3 years of academic credit. Classes are usually smaller than undergraduate classes and seminars are common. Typically, students must study articles in scholarly journals as well as textbooks; research papers are usually required. Graduate students have closer contact with their professors and other students in their departments than do undergraduates, but usually have less contact with other parts of university life. They tend to live off campus, are

often married, and, in many cases, have jobs or assistantship duties in addition to their studies.

Doctoral students usually specialize in a subfield of their discipline. In physics, for example, the student may concentrate on acoustics; in history, on the American Civil War. However, because a doctoral recipient must have a good knowledge of all aspects of a field, comprehensive examinations on all core or major areas of the discipline must be passed. The nature of these exams—whether oral or written, the sequence in which they are taken, the number of times that they may be retaken in case of failure—differs significantly from school to school and from department to department. These exams, together with the requirement that at least a B average be maintained (rather than the C average of the undergraduate school), make doctoral coursework more demanding and challenging than undergraduate courses. Most graduate students gladly spend the additional time required studying and conducting research, however, because the material is so directely related to their major interest.

The dissertation poses a difficult obstacle for many doctoral candidates. The dissertation is a report of original research conducted by the candidate to answer some significant question in the field; it sets forth an original hypothesis or proposes a model and then tests it. In order to test the hypothesis, the student in the sciences or engineering must usually undertake laboratory work, and the student in the humanities must embark on an extensive study of original documents or published material. While conducting the research and preparing the dissertation, the student is guided and advised by a faculty member.

Completing the dissertation usually takes the equivalent of 1 or 2 years of full-time work. The amount of time required varies depending on the candidate's other obligations, the subject of the dissertation, and the diligence of the student. Some students find shifting from the structured environment of classrooms and examinations to the uncertainties of research difficult. As a result, many candidates who have completed their coursework don't complete their dissertation. Colloquially, they are called ABD's (All But Dissertation). Although an ABD is not a degree, many employers view an ABD holder as having a semi-official status between that of a master's degree and doctorate holder.

Although a Ph.D. program can be completed in 3 or 4 years of uninterrupted study, it almost always takes longer. For doctorate recipients in

1983 (the latest data available), the median time spent as registered students after receiving a bachelor's degree was 6.6 years. However, the time varied by field. Students in the natural sciences and engineering took less time on average than students in other fields. Because few people pursue a doctorate nonstop after leaving college, the median age of those awarded a doctorate was almost 33.

IS A MASTER'S DEGREE REQUIRED?

Contrary to what many believe, a master's degree is not required for entrance into most Ph.D. programs. Although about 80 percent of those awarded a Ph.D. in 1983 had obtained a master's first, some students—especially in chemistry and biochemistry—go directly from the bachelor's degree to the Ph.D. and never receive one.

The master's degree is awarded in its own right. Most are awarded to students who do not intend to go on for their doctorate; however, normal progress toward a Ph.D. usually involves fulfilling the requirements for a master's degree as well. For example, acceptance as a candidate for the doctorate may require completion of a certain number of courses and passing certain tests; completion of these same requirements may warrant the award of the master's degree.

Earning a master's degree might necessitate completing projects that do not contribute directly toward progress in a Ph.D. program, however. For example, a master's thesis representing 500 or more hours of research may be required; while writing a master's thesis is often of general benefit to the student, the content of the thesis may not be useful at later stages of a doctorate program. Therefore, students who are sure they will continue their studies up to the doctorate in the same institution may save time by enrolling in a Ph.D. program at the start rather than first starting out in a master's degree program.

POSTDOCTORAL STUDY

Although the Ph.D. is the highest academic degree awarded, obtaining it does not necessarily mean the end of one's studies. It has become increasingly common for new Ph.D.'s, especially in the natural sciences, to spend a period of time—often 2 years—doing postdoctoral research and study. Postdoctoral fellows usually perform research, often on a topic of interest to an institution, in return for financial support in the form of a postdoctoral fellowship. In some fields, postdoctoral research is becoming almost a necessity because these areas have become so advanced that the regular doctoral program doesn't afford enough time to become fully knowledgeable about the field and proficient in research. Some recent Ph.D.'s hold postdoctoral positions while they search for a permanent job that suits their interests.

FINANCIAL SUPPORT

The cost of obtaining a Ph.D. is considerable because of the long period involved. Tuition, housing, travel to a distant university, and child care must be paid for somehow. A substantial cost of graduate education in addition to out-of-pocket expenses is the income that students would have earned had they sought employment immediately after college. Because new employees typically receive fairly rapid promotions and salary increases, the amount of this lost income rises every year the student remains in graduate school.

A complex system of financial assistance has evolved that provides some or all of the tuition and living expenses for most graduate students. The sources of financial assistance vary greatly. Most students rely on a combination of types of financial support, including savings, loans, earnings from part- or full-time jobs, family contributions, and their spouse's earnings. Assistantships and fellowships are the most common sources of income other than earnings.

Assistantships. Basically, an assistantship is a part-time job. The student provides services to the university in return for a small salary and reduction or elimination of tuition. Because the job is in the student's own field, there is some educational benefit to the student from this work. The work experience can also be important when the student seeks full-time employment. There are two kinds of assistantships—teaching and research. The number awarded and the standards for the award vary widely from institution to institution and from department to department.

A teaching assistant teaches one or more courses, usually lower level undergraduate courses. Sometimes, duties are restricted to grading tests or providing tutorial services. Other times, the assistant might conduct the laboratory sessions of a course taught by a professor. In many cases, the assistant has almost all the duties of a regular faculty member, including preparing the syllabus, developing lectures, designing assignments, and evaluating the class's progress. Teaching assistantships are common in most fields.

Research assistants work in laboratories, libraries, or offices, assisting the faculty in performing research. Duties can range from preparing bibliographies to conducting experiments. The availability of these assistantships varies by field; they are common in science and engineering, less common in social sciences, and relatively rare in the humanities.

Fellowships.   Fellowships are similar to scholarships in undergraduate school in that there are usually no work requirements. Fellowships, which can cover tuition and living expenses, are primarily awarded by universities but are also available from other sources, notably the National Institutes of Health (NIH) and the National Science Foundation (NSF), both of which are Federal agencies. NSF and NIH also award traineeships, which are similar to fellowships except that the funds are not awarded directly to the student but are distributed by the universities. NSF and NIH fellowships and traineeships are concentrated in engineering and the physical, life, and social sciences.

PH.D. EMPLOYMENT CONDITIONS

Most Ph.D. programs are designed to prepare one for college or university faculty employment by providing a thorough knowledge of a subject and the skills to do research. Until recent years, the major—and, in some fields, almost the only—employers of Ph.D.'s were colleges and universities. Therefore, trends in college enrollments have had an important effect on employment opportunities for Ph.D.'s.

During the 1960's, undergraduate enrollments grew rapidly from 3.6 million in 1960 to 7.9 million in 1970 as the post-World War II baby boom generation reached college age. College enrollments also were inflated during this period by an increase in the percentage of the college-age population who attended college. Growth in enrollments was considerably slower in the 1970's, and it is expected that enrollments will decline beginning in the mid-1980's because of fewer births after the mid-1960's.

The large expansion of college enrollments in the 1960's created a high demand for new faculty. Enrollments in Ph.D. programs responded to this demand, and many of the new bachelor's degree holders who were available continued into graduate school. In addition, Federal and other support for graduate studies increased. However, when growth in enrollments started to slow around 1970, colleges and universities greatly reduced their hiring; and new Ph.D.'s in many fields have had difficulty obtaining permanent academic employment since that time. Natural scientists, partly because of opportunities in industry and government, have had better employment prospects than social scientists and humanities Ph.D.'s, who have historically had fewer opportunities outside colleges and universities. The situation has been different for Ph.D. engineers and computer scientists. They have been in such high demand in industry and other areas in recent years that they have often been lured away from the classroom by much higher salaries in industry. This has resulted in a shortage of college faculty in engineering and computer science even though surpluses existed in other fields.

LIFE AS A FACULTY MEMBER

Teaching or conducting research is the primary work activity of most Ph.D.'s, and more than half work in colleges and universities. The teaching of undergraduates and course preparation are important parts of faculty members' duties; although 4-year college and university faculty members spent less than half their time in instruction and course preparation, additional time was spent on duties closely related to teaching, such as advising students. These estimates are only averages, of course. Some faculty may spend most of their time doing research, and others—department heads, for example—may devote a considerable amount of time to administration.

Although research consumes less than a fifth of the average faculty member's time, it is typically a very important factor in a faculty member's career. He or she must produce research findings of sufficient quality to be published in scholarly journals. The publication of research results is taken as evidence that the faculty member is staying abreast of and contributing to progress in his or her field and adding to the reputation of the institution. "Publish or perish" is the rule in many institutions.

Many faculty members obtain grants or contracts—often from the Federal Government—to support part or all of their research. In some institutions or academic departments, grants and contracts are an important source of funds. Professors who are able to obtain contracts because of their prominence in a field are highly regarded; their efforts bring greater recognition to the school.

An important part of the traditional academic career is the attainment of tenure. In the traditional academic career, a new Ph.D. is hired with the rank of instructor or, more usually, assistant professor. After a certain period (usually 7 years), the faculty member's teaching record, research projects, and overall contribution to the school are reviewed; tenure is granted if the review is favorable.

Once granted tenure, a professor cannot ordinarily be fired and is likely to continue with that institution for the remainder of his or her career. A faculty member who is denied tenure usually must obtain a job elsewhere. The purpose of tenure is to protect the faculty's academic freedom; that is, it enables the faculty member to teach and conduct research free from the fear of being fired for advocating unpopular ideas. It also gives both faculty members and their institutions the stability needed for effective research and teaching.

In recent years, however, there have been many pressures on higher educational institutions and their faculty that have forced modifications to the traditional faculty career system. As noted earlier, enrollments, which have leveled off, are projected to decline, which will result in lower tuition income. Inflation increased costs faster than tuition and fees could be raised, and Federal and State funds to support higher education were greatly reduced. Government funds supplied 62.5 percent of costs in public 4-year institutions in 1970–71; this was reduced to 57.6 percent in 1981–82. In private 4-year institutions, the reduction was from 24.9 to 19.9 percent over the same period. Furthermore, a large proportion of most institutions' faculties already have tenure, which compounds these problems. In 1983, 62 percent of science, engineering, and social science faculty and 70 percent of humanities faculty had tenure. Because much of the faculty was hired during the 1960's, the rate of deaths and retirements is relatively low. Therefore, college administrators often find themselves under pressure to reduce costs but have little maneuvering room when some fields—engineering and computer science, for example—become more popular at the expense of other fields, such as English literature or foreign languages. When this happens, tenured staff in the less popular fields cannot be shifted to the more popular ones.

Many of the strategies adopted by colleges and universities to cope with these pressures have had adverse consequences for new Ph.D.'s. The major strategy has been to restrict the hiring of new faculty members, especially in the humanities and social sciences, which has resulted in intense competition in some fields for the few available openings. Colleges and universities have also chosen to create temporary, nontenure-track positions for many of the new faculty members they do hire. Because faculty members holding temporary positions must often leave when their contract expires, many have had a series of temporary jobs at colleges and universities all across the country, becoming what have been called academic nomads.

Another strategy used by colleges and universities to reduce costs is to increase the use of part-time faculty, who usually cost the college less per course taught than full-time faculty. Some part-timers are new Ph.D.'s unable to obtain a tenure-track position. Many others work full time in industry or government jobs and teach a course or two on the side.

Even if a new Ph.D. obtains a satisfactory tenure-track faculty position, a variety of changes in campus life caused by cost pressures and steady or declining enrollments have made the faculty in many institutions less satisfied with their jobs than in the past. Academic salaries have not kept up with inflation, the pressure to produce publishable research results and to obtain research grants and contracts has increased, laboratory equipment has become increasingly out of date, and, in some cases, working conditions have been adversely affected by buildings that are deteriorating due to inadequate maintenance or by students who are unprepared for college-level work.

OPPORTUNITIES OUTSIDE ACADEMIA

A large proportion of doctoral degree holders do not work in higher education. Although doctoral programs have traditionally concentrated on preparing their students for life as a faculty member, Ph.D.'s in some fields are in demand by employers other than universities. Scientific and engineering research is an essential activity in industry and government, and large proportions of Ph.D.'s in science and engineering have always worked there. Growth in industrial research and development spending since the early 1960's has resulted in more Ph.D.'s than ever who work outside academia.

Many scientists and engineers with doctorates prefer nonacademic work for several reasons. The pay is usually higher—often much higher—in industry than in colleges and universities. Of perhaps more importance to many, industrial research labs often have more up-to-date equipment than universities. Another advantage to those who wish to conduct research is that, in industry, without teaching and administrative duties, one can spend full time on research.

Prior to the early 1970's, many employers in industry and government were reluctant to hire Ph.D.'s in the social sciences and humanities. It was assumed they would not be satisfied with their jobs and would leave when a faculty vacancy became available. Some new Ph.D.'s, after experiencing the disappointment of being unable to obtain a faculty job, became even more distressed when they found they almost had to hide the fact that they had a Ph.D. when looking for a nonacademic job. However, in recent years, things have changed. Many employers have found that humanities and social science Ph.D.'s are valuable employees. They are bright, are trained in research methods, and have excellent communications skills. Similarly, the attitudes of new Ph.D.'s have also changed. Because many new Ph.D.'s are well aware of the poor prospects of academic employment, they are more receptive to nontraditional types of employment.

WHAT PH.D.'S EARN

Average annual salaries for Ph.D.'s in 1983 varied considerably by the field of doctorate, from around $30,000 in humanities fields to over $46,000 in engineering. Salaries paid by business and industry were higher than those paid by educational institutions for most fields, but not for the humanities. The salaries in several other occupations can serve for a comparison: Secondary school teachers in public schools earned an average of $21,100 during the 1982–83 school year; experienced engineers, most of whom have a bachelor's or master's degree, earned average salaries of about $36,700 in 1983. Others with at least 3 years of postbaccalaureate training earned more. Experienced salaried lawyers averaged from $40,000 to $50,000 in 1983. The average income of dentists in 1982 was about $55,000 and the average of all physicians' net incomes in 1982 was over $100,000.

FUTURE EMPLOYMENT OPPORTUNITIES

For at least the next 10 years, employment prospects for college and university faculty, which already are poor in most fields, probably will worsen as college enrollments decline. The number of 18- to 21-year-olds, the age group that traditionally has supplied most undergraduates, is expected to decline over the period because of fewer births after the mid-1960's. Until after the mid-1990's, there are likely to be few tenure-track openings, at least outside of engineering and some of the sciences. In fact, there are fears that lower enrollments might force some colleges to lay off tenured professors, something that has been almost unheard of in the academic world. However, opportunities in business and government for Ph.D.'s in science and engineering fields should be favorable.

There is some good news over the long term for those presently thinking of pursuing a Ph.D. By the late 1990's, employment conditions for Ph.D.'s should improve. Although this seems like a long time away, the average doctorate recipient earned a bachelor's degree some 10 years earlier. The improvement in employment conditions would therefore take place by the time today's high school seniors become Ph.D. candidates.

Employment prospects for Ph.D.'s are expected to improve in the late 1990's for several reasons. First, the children born to the baby-boom generation will be old enough for college by then; the college-age population and, thus, enrollments, are expected to start to increase from the low point around 1995. Second, demand for people with doctorates is likely to continue to increase in nonacademic areas because of the increasingly higher levels of technology and complexity of industry and government. Third, and perhaps most important, the very large number of college faculty hired during the 1960's will begin retiring by the late 1990's.

Currently, most retiring faculty members were hired before 1960. Faculty members hired during the 1960's will begin retiring in the mid- to late 1990's. This will create a very large number of openings because the number of faculty more than doubled between 1960 and 1970. Conditions may improve sooner in some fields than in others, depending on the age of the faculty, the number of students choosing a field as a major, and nonacademic demand.

Because the employment outlook for Ph.D.'s will vary considerably by field, The *Occupational Outlook Handbook* should be consulted for employment outlook information on specific fields. The *Handbook* will also provide information on the nature of the work, working conditions, and earnings for many occupations that Ph.D.'s enter.

COMPREHENSION QUESTIONS

_____ 1. The doctoral dissertation consists of
   a. a series of written and oral examinations.
   b. 20 units of advanced university courses in the candidate's field.
   c. a report on original research conducted by the candidate to answer some significant question.
   d. one three-day written examination.

_____ 2. Students in the doctoral program usually
   a. specialize in a subfield of their discipline.
   b. do not specialize in any particular area in their discipline.
   c. take 20 postgraduate courses that are of a general nature.
   d. fulfill advanced general education requirements.

_____ 3. An assistantship is
   a. a part-time job as a teacher or researcher awarded to doctoral students.
   b. the name of the status of all doctoral students.
   c. an entry-level teaching position that requires a completed doctoral degree.
   d. a scholarship for doctoral students.

_____ 4. A fellowship is a
   a. beginning teaching position.
   b. part-time job awarded to doctoral students.
   c. the name of the status for all doctoral students.
   d. money grant, like a scholarship, awarded to doctoral students.

_____ 5. Most Ph.D.'s find employment as
   a. writers.
   b. managers in industry.
   c. college or university professors.
   d. managers in governmental positions.

_____ 6. If a Ph.D. becomes a professor, he/she usually can attain tenure in
   a. 10 years.
   b. 2 years.
   c. 3 years.
   d. 7 years.

_____ 7. The salary a Ph.D. can expect is usually higher
   a. in industry.
   b. as a professor.
   c. than a medical doctor.
   d. than a salaried lawyer.

_____ 8. By the late 1990s, employment for the Ph.D.'s is expected to
   a. be more numerous than now.
   b. be less numerous than now.
   c. stay about the same as now.
   d. be nonexistent.

_____ 9. The student who works on the doctorate with no interruptions can often complete the program in
   a. 10 years.
   b. 1–2 years.
   c. 3–4 years.
   d. 7–8 years.

_____ 10. A candidate who completes all the coursework but not the dissertation is referred to as a
   a. predoctorate.
   b. almost doctorate.
   c. Master of Philosophy.
   d. ABD.

Allow 10 points per correct answer.   Your score _____ %
Number of words: 4180.   Your rate _____
Answer key is on page 272.
Record your rate and comprehension score on your Course Data Sheet.

THE INCREDIBLE JOURNEY
COMPREHENSION QUESTIONS

_____ 1. The journey took place in
   a. Northern United States.
   b. Alaska.
   c. Canada.
   d. Southern California.

_____ 2. The main animal characters were the
   a. Siamese cat, Labrador retriever, bull terrier.
   b. Burmese cat, collie, cocker spaniel.
   c. striped cat, boxer, poodle.
   d. tabby cat, German shepherd, Doberman pinscher.

_____ 3. The housekeeper, Mrs. Oakes, was not overly concerned when she found the animals gone because she thought that they
   a. had been picked up by their owner.
   b. were with Longridge.
   c. were playfully hiding from her.
   d. deserved to be punished.

_____ 4. The Indians treated the old dog nicely because they
   a. were always kind to animals.
   b. were afraid of the cat who watched over the dog.
   c. hoped to catch the animals and keep them.
   d. thought the dog was sent by the Spirits to test them.

_____ 5. The cat was saved from drowning by
   a. a girl and her family.
   b. the old dog.
   c. the young dog.
   d. the Indians.

_____ 6. The young dog was badly wounded by
   a. a lynx.
   b. a wolf.
   c. an angry farmer.
   d. porcupine quills.

_____ 7. The animals were traveling to
   a. the Hunters.
   b. Longridge's home.
   c. someplace warmer and friendlier.
   d. anyplace far away from Mrs. Oakes.

_____ 8. The number of miles they traveled was
   a. 1,000.
   b. 500.
   c. 300.
   d. 100.

_____ 9. On the journey, the animals fought with a
   a. snake and lion.
   b. wolf and bear.
   c. bear and collie.
   d. buzzard and beaver.

_____ 10. In the end
   a. all three arrived safely.
   b. the young dog and cat arrived; the old dog died.
   c. the cat died.
   d. the young dog died.

Allow 10 points per correct answer.   *Your score* _____ %
Number of words: 33,500.   *Your rate* _____
Answer key is on page 272.
Record rate and comprehension score on Course Data Sheet.

GENERAL NOVEL COMPREHENSION QUESTIONS

(To be used only when reading a novel other than *The Incredible Journey*.)

Title _____   Author _____

1. Name the main character(s). _____

2. Where does the story take place? _____

   _____

3. Approximately when does the story take place? _____

4. Name two other characters. (1) _____

   (2) _____

5. What type of story is it (love story, adventure, science fiction, war story,

   fantasy, etc.)? _____

6. Briefly summarize the situation at the beginning of the story.

   _____

   _____

   _____

7. List three things that happen to the main character.

   (1) _____

   (2) _____

   (3) _____

8. State the relationship(s) between the main character and at least one other

   character (husband and wife, father and son, friends, etc). _____

9. How does the story end? _____
_____
_____

10. Write one sentence that tells what this whole story illustrates (author's message). _____
_____

Directions: *You may wish to look back into the story to find out if you wrote the correct answers. If you do, give yourself 10 points for each correct answer.*

If you do not correct your answer sheet, estimate your understanding of the story by writing "excellent," "good," "fair," or "poor" in the place for your score.

Your score _____ %

Total number of words _____   *Your rate* _____

To find your rate, refer to directions in Chapter 8, page 80. Record title, rate and comprehension score on Course Data Sheet.

11

Speed Research Reading

Materials:
- Two library books on the same subject
- Ten 3 x 5 note cards
- Drill book, previously read (A good one is *The Incredible Journey*.)
- Reading:
    Dr. Jekyll and Mr. Hyde, or another novel of approximately 33,000 words

Objective:
- To learn how to do research reading rapidly

DRILL PRACTICE ;

As usual, do eye-pacing drills before beginning the actual lesson. In a previously read book (*The Incredible Journey* or another novel), drill for one minute, always trying to move your eyes faster than in earlier drills, faster than either your reading or skimming rates. Use soft focus by gliding your eyes over the print, not paying attention to particular words. Do not use the key word subvocalization in drills; you may still attain the ability to visualize by continuing to give your eyes this rapid practice. Relax; keep your mind free of outside thoughts. Whatever thoughts do enter your mind accept as coming from the book.

Ready? Begin (1 minute). Stop. Write your recall.

Count the number of pages you covered. Now add an equal number so that this time you will have to go twice as fast to reach this goal. Back at the beginning. Ready? Begin (10 seconds. . .1 minute). Stop. Add to your recall.

If you didn't finish all the pages, try to finish this time. If you did finish, add ten more pages. If there aren't enough pages in the book to complete your goal, just start over again when you get to the end of the book. Ready? Begin (10 seconds. . .1 minute). Stop. Add to your recall.

Add ten more pages. Ready? Begin (10 seconds. . .1 minute). Stop. Add to your recall.

This time take a drill rate. Start at the beginning of the story. If you have to go over the book more than one time, be sure to still count *all* the pages you covered to get your drill rate. Ready? Begin(1 minute). Stop. Figure your rate and record it on your Course Data Sheet.

RESEARCHING

Researching through reading is the act of finding out more about a subject by reading about it or investigating the subject in some way, using books as sources of information. The purpose of the research may be to write a paper on the subject or just to become more knowledgeable about it.

Thorough research usually requires getting information from several books, each of which may also contain information irrelevant to your specific topic. A good comprehension reading of each source book would be time-consuming, inefficient, and unnecessary. Finding the information you need for your topic and reading only those portions is a much more practical, efficient, and rapid way to research.

The actual writing of a research paper is a

lengthy, complex process that includes much more than reading sources, and the total process will not be discussed here. For more complete information on writing research papers consult a good English handbook. Our concern is limited to how to do the reading portion of the research process efficiently and rapidly.

Method for Rapid Research

Research reading combines the use of skimming and scanning techniques (see Chapter 10) and great flexibility in reading rates (see Chapter 7).

Research reading consists of three basic steps: (1) survey; (2) one very flexible reading in which you mark portions that deal with your topic; and (3) rereading of marked parts for taking notes.

1. Survey. Read the title page and the date of publication to see if this source has current information. For some topics, data become outdated quickly. Skim the preface and introduction to find out the plan of the book and to be certain the author is an authority on the subject. Read the table of contents to verify that the book contains information on your topic. Notice if there are whole chapters totally devoted to your topic.

2. Read selectively and with great flexibility in rate. If you found that only certain chapters deal with your topic, read those only.

   If it appears that information on your topic is spread throughout the book, go through the entire book.

   Reading for research is very flexible. You *skim,* looking for ideas or quotes on your topic. In skimming you read at a very rapid rate to follow the sequence of the author's main ideas without concern for the general details. When you spot a main idea that appears to contain a good quote or data you can use, you slow down to a rate that will give you good comprehension and read it and those details associated with it. If you think this portion will be useful to you, place a light pencil dot in the margin. Then continue skimming rapidly until you find another idea or quote, slow down to read it and mark it, and go on until you have finished the book.

   If the book or chapter contains material on your topic and you expect to find a lot of information you can use, slow down to read the beginnings of chapters, subsections, and paragraphs. At the beginnings you will learn the main idea of the chapter, section, or paragraph, and this will tell you if it contains information you want. If it does, be alert for the information. If the main idea indicates that this portion will not be of value to you, quickly skim it or skip it entirely.

   If the research book is not really on your topic, but you expect there may be some specific information you can use and you don't know exactly where to find it, *scanning,* rather than skimming, may be more helpful. In scanning, you read at a very rapid rate, looking for specific information that relates to your topic only, and you are not necessarily concerned with the author's main ideas, unless they contain the information for which you are looking. Sometimes they do, but other times your information is contained in the details. Decide on how a reference to your topic might be stated: the key words of your topic or synonyms for it. Then scan, looking for those key words or synonyms. When you see them, slow down to a good comprehension rate and read and mark that portion. Finish the book in this manner.

   During the skimming or scanning, do not stop to take notes; it will interrupt your train of thought. Besides, most authors repeat their most important ideas several times during the course of a book. If you take a note early in the book, you may later find that same idea presented in a much more quotable way. By waiting until you have completely finished the book, you will find that you know more about the subject and that particular book and are in a much better position to determine what is really important; and you will be able to take better and more meaningful notes.

3. Reread selectively and take notes. After completing the book, go back to the beginning and go through the book page by page looking for each marked part. Reread each marked part and decide if it is worthy of a note. If it is, write an abbreviated title of the book as a heading at the top of a 3 × 5 note card. Write the page number (you will need it if you later plan to have footnotes for a paper). Either quote the book exactly or restate the idea in your own words. If you quote, use quotation marks. Write only one item of information on each card and do not write on the back of the card. Erase your mark in the book and proceed to your next mark, repeating the

process until you have finished the entire book.

That's it: You are finished with the book, you have the notes you need, and you didn't waste time reading what you didn't need.

Practice in Research Reading

Decide on a topic. Choose one that is sure to be contained in the two books you checked out of the library. Pick a very simple one. Don't spend a lot of time choosing. It's the *method* of reading that you want to practice now.

Follow the preceding directions. Do each of the three steps. Take at least five notes per book for this practice.

Fill out the Research Report on page 113.

FOURTH NOVEL READING

Read the book, *Dr. Jekyll and Mr. Hyde*. Preview by skimming on your own, the first five pages, five pages at random in two places in the book, and the last five pages. Answer the usual questions (refer to "Summary of procedure for reading the novel," on page 77). Use flexibility, especially at beginnings. If you cannot visualize, subvocalize some of the words, without slowing down to do this.

Today, reach your bookmark, placed at the halfwaypoint, in fifteen minutes or less.

In answering the questions, *scan* for any answers you do not know. This should give you a high comprehension score!

SUMMARY

Research reading is very flexible. You skim or scan the entire material, slowing down to read and mark the ideas relevant to your topic. You continue in this way until the book is finished. Then you go back to each marked part, reread that portion, take a note on it, and erase your mark.

RESEARCH REPORT

Name _____ Date _____

1. My research topic is _____

_____

2. The books I am using for research are

   A. Title _____

   Author _____

   Date of publication _____

   Hour: Minutes:

   Time I finished research in this book:

   Time I started research in this book: _____

   Total time spent:

   I took _____ notes from this book.

   I went through the entire book. Yes _____ No _____

   I skimmed _____ chapters only. I scanned _____ chapters.

   B. Title _____

   Author _____

   Date of publication _____

   Hour: Minutes:

   Time I finished research in this book:

   Time I started research in this book: _____

   Total time spent:

   I took _____ notes from this book.

   I went through the entire book. Yes _____ No _____

   I skimmed _____ chapters only. I scanned _____ chapters.

_____ 1. Dr. Henry Jekyll was
   a. completely good and moral.
   b. both good and evil.
   c. completely evil.
   d. a hypocrite.

_____ 2. Edward Hyde was
   a. completely good and moral.
   b. both good and evil.
   c. completely evil.
   d. a hypocrite.

_____ 3. Dr. Jekyll had written a will leaving everything to
   a. Utterson.
   b. Lanyon.
   c. Poole.
   d. Hyde.

_____ 4. For the past ten years Dr. Jekyll had been involved in
   a. teaching at the university.
   b. writing his autobiography.
   c. helping the sick poor.
   d. conducting unknown experiments.

_____ 5. The primary clue in the brutal murder of Sir Danvers Carew was a
   a. cane Utterson had given to Jekyll.
   b. hat belonging to Hyde.
   c. letter written by Sir Carew.
   d. confession left by Hyde.

_____ 6. At first, Dr. Jekyll became Mr. Hyde by
   a. drinking a special potion.
   b. strongly willing the change to take place.
   c. putting himself into a trance.
   d. purposely doing something evil.

_____ 7. Later, Dr. Jekyll became Mr. Hyde by
   a. drinking a double dose of a special potion.
   b. willing the change to take place.
   c. desiring to do something evil.
   d. leaving the house.

_____ 8. Through use, Hyde became
   a. weakened and less dominant.
   b. less evil.
   c. more like Dr. Jekyll.
   d. more dominant and highly developed.

_____ 9. In the end, Dr. Jekyll
   a. committed suicide.
   b. got rid of Hyde.
   c. had himself committed to an insane asylum.
   d. continued his dual life.

_____ 10. One of the author's messages appears to be:
a. people have no control over their evil natures.
b. when one continually gives in to one's evil nature, loss of control eventually occurs.
c. people would have no evil natures if they would not delve into realms of the unknown.
d. good always wins over evil.

Allow 10 points per correct answer.   *Your rate* _____ %
Number of words: 33,000   *Your score* _____
Answer key is on page 272.
Record rate and comprehension score on Course Data Sheet.

GENERAL NOVEL COMPREHENSION QUESTIONS

(Use only if reading a novel other than *Dr. Jekyll and Mr. Hyde*.)

Title _____ Author _____

1. Name the main character(s). _____

_____

2. Where does the story take place? _____

_____

3. Approximately when does the story take place? _____

4. Name two other characters. (1) _____

(2) _____

5. What type of story is it (love story, adventure, science fiction, war story,

fantasy, etc.)? _____

6. Briefly summarize the situation at the beginning of the story.

_____

_____

_____

7. List three things that happen to the main character.

(1) _____

(2) _____

(3) _____

8. State the relationship(s) between the main character and at least one other

character (husband and wife, father and son, friends, etc). _____

9. How does the story end? _____

_____

_____

10. Write one sentence that tells what this whole story illustrates (author's message). _____

_____

Directions: *You may wish to look back into the story to find out if you wrote the correct answers. If you do, give yourself 10 points for each correct answer.*

If you do not correct your answer sheet, estimate your understanding of the story by writing "excellent," "good," "fair," or "poor" in the place for your score.

Your score _____ %

Total number of words _____   *Your rate* _____

To find your rate, refer to directions in Chapter 8, page 80. Record title, rate, and score on Course Data Sheet.

12

Finding Your Level of Best Comprehension

Materials:
- Readings:
  "Career Charisma"
  "Money: Our Most Intimate Relationship"
  The Call of the Wild or another 35,000 page novel
- New drill book

Objective:
- To learn how to find your level of best comprehension

DRILL PRACTICE

Using a book you have not read before, drill as fast as you can, faster than any previous time. You will have two minutes; see how far you can get. Ready? Begin (2 minutes). Stop. Begin a recall sheet.

Now, see if you can read the same amount of material in half the time, one minute. That means you will have to start out twice as fast and keep up that pace for the whole time! Ready? Begin (10 seconds. . . 1 minute). Stop. Add to your recall.

This time, going over the same material, you will have only one-half minute to finish. Again, you will have to double your rate to finish. Really try! Ready at the beginning? Begin (5 seconds. . . 30 seconds). Stop. Add to your recall again.

Turn to new material. Starting at the top of a page, you will go as fast as you have been, or faster if you can. This time you will take your drill rate. Ready? Begin (1 minute). Stop. Figure your rate and record it on your Course Data Sheet.

Find a partner and tell what you think this story was about. Just let the story come out spontaneously; don't be concerned with accuracy. If you are doing this alone, write it down.

LEVEL OF BEST COMPREHENSION

You have learned that a flexible reading rate improves your comprehension. You know that you should read difficult material more slowly than easy material. In this chapter you will learn a technique that will enable you to determine more specifically how fast or how slowly you should be reading any type of material so that you are always taking advantage of the highest reading rate of which you are capable without sacrificing comprehension.

Several factors influence the rate at which you can read with good comprehension, the most important of which are the difficulty of the vocabulary, the complexity of the sentence structure, and your previous knowledge of the subject. Your recognition of these factors in the preview of the material will better prepare you to accept the necessary rate variations from one type of material to another.

Method

Finding your level of best comprehension is very simple. In the preview, you try to sense the difficulty of the material by noticing if there are many long words and long and involved sentences. Is the subject one about which you know a lot or nothing? Do you understand the ideas easily in your skimming? By the end of the preview you should have determined if this material will be easy or difficult. Based on this knowledge, you make a tentative decision about how rapidly you can expect to read it.

Then you begin to read the material for good comprehension at a rate you expect will be appropriate. If you understand what you are reading, you immediately speed up until you lose comprehension; then you slow down until you gain comprehension again so that you are reading with comprehension at the highest rate you can for this material. If, however, when you begin to read you do not understand what you are reading, you have started at too high a rate and all you need to do is slow down until you do understand.

After you have found your level for best comprehension, you still use flexibility, slowing down on the hard parts and speeding up on the easy parts. That is, you will actually be reading within a range of rates that will sometimes be faster than your level of best comprehension and sometimes slower, but will hover around that level. In easy materials the range will be close to your fastest rates, and in difficult materials the range will be much lower.

When you first begin to use this technique, you should find your level of best comprehension several times during the course of any reading because your tendency will be to slow down on the hard parts and to stay at that slower rate. Whenever you feel that you have been reading slowly for a long time, follow these two easy steps to get back up to your level of best comprehension (see Figure 12-1).

DRILL PRACTICE IN FINDING LEVEL OF BEST COMPREHENSION

Return to the portion of your drill book on which you took your drill rate today. Now, you will reread this portion for comprehension. You will also practice finding your level of best comprehension. Begin to read the same portion of the story at what you would consider a normal reading rate for this material. If, when you start reading, you understand the material, slowly speed up until you begin to lose comprehension, and then, slowly slow down until you gain it again. If, when you start reading, you do *not* understand the story, slow down gradually until you gain comprehension. In each case you will have found your level of best comprehension. Then continue at that general rate using flexibility by slowing down where you need to, to retain comprehension, and speeding up where you find the material easier.

You will have two minutes in which to read the same number of pages you just read in one minute. If you finish the allotted pages before time is called, continue reading. Begin (2 minutes). Stop. Write down what you can remember, if you are doing this alone. If you told a partner your drill story, revise that story and tell it to your partner again.

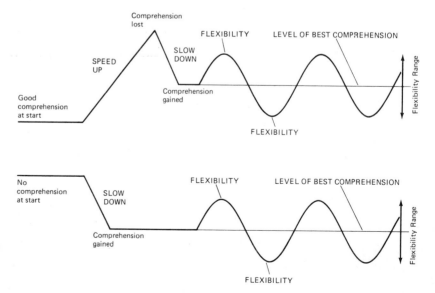

Figure 12-1　Finding Your Level of Best Comprehension

READING PRACTICE

Read the article "Career Charisma" on page 120. Preview by skimming the entire article at your own pace. Pay special attention to the beginning of the article and the beginning of each paragraph. Recognize the difficulty level of the article. Recall what you already know about the subject.

Read the article. Use the method to find your level of best comprehension at the beginning and several times during the reading to be sure that you have not slowed down more than necessary. Use flexibility constantly as you read: Slow down slightly at the beginning of each paragraph and any place that appears to contain an important idea or difficult part. Do not stay at the slow rate; speed up again immediately.

Use the numbered directions below for reading the story.

Reading Sequence Directions

1. Record your starting time.
2. Begin reading. Immediately find your level of best comprehension, and slow down and speed up as the material requires to attain understanding. Find your level of best comprehension several times during the reading, especially if you suspect that you may be reading too slowly.
3. Record the finishing time.
4. Answer questions. Correct answers.
5. Compute your rate and comprehension score.
6. Record rate and comprehension score on your Course Data Sheet.
7. Hold a class discussion of the story or scan the story to find the answers to the questions you missed.

As another reading practice in finding your level of best comprehension, read the article, "Money: Our Most Intimate Relationship" on page 127. Preview and read this article in the same manner as you did "Career Charisma," and follow the reading sequence directions.

FIFTH NOVEL READING

Read *The Call of the Wild,* or another novel of about 35,000 words.

Preview by skimming the first and last five pages and five pages in two random spots. Answer the usual questions and follow the instructions, "Summary of procedure for reading the novel," page 77.

In reading, find your level of best comprehension at the beginning and at least five other times throughout the book. Use flexibility slowing on beginnings and whenever you don't understand. Continue to try to visualize by keeping your mind clear of outside thoughts and allowing the ideas from the book to enter. If you can't visualize, subvocalize some of the words. Reach your bookmark at the halfway point in less than fifteen minutes.

In answering the questions, *scan* for any answers you do not know.

SUMMARY

Each type of material can be read with good comprehension at the highest possible speed by finding your level of best comprehension. This can be done by speeding up until comprehension is lost and then slowing down until it is gained again. At this highest rate for good comprehension, you still apply flexibility, so that you are reading faster over the easy parts and more slowly over the hard parts.

CAREER CHARISMA

Phyllis Schneider

What makes a superstar able to rise so rapidly to the top? Many times it isn't talent, training or track record—it's a certain attitude, enthusiasm, confidence. Call it. . . .

The real winners in business (and in life, for that matter), the women and men who are tapped for golden career opportunities, often have something extra. Some observers call it "charisma," others say "vision." But whatever one calls it, understanding what fuels these early successes is important for everyone who has high goals for her future.

The people with charmed careers have a way of

looking at the world that makes top management feel they can do almost anything superbly, that imbues everybody with whom they work with a kind of enthusiastic, winning spirit. Their success is as much a matter of attitude as of hard work and talent. They are optimists. That optimism is astonishingly powerful, and it can be cultivated.

Although Norman Vincent Peale has championed the virtues of "positive thinking" for more than 35 years, only recently have serious researchers started to explore the ways optimism affects not only one's health and longevity but career success as well.

A number of studies confirm what Peale intuitively knew was correct: The optimist almost invariably has an edge over her less enthusiastic colleagues. And for good reason: It is the secret of her charismatic effect on others.

WHAT RESEARCH SHOWS

In one of the most important studies to date, Martin Seligman, PhD, professor of psychology at the University of Pennsylvania, surveyed representatives of a major life-insurance company and found that outlook dramatically affected performance. Among the long-term reps, those who confidently expected a good outcome sold 37 percent more insurance than those with negative attitudes. Attitude also had a powerful effect on new hires: The optimists among them sold 20 percent more.

Impressed by Seligman's study, the insurance company hired 100 people who had failed the standard industry entrance test but scored high on optimism. The move paid off: These people sold 10 percent more insurance than the average rep.

Seligman links a person's tendency toward optimism—or pessimism—to what he terms "explanatory style." When things go wrong, the pessimist tends to blame herself, saying, for example, "No wonder this product flopped—I'm terrible at marketing." The optimist, says Seligman, explains her setbacks in terms of outside forces. "Of course we weren't able to sell that product," she's likely to tell herself. "The stores did a lousy job promoting it! Now I know we've got to put more effort into motivating the stores to push the product."

A similar dynamic shows up when things go well, Seligman explains. The pessimist explains her success in terms of chance: "It was nothing. Just luck." The optimist accepts the kudos and tells herself, "I knew my hard work would pay off."

This doesn't mean that optimists are unrealistic about themselves or their situation. Industrial psychologist Howard P. Stevens defines true optimism as "the middle ground between two other attitudes. On one end, you have naïveté, or viewing the world through rose-colored glasses," he says. "At the opposite pole is pessimism or fatalism.

"Naïveté and pessimism are actually coming from

the same place," explains Stevens, "a belief that some outside force is totally in control of your life, that something or someone will guide or thwart you, be it city hall, your boss, your company. The optimist believes power or control comes from within herself, that she's ultimately responsible for her own success. And she knows how to keep the power going." Understanding how these forces operate can help you harness your feelings to make your career take off.

THE WAY YOU SEE YOURSELF CAN TRANSFORM YOUR CAREER

It isn't all rose-colored glasses. New research by Shelley Taylor, PhD, of the University of California at Los Angeles, and Jonathon Brown, PhD, of Southern Methodist University, in Dallas, suggests that positive illusions create self-fulfilling prophecies that propel those who hold them to achieve. Such people will work harder and longer, and their perseverance allows them to do better.

Simply put: A negative attitude imprisons you, while a positive outlook empowers you. That is the magic of career charisma. Herbert J. Freudenberger, PhD, the psychoanalyst who coined the term "burnout" and now helps corporations set up motivational programs, points out, "Losers tend to view themselves as losers, while winners see themselves as winners. What's more, you transmit your feelings about yourself to others. If you perceive yourself as a winner, you'll convey a certain attitude of self-confidence that others will pick up on."

Your internal image can have a compelling external effect. "Our expectations about ourselves and situations not only affect how we see reality," Freudenberger emphasizes, "they affect reality itself." For instance, an optimistic mind-set can give you a big advantage in hiring situations. Donald C. Williams, who heads an executive-recruiting firm that places company presidents and CEOs, says, "A placement can be based heavily on chemistry between boss and candidate." (The best choices are 50 percent chemistry and 50 percent track record, he adds.)

An applicant's effervescence, personality, presence, enthusiasm—these add up to the "chemistry" that often determines which of two equally qualified candidates walks off with the plum job.

PROFILES IN CHARISMA

Sally Frame-Kasaks, 43, has exuded that kind of magnetism from early in her professional life. At 26 Frame-Kasaks, currently chairman and CEO of the Talbots chain of specialty stores, became a full buyer in retailing. At 38 she was hired as president of Ann Taylor.

This pattern has characterized her career. When Sidney Mayer, senior vice president for merchandise planning and coordination at Saks Fifth Avenue, interviewed Frame-Kasaks in 1976, he says he knew "fairly soon into the interview that I was going to hire her—and for a job she didn't have a great deal of product familiarity with. She was a fashion director from the sportswear area at Garfinckel's, and I was looking for a line-operations person to manage our intimate-apparel division."

She beat out the other candidates for the vice president spot because "everything else about her was right," says Mayer. "Her knowledge, her dedication to quality—and her presence, her personality. She had an effervescence that just didn't quit."

SELF-FULFILLING PROPHECIES

But enthusiasm doesn't operate only in job interviews. Daily life provides plenty of opportunities. "I always loved change, something new. Change is a challenge, an excitement," says Dawn Sibley, 48, executive vice president, director of media and communications services for Ally & Gargano Advertising, in New York. Sibley, who was named a vice president of Ted Bates Worldwide, Inc., at 30, is another exemplar of how to create the best possible reality, even in difficult circumstances.

As senior vice president of MCA Advertising, a division of Marketing Corporation of America, in Westport, Connecticut, Sibley skillfully guided her group through Marketing Corporation's 1986 merger with Ally & Gargano. "She constantly encouraged us to focus on the overall positive aspects of the merger for our agency," says Patrice Listfield, the agency's vice president, associate media director. "There was resistance from others. People rarely react well to change, but because of Dawn's positive vision and her constant encouragement, our department came through better than any other group."

Sibley herself recalls that "during the MCA merger situation I was very positive about it right away. I was the first person in the organization to get my department reorganized."

CONVERTING FEAR INTO CHALLENGE

Viewing nine out of ten problems as solvable, focusing on desired results rather than possible failures and calling on self-confidence empower people to step forward and assume risks they would never attempt if they were fearful.

And risk-taking is crucial to career success ("If you're afraid to try something new," says Dawn Sibley, "you'll never go anywhere.") It's also one of the hallmarks of a leader, says Howard Stevens, who works with Fortune 500 companies to identify and develop potential leaders.

"The aggressively optimistic person converts fear into challenge," explains Stevens, "and the feeling becomes exhilarating. They look forward to it again." He adds that "to become successful, you have to be on the cutting edge. You have to risk being the first one to do

something and to be willing to take the heat if it doesn't work out."

Amy Hirsh, 35, who was confident enough as a student to turn a chance on-the-street meeting with television personality Dick Cavett into lunch and an invitation to intern on his show, has made meeting challenges a way of life. Hirsh went on from the Cavett show to a stellar career in television. At 33, for example, she was named a senior producer at *Good Morning America (GMA)*, supervising more than 100 people.

Colleagues describe her as "incredibly cool under pressure," a useful trait in live television, with its split-second decisions. Her self-confident willingness to trust her instincts propelled her to the top astonishingly rapidly.

During the TWA hostage crisis in 1985, for example, Hirsh and her team were trying to get "a phoner to Nabih Berri, one of the quote/unquote negotiators" so they could tape an interview. "If the wrong things were said on the air, the whole thing could blow up," says Hirsh, who worried about how an interview would affect the lives of the hostages. The call to Berri came through just as *GMA* went on the air.

"I could have decided to hang up, but my instincts as a producer told me to go through with it," she recalls. "Once the interview started, I also felt we couldn't say, 'Hold on, Mr. Berri. We have to go to a commercial break.' I ran the interview through all commercials for the next 40 minutes. A vice president of ABC was standing in the control room with me, and he wasn't at all pleased by my decision to program through commercials, but I stood my ground."

The interview was major news. "We scooped [CBS's] Dan Rather, who was trying to get through to Berri at the same time and was put on hold," Hirsh remembers. "The next day we were on the front page of every major newspaper in the country."

That ability to make a tough call was one of the reasons Hirsh was appointed interim executive producer of *GMA* 14 months later when her boss left the program. She was only 34.

Hirsh's latest move? A change of coasts and career. Early this year she left *Good Morning America* ("I'd done everything I could do there!") to become a producer for ABC Circle Films in Los Angeles. "It's a wonderful challenge," she says. "I'm staying in television—and with ABC—but I'll be doing something very different: coming up with and developing ideas for TV movies and then producing the films.

I'm practicing what I've preached for so long to my employees: You've got to motivate yourself to go two steps beyond what you think you can do in order to succeed."

BECOMING AN OPTIMIST

How do charismatic optimists get that way—and is it catching?

"Sally Frame is one of the most energetic, 'up'

people I've seen in my entire retail career," says a former colleague. Frame-Kasaks (she married last year) credits her parents for instilling her with a "can do" attitude.

"My mother was gregarious, effervescent. Dad was contemplative and more reserved, but he gave me the feeling that I could do anything," she remembers. "One night when I was 12 or 13, we were walking our dog and Dad was explaining the constellations to me.

" 'I want to be the first woman on Venus,' I announced. He looked at me, then began to seriously construct a game plan. First, he said, I'd have to study physics and astronomy. The next thing I knew, he had me mentally enrolled in engineering school. He never laughed at my 'dream of the moment.' He just seemed to assume—and made me assume—I could accomplish anything I set my mind to."

Experiences like this help create the confidence and optimism that is key to personal magnetism. Researchers believe that where a person lands on the optimism/pessimism scale is shaped during childhood by influential adults, especially parents and teachers. Seligman feels that a person's "explanatory style" remains relatively stable over a lifetime. Other experts, including Freudenberger, disagree—fortunately for those not blessed with parents like the Frames.

"A person's optimism level changes over the years—depending on what's happening in their life (both personal and professional), the type of people they work and socialize with and how determined they are to motivate themselves," Freudenberger says.

The charisma that makes optimists so exciting to work for (and to have work for you) inspires co-workers to accomplish more than they had thought possible. Optimism is contagious. One good way to develop this winner's attitude is to work for someone who has it, so you can catch it.

THE OPTIMISTIC OFFICE

"The boss who delegates and encourages employees to take risks promotes optimism and, in turn, good business," Freudenberger emphasizes. "Because the employees feel good about themselves, they have a sense of control over their careers, and they're more likely to go the distance." The explanatory style that encourages creativity can be a manager's greatest asset.

"When Dawn Sibley walked into a room, things began to happen," says Eileen Logan, a sales associate at Hunneman and Company Realtors, in Boston, who worked for her at Ted Bates Advertising in the mid-'70s. "Her very presence made people feel optimistic and motivated."

Roberta Dougherty, a political editor for *CBS This Morning*, speaks similarly of Amy Hirsh, her boss at *Good Morning America:* "Amy is very comfortable at the center of things. She just naturally took to the role of boss." And she enjoyed it.

Perhaps that's part of the reason people want to go

the distance for Hirsh. That, and her talent for making others feel they can accomplish any task she hands them: "Amy would walk into my office and sketch a big star on my drawing board," says Stephen Lewis, *GMA*'s editorial producer. "Then she'd write the names of various hot celebrities in the star and say, 'I want these people for the show: Donald Trump, Beverly Sills, George Steinbrenner, Elizabeth Taylor.'

"She made us go one step beyond trying. She'd smile and say, 'I know you can do it.' She made you feel as though you were doing it for her, and you wanted to because she cared so much about the show."

Frame-Kasaks got a similar leg up from an early boss who approved a major buying plan she developed. "When I showed him my plan, he gulped, then signed off on the orders. We projected substantial liability, but they converted into extremely good sales." Soon after that she was promoted to full buyer.

Years later, when Frame-Kasaks was a department-store VP, a junior buyer confronted her with a small item that was selling well. "She wanted to reorder a substantial number," Frame-Kasaks recalls. "Suddenly I remembered my experience so long ago when someone put incredible trust in my judgment, and I sat down with her to develop a sales plan. I felt a little apprehensive as I signed off on the orders, and I never fully revealed the magnitude of the investment to my bosses. But I had faith in this buyer. The rest is history: The item turned out to be one of the most successful things the store ever carried, and it made a tremendous profit. The experience gave me certain credibility with my people, who began to take more risks with me, coming up with more creative ideas."

AN OPTIMISTIC BOSS CAN CHANGE YOUR CAREER

A boss who makes you feel you can accomplish anything can exert a career-transforming force on your future.

Two years after joining entrepreneur Maurice Lewitt at his health-services company (now called Nu-Med Medical, Inc.) in 1970, Carol Schardt had added managerial functions to her original job as executive secretary. Now vice president, investor relations and corporate communications, for the Encino, California, firm (which owns acute-care and psychiatric hospitals in the US), Schardt, 48, has both benefited from a charismatic boss and learned to become one.

When Lewitt asked her to set up and supervise an in-house graphic design department as part of the corporate communications function, Schardt initially balked. "But he kept telling me, 'You can do it, Carol,' " Schardt, who believes that any success in business is based on 50 percent talent and 50 percent positive thinking, rose to the challenge.

In the process she also changed the career of another Nu-Med employee, Deborah Wilson. In search of a new career, Wilson had started to study design at UCLA. "Carol encouraged me, and she also got the company to pay for my tuition," Wilson says. "She felt I was talented and helped me explore those talents." Several years later when Schardt was tapped to set up the design department, she hired Wilson as its director.

"Carol's enthusiasm about the new department and my new career was contagious," Wilson recalls. "She said, 'I have confidence in you. You can do it.' She even took a six-week course in graphic art with me so that *she* would have a good understanding of the basics of the operation.

"Someone who's a motivator doesn't do things for you," says Wilson. "They give you the opportunity—and the belief in yourself—to make things happen."

ELIMINATE THE NEGATIVE

The flip side of contagious attitudes is the damage an overanxious, negative boss can do—not just to her own career but to the self-image and future success of those who work for her. Leaving a negative boss could be the best thing an employee can do for her career growth.

"What's amazing," says Freudenberger, "is the degree to which the boss's attitude can trickle down. Whenever I see a morale or attitudinal problem in a corporation, I ask the employees to list the personality characteristics of the boss. In almost every instance the boss takes a consistently negative stance in his day-to-day dealings with the workers."

Sibley, who says she once inherited—and had to re-inspire—an entire group of unenthusiastic media people, feels office pessimists (bosses and employees) often don't realize that they're operating defensively or self-defeatingly.

"Some are pessimists because of the way they were raised," she says. "Others do it for the attention—they're whiners. Still others want to be persuaded that your idea or the company's idea is a good one. You have to invest a certain amount of time in these people to help them recognize they've got an attitude problem that's holding them back."

Sibley tells the story of a young media executive she hired a few years back. "This fellow had a tremendously negative outlook on everything when he started working for me," says Sibley, "and it got to the point where other groups didn't want to work with him. I used his employee evaluation to sit him down and tell him, in the most positive terms, how he could improve his work *and* his attitude.

"He was startled to hear that others perceived him as being negative; he felt he was a fairly optimistic person. As we talked he revealed that his boss of the previous five years had been a real pessimist, and he thinks he may have inadvertently taken on his boss's attitude."

Sibley worked with her employee to help him find ways to redirect his thinking toward a more positive approach, giving him the encouragement and positive feedback he desperately needed as well as helping to cultivate his self-esteem. "Now he's doing terrifically," she reports. "People like to work with him, and he's basically a happier person. I know *I'm* a lot happier because he's working out!"

POSITIVE REINFORCEMENT

The final piece of the puzzle is personal, not professional. The people who are truly successful have taken the time to "develop a well-rounded life that includes *many* positive areas, not just one," says Howard Stevens, who has worked with many successful executives through his consulting firm, the H. R. Chally Group, in Dayton, Ohio. "You need more than your job to feel fulfilled. Fulfillment comes from achievements on the job front and in community and family life as well."

A multifaceted life may well be the optimist's psychological safety net: If you suffer a defeat in one area, you're sustained by your successes in the others. Since few people go through the years without facing any reversals at all, making room for variety is worth the extra complexity such a life entails.

Carol Schardt, who believes that lifelong learning keeps one motivated and challenged, recently completed her degree in business administration after attending school part-time for years. "I was already a VP in my company," says Schardt. "Technically I didn't need to finish my education, but I did it for myself." Schardt also devotes many hours to fund-raising projects for Villa Esperanza, a home for mentally disabled children and adults.

Dawn Sibley, who says, "I've always liked myself, but not to the extent I do now," adds that "success has definitely played a part in my happiness and sense of self-esteem; success *is* ego-building." But she, too, feels that a well-rounded life is essential. "My friends are very important to me," says Sibley, "and I socialize a lot." She also was recently elected to the post of president of the local residents association.

"I've always recognized that there was more to life than work, even though I derive tremendous satisfaction and a sense of accomplishment from my career," says Sally Frame-Kasaks. "I consider myself a very fortunate person. I've got the career I always wanted, but I've also got a good support system—loving friends and family. [In June 1987 she married for the first time and became an "instant stepparent" to her husband's two daughters.] I really believe you must make room in your life for many things."

A stellar career, a loving family and good friends have given Frame-Kasaks "the confidence to go forward and try new things. I honestly think I could suffer a severe setback, I could lose my job tomorrow, and though I might not come out on top, I'd emerge pretty well intact. I think I'm a 'winner' in the broadest sense of the word."

And that's what optimism—and success—are all about.

10 WAYS YOU CAN DEVELOP AN OPTIMIST'S EYE

"Success is 98 percent sweat and only 2 percent genius," says Howard Stevens, founder and chairman of the H. R. Challey Group, a top management-consulting firm. "And optimism is the fuel that makes you persevere."

But what if on an otpimism scale of one to ten, you find yourself stuck somewhere between two and three or waffling between four and seven? Can you move closer to the optimistic end of the scale—and stay there? Absolutely. Here is Steven's ten-part program for redirecting your thinking toward the positive.

1. **Consciously set goals,** small ones you're 90 percent sure you'll succeed at, and work toward them. Five out of ten people avoid setting goals because they're afraid they'll feel bad if they don't reach them. As you reach your goals, set new ones. You'll find yourself striving to meet larger, more difficult challenges.

2. **Acquire a sense of control by doing your homework.** Be aware of all the outside forces that play into the goal you're trying to reach. Knowing who your competitors are, who's tackled a similar project before, how much the project will cost, which colleagues are likely to resist or support you, will make you feel more on top of the situation. Developing a well-thought-out plan will give you more confidence and enthusiasm about your goal or project.

3. **Anticipate success.** Fantasize about what winning will feel, taste and look like (do this several times daily, in the shower, on your way home from work, as you fall asleep). Imaging, or seeing yourself as succeeding, is a particularly powerful tool. Olympic athletes, especially slalom skiers and divers, use imaging techniques to psych themselves for a win. For instance, a skier fantasizes about winning in advance: She sees herself making a perfect run down the slope, superbly negotiating all the curves.

4. **Create a psychological safety net**—it's much easier to walk across a tightrope if you know there's a safety net underneath. Imagine the worst possible outcome that could occur, and have a solution or alternate plan ready. For example, if you're making a difficult presentation to your company's management group, fantasize about all the things that could go wrong and create solutions. Having solutions gives you a sense of control, and knowing you could survive the worst reinforces your self-confidence. This motivation technique is called "experiencing it through," and it's been found to be one of the most effective methods of redirecting your thinking.

5. **Be good to yourself.** Motivate yourself through a long and difficult project by dividing it into steps and rewarding yourself after each one. Increase the value of the reward when the going gets tough. You might start by giving yourself bath oil or the latest Dick Francis mystery, then a new suit—and when your motivation really sags or the task at hand is particularly arduous or unappealing, promise yourself a trip or a spa weekend as soon as you complete it.

6. **Surround yourself with successful, positive people.** Success and optimism are contagious. So are pessimism and failure. You're cutting your own throat if you constantly associate with people who are negative or have a "loser" attitude.

7. **Don't fight negative thoughts.** Accept them, then replace them by moving on to the next task. (Suppressing negative thoughts only makes them resurface.)

8. **Keep your body tuned.** A 30-minute aerobic workout five times a week—or even three times—is a good way to relieve stress and create a feeling of well-being. (Researchers now know that exercise causes the brain to release endorphins, natural opiates that promote this feeling.) A body in good working order also gives you stamina—you'll be able to put in longer hours and still have energy.

9. **Look good to feel good.** Being well dressed and well groomed (everything from a weekly manicure to the right makeup) helps boost your confidence—and the confidence of others in you.

10. **Don't live at the office.** A satisfying family/social life can sustain you through the stress of a tough week and give you perspective. In addition, having important roles in your life outside work reduces the anxiety of having all your emotional eggs in one basket. Community or charity work also can make you feel powerful and worthwhile in ways totally separate from your corporate self.

COMPREHENSION QUESTIONS

_____ 1. This article states that the secret of career charisma is
   a. hard work.
   b. optimism.
   c. dedication.
   d. education.

_____ 2. This author says that the way you see yourself internally
a. has no affect upon the way reality turns out.
b. is your secret that others don't know.
c. should be ignored to achieve success.
d. has a serious affect upon outside reality.

_____ 3. One powerful way to cope with the fear of taking risks is to
a. use self-confidence to turn fear into challenge.
b. ignore the fact that it is a risk.
c. pray that you are lucky.
d. get others to assume responsibility.

_____ 4. The charismatic attitude
a. has never been adequately defined.
b. only affects the one who possesses it.
c. is contagious.
d. is greatly overrated.

_____ 5. From the examples cited, you can conclude that the most important characteristic for success is
a. recognition of your faults.
b. feeling like a winner.
c. having relevant experiences so that you know what to do.
d. having the ability to cultivate friends in high places who can help you.

_____ 6. Truly successful people
a. realize that one's job should rule one's life.
b. also achieve fulfillment in family and community.
c. shield their employees from having to take risks.
d. are willing to settle for less in personal life to have more professionally.

_____ 7. One suggestion for developing a positive attitude is to
a. accentuate the positive by ignoring problems.
b. fight negative thoughts.
c. repeatedly imagine yourself succeeding.
d. be the most positive person in a group of pessimists.

_____ 8. Another suggestion to create confidence is to
a. keep on top of problems by spending lots of extra time at the office.
b. surround yourself with less confident people who compliment you often.
c. avoid setting small goals that don't challenge you.
d. find alternate solutions to possible problems before they occur.

_____ 9. A motivational technique suggested is to
a. reward yourself frequently.
b. punish yourself for failures.
c. set up a competition with a fellow worker.
d. keep yourself from wearing that new outfit until you have a success.

_____ 10. From this article, you can conclude that
a. if you didn't get charisma growing up, you will never have it completely.
b. career charisma only affects your job performance.
c. you can develop effective career charisma now.
d. how you appear to others is more important professionally than how
you feel.

Allow 10 points per correct answer.   Your score _____ %
Number of words: 3700   Your rate _____
Answer key is on page 272.
Record your rate and comprehension score on Course Data Sheet.

MONEY: OUR MOST INTIMATE RELATIONSHIP

Junius Adams

When is a dollar not a dollar? Almost always, say experts, because for most of us, it's merely a stand-in for more slippery essentials—power, security, even love. Now, discover just how cash colors your life.

Gloria, a $34,000-a-year executive with more than $100,000 stashed away in savings accounts, is in a housewares store, looking for a new teapot—her old one lost its spout this morning. She finds just the thing, a nice-looking pot marked down from $15.99 to $9.99, but then has a change of heart. It hurts Gloria, almost physically, to part with the money. Instead, she purchases a fifty-nine-cent tube of glue. Perhaps she can stick the spout back on and extend the life of her teapot a few more years. . . .

Susan, a $16,000-a-year secretary with no savings and $900 due on her credit card, has just treated her friend Kim to a birthday lunch. They are dining at a fairly pricey restaurant new to them, where the food has turned out to be mediocre and the service slow. For a moment, she's tempted to give the waiter a very small tip or perhaps none at all. Then she thinks, Poor man, it's not his fault the kitchen was slow. Sympathetic, she leaves a 25 percent tip. . . .

One of the most vital bonds in most people's lives is also one of the least discussed: their relationship with money. Ask an acquaintance about her sex life, psychiatric history, secrets, and fantasies, and she'll tell freely. Ask her what her income is or how much she has in the bank, however, and she's apt to be shocked at this attempted invasion of her privacy. Money may well be the last taboo topic in an ever more open society.

For most people, the subject is at least highly charged. "Money is more important as a symbol than as an actuality," explains Linda Barbanel, a New York psychoanalyst who specializes in the psychology of money. "For women especially, money, and security are very closely intertwined; money gives them a feeling of safety. With men, money tends to be intertwined with power. They prize money, because it gives them the feeling of having clout."

Few of us are even *sane*, much less objective, about money, according to California psychologists Herb Goldberg and Robert T. Lewis, authors of *Money Madness*. One person will scrimp, another fling cash around like a sailor on payday. What causes these differing attitudes? In part, it is childhood conditioning. The child reacts to the family situation—rich or poor, secure or insecure—either by absorbing and duplicating the parental pattern of money management or by rebelling against it. Inherent temperament also plays a role: A sensitive, fearful person may react to early experiences of poverty by becoming financially anxious—eager to save and reluctant to spend—while her more adventurous, devil-may-care sibling turns into a high-rolling gambler and spendthrift.

Although money signifies different things to differ-ent people, say Goldberg and Lewis, four basic meanings apply almost universally: money-as-security, money-as-freedom, money-as-love, and money-as-power.

Let's examine these categories more closely—you might find *your* fiscal style in one or more of them.

THE SECURITY SEEKERS

Experience has left the security seeker mistrustful of people; money, she finds, is far more reliable. Equating emotional security with financial security, she spends sparingly and seeks safety in owning property and having a large savings account.

Marcia is a pseudonym for a well-known television personality, someone whose real name you would recognize instantly. In her late thirties, she has a six-figure income and is married to an entertainment executive who earns even more. They live in a magnificent apartment overlooking Central Park, entertain lavishly, and are frequent world travelers. Marcia's annual expenditures for clothing, hairdressers, and beauty treatments are larger than the income of many middle-class families.

Despite her affluent life-style, she describes herself as "frugal—cheap, if you want to use the word."

Marcia hates to buy anything at the full retail price and will go to endless trouble to track down the manufacturer or distributor and obtain an item at wholesale. She refuses to take taxis, relying instead on public transportation. She will never, ever throw out a soda bottle that can be returned for a five-cent deposit. Although she gives over one hundred presents a year to friends and associates, most of these are either "recycled" (gifts someone gave *her*) or showy but inexpensive objects she buys in quantity from a wholesaler.

Marcia expends many hours in making these petty economies, some of which she acknowledges are "tacky," but she regards them as valid nevertheless. "If I hadn't been scared to death about money all my life, I would have never survived so well," she says. Her husband, a generous, openhanded person, disapproves of her stinginess. "We're a good balance for each other," she explains. "He prevents me from being too dreadfully cheap, and I make sure he puts our money into safe, conservative investments."

She grew up in relative poverty. Her father died in an accident when she was ten, and her sister later became crippled by a neurological disorder. At sixteen, Marcia had to get a job to help support her family. For years, she toiled in various low-level jobs and, at one point, came down with ulcerative colitis "from worrying about bills." Although she's since achieved financial success, the psychological scars of those early times are still upon her. "In my experience," she says, "the people who criticize my frugality are the same people who never pick up a restaurant check and would be very happy to let me be Miss Wonderful and pay all their bills. I have a great tenderness toward money, a great respect for it. I'm proud of the fact that I've been a good manager."

For years, Sherry, a thirty-one-year-old free-lance illustrator, has been putting every penny she can into her savings. Although not in an upper-income bracket (she grosses about $25,000 a year), she has accumulated a small fortune in the last decade. Sherry does not own a car. She does not smoke or drink. "When I see someone buy a carton of cigarettes or run up a ten-dollar tab for booze," she says, "I get a small feeling of satisfaction—that's ten dollars *I'm* not spending." She buys most of her clothing at discount outlets that offer 50 to 70 percent off, making sure she gets "classic designs I can wear for years." These penny-watching tactics have paid off. She is now worth over $150,000.

Sherry, too, lost her father early, when he abandoned the family, whose finances thereafter were quite chaotic. "Many of my early memories are of money problems," she says. "We couldn't shop in certain stores or even walk past them, because my mother owed the shopkeeper money. Bill collectors were constantly coming to our door—I was *terrified* of them." Ever since, Sherry has striven to be solvent, to avoid debt, and to pay bills immediately and in full.

"Of course, money means security," she acknowledges. "It's the only thing around that offers *any*. Even so, I don't feel safe. I just think there may be some cataclysmic event, and all this money I've saved will turn to dust. I would never invest in the stock market—the risk of losing is so horrendous that I feel inhibited about any form of speculation. I am, however, going to put some of my money into real estate one of these days. That's something I feel fairly safe about."

Someone who finds security in money, according to psychoanalyst Linda Barbanel, probably had a lack of both money and love in her background. Says Barbanel, "From this background comes a lot of worry and fear about the future. This tends to be worse with women than with men, because women, whether rich or poor, are used to being on the dole—from their fathers or brothers if not the welfare department. We are used to counting our small change, to making small expenditures. Big-ticket items like cars or IRAs make us nervous. Even when we get married and start bringing in a second income, we tend to take care of the small chores, the small expenses. The security-minded woman runs to the bank the minute she gets her paycheck and socks it away, buys all kinds of insurance, and will deny herself pleasures in order to save money. She's a big bargain hunter too. What she's trying to do is show that she can survive in a tough, cruel world by stretching a buck better than the next person."

THE FREEDOM LOVERS

A horror of being oppressed or constricted motivates some women to accumulate money and, in doing so, "buy" freedom. Financial independence, they believe, will allow them to feel less bound to a job, husband, or lover.

Veronica, a thirty-three-year-old cosmetics executive, is as thrifty as Marcia and Sherry. Luxury cars, $150 pairs of shoes, and expensive resort vacations don't tempt her. What she *does* with all the money she refuses to spend, however, would give a security seeker heart failure. For years, she's been investing large sums of money in the stock market—"speculative stocks mostly. I'm a gambler, and I get pleasure out of seeing my holdings go up and down." Veronica feels more at home with large expenditures than with small ones. "It doesn't bother me to write big checks, but I hate to pay the electric bill—I always feel they're probably cheating me out of ninety-two cents."

Veronica is after independence. "Ever since childhood, I've resented the fact that I *had* to work, that I could be tied down by financial need. I wanted to feel self-sufficient enough that if a job wasn't going right I could say, 'Screw you, I quit!' " Even with Jim, her live-in lover, she maintains complete financial separation. "Anything we buy for the house, groceries and so on, we write down on a little pad. At the end of the month, we settle up. I would never consider pooling funds, never—he's a disaster with money."

Veronica has played with her money so well that she *could* afford to live without working, but she has no intention of quitting her job. "For now, it's enough just to know that freedom is *available*."

Three years ago, Vicki was the lead singer of a now-famous rock group. She quit, she says, because "I couldn't tolerate the life. We were totally regimented by our manager—go here, go there, do this, do that. I hardly ever had a moment to myself, especially when we were on the road." Today, at twenty-six, Vicki lives in a walk-up apartment in New York's East Village, on an income she cheerfully describes as "well below the poverty level." She no longer performs ("I don't even own a guitar"), and supports herself by designing and making one-of-a-kind blouses that she sells to boutiques and private customers.

"My friends keep reminding me I'd be rich if I had stayed with the group, but I answer, 'So what?' Money is tyranny. The more you have, the more hemmed in you are. I'm happier now, really in control of my life. I'm a vegetarian—I can cook up a terrific meal with ten cents' worth of vegetables and a handful of brown rice. I make my own clothes. Most of the things I like to do, like going to museums and galleries, visiting friends, and just strolling the streets, don't cost much. Who needs money?" Vicki's only regret is having disappointed her parents. "They're convinced that only a junkie or mental case could live the way I do. They keep offering to send me to a shrink, so I'll come to my senses and go marry some

CPA." That's not likely to happen; marriage, says Vicki, "is the last thing I want. In fact, when a guy starts getting too serious with me, I usually break off with him."

Freedom lovers detest being coerced or put under any kind of obligation. Commands or suggestions that threaten their autonomy raise their hackles, and continued nagging can spark outright rebellion. A freedom lover wants to do things *her* way, not yours. Those like Veronica seek to neutralize the threat by becoming well-to-do. Others, like Vicki, will embrace a low-income lifestyle. Yet a third group will assert their "independence" by running up huge bills they don't intend to pay, writing bad checks, stealing, swindling, and even committing armed robbery.

Love, sex, and marriage, too, are threats to autonomy, and freedom seekers tend to feel uncomfortably submerged when a relationship becomes too intimate. Some freedom lovers will remain celibate; others opt for an arm's-length relationship—equal but unmerged. Still others (men more often than women) will take on a passive, submissive mate who seems unthreatening. Although independence is what freedom lovers claim to seek, say psychologists Herb Goldberg and Robert Lewis, they actually have "strong dependency hunger, but devote an inordinate amount of energy to denying it and pretending it doesn't exist."

THE LOVE MONGERS

Typically, a love monger's parents, unable to show their caring openly, used toys, candy, and money as gestures of affection or approval. Once grown, she continues the pattern, offering money or gifts to *purchase* love from those she wants to please and withholding them from those she rejects. She may also "love" herself by splurging on luxuries, or demand money or gifts from others as proof that they love her.

Leslie, a twenty-seven-year-old actress and model, is renowned among her friends for her generosity and hospitality. In financial trouble? Leslie will come to the rescue, even if she has to dip into her savings or borrow from a third party. Temporarily broke and homeless? Leslie will take you in and provide food and shelter. Having a birthday? Trust your dear friend to throw open her apartment, invite all your pals, and serve copious food and drink.

She does all this on a rather modest income; Leslie is well regarded professionally but hardly overloaded with acting parts or modeling assignments. Thanks to her male admirers, however—she always has at least two or three on tap—she manages to spend more money than she earns. Some of these men are her lovers, some not, but all have certain traits in common: They are middle-aged, indulgent, and well-heeled. They're also trained, by Leslie, to be generous. After inviting one to a dinner party, she's apt to say, "And, by the way, get here early and bring twelve lobsters." When one of her friends was threatened with an eviction for falling behind on her payments, she

inveigled a former lover into paying two months' rent for the girl, whom he had never met.

Although Leslie's parents were comfortably well off, they treated their children in a niggardly fashion. "My sister and I always had smaller allowances than any of our friends," she recalls. "Yet every time we were paid this pittance, we were expected to be extravagantly grateful. My mother even demanded gratitude for *food*. She would say things like 'I hope you realize how hard your poor father had to work to buy you this bowl of cornflakes.' I promised myself that when I grew up, I would be generous with everybody and try to make them feel good instead of bad."

Agnes, a twenty-eight-year-old legal secretary, spends more of her thirty-thousand-dollar-a-year income on other people than she does on herself. She's so eager to please, in fact, that she's an embarrassment to many of her friends; she's apt to show up at a casual dinner with a huge bouquet of flowers and a twenty-dollar bottle of wine, or give an expensive art book to a friend who simply mentioned she'd like to have it. If you give her a gift, no matter how insignificant, she'll be ecstatically grateful, then reproach you for wasting money on her.

Agnes can't be bothered with bargain hunting—she shops at stores where the clerks are friendly and the owners know her by name. Despite her frequent and sometimes extravagant gift buying, Agnes lives well within her income and has about twenty-two thousand dollars in savings plus another eight thousand dollars in an IRA.

Basically, says Linda Barbanel, the love monger is someone who feels both unloved and unlovable. Money in itself has little importance to her. Its value is as a token or proof of love. Too insecure to risk direct involvement, she sees love as a transaction in which money is used to purchase affection or approval. She may be genuinely fond of someone but won't feel she's shown those feelings until she's paid the bill. The old aunt who regularly sends you two hundred dollars for your birthday when a card would have sufficed is a love buyer. So, too, is the man who would never dream of offering you one perfect rose—he always gives at least three dozen.

Then there are the love sellers—people who need to have money (the amount isn't too important) lavished on *them* in order to feel loved. Another person in this category is the love waif, who seems almost to relish financial tribulations: being stranded somewhere, menaced with eviction, threatened with having her car repossessed. Every time a savior comes to her rescue, she feels a rush of love—which is a strong motivation for remaining financially irresponsible.

THE POWER BROKERS

To these people, money symbolizes power. With it, status, importance, domination, and control are theirs. They prize money for its clout, its ability to clear away obstacles and help them assert themselves.

Jane, a thirty-one-year-old attorney, is proud that in addition to being the only female lawyer in her firm, she is the youngest person ever to be made a full partner. Heavily in debt, she lives in luxury. Her new co-op apartment, furnished by a voguish name decorator, is cleaned by a maid every day. A part-time chef prepares the meals at Jane's frequent dinner parties, to which only the wealthy, prominent, and politically powerful are welcomed. Her clothes come from the most expensive boutiques and department stores in the city.

"There's method in my madness," says Jane. "I'm living beyond my means right now, but my social life has helped me meet some very influential people. Already, I've brought several big clients into the firm. I expect my income to triple within the next two to three years. Money breeds money, you know—you have to spend it to make it."

Jane is unmarried and does not have a steady boyfriend. She dates casually from time to time—usually successful, older men who are more escorts than lovers. "I don't have time for a serious relationship right now," she says.

Jane describes her parents as "little people, mentally and emotionally—very timid and inoffensive. I was always exasperated with them when I was growing up. They wanted me to make a nice, safe marriage and then go hide under a rock somewhere for the rest of my life. They thought it was terribly reckless and unfeminine of me to enter law school. Actually, I've modeled my life on them—everything they've done with their lives, I do in reverse."

Cynthia, a twenty-eight-year-old New York City advertising copywriter, drives a Porsche, dresses in Donna Karan and Calvin Klein, and lives in a small but plush apartment on Manhattan's Upper West Side. Too impatient to pinch pennies, she buys her groceries in a high-priced but convenient market, takes taxis everywhere, and dines regularly in expensive restaurants. Economizing is beneath her. "My salary is over sixty thousand dollars, and in my spare time, I do freelance work for several other companies," she says. "Why should I bother trying to save money when I can moonlight and earn fifty to one hundred dollars an hour?"

In her off hours, Cynthia hangs out with a gang of well-to-do young fun lovers who all patronize the same restaurants-of-the-hour and fill up Nell's and the Palladium. A number in the crowd are European, especially the men. Cynthia has had affairs with an Italian count and a German millionaire playboy. Her name is sometimes mentioned in the gossip columns. "I admit it, I'm an elitist," she says. "I like to be around high-level, high-profile people." She expects to meet the right man soon, but she's certain he won't be European. "They're simply not serious enough about their careers. My guy, when I find him, will be American—someone who's done at least as well in life as I have," she explains.

Cynthia grew up in an exclusive town in New Jersey, the only daughter of a wealthy hardware merchant. Her parents sent her to top schools and were anxious for her to be a big success. Even today, when she doesn't really need it, they are eager to assist her financially.

A power seeker, say Goldberg and Lewis, can't be too rich or too powerful. Not all power seekers are as successful as Cynthia and Jane, but they do share the same motives: They are reacting to inner feelings of vulnerability and insignificance and must prove themselves, not just once but over and over.

Some, like Jane, are almost indifferent to money. They use it as a tool, quite cold-bloodedly, and are willing to risk bankruptcy in order to get the best possible leverage from their bucks. Others, like Cynthia, see money as an end in itself, a badge of status that is of no use if not flaunted. Cynthia can be described, though she hates the word, as a yuppie.

"Like it or not," says Linda Barbanel, "the yuppies are your contemporary power gang. These people have been indulged and spoiled all their lives. Their parents are from the insecure generation that followed the Depression. They wanted their children to feel the freedom they never did while growing up, to have all the advantages, and to do better than they did. Meanwhile, the kids grow up thinking, yes, they deserve the best, can have whatever they want, and by God, are going to get it. They're the ones who fall for the designer labels and the name brands and must live in the most fashionable neighborhoods. They want everything from their underwear to their automobiles to proclaim their superior status. If you're a yuppie, the big problem is that there are too many of you. Sooner or later, you'll discover there's not enough money or success to go around."

MIX AND MATCH

Few of us fit neatly into any category, of course. Some are spendthrifts in one area, tightwads in another, security minded in certain situations, love purchasers in certain others. These shifting attitudes are often the result of contradictory money styles that exist within the family or of other special circumstances in our upbringing.

Mindy, for instance, is the daughter of a big-spending power broker and a penny-pinching, security-minded mother. Her main impulse is to be a love buyer, but her acts of generosity are frequently spoiled by guilt pangs, and the emotional conflict makes her seem selfish, grudging, and censorious, rather than giving, to the recipient.

"No matter what the fiscal style is, there's an explanation for it," says Barbanel. "We understand what the recipe is, what family background is necessary to create a certain type of person." One reason psychologists such as Barbanel, Goldberg, and Lewis enjoy zeroing in on money patterns is that unlike certain other habits—such as the sexual—they are easy to trace yet just as meaningful.

Also figuring into your fiscal style is your basic

money anxiety, which, according to financial consultants Don and Joan German, authors of *Ninety Days to Financial Fitness,* must be heeded when planning an investment program. Would you suffer heart palpitations if required to walk three blocks to the bank carrying two thousand dollars in cash? Would you be appalled if a stock you owned suddenly dropped eight or ten points? Do you become worried about your own savings when you hear that a bank in some other state has failed? If so, your money anxiety is high, and you should invest only in safe, insured bank deposits, government bonds, and blue-chip securities—and stay away from investments that, no matter how sound and sensible, would cause you to lose sleep at night. If none of the above ruffles you, you can afford, emotionally, to invest in speculative-growth stocks, commodity futures, and market-index options.

WHO WILL GET RICH?

People from poor families have more to overcome than just financial disadvantages in their struggle to secure riches. The affluent, comfortable with a prosperous life, feel it quite natural to seek a career that offers large financial rewards. Those from poor backgrounds almost invariably must rebel against the family pattern and say, "I refuse to live like this." Even a middle-class person who's trying to become truly wealthy must first break a certain family mold of financial patterns and expectations.

The very rich and very poor do, however, have something in common that may make leaping the gap somewhat easier. Whereas a middle-income person must constantly make choices—"Shall I buy a new car or take a trip to Europe?"—people in the upper and lower brackets do not. The rich person can have both; the poor person can afford neither.

With a balanced attitude, say Goldberg and Lewis, you would neither worship nor denounce the almighty dollar, would control it rather than be controlled *by* it, and would use it constructively to enhance your own life and the lives of those around you. Do you fall short of this ideal? If so, you are perfectly normal in your irrationality. Do, however, give some thought to your particular brand of craziness; dissecting it is the first step toward becoming less anxious and more sensible about the way you earn, save, and splurge.

COMPREHENSION QUESTIONS

_____ 1. According to this article, security seekers
    a. put their trust in others.
    b. are looking for power over others.
    c. put their trust in the stock market's ability to generate profit.
    d. mistrust people.

_____ 2. Security seekers are trying to
    a. win influential friends.
    b. prove they can survive by economizing better than others.
    c. buy love.
    d. gain a high social status.

_____ 3. The author says the freedom lovers
    a. have strong dependency needs.
    b. always live beyond their means.
    c. love intimate relationships.
    d. usually embrace a very low-income lifestyle.

_____ 4. The love mongers
    a. feel unloved and unlovable.
    b. must keep a large money reserve to feel loved.
    c. always give money to anyone who asks.
    d. will not give a gift unless given one first.

_____ 5. The power brokers
    a. are always successful.
    b. have inner feelings of being important.
    c. must prove themselves over and over.
    d. usually come from a deprived environment.

_____ 6. Many people are a mix of attitudes towards money as a result of
   a. contradictory money styles that existed within their families during their childhood.
   b. one major experience during adulthood.
   c. the contradictory information they received in school.
   d. the influences of contrasting style of a mate.

_____ 7. Regarding your money style, this article suggests that you
   a. change to one of the other better styles.
   b. recognize it in planning an investment program.
   c. be totally consistent to one style to gain the most benefits.
   d. ignore it to keep from worrying.

_____ 8. Regarding becoming truly rich, the author says that what is necessary for the middle-class and poor is a
   a. better education.
   b. group of influential friends.
   c. recognition of money styles.
   d. breaking of the family financial patterns.

_____ 9. The author concludes that being irrational in your use of money
   a. is a symptom of psychological problems.
   b. always leads to financial ruin.
   c. is perfectly normal.
   d. makes life more interesting and fun.

_____ 10. You could come to the conclusion that with the information given you can
   a. totally break your spending and saving habits.
   b. analyze your friends' styles with accuracy.
   c. give money a less important role in your life.
   d. work toward more constructive use of money in your life.

Allow 10 points per correct answer.   *Your score* _____ %
Number of words: 4500   *Your rate* _____
Answer key is on page 272.
Record your rate and comprehension score on Course Data Sheet.

THE CALL OF THE WILD
COMPREHENSION QUESTIONS

_____ 1. Buck's position changed from ruler of a large ranch to worker in a dog team when
   a. Judge Miller sold him.
   b. he ran away.
   c. he was lost.
   d. the gardener's helper sold him.

_____ 2. In this new life Buck had reason to fear
   a. only the men, not the other dogs.
   b. only the other dogs, not the men.
   c. both the men and the other dogs.
   d. only the wolves and other wild beasts.

_____ 3. Regarding Buck's morals, he
   a. could not kill or steal because of his earlier training.
   b. learned to kill out of necessity, but felt guilt and remorse.
   c. learned to kill and enjoyed it.
   d. learned to steal but could not learn to kill.

_____ 4. On the dog team Buck became
   a. the leader.
   b. second in command.
   c. the rear dog.
   d. a side dog.

_____ 5. During the course of the story, on the dog team Buck traveled
   a. 500 miles.
   b. 1,500 miles.
   c. 3,000 miles.
   d. 10,000 miles.

_____ 6. Buck's relationship with John Thornton was one of
   a. great mutual love.
   b. fear: Buck's fear of Thornton's club and Thornton's fear of Buck's
      ferocious strength.
   c. need: Thornton's need of a watchdog and Buck's need of a home.
   d. hate: Buck's hatred of all men and Thornton's hatred of dogs.

_____ 7. Thornton made a bet with Mathewson that Buck could
   a. run faster than Mathewson's dog.
   b. win a dog fight.
   c. pull a loaded sled faster than Mathewson's dog.
   d. pull a sled loaded with 1,000 pounds for 100 yards.

_____ 8. At the end of the story Buck
   a. is killed.
   b. joins a wild wolf pack.
   c. is sold to another gold prospector.
   d. roams alone in the wilderness for the rest of his life.

_____ 9. An important idea that the author, Jack London, is illustrating in this story
   is that
   a. animals are very different from people.
   b. an animal born in a civilized world is more gentle than his brothers born
      in the wilderness.
   c. a creature retains a subconscious memory of his ancestors that can be-
      come active in him under the right circumstances.
   d. most men are cruel to animals.

_____ 10. Animals who became too old or sick to perform their duties wanted to
   a. be left behind.
   b. be sent to a hospital for old and sick dogs.
   c. continue in the work they had known.
   d. lie around and do nothing.

Allow 10 points per correct answer.   Your score _____ %
Number of words: 35,000   Your rate _____
Answer key is on page 272.
Record rate and comprehension score on Course Data Sheet.

GENERAL NOVEL COMPREHENSION QUESTIONS

(To be used only when reading a novel other than *The Call of the Wild*)

Title _____ Author _____

1. Name the main character(s). _____

   _____

2. Where does the story take place? _____

   _____

3. Approximately when does the story take place? _____

4. Name two other characters. (1) _____

   (2) _____

5. What type of story is it (love story, adventure, science fiction, war story,

   fantasy, etc.)? _____

6. Briefly summarize the situation at the beginning of the story.

   _____

   _____

   _____

7. List three things that happen to the main character.

   (1) _____

   (2) _____

   (3) _____

8. State the relationship(s) between the main character and at least one other

   character (husband and wife, father and son, friends, etc). _____

9. How does the story end? _____

   _____

   _____

10. Write one sentence that tells what this whole story illustrates (author's

    message). _____

    _____

Directions: *You may wish to look back into the story to find out if you wrote the correct answers. If you do, give yourself 10 points for each correct answer.*

If you do not correct your answer sheet, estimate your understanding of the story by writing "excellent," "good," "fair," or "poor" in the place for your score.

Your score _____ %

Total number of words _____   Your rate _____

To find your rate, refer to directions in Chapter 8, page 80. Record title, rate, and comprehension score on Course Data Sheet.

13

The Basic Speed-Study Method

Materials: • Readings:
"Robots and Beyond: The Age of Intelligent Machines"
What to Say When You Talk to Your Self, or another 50,000 word nonfiction book
• Drill book
• Advanced additional reading report: fiction book
• Advanced additional reading report: nonfiction book
• Advanced additional reading report: articles

Objectiives: • To learn the speed-study method
• To learn how to apply the speed-study method to nonfiction
• To understand how to do the advanced additional reading

Your primary emphasis up to now has been your attainment of the highest reading rates of which you are capable, regardless of any decreases in comprehension. You have been learning a new reading habit of faster eye pacing. But, of course, speed alone is not enough. When you can understand what you read rapidly, then you are truly speed reading.

From this point on, your emphasis will shift to improvement in comprehension skills as you continue to use your rapid-reading techniques on various types of difficult college-level materials. Most of the following chapters will assume that you are reading for purposes of study, a type of reading in which you must know the material thoroughly. Special techniques will be presented for reading in depth, coping with specialized vocabularies, critical reading, reading in special academic areas, and reading for enjoyment.

You should cut out Course Data Sheet 2, in the Appendix, page 269. This new sheet provides the proper format to record the new type of materials.

Eye-pacing drills will continue, and each week you will take the customary drill rate. You may expect that your drill rates will continue to increase, but not as dramatically as before.

The new speed-reading techniques that will be introduced probably will not increase your reading rate; they are intended to increase your comprehension. Keep in mind that the materials will all be on the college level, and the questions on these materials will be more difficult than in earlier chapters. Therefore, a comprehension score of 80 percent actually indicates better comprehension than the same score on any previously used materials.

The required additional reading for this and subsequent chapters will be different from what you have been doing and will not be a weekly requirement. By now, you should be using your rapid-reading techniques on all your reading, and therefore practicing regularly is no longer a motivational requirement. The details of the new assignments are discussed on page 140.

By the end of this second half of the book, you will have acquired all the skills and reinforcement of these skills necessary to use speed reading effectively on any type of reading you are likely to encounter.

DRILL PRACTICE

Do the same drills that you did at the beginning of Chapter 11, page 109. Then, take a drill rate for this week. *(The Call of The Wild* is a good book to use.)

STUDYING

Webster's New World Dictionary defines *studying* as follows: "to apply one's mind to attentively; try to learn or understand by reading, thinking, etc.; to examine or investigate carefully; to scrutinize; to read so as to know and understand it."* Studying, then, by definition, requires more than just the ability to read any given writing; it requires some purposeful method that leads to a complete and thorough understanding of the ideas contained in the writing. This chapter will present a method that will enable you to make the transition from "just reading" to "studying."

Studying usually cannot be accomplished adequately by completing one reading of the material only, no matter how slowly or attentively that reading is done. Thus, experts on study skills recommend a method or process of reading that includes three basic elements: preparation for reading, the actual reading, and a review of the important points. Speed reading for study purposes must follow these sound principles if thorough understanding of the material is to be attained. Although the underlying process of studying, therefore, is basically the same for slow or rapid reading, each segment of the study process is accomplished in considerably less time when the speed-reading method is used. We call this unification of speed reading with the study method *speed studying*.

All the previous chapters have been preparation for speed studying. In speed studying you will integrate rapidly paced eye movements, skimming, scanning, finding your level of best comprehension, flexibility, marking a text, recognizing the author's organizational pattern as an aid to understanding and remembering, and thinking in images or ideas. It all comes together as these techniques are applied within the context of an approved and tested study system.

Just as it was important for you to practice each of the preparatory skills until you could use it well, it is now important to practice their unification in the study system until you can speed study easily and with confidence. Therefore, most of the practice readings you will do during the remainder of the book will be exercises in speed studying. The following detailed description of the speed-study process set forth should be followed for *all* materials read hereafter, except where you

Webster's New World Dictionary, Second College Edition (New York: William Collins & World Publishing Co., Inc., 1974), p. 1,414.

are specifically instructed otherwise. As you study the works that follow in this and later chapters, you may wish to reread this description to be certain that you are following the sequence properly for maximum results.

In later chapters certain additional information will be provided to help you speed study specific types of material such as history. However, the basic process and sequence will remain the same for all study materials.

At this point I caution you to recognize that the most effective study method will vary for each individual. Some people find that they must write things down to learn them; these people should take notes or make an outline of the material. Others find that rereading the material many times works best for them; these people should do many postviews.

The study method presented here is a basic one, to be used as a starting point. If you have already devised a good study method that works for you, incorporate these ideas into your method in a way that suits you best. If you presently have no study method, begin by using this method exactly as presented and then experiment by adding note-taking and several postviews until you are satisfied with your results. You need a method for studying that fits your individual characteristics. Start to find it now!

Method for Speed Studying

1. **Survey** Look at the front and back covers and title. Read the preface and introduction. Read the contents. If there is a glossary in the back of the book, skim down and read definitions of words or terms that are unfamiliar to you. Skim the first few pages and the last few pages. Make a tentative decision on the most efficient method of previewing this material. (See Preview and Postview Methods, following.)

2. **Preview** Previewing for study is usually a skimming of the entire material, that is, going at a rate faster than a reading rate to get the main ideas only, not the details. For our purposes, you will time this skim-preview so that you can figure out your preview rate. You may sometimes choose one of the other preview methods that follow, but only when you are very familiar with the topic of the material or when the material appears to be easy for you.

   In previewing nonfiction (informational material), pay special attention to chapter titles and section titles. Look for main ideas especially at the beginning of chapters, sections, and paragraphs. As you skim, arrange your hand-pacing pattern so that you go under the first line of each paragraph. Look for clues to the organizational pattern and come to a tentative conclusion about what pattern the author used. Formulate a tentative thesis statement (main idea of entire work).

In previewing fiction (stories), look for the names of the characters, where and when the story takes place, and the general sequence of events.

In all previewing, try to sense the difficulty of the material by noticing if there are a lot of big words and the length and complexity of the sentences.

When preview is completed, answer the special preview questions, correct your answers with the answer key in the Appendix, compute your rate and comprehension score, and record them in the *Preview* columns on your Course Data Sheet 2.

3. **Good Comprehension Reading** The term Good Comprehension will be used hereafter specifically to refer to the reading of any material for maximum meaning, as opposed to the preview which is preparation for reading, and the postview which is reinforcement of the reading; this term should not be confused with the general term "comprehension," which refers to your ability to understand.

The good comprehension reading is a slower reading, in which you want to understand the details and how they relate to the main idea. It is timed. First, find your level of best comprehension. Use flexibility. Mark the text for main ideas, parts not understood, and questions you have about the material. Look for the important details that back up the main idea. Recognize the pattern the author used to organize the material (his or her blueprint), which will help you relate the details to the main idea. You may wish to revise the thesis statement you formulated in the preview. Make a tentative decision on the most efficient method of postviewing the material. (See Preview and Postview Methods.) Answer the good comprehension questions. Correct answers with the answer key in the Appendix. Compute your rate and comprehension score for this reading and record them in the *Good Comprehension* columns on your Course Data Sheet 2.

4. **Postview** This is a very flexible reading, sometimes timed. You may use a skimming or a scanning technique depending on your purpose for postviewing. If your purpose is to reinforce the ideas you learned in the preview and good comprehension readings, you should skim the material, slowing down on the marked parts. However, if your purpose is to find answers to questions, you should scan, looking for the specific information.

You do not always need to postview the entire work. The portions of the work you understood well can be skipped and only the difficult parts gone over again one or more times. Refer to "Postview Methods" below for choices in ways to postview.

In the postview reading react to the material, form opinions, come to conclusions, make inferences—all based on facts presented in the material. Pay attention to the author's style.

Also, look for the answers to questions missed on the preview and good comprehension readings. When the material is especially difficult, you may postview before answering the comprehension questions, and more than one postview may be needed. Answer the postview questions, if there are any. Correct answers. Record your rate (if taken) and comprehension score on your Course Data Sheet 2 in the *Postview* columns.

On easy material, postview is optional.

Speed-Study Sequence Outline

1. Survey.
2. Record starting time for Preview.
3. Preview: skim.
4. Record finishing time.
5. Answer Preview questions; correct.
6. Compute rate and score; record on Course Data Sheet.
7. Record starting time for Good Comprehension Reading.
8. Good Comprehension Reading: level of best comprehension, flexibility, marking text.
9. Record finishing time.
10. Answer Good Comprehension questions; correct.
11. Compute rate and score; record on Course Data Sheet.
12. Record starting time for Postview.
13. Postview: skim, reread ideas, find answers to missed questions, react.

Nonfiction chart

Level	Comprehension
SURVEY	Introduction/Conclusion/Titles/Pictures/Covers/Contents/Glossary/etc.
PREVIEW—FAST	Thesis (Key idea) of whole piece Main ideas: Chapter Headings Questions Introduction/Conclusion Beginnings of Paragraphs (Topic Sentences) Clues to Organizational Pattern
GOOD COMPREHENSION— SLOWER Mark: Main Ideas Questions Not Understood	Continue with Main Ideas Get *details* and relationships of them to main ideas Some possible Relationships (Organizations): 1. Compare/Contrast 2. Example 3. Time/Space 4. Information (Statistics) 5. Definition 6. Cause/Effect 7. Explanation 8. Analysis
POSTVIEW—FAST, FLEXIBLE Do if: Need reinforcement Opinion Open to question Author's conclusions vague Missed something	Skim or Scan: 1. Look for parts that need to be filled in. Slow down to reread. 2. Reinforce important ideas. Read and react: 1. Get correct conclusions of author (based on what *he* said). 2. Your own judgments based on facts as presented. 3. Style of work.

14. Record finishing time.
15. Answer Postview questions; correct.
16. Compute rate and score; record on Course Data Sheet 2.

PREVIEW AND POSTVIEW METHODS

Every preview and postview need not be a complete reading of all the material. You should choose the best method for you for the particular material, which will depend on your previous knowledge of the subject, the complexity of the material, and how thoroughly you must know it.

Following is a list of preview and postview methods from which you may choose. In the survey you can recognize if the work is on a subject that is familiar to you and if it appears to contain only one main idea or is more complex, with several main ideas and many important details. Make a tentative decision about which method you should use. If, after you begin, you find that you made a mistake in your choice, you can easily switch to another method. For example, if you decided to skim only a few pages at the beginning and at the end (method 1) and as you preview you realize you are not getting enough information because the material is more difficult than you expected, just continue to skim the entire work (method 3) or until you understand the main idea of the work; then you can switch to skimming the beginning of each chapter or section (method 4).

Do not choose your postview method until you have finished your good comprehension reading. By then you will know what else you need to do to understand the material thoroughly. However, once again, if you make the wrong choice, you can switch to another method.

Preview Methods

1. Skim the first few pages and the last few pages.

2. Skim the first five pages, five pages at random at two or three places in the work, and the last five pages.
3. Skim the entire work.
4. Skim the beginning of each chapter of a book or each subsection of an article. If it appears easy and you recognize the main idea of the chapter or subsection, skip the rest of the chapter or subsection. Skim the beginning of the next chapter or subsection; if it is easy and you recognize the main idea, skip to the beginning of the next chapter or subsection. Continue on through the entire work in this manner. The more difficult and complex chapters or subsections should be skimmed in their entirety.

Postview Methods

1. Skim the entire work, slowing on marked parts and information for which you are looking.
2. Skip from marked part to marked part; reread only these.
3. Reread difficult chapters or sections only.
4. Scan for answers to missed questions or special information.
5. Postview, using any method, before answering the comprehension questions. You may need to postview several times.

For condensed information on the speed-study method, read the charts on pages 138 and 154.

Speed-Study Practice: Article

The first article for practice in speed studying is "Robots and Beyond: The Age of Intelligent Machines" on page 140.

Go through the entire speed-study process with this article. For this practice, preview by skimming the entire article. Remember that in nonfiction you should recognize the main idea and get a general idea of what the article is about in the preview. Be sure to mark the important parts in the good comprehension reading. Postview by skimming the entire article, paying special attention to the parts you marked as important. Preview, good comprehension, and postview readings should be timed so that you can figure out your rate for each and record them on your Course Data Sheet. There are questions for each reading so that you will also have three comprehension scores to record.

Follow the speed-study sequence outline on page 137 and refer to the detailed description of each step if you need to. You will be completely on your own during the entire process. See how thoroughly you can know the information in the article by applying the steps in the study process as well as you can.

Self-Evaluation

In order to judge whether or not you are using the new speed study method properly, look at all the rates you recorded on your Course Data Sheet for this article. The preview rate should be considerably faster than the good comprehension rate. If it isn't, you are not previewing but trying to do a good comprehension reading twice. Decide that the next time you will actually preview in the first reading by going faster. This preview reading is intended as a preparation for the actual reading.

The proper rate for a postview is more difficult to evaluate because it will depend on how much of the material you needed to reread for complete understanding. However, generally it should fall somewhere between the preview rate and the good comprehension rate. If there were many sections that required slowing down to reread, the rate will naturally be slower than if you only had to reread a few portions.

Speed-Study Practice: Nonfiction Book

Use the four-step speed-study method described in this chapter on the nonfiction book, *What to Say When You Talk to Your Self,* or another nonfiction book of at least 50,000 words that is suitable for study. Follow the "Speed-Study Sequence Outline" on page 137 so that you will know the order of each step. Review how each step is done by rereading the steps of the method and referring to the "Nonfiction Chart."

Allow two hours or two reading sessions for speed-studying each book. In the first session you should complete the survey and the preview-skim reading of the entire book and answer the preview questions.

In longer works you will find it difficult to keep up a skimming pace throughout the preview. Your tendency will be to slow down to read the work. Keep in mind that you are only preparing to read the work, and keep the pace fast!

In the second session do the good comprehension reading and the postview(s). For the good comprehension reading remember to find your level of best comprehension, use flexibility, and mark the text. Answer the good comprehension questions after that reading and the postview questions after the postview.

After completing the entire method, evaluate your use of the speed-study method. Is the preview the fastest rate? Is the good comprehension rate the slowest (not slow, only slower than the preview)? Be sure that you are using the method *properly* for best study results!

If you are reading a nonfiction book other than *What to Say When You Talk to Your Self,* answer the "Advanced Nonfiction General Questions" at the end of this chapter, preview, good comprehension and postview sets.

Additional Reading Assignments

From now on, for the additional reading outside of class you will read one fiction book, one nonfiction book, and two articles—a total of two books and two articles that should be completed by the time you finish this book (not every week). Read them according to the directions on the report sheets which follow the speed-study process that you have been practicing in this chapter.

Choose materials in which you are interested. They may be materials you would ordinarily read anyway or those you must read for other purposes. The only requirement is that they be read according to the instructions for the speed-study process.

For each book or article you read, fill out a separate report sheet answering all the questions that you can. If a question does not apply to the material you are reading, skip it. Be sure to figure your rates for each reading and record them in the proper places.

All the additional reading report sheets you will need are in the Appendix starting on page 263.

SUMMARY

All materials that must be understood completely should be read by using a study process incorporating valid study techniques with the speed-reading techniques learned in all the previous chapters: skimming for preview; best comprehension reading level; flexibility; marking a text; and scanning for better understanding of difficult areas.

ROBOTS AND BEYOND: THE AGE OF INTELLIGENT MACHINES

Kendra R. Bonnett

"I can't define a robot, but I know one when I see it."
—Joseph Engelberger, founder of *Unimation*

It is difficult to say just when the first robot was built. For one thing, a lot depends on your definition. If you believe, for example, that a robot is any machine that performs work, then you might consider bicycles in your classification. On the other hand, you might agree with the definition used by the *Robot Institute of America:* "A robot is a reprogrammable, multifunctional manipulator designed to move material, parts, tools, or specialized devices through variable programmed motions for the performance of a variety of tasks." The second is certainly the more specific of the two definitions and sounds very much like the industrial robot arms used in factories around the world. But even this does not adequately satisfy the question, what is a robot.

You might be surprised to know that scientists working in the fields of robotics and artificial intelligence (AI) disagree on issues ranging from proper terminology to technological procedures. Take sensors: Robots need sen-

sors to function within their environment. Sensors give robots information on what they see (vision system), what they touch (pressure and touch sensors), and what they hear (sound sensor and speech recognition system). And yet, scientists cannot agree on the best model for sensor design. Should robot sensors try to replicate the human senses of sight, touch and hearing, or should the model be some electro-mechanical design that functions very differently from any biological system?

Whichever side you favor, you will be agreeing and disagreeing with some of the best scientific minds of our time, and a few scientists will even agree with you if you say, who cares, so long as the robot works. You have to expect this sort of wild disagreement when you are working in such a new field with so many unanswered questions. You also must be prepared to change your mind when new evidence is discovered. In the case of the sensors, for example, you can easily argue either side:

Human/biological model The process of closely replicating human functions helps us to unlock some of the mysteries of the human body, which, in turn, may have ramifications for medicine and the creation of articial organs. For example, scientists have learned that certain cells in our body process and interpret data independent of the brain. Robotics experts are now experimenting with smart sensors (sensors with microchips) to relieve the processing strain on the main computer. Perhaps someday similar smart sensors will be implanted in our bodies to replace ailing sensory organs.

New Model The process of creating a new system may provide us with better ways to do things and result in systems that will help humans to see, hear, and think better and faster than ever before. The discovery of a vision system not based on the human eye, but that allows a machine to see images more clearly, might help visually-impaired people regain their sight.

Perhaps, then, the best solution is to keep an open mind as you explore the world of robotics and intelligent machines.

MECHANICAL BEGINNINGS

The human obsession for building mechanical figures in our own image is almost as old as the human species itself. Mythology is full of stories of inanimate objects being endowed with the characteristics of man and beast. The Egyptian statue of the slain Memnon—victim of the Trojan War—was rumored to speak when the first rays of dawn's light shone. The Greek myths describe statues created by the inventor Daedalus to stand guard outside the Labyrinth on the island of Crete. The Greeks thought that the statues were powered by quicksilver or Mercury, making them so realistic that the statues had to be chained to keep them from running away.

Similar stories are scattered throughout history. The famous Bavarian philosopher Albertus Magnus is said to have spent almost 30 years of his life creating a walking, talking automaton that supposedly worked as his servant. One version of the legend claims that it could answer the door and greet a visitor; another that the figure was a beautiful, talking woman. When Thomas Aquinas, later canonized as a saint, saw the automaton, he said it was bewitched and destroyed it as the work of the Devil!

The response was quite different at the 1939 New York World's Fair as crowds swarmed around the Westinghouse Electric exhibit trying to catch a glimpse of *Elektro* and a mechanical dog named *Sparko*. *Elektro* moved its fingers and arms, walked (really rolled), and produced great puffs of smoke—twenty-six movements in all. The faithful *Sparko* barked, begged, and wagged its tail. But even these amazing characters were only remote-controlled machines designed to perform a se-

ries of predetermined movements. They were not robots—by any stretch of the definition.

For all the ancient stories about mechanical figures, water clocks, and automatons, the term robot is still relatively new. It only came into usage in 1921 with the production of Czech playwright Karel Capek's play *R.U.R. (Rossum's Universal Robots)*. The word *robot* comes from the Czechoslovakian word *robotta*, meaning degrading, menial work or involuntary servitude, and was used to describe the mechanical workers in the play.

THE ROBOT AGE BEGINS

The earliest attempts to recreate man focused on physical features—to make a creature that looked human and appeared to act human. Today, you have only to look at the array of mechanical entertainment robots, called showbots, or the Hollywood creations, like C3PO, to realize that people's fascination with humanoids is as strong as ever. Scientists and robot experts, however, have other objectives—the primary one being artificial intelligence and the related fields of sensory, vision, and mobility research.

In the 50s scientists experimented with robots and robot devices, which while they did not appear human, emulated human or, more precisely, animal behavior. *LEARM*, modeled to look and respond like a common flatworm, was an early electronic learning machine designed to study patterns and processes of learning. Scientists had been experimenting with real flatworms and earthworms, training them to find their way through a T-shaped maze. They wanted to know if a mechanical worm, with three switches positioned on its head, could be taught to find its way in the maze. At first *LEARM* moved at random, but touching one of the switches against the wall "rewarded" the robot with a small electrical charge. *LEARM* stored in memory the patterns of movement that resulted in reward and, in effect, learned the maze. This was an early experiment in artificial intelligence and demonstrated that simple thought processes could be created electronically.

The first researchers interested in thinking and learning machines came from many fields—philosophy, psychology, medicine, mathematics, biology and engineering. In the summer of 1956 a small group of them held a conference at Dartmouth College in New Hampshire to discuss and share ideas about this emerging science of artificial intelligence. Leading AI experts like M.I.T. Professor Marvin Minsky and Professor John McCarthy of Stanford came out of this era. In the 1950s, they were eager young men, somewhat naive, who thought they could solve the mysteries of human-thinking processes and get the rest of the scientific community to accept their findings.

Today, three decades later, significant progress has been made. Computing capability (measured in terms of memory, processing speed, size and portability of equipment) has helped make this possible. The other component is the men and women whose dedication, imagination, creativity and vision enable them to search for the link between human thought and intelligent machines.

AI research is helping engineers give machines the capability to function according to decisions made independently of human involvement. This is an important development if robots are ever to do the wonderful things we like to imagine. When a process is simple, a computer program based on an *algorithm* or set of step-by-step instructions can usually handle the problem. For example, the algorithm for making a bed would be the sum of all the steps taken to straighten the sheets, tuck in the blanket, pull up the spread and fluff the pillows. Technically you could teach a robot to make a bed.

But what happens to the algorithm when your dog Spot decides to take a nap on the bed? Will the robot know how to handle the dog, or will it just make up the bed with Spot in it? Also, you cannot possibly account for every condition or situation. Your mother may pile clean clothes on the bed, your sister may return your tennis racket and throw it on the bed, and so on. One solution is to create a program that allows the robot to make some decisions about items on the bed. You could provide the robot with a set of general rules for identifying clothes, dogs, sports equipment and other household items and a set of instructions telling it what to do with each. Your robot now becomes an *expert system* capable of handling most of the situations in the course of making a bed.

But this expert system is only able to make beds. You would need different expert systems for vacuuming, window washing, and cooking. Another, more global solution, one that is still part of AI, is to create a system that *learns* to make a bed. That learning can occur from processing verbal instructions, watching a person make a bed, by trial-and-error, or by a combination of all three. The important thing is that a robot so programmed could learn virtually any task, and that is the goal of AI experts—but all this takes time. Robots have already shown they can solve maze problems and other simple tasks and they can function as expert systems. No doubt the other capabilities will come.

THE BETTER TO SEE YOU

While some scientists concentrate on machine learning, others are trying to endow robots with better vision systems. Robots do not have eyes; they view images through television cameras and convert the picture into a digital signal. The process, called *digitizing*, divides an image up into tiny squares called picture elements or *pixels*. Computer graphics are processed the same way—nothing but hundreds of little squares that are turned on or off depending on the picture. The clarity or resolution of an image depends on the number and size of the pixels. More and smaller pixels result in a sharper picture.

There are three basic ways that robots see, that is interpret, an image. These are gray-scale, binary and three-dimensional imaging. **Gray-scaling** is most commonly used in industrial applications requiring a system that can recognize objects and inspect materials for flaws. Pixels range in luminance from white to black with a range of grays in between. Details are depicted by a range of tones and the picture resembles a fuzzy black-and-white photograph.

Binary imaging eliminates the gray scale: a pixel is either on or it is off. The outline of an object will be clear, but all interior features are lost. The process is cheaper and requires less data storage, but it also has very limited capacity. For example, a binary system cannot recognize the subtle but distinct differences between a golf ball and a ping-pong ball. Nor can it distinguish between objects that overlap or touch, which is often the case on an assembly line.

Three-dimensional imaging is the most expensive of all, but when perfected this will most closely resemble human vision. The cost of equipment (two cameras for stereo vision) and length of processing time still make three-dimensional imaging impractical for most industrial applications. But scientists are working on short cuts to image analysis that will make this a useful tool.

ROBOTS ON THE MOVE

Ever since you were a baby, walking has been one of the easier things you do. But consider the process, the simple sequence of throwing one leg forward and landing on a foot involves hundreds of sensor-motor messages. The balance sensors in the inner ear communicate to the balance control center in the brain. The motor control areas of the brain's cortex, in turn, send messages to the muscles in the leg, foot, and back. Similarly, the nerves in the joints and muscles relay messages back to the brain. Oh, do not forget that all this time your eyes are scanning the ground for obstacles and hazards in your path.

And you thought walking was as easy as putting one foot in front of the other. It is no wonder then that many robot designers prefer to conserve precious data processing power for other tasks and either restrict their robot designs to immobile units or to mobile units with wheels and tractor-type treads.

Research scientists, however, keep working on walking machines. They know that the fastest way to cross rough ground is on legs, but as yet no wheel or tread vehicle has come close to crossing open terrain as quickly as a horse. Although the Japanese scientists at Waseda University in Tokyo have a two-legged model, called *WL-1ORD*, that successfully demonstrates dynamic walking in a machine, most of the research designs feature robots with four or six legs.

In 1983, Odetics, Inc, introduced a six-legged robot called *ODEX I*. This robot is extremely agile and stable. With six legs, even while walking *ODEX* can always have at least three legs on the ground—like a tripod. *ODEX* can navigate virtually any terrain and move along at a rate of two miles an hour. It cannot run races with a horse yet, but it does represent great advances in robot mobility.

Besides increasing the range of possible applications for robots, mobility research is helping paraplegic people. Robotic legs for amputees and exoskeletons for paralysis victims may restore mobility to many handicapped people. Furthermore, mobile robots can serve severely disabled people by fetching objects, feeding and grooming. Veterans hospitals are putting considerable time and money into this phase of robotic research. The following statement comes from a report by the Veterans Administration Medical Center in Palo Alto, California: *In the process of proving that robotics technology is appropriate and feasible, it became clear that mobility was a key requirement for a truly useful rehabilitative device.*

ROBOTS AT WORK

In 1960 Joseph Engelberger and George Devol installed the first industrial robot in the United States. It was a blind, dumb workhorse used to move objects from one location to another. Still, here was a machine that had the potential to work 24 hours a day, never get tired of even the most boring jobs, and perform the same task the same way the 10,000th time as it did the first time. It was a beginning. Today there are some 15,000 industrial robots used in the United States, and that number is expected to increase to 35,000 by 1990.

When we think of robots at work we usually picture the industrial arm welding, painting, or assembling cars. The auto industry is still the largest user of robots, but other applications are being explored. As robots have better vision, greater mobility, more sensing capability, and become more intelligent we will see many more unusual applications. Even today, robots are doing demolition work . . . inspecting paint on a new car in 1.2 minutes (it takes a human 45 minutes) . . . repairing underwater cables . . . playing chess well enough to become official chess masters . . . serving as organ accompanist with the symphony . . . and more.

At the University of Western Australia, scientists have been working with the wool industry to make sheep shearing a more cost-effective procedure. Inflation and the rising price of labor threatens to prevent the wool industry from competing with the producers of other textile fibers. Scientists are trying to create a machine that is a fast, accurate and efficient alternative to shearing by hand. The result is the *SM* robot, which consists of a restraining cradle to hold a sheep and a robot arm equipped with pressure sensors, vision, and a cutting head (end effector). The sensors are designed to keep the cutting head a prescribed distance from the animal's skin. To be effective, these sensors must be quick to react to bumps in a sheep's skin as well as to any movement, including breathing, the animal makes.

The robot, in its various designs, has sheared some 500 sheep since 1979, but has still not reached a level of performance that makes it an acceptable alternative to hand shearing. Both the robot's developers and people in the wool industry eventually expect to shear 97% of a sheep's wool in three minutes without injuring the animal—a goal that is still a couple of years away.

For our second application, we take to the sky with a most unusual robot and its creator, Paul B. MacCready, a man who has spent much of his life doing the impossible with flying machines. He has won prizes and praise for his human-powered and solar-powered planes. In 1984 he took on the task of creating a flying, wing-flapping replica of a dinosaur . . . pterosaur (a giant, flying reptile) to be exact.

When the fossil of *Quetzalcoatulus northopi* (pterosaur) was discovered in West Texas in 1972, paleontologists wanted to know how this giant reptile with a wing span of 36 feet and no tail could fly. The National Air and Space Museum contracted with MacCready's company, Aero-Vironment, Inc. in Monrovia, California, to develop a flying model.

The model, built to half scale with a wing span of 18 feet and total weight of 36 pounds, is really a flying robot, even though it does not do human work and it is not reprogrammable. The robot is a machine dedicated to the task of flying, but it does so in a manner emulating the instinctive action and reaction of the ancient reptile itself. Through a system of gyroscopes, wind speed sensors, special motors and a small, on-board computer, the robot pterosaur can monitor its speed, wing angle, and position. The information received through sensors (feedback) is used to control flapping, twist, and sweep of its wings. Powered by rechargeable nickel cadmium batteries and elastic bands, the robot can fly on its own for about five minutes.

Finally, robot technology helps neurosurgeons at the Long Beach (California) Memorial Medical Center perform brain surgery and take tissue samples from patients suspected to have brain tumors. A small robot arm is interfaced to a computer and a CAT scanner (which takes digitized, three-dimensional images of the brain). Once a doctor identifies the tumor from the CAT scan image and locates the exact spot for surgery, the computer calculates the coordinates and positions the robot arm. The system is accurate to within two-thousandths of an inch and can determine the best angle for entering the skull. The robot does not do the actual surgery, since doctors fear a power surge might cause the robot to move the wrong way while cutting. They turn the robot off, secure it in position and apply pressure by hand to the knife (held in the robot's gripper). The procedure is so accurate that patients require only a local anesthesia and can usually go home the day after surgery (recovery used to take a week or longer).

IS THERE A FUTURE FOR INTELLIGENT MACHINES?

With social and physical scientists exhibiting increasing interest in artificial intelligence and intelligent machines, we can expect to see continued improvements in robotics. Most of us will see these advances in terms of applications. If, for example, we soon see robots vacuuming airport lobbies and mowing the lawn, as Dr. James Crowley of Carnegie-Mellon University claims, we will know that science has made some significant breakthroughs in navigation.

Just how quickly the breakthroughs will come is hard to say. But, remember that robots have passed through four generations in only a little more than 30 years. Since 1950 robots have evolved from crude platforms, through blind and dumb industrial workhorses, to machines with vision, some decision-making capability and, in some cases, mobility. The fifth generation will be robots with artificial intelligence.

But will society be ready for these breakthroughs? Will they feel comfortable with machines that can think, learn, and even originate ideas? Creating intelligent robots may, in fact, turn out to be easier than preparing people to accept these machines. As Professor Marvin Minsky admitted, *I have mixed feelings about whether society could tolerate intelligent machines. It was three hundred years from Newton to Einstein, and mechanics developed very nicely . . . If artificial intelligence came in ten years, it might be an intolerable thing for most people.*

PREVIEW QUESTIONS

_____ 1. Building mechanical figures with human characteristics
   a. is a twentieth-century invention.
   b. began in the 1850s.
   c. was invented in Czechoslovakia.
   d. is almost as old as the human species itself.

_____ 2. Robots see by means of
   a. rudimentary eyes.
   b. still cameras.
   c. television cameras.
   d. light detectors.

_____ 3. Scientists have found that making robots that can walk is
   a. a simple process.
   b. an extremely complex process.
   c. impossible at the present time.
   d. of no value.

_____ 4. Today, true robots are
   a. being used to perform varied tasks.
   b. only used in scientific research.
   c. only used in industry.
   d. in the experimental stages only.

_____ 5. This article emphasizes information on
   a. how to build a robot.
   b. the current status of the robotics field.
   c. what the robot will be like one hundred years from now.
   d. the intricate internal electronics of robots.

Allow 20 points per correct answer.   Your score _____ %
Number of words: 3800   Your rate _____
Answer key is on page 272.
Record rate and comprehension score on Course Data Sheet 2 in the Preview columns.

GOOD COMPREHENSION QUESTIONS

_____ 1. The terminology and technical procedures in the field of robotics
    a. are not agreed upon.
    b. are firmly set and agreed upon.
    c. were invented by Herman Robot.
    d. are the same as used in the computer field.

_____ 2. By using the biological human-type sensors, scientists will
    a. unquestionably make the best sensors possible.
    b. be taking the easy way.
    c. follow a course doomed to fail.
    d. help unlock some of the mysteries of the human body.

_____ 3. By creating a new model for the robotic sensors, scientists
    a. will be taking the easy way.
    b. will follow a course doomed to fail.
    c. must first invent new computer technology.
    d. may find the technology to help humans improve their own sensor functions.

_____ 4. The term robot originally meant
    a. electronically-powered machine.
    b. degrading, menial work.
    c. automatic worker.
    d. bionic humanoid.

_____ 5. According to this article, robots today can
    a. learn many complex expert systems, such as bedmaking.
    b. use programmed general rules and instructions to execute expert systems.
    c. set up their own step-by-step instructions to execute expert systems.
    d. invent solutions to problems by "thinking."

_____ 6. The most commonly used method for robotic vision for robots used in industry is
    a. three-dimensional imaging.
    b. Binary imaging.
    c. Gray-scaling.
    d. optical tri-vision.

_____ 7. Most robots today move by means of
    a. wheels or tractor-type treads.
    b. six legs.
    c. four legs.
    d. springs.

_____ 8. One of the uses of robots today discussed in this article is
    a. to assist in performing brain surgery.
    b. that of creating poetry.
    c. to assist in flying an airplane.
    d. reading to the blind.

_____ 3. What you say aloud to others is considered
   a. outside the realm of self-talk.
   b. a self-directive to your subconscious.
   c. more influential to others than to yourself.
   d. of no consequence as a self-talk directive.

_____ 4. The subconscious part of the mind is believed to
   a. evaluate all information.
   b. be directed by our conscious mind.
   c. have little influence over our attitudes.
   d. accept all input as true and real.

_____ 5. The self-management sequence referred to shows each step creating the next step of the sequence. These creations are in this order:
   a. attitudes create beliefs which create programming.
   b. actions create attitudes which create beliefs.
   c. feelings create beliefs which create attitudes.
   d. programming creates beliefs which create attitudes.

_____ 6. Self-talk for the purpose of habit changing should be stated as
   a. a desire you want to take place in the future.
   b. though the change has already taken place.
   c. a simple phrase giving direction.
   d. a promise of what you will do.

_____ 7. Self-talk that deals with tackling an unpleasant situation that cannot be changed is best handled by
   a. self-talking a precise, lengthy script telling why you should face the situation.
   b. recalling how you handled earlier incidents of a similar nature.
   c. making an instant adjustment to how you look at the situation.
   d. telling yourself ways that you will change the situation in the future.

_____ 8. In order to prepare your own effective self-talk scripts, follow the author's checklist, which includes all of the following *except*
   a. stating it in the present tense.
   b. making it specific.
   c. making it use a lot of thought processes.
   d. making it personal and honest.

_____ 9. For motivation to work effectively over a long period of time, it must
   a. be repeated over and over.
   b. come from a source within yourself.
   c. come from a charismatic, authoritative figure in your life.
   d. utilize some mental ability.

_____ 10. This author states that your subconscious will
   a. always arrange to do what is best for you.
   b. ignore all directions except those reinforced from childhood.
   c. reject information that is false.
   d. do exactly and literally what you tell it to do.

Allow 10 points per correct answer.   Your score _____ %
Number of words: 74,000   Your rate _____
Answer key is on page 272.
Record rate and comprehension score on Course Data Sheet 2 in the Good Comprehension columns.

WHAT TO SAY WHEN YOU TALK TO YOUR SELF
POSTVIEW QUESTIONS

_____ 1. An example of self-talk to stop smoking that would get optimum results is the following:
- a. "I will stop smoking."
- b. "I am a nonsmoker."
- c. "I know I should stop smoking."
- d. "I want to stop smoking."

_____ 2. A good example of self-talk to handle the immediate unpleasant situation of going to work would be:
- a. "I am going to enjoy work today."
- b. "Since I hate my job, I will find a different one."
- c. "I should not have to do things I don't like."
- d. "People like me."

_____ 3. From the information provided, you could conclude that this author believes that
- a. it is best to accept yourself as you are and not expect perfection.
- b. you can make some changes in yourself, but not significant ones.
- c. you can change yourself significantly only with professional help.
- d. you are capable of re-creating yourself as you want to be.

_____ 4. The self-talk techniques are essentially based on the assumption that your subconscious
- a. wants change.
- b. will change easily by just telling it what you want.
- c. only has powers that you consciously give it.
- d. believes and acts on whatever it is repeatedly told.

_____ 5. The author concludes that with positive self-talk techniques you
- a. take responsibility for your life.
- b. free yourself from responsibility.
- c. are unconcerned with who takes responsibility.
- d. give responsibility to a higher power.

Allow 20 points per correct answer.   _Your score_ _____ %
Number of words: 74,000   _Your rate_ _____
Answer key is on page 272.
Record rate and comprehension score on Course Data Sheet 2 in the Postview columns.

ADVANCED NONFICTION
GENERAL PREVIEW QUESTIONS

Title _____ Author _____

1. Which of the following does this book contain ("yes or "no," 2½ points each)?

_____ a. preface		_____ e. index
_____ b. introduction		_____ f. bibliography
_____ c. table of contents		_____ g. data on the author
_____ d. glossary		_____ h. maps, charts, graphs

2. Explain the meaning of the title. _____

_____

3. What type of book is it (history, scientific, "how to," biography, textbook, etc.)? _____

4. What is the subject of this book? _____

_____

5. What does the writer's purpose appear to be (check one)?

_____ a. to explain factual information on the subject

_____ b. to report what happened

_____ c. to give *his* or *her* ideas on the subject

_____ d. to persuade you to take some action

_____ e. to teach you how to perform some act

Correct by scanning to find the answers in the book.

Allow 20 points per correct answer. (Each part of question one is worth 2½ points.)

Figure out the number of words in the book. _____

Your score _____ %
Your rate _____

ADVANCED NONFICTION
GENERAL GOOD COMPREHENSION QUESTIONS

1. Write one sentence stating the most important thing the author says about the subject of this book (the main idea). _____

_____

2. Write two short sentences stating two other important things brought out in this book.

(1) _____

(2) _____

3. At the end, does the author state a conclusion? _____ What is it? _____

_____

4. What is the most interesting thing you learned from this book? _____

_____

5. What is the most useful thing you learned from this book? _____

_____

6. Write a short summary of the information this book covers. _____

_____

_____

_____

7. List three important details the author gives to support the main idea.

    (1) _____

    (2) _____

    (3) _____

8. Is this book written according to a logical, sequential time order (what happened first, second, third, etc.), or does it jump around in time? _____

9. Does the author refer to or quote authorities or sources in this field of knowledge, or is the information presented as all his or her ideas? _____

10. From the information given in this book, what conclusion can *you* come to?

    _____

Correct by finding the answers in the book.
Allow 10 points per correct answer.   *Your score* _____ %
Number of words _____   *Your rate* _____

ADVANCED NONFICTION
GENERAL POSTVIEW

Postview by skimming and scanning for the answers to the preview and good comprehension questions. Score the tests. Record title, rates, and comprehension scores on Course Data Sheet 2 in the appropriate columns.

14

Speed Studying Fiction

Materials:
- Readings:
  "The Outcasts of Poker Flat"
  Fahrenheit 451 or another adult novel of 50,000 words
- Drill book

Objectives:
- To learn how to apply the speed-study method to fiction
- To learn how to use the speed-study techniques for analyzing literature

DRILL PRACTICE

Repeat the drills at the beginning of Chapter 12, page 118, only this time go much faster. Take your drill rate for this week.

STUDYING FICTION

In studying fiction it is not enough just to know and remember the story—you must also understand the total meaning of the work. To arrive at the total meaning, the separate parts must first be understood. Then the sum total of the significances of these parts equals the theme. Thus, unlike nonfiction, the theme is recognized last.

Stories are made up of component parts, called the elements of fiction, and these include characters, plot, setting, point of view, symbols, style, and theme. Each part must be recognized and its significance or contribution to the meaning of the story must be figured out. Only then can the true meaning of the literary work be consciously known and put into words. A less extensive study will leave you with only vague impressions of meaning but not definite meaning. Studying each element of the story to arrive at the meaning of the whole work is called analysis.

In this chapter a method will be presented that will help you to use your speed-studying techniques to analyze stories. However, because of limitations of time, only a superficial explanation of each element of fiction is possible. Literature courses discuss them at length and in depth. Therefore, if you don't completely understand each element, don't be concerned. Your primary purpose at this time is to understand the reading method that you should use whenever you need to analyze a work.

GLOSSARY OF LITERARY TERMS: ELEMENTS OF FICTION

Use this glossary in conjunction with the Fiction Chart on page 154.

Characters The imaginary people of the story. Like real people, they are described, have individual qualities of character, reasons or motivations for what they do, and bear relationships to each other. However, authors can make their imaginary characters whatever they wish; they can give them any qualities. They choose everything about them to suit their purpose and to illustrate the main idea (theme) of the story.

In "To Build a Fire" the author, Jack London, chose to make the main character, Tom Vincent, young, "big-boned and big-muscled," healthy, strong, and fearless to illustrate the theme that when pitted against the freezing cold of the Klondike, not even a strong young man can escape its terror.

Conflict   The problem around which the story revolves. Conflict can be between two characters, two groups of people, a character and society, or within a character between two aspects of himself or herself. During the course of the story, it appears first that one side will win; then there is a shift and the other side appears to be winning. This back and forth movement creates suspense and continues until the end when the conflict reaches a climax and may or may not be completely resolved.

In *The Old Man and the Sea* the old man is in conflict with the forces of nature, represented by the sea, the fish, and his own old age. In his battles with these natural forces, many times he appears to be losing the battle, and many times it looks as though he might win. At the climax, he does beat the fish, only to lose it to another natural force, the sharks. In the end it appears that he is beaten, but we, as the readers, are left with the feeling that he is not finished yet, that he will go out and try again. The conflict is not totally resolved.

Point of View   The place from which the reader is allowed to view the story. It is recognized by asking, Who is telling the story? What is the relationship of that person to the story? If a character in the story is the narrator, the story is said to be in the first person, an "I" story. If the author is telling the story, the point of view may be omniscient, limited omniscient, or objective. When omniscient, authors allow themselves the power to tell you what is in the minds of the characters. When limited omniscient, authors restrict themselves to telling you what is in the mind of only one character, usually the main character. When objective, authors tell the story as observers and do not tell you the thoughts of any of the characters.

Authors choose the point of view they feel will reveal their story in a manner most suited to their purpose. Frequently it is significant to the total meaning and understanding of the story.

"The Adventure of the Speckled Band" is told in the first person by Dr. Watson, a lesser character in the story. Revealing the story in this way heightens the suspense. If Sherlock Holmes or the author were to tell the story, the reader would have access to the clues too soon.

In "The Tell-Tale Heart" the main character narrates the story, also in the first person. Since the story is what the character is thinking, the reader must know what is going on in his mind. Although the author could have chosen the omniscient point of view and thereby told us the character's thoughts, the story would have lost some of the effect of horror by placing another person, the author, between the events and the reader.

So you see, the author chooses the point of view for good artistic reasons.

Plot   A series of events that form the action of the story. The "action" need not be physical movement, it can be movement of ideas within a character. When you tell someone what the story was about, what happened, you are telling the plot. The conflict is part of the plot.

Setting   The time, place, and environment of the story, and also the culture and emotional atmosphere. The setting is especially important when it influences the actions of the characters.

In *The Old Man and the Sea* and "To Build a Fire," the settings are important because they supply the opposing forces of the conflict, which in these stories is nature.

Style   The way authors write. It includes their arrangement and choice of words, the rhythm of their language, how they achieve emphasis, and the arrangement of their ideas—in fact, everything that goes into the individuality of their writing.

Edgar Allen Poe's style includes big words, long and involved sentences, and the mood of terror.

Symbol   Something that stands for something else. Symbols suggest complex ideas and feelings. It is a device used in literature to allow the author to suggest several meanings with a single object or image. These suggested meanings add to the reader's experience of the story in a way that putting the idea or feelings into words could not do.

The fish in *The Old Man and the Sea* is a symbol for many ideas: the forces of nature, the vast unknown of the sea, the youth and strength that the old man no longer possesses, the challenges and struggles of life (the sea representing life), the fight each creature puts up to survive, the respect each creature deserves—to name only some of the symbolic meanings.

The dog, Buck, in *The Call of the Wild* symbolizes all creatures, including man.

All of these symbols contribute to the comments the authors are making about life—their themes, what they are illustrating by their stories.

Theme   Sometimes called *thesis*, this is the main idea that the author is trying to get across to the reader. It may be put into words somewhere in the story, or it may be implied. It is always a general statement about life that is being illustrated by the narration of the specific situation and specific characters in the story. All the elements of the story—in fact, everything in the story—must back up or substantiate the theme. If they don't, you haven't the real theme of the story.

In *The Call of the Wild* Jack London has illustrated his theme that deep within all creatures, man and animals, is the unlearned, instinctual pull back to our prehistoric beginnings that will surface under certain circumstances and wipe out all the learned, "civilized" behavior.

The dog, Buck, is given human characteristics and is meant to represent (symbolize) humans as well as animals. Although Buck was born into and brought up in a gentle, civilized environment, when his survival is at stake he gradually becomes more and more fierce and wild until he actually joins a wolf pack, his uncivilized brothers; he instinctually reverts to a prehistoric wild state.

METHOD FOR READING FICTION

In reading stories for in-depth understanding, you follow the basic four-step speed study method. The fiction chart indicates what kind of information you should try to obtain in each step. The short glossary of terms will help you understand more specifically to what that information refers.

Sometimes four speed-study steps are not enough. When the story is complex or whenever you must do a complete analysis, more steps may be needed. In such cases it is advisable to do additional postview skimmings, scannings, or readings in which you specifically pay attention to only

Fiction Chart

Element	Preview	Good Comprehension	Postview (May need to do one for each element)
PLOT (Action of story)	Outline—what happens	Get details Identify Conflict	Know significance of conflict or problem
CHARACTERS	Introduction: Who? Description Relationships	Qualities Motivations	Know significance of characters, actions, and relationships
SETTING	Facts: Where When Culture Environment	Details that influence story (if applies)	
POINT OF VIEW	Look for it: Internal (1st or 3rd) External (Omniscient or Objec- tive)	Figure out	Is it significant?
THEME		Collect facts that are building up to it	Figure it out—must be logical assumption. Incidents and characters must support it.
SYMBOLS		Identify important ones	Figure out significance
STYLE	Biography of author (if applies)	Identify	Critical analysis and comparison

one element at a time and gather data on that element so that you can come to a conclusion about its significance. For instance, if you were to analyze the symbols in a story, after the good comprehension reading you should write down a list of possible symbols you saw in the story. Then, you should postview-skim the story, just looking for those symbols, others you may have missed, and clues to their meanings and significances. Mark them as you reread. Use any mark you wish, but one that is easily identifiable is the first letter of the symbol. (Example: If a horse is used as a symbol, write an *H* in the margin every time you see it or any information about it.) Add to your list any new symbols. Write down their meanings. You might even have to scan the marked parts again to fill in information on meanings and significances.

If you don't understand the point of view, theme, or any element well enough to analyze the story, you should do a separate postview-skim for information on each of these elements. You might need to skim once for point of view, once for theme, and so on. Difficult stories might need to be reread many times before a complete analysis can be done. However, many readings are required for this type of thoroughness even when you are reading slowly. At least you can do each reading rapidly.

SPEED-STUDY PRACTICE: THE SHORT STORY

Use the four-step speed-study method for speed studying the story, "The Outcasts of Poker Flat" on page 156. Refer to the "Speed-Study Sequence Outline" on page 137 to recall the order of the steps in the process. Refer to the Fiction Chart to know what information you should be looking for in each of the four steps.

Preview-skim the entire story, looking for the outline of the plot and getting general information on some of the elements of fiction such as the characters, setting, and point of view. Answer the preview questions.

Do a good comprehension reading, looking for details on the elements of fiction; refer to the chart for specifics. Find your level of best comprehension, use flexibility, mark the important details. Answer the good comprehension questions.

Do a complete postview, skimming and slowing on marked parts and on parts that will contribute to your knowledge of why the author chose to use each of the elements in the manner that he or she did (significances). Answer the postview questions. If you cannot answer any postview question,

postview again to find the answer. It is important that you understand all of the parts (elements) of the story so that you can become aware of the author's theme or message by the time you are finished.

Self-Evaluation

Constantly evaluate your use of the speed-study method. Is the preview the fastest? Is the good comprehension slower than the preview? Is the postview somewhere between the two rates? If not, you need to modify the way you are using the method to get the best results.

Speed-Study Practice: The Novel

For practice in speed studying longer fiction use the novel *Fahrenheit 451* or another novel of about 50,000 words.

Apply the four-step speed-study method as modified slightly in the following instructions. The modification is in the manner of postviewing, so pay special attention to those instructions. Refer to information given earlier in this chapter and in the chart for fiction to be sure of what kind of data you look for in each of the four steps.

You should allow two reading sessions or two hours to complete this practice reading. In the first session you should complete the survey and the preview-skim reading of the entire book and answer the preview questions.

In longer works such as a novel, you will find it more difficult to keep up a skimming pace throughout the preview. Your tendency will be to slow down to read the story. Keep in mind that you are only preparing for the reading, and keep the pace fast!

In the second session do the good comprehension reading and the postview(s). For the good comprehension reading, remember to find your level of best comprehension, use flexibility, and mark the text. Answer the questions for this reading.

Now we come to the change in the basic speed-study method—the postview. Ordinarily, for literature you would postview at least once for each element of fiction, looking for information to help you understand the significance of that element as used in this particular work. But since you are probably not a literature student, you will not be expected to do this type of analysis. Instead, for this practice you will read the postview questions first and try to answer them; they deal with significance that you should try to figure out from the story. If you cannot answer a question or are unsure of the answer, postview to find it in one of the following ways: (1) start at the beginning of the story and skim until you feel you have enough information to answer the question; or (2) use the chapter titles to pick out the sections most likely to contain the answer you seek, and skim these sections only; or (3) try to recall where in the book you saw information to answer the question (beginning, middle, end) and skim that part only. You may have to postview several times, once for each question. You cannot time this type of a postview because you will not be going over the entire book in any one postview reading. Therefore, you cannot figure out your postview rate, but you should have a very high postview comprehension score because you will find the answers!

At the end of this chapter you will find three sets of questions for *Fahrenheit 451* and three sets for a general novel. Use the general set of questions if you are reading a novel other than *Fahrenheit 451*. The procedure and method are the same in either case.

Evaluate your rates. Was the preview rate considerably higher than your reading rate this time? For proper studying, it is essential to preview so that a total concept of the work is perceived by answering test questions, formulating questions of your own, or just getting a sense of what the book is about. Thus in the actual reading the details will fit more readily into the organized whole.

SUMMARY

To understand the meaning of a literary work, you must recognize the component parts and understand their significance to the story. In complex stories a separate postview for each element may be needed for recognition and understanding of its significance.

THE OUTCASTS OF POKER FLAT

Bret Harte

As Mr. John Oakhurst, gambler, stepped into the main street of Poker Flat on the morning of the twenty-third of November, 1850, he was conscious of a change in its moral atmosphere since the preceding night. Two or three men, conversing earnestly together, ceased as he approached, and exchanged significant glances. There was a Sabbath lull in the air, which, in a settlement unused to Sabbath influences, looked ominous.

Mr. Oakhurst's calm, handsome face betrayed small concern in these indications. Whether he was conscious of any predisposing cause, was another question. "I reckon they're after somebody," he reflected; "likely it's me." He returned to his pocket the handkerchief with which he had been whipping away the red dust of Poker Flat from his neat boots, and quietly discharged his mind of any further conjecture.

In point of fact, Poker Flat was "after somebody." It had lately suffered the loss of several thousand dollars, two valuable horses, and a prominent citizen. It was experiencing a spasm of virtuous reaction, quite as lawless and ungovernable as any of the acts that had provoked it. A secret commmittee had determined to rid the town of all improper persons. This was done permanently in regard of two men who were then hanging from the boughs of a sycamore in the gulch, and temporarily in the banishment of certain other objectionable characters. I regret to say that some of these were ladies. It is but due to the sex, however, to state that their impropriety was professional, and it was only in such easily established standards of evil that Poker Flat ventured to sit in judgment.

Mr. Oakhurst was right in supposing that he was included in this category. A few of the committee had urged hanging him as a possible example, and a sure method of reimbursing themselves from his pockets of the sums he had won from them. "It's agin justice," said Jim Wheeler, "to let this yer young man from Roaring Camp—an entire stranger—carry away our money." But a crude sentiment of equity residing in the breasts of those who had been fortunate enough to win from Mr. Oakhurst overruled this narrower local prejudice.

Mr. Oakhurst received his sentence with philosophic calmness, none the less cooly that he was aware of the hesitation of his judges. He was too much of a gambler not to accept Fate. With him life was at best an uncertain game, and he recognized the usual percentage in favor of the dealer.

A body of armed men accompanied the deported wickedness of Poker Flat to the outskirts of the settlement. Besides Mr. Oakhurst, who was known to be a coolly desperate man, and for whose intimidation the armed escort was intended, the expatriated party consisted of a young woman familiarly known as "The Duchess"; another, who had won the title of "Mother Shipton"; and "Uncle Billy," a suspected sluice-robber and confirmed drunkard. The cavalcade provoked no comments from the spectators, nor was any word uttered by the escort. Only, when the gulch which marked the uttermost limit of Poker Flat was reached, the leader spoke briefly and to the point. The exiles were forbidden to return at the peril of their lives.

As the escort disappeared, their pent-up feelings found vent in a few hysterical tears from the Duchess, some bad language from Mother Shipton, and a Parthian volley of expletives from Uncle Billy. The philosophic Oakhurst alone remained silent. He listened calmly to Mother Shipton's desire to cut somebody's heart out, to the repeated statements of the Duchess that she would die in the road, and to the alarming oaths that seemed to be bumped out of Uncle Billy as he rode forward. With the easy good-humor characteristic of his class, he insisted upon exchanging his own riding-horse, "Five Spot," for the sorry mule which the Duchess rode. But even this act did not draw the party into any closer sympathy. The young woman readjusted her somewhat draggled plumes with a feeble, faded coquetry; Mother Shipton eyed the possessor of "Five Spot" with malevolence, and Uncle Billy included the whole party in one sweeping anathema.

The road to Sandy Bar—a camp that, not having as yet experienced the regenerating influences of Poker Flat, consequently seemed to offer some invitation to the emigrants—lay over a steep mountain range. It was distant a day's severe travel. In that advanced season, the party soon passed out of the moist, temperate regions of the foot-hills into the dry, cold, bracing air of the Sierras. The trail was narrow and difficult. At noon the Duchess, rolling out of her saddle upon the ground, declared her intention of going no farther, and the party halted.

The spot was singularly wild and impressive. A wooded amphitheatre surrounded on three sides by precipitous cliffs of naked granite, sloped gently toward the crest of another precipice that overlooked the valley. It was, undoubtedly, the most suitable spot for a camp, had camping been advisable. But Mr. Oakhurst knew that scarcely half the journey to Sandy Bar was accomplished, and the party were not equipped or provisioned for delay. This fact he pointed out to his companions curtly, with a philosophic commentary on the folly of "throwing up their hand before the game was played out." But they were furnished with liquor, which in this emergency stood them in place of food, fuel, rest, and prescience. In spite of his remonstrances, it was not long before they were more or less under its influence. Uncle Billy passed rapidly from a belicose state into one of stupor, the Duchess became maudlin, and Mother Shipton snored. Mr. Oakhurst alone remained erect, leaning against a rock, calmly surveying them.

Mr. Oakhurst did not drink. It interfered with a profession which required coolness, impassiveness, and presence of mind, and, in his own language, he "couldn't afford it." As he gazed at his recumbent fellow-exiles, the loneliness begotten of his pariah-trade, his habits of life, his very vices, for the first time seriously oppressed him. He bestirred himself in dusting his black clothes, washing his hands and face, and other acts characteristic of his studiously neat habits, and for a moment forgot his annoyance. The thought of deserting his weaker and more pitiable companions never perhaps occurred to him. Yet he could not help feeling the want of that excitement which, singularly enough, was most conducive to that calm equanimity for which he was notorious.

He looked at the gloomy walls that rose a thousand feet sheer above the circling pines around him; at the sky, ominously clouded; at the valley below, already deepening into shadow. And, doing so, suddenly he heard his own name called.

A horseman slowly ascended the trail. In the fresh, open face of the new-comer Mr. Oakhurst recognized Tom Simson, otherwise known as "The Innocent" of Sandy Bar. He had met him some months before over a "little game," and had, with perfect equanimity, won the entire fortune—amounting to some forty dollars—of that guileless youth. After the game was finished, Mr. Oakhurst drew the youthful speculator behind the door and thus addressed him: "Tommy, you're a good little man, but you can't gamble worth a cent. Don't try it over again." He then handed him his money back, pushed him gently from the room, and so made a devoted slave of Tom Simson.

There was a remembrance of this in his boyish and enthusiastic greeting of Mr. Oakhurst. He had started, he said, to go to Poker Flat to seek his fortune. "Alone?" No, not exactly alone; in fact (a giggle), he had run away with Piney Woods. Didn't Mr. Oakhurst remember Piney? She that used to wait on the table at the Temperance House? They had been engaged a long time, but old Jake Woods had objected, and so they had run away, and were going to Poker Flat to be married, and here they were. And they were tired out, and how lucky it was they had found a place to camp and company. All this the Innocent delivered rapidly, while Piney, a stout, comely damsel of fifteen, emerged from behind the pinetree, where she had been blushing unseen, and rode to the side of her lover.

Mr. Oakhurst seldom troubled himself with sentiment, still less with propriety; but he had a vague idea that the situation was not fortunate. He retained, however, his presence of mind sufficiently to kick Uncle Billy, who was about to say something, and Uncle Billy was sober enough to recognize in Mr. Oakhurst's kick a superior power that would not bear trifling. He then endeavored to dissuade Tom Simson from delaying further, but in vain. He even pointed out the fact that there was no provision, no means of making a camp. But, unluckily, the Innocent met this objection by assuring the party that he was provided with an extra mule loaded with provisions and by the discovery of a rude attempt at a loghouse near the trail. "Piney can stay with Mrs. Oakhurst," said the Innocent, pointing to the Duchess, "and I can shift for myself."

Nothing but Mr. Oakhurst's admonishing foot saved Uncle Billy from bursting into a roar of laughter. As it was, he felt compelled to retire up the cañon until he could recover his gravity. There he confided the joke to the tall pine-trees, with many slaps of his leg, contortions of his face, and the usual profanity. But when he returned to the party, he found them seated by a fire—for the air had grown strangely chill and the sky overcast—in apparently amicable conversation. Piney was actually talking in an impulsive, girlish fashion to the Duchess, who was listening with an interest and animation she had not shown for many days. The Innocent was holding forth, apparently with equal effect, to Mr. Oakhurst and Mother Shipton, who was actually relaxing into amiability. "Is this yer a d—d picnic?" said Uncle

Billy, with inward scorn, as he surveyed the sylvan group, the glancing firelight, and the tethered animals in the foreground. Suddenly an idea mingled with the alcoholic fumes that disturbed his brain. It was apparently of a jocular nature, for he felt impelled to slap his leg again and cram his fist into his mouth.

As the shadows crept slowly up the mountain, a slight breeze rocked the tops of the pine-trees, and moaned through their long and gloomy aisles. The ruined cabin, patched and covered with pine-boughs, was set apart for the ladies. As the lovers parted, they unaffectedly exchanged a kiss, so honest and sincere that it might have been heard above the swaying pines. The frail Duchess and the malevolent Mother Shipton were probably too stunned to remark upon this last evidence of simplicity, and so turned without a word to the hut. The fire was replenished, the men lay down before the door, and in a few minutes were asleep.

Mr. Oakhurst was a light sleeper. Toward morning he awoke benumbed and cold. As he stirred the dying fire, the wind, which was now blowing strongly, brought to his cheek that which caused the blood to leave it,— snow!

He started to his feet with the intention of awakening the sleepers, for there was no time to lose. But turning to where Uncle Billy had been lying, he found him gone. A suspicion leaped to his brain and a curse to his lips. He ran to the spot where the mules had been tethered; they were no longer there. The tracks were already rapidly disappearing in the snow.

The momentary excitement brought Mr. Oakhurst back to the fire with his usual calm. He did not waken the sleepers. The Innocent slumbered peacefully, with a smile on his good-humored, freckled face; the virgin Piney slept beside her frailer sisters as sweetly as though attended by celestial guardians, and Mr. Oakhurst, drawing his blanket over his shoulders, stroked his mustaches and waited for the dawn. It came slowly in a whirling mist of snow-flakes, that dazzled and confused the eye. What could be seen of the landscape appeared magically changed. He looked over the valley, and summed up the present and future in two words,—"snowed in!"

A careful inventory of the provisions, which, fortunately for the party, had been stored within the hut, and so escaped the felonious fingers of Uncle Billy, disclosed the fact that with care and prudence they might last ten days longer. "That is," said Mr. Oakhurst, *sotto voce* to the Innocent, "if you're willing to board us. If you ain't—and perhaps you'd better not—you can wait till Uncle Billy gets back with provisions." For some occult reason, Mr. Oakhurst could not bring himself to disclose Uncle Billy's rascality, and so offered the hypothesis that he had wandered from the camp and had accidentally stampeded the animals. He dropped a warning to the Duchess and Mother Shipton, who of course knew the facts of their associate's defection. "They'll find out the truth about us *all* when they find out anything," he added, significantly, "and there's no good frightening them now."

Tom Simson not only put all his worldly store at the disposal of Mr. Oakhurst, but seemed to enjoy the prospect of their enforced seclusion. "We'll have a good camp for a week, and then the snow'll melt, and we'll all go back together." The cheerful gayety of the young

man, and Mr. Oakhurst's calm infected the others. The Innocent, with the aid of pineboughs, extemporized a thatch for the roofless cabin, and the Duchess directed Piney in the rearrangement of the interior with a taste and tact that opened the blue eyes of that provincial maiden to their fullest extent. "I reckon now you're used to fine things at Poker Flat," said Piney. The Duchess turned away sharply to conceal something that reddened her cheeks through its professional tint, and Mother Shipton requested Piney not to "chatter." But when Mr. Oakhurst returned from a weary search for the trail, he heard the sound of happy laughter echoed from the rocks. He stopped in some alarm, and his thoughts first naturally reverted to the whiskey, which he had prudently *cachéd*. "And yet it don't somehow sound like whiskey," said the gambler. It was not until he caught sight of the blazing fire through the still-blinding storm and the group around it that he settled to the conviction that it was "square fun."

Whether Mr. Oakhurst had *cachéd* his cards with the whiskey as something debarred the free access of the community, I cannot say. It was certain that, in Mother Shipton's words, he "didn't say cards once" during that evening. Haply the time was beguiled by an accordion, produced somewhat ostentatiously by Tom Simson from his pack. Notwithstanding some difficulties attending the manipulation of this instrument, Piney Woods managed to pluck several reluctant melodies from its keys, to an accompaniment by the Innocent on a pair of bone castinets. But the crowning festivity of the evening was reached in a rude camp-meeting hymn, which the lovers, joining hands, sang with great earnestness and vociferation. I fear that a certain defiant tone and Covenanter's swing to its chorus, rather than any devotional quality, caused it speedily to infect the others, who at last joined in the refrain:—

> "I'm proud to live in the service of the Lord,
> And I'm bound to die in His army."

The pines rocked, the storm eddied and whirled above the miserable group, and the flames of their altar leaped heavenward, as if in token of the vow.

At midnight the storm abated, the rolling clouds parted, and the stars glittered keenly above the sleeping camp. Mr. Oakhurst, whose professional habits had enabled him to live on the smallest possible amount of sleep, in dividing the watch with Tom Simson, somehow managed to take upon himself the greater part of that duty. He excused himself to the Innocent, by saying that he had "often been a week without sleep." "Doing what?" asked Tom. "Poker!" replied Oakhurst, sententiously; "when a man gets a streak of luck,—nigger-luck,—he don't get tired. The luck gives in first. Luck," continued the gambler, reflectively, "is a mighty queer thing. All you know about it for certain is that it's bound to change. And it's finding out when it's going to change that makes you. We've had a streak of bad luck since we left Poker Flat,—you come along, and slap you get into it, too. If you can hold your cards right along you're all right. For," added the gambler, with cheerful irrelevance,—

> " 'I'm proud to live in the service of the Lord,
> And I'm bound to die in His army.' "

The third day came, and the sun, looking through the white-curtained valley, saw the outcasts divide their slowly decreasing store of provisions for the morning meal. It was one of the peculiarities of that mountain climate that its rays diffused a kindly warmth over the wintry landscape, as if in regretful commiseration of the past. But it revealed drift on drift of snow piled high around the hut,—a hopeless, uncharted, trackless sea of white lying below the rocky shores to which the castaways still clung. Through the marvellously clear air the smoke of the pastoral village of Poker Flat rose miles away. Mother Shipton saw it, and from a remote pinnacle of her rocky fastness, hurled in that direction a final malediction. It was her last vituperative attempt, and perhaps for that reason was invested with a certain degree of sublimity. It did her good, she privately informed the Duchess. "Just you go out there and cuss, and see." She then set herself to the task of amusing "the child," as she and the Duchess were pleased to call Piney. Piney was no chicken, but it was a soothing and original theory of the pair thus to account for the fact that she didn't swear and wasn't improper.

When night crept up again through the gorges, the reedy notes of the accordion rose and fell in fitful spasms and long-drawn gasps by the flickering camp-fire. But music failed to fill entirely the aching void left by insufficient food, and a new diversion was proposed by Piney,—story-telling. Neither Mr. Oakhurst nor his female companions caring to relate their personal experiences, this plan would have failed, too, but for the Innocent. Some months before he had chanced upon a stray copy of Mr. Pope's ingenious translation of the Iliad. He now proposed to narrate the principal incidents of that poem—having thoroughly mastered the argument and fairly forgotten the words—in the current vernacular of Sandy Bar. And so for the rest of that night the Homeric demigods again walked the earth. Trojan bully and wily Greek wrestled in the winds, and the great pines in the cañon seemed to bow to the wrath of the son of Peleus. Mr. Oakhurst listened with quiet satisfaction. Most especially was he interested in the fate of "Ashheels," as the Innocent persisted in denominating the "swift-footed Achilles."

So with small food and much of Homer and the accordion, a week passed over the heads of the outcasts. The sun again forsook them, and again from leaden skies the snow-flakes were sifted over the land. Day by day closer around them drew the snowy circle, until at last they looked from their prison over drifted walls of dazzling white, that towered twenty feet above their heads. It became more and more difficult to replenish their fires, even from the fallen trees beside them, now half hidden in the drifts. And yet no one complained. The lovers turned from the dreary prospect and looked into each other's eyes, and were happy. Mr. Oakhurst settled himself coolly to the losing game before him. The Duchess, more cheerful than she had been, assumed the care of Piney. Only Mother Shipton—once the strongest of the party—seemed to sicken and fade. At midnight on the tenth day she called Oakhurst to her side. "I'm going," she said, in a voice of querulous weakness, "but don't say anything about it. Don't waken the kids. Take the bundle from under my head and open it." Mr. Oakhurst did so. It contained Mother Shipton's rations for the last week, untouched. "Give 'em to the child," she said, pointing to the sleeping Piney. "You've starved yourself," said the gambler. "That's what they call it," said the woman, querulously, as she lay down again, and, turning her face to the wall, passed quietly away.

The accordion and the bones were put aside that day, and Homer was forgotten. When the body of Mother Shipton had been committed to the snow, Mr. Oakhurst took the Innocent aside, and showed him a pair of snow-shoes, which he had fashioned from the old pack-saddle. "There's one chance in a hundred to save her yet," he said, pointing to Piney; "but it's there," he added, pointing toward Poker Flat. "If you can reach there in two days she's safe." "And you?" asked Tom Simson. "I'll stay here," was the curt reply.

The lovers parted with a long embrace. "You are not going, too?" said the Duchess, as she saw Mr. Oakhurst apparently waiting to accompany him. "As far as the cañon," he replied. He turned suddenly, and kissed the Duchess, leaving her pallid face aflame, and her trembling limbs rigid with amazement.

Night came, but not Mr. Oakhurst. It brought the storm again and the whirling snow. Then the Duchess, feeding the fire, found that some one had quietly piled beside the hut enough fuel to last a few days longer. The tears rose to her eyes, but she hid them from Piney.

The women slept but little. In the morning, looking into each other's faces, they read their fate. Neither spoke; but Piney, accepting the position of the stronger, drew near and placed her arm around the Duchess's waist. They kept this attitude for the rest of the day. That night the storm reached its greatest fury, and, rending asunder the protecting pines, invaded the very hut.

Toward morning they found themselves unable to feed the fire, which gradually died away. As the embers slowly blackened, the Duchess crept closer to Piney, and broke the silence of many hours: "Piney, can you pray?" "No, dear," said Piney, simply. The Duchess, without knowing exactly why, felt relieved, and, putting her head upon Piney's shoulder, spoke no more. And so reclining, the younger and purer pillowing the head of her soiled sister upon her virgin breast, they fell asleep.

The wind lulled as if it feared to waken them. Feathery drifts of snow, shaken from the long pine-boughs, flew like white-winged birds, and settled about them as they slept. The moon through the rifted clouds looked down upon what had been the camp. But all human stain, all trace of earthly travail, was hidden beneath the spotless mantle mercifully flung from above.

They slept all that day and the next, nor did they waken when voices and footsteps broke the silence of the camp. And when pitying fingers brushed the snow from their wan faces, you could scarcely have told from the equal peace that dwelt upon them, which was she that had sinned. Even the law of Poker Flat recognized this, and turned away, leaving them still locked in each other's arms.

But at the head of the gulch, on one of the largest pine-trees, they found the deuce of clubs pinned to the bark with a bowie-knife. It bore the following, written in pencil, in a firm hand:—

†
BENEATH THIS TREE
LIES THE BODY
OF
JOHN OAKHURST,
WHO STRUCK A STREAK OF BAD LUCK
ON THE 23RD OF NOVEMBER, 1850,
AND
HANDED IN HIS CHECKS
ON THE 7TH DECEMBER, 1850.
†

And pulseless and cold, with a Derringer by his side and a bullet in his heart, though still calm as in life, beneath the snow lay he who was at once the strongest and yet the weakest of the outcasts of Poker Flat.

PREVIEW QUESTIONS

_____ 1. Who is *not* a character in this story?
   a. Tom Simson.
   b. Piney Woods.
   c. John Oakhurst.
   d. Billy Budd.
   e. Mother Shipton.

_____ 2. The story takes place in the year
   a. 1950.
   b. 1850.
   c. 1975.
   d. 1792.

_____ 3. Most of the story takes place in
   a. Poker Flat.
   b. Roaring Camp.
   c. the Sierra Mountains.
   d. Sandy Bar.

_____ 4. The story covers a period of about
   a. one year.
   b. two days.
   c. two weeks.
   d. one day.

_____ 5. An important aspect of the setting was the
   a. snow.
   b. rain.
   c. cabin.
   d. excessive heat.

Allow 20 points per correct answer.   *Your score* _____ %
Number of words: 4100   *Your rate* _____
Answer key is on page 272.
Record rate and comprehension score on Course Data Sheet in Preview columns.

GOOD COMPREHENSION QUESTIONS

_____ 1. John Oakhurst was not hanged because
   a. he apologized to the important townspeople.
   b. those who had won money from him overruled this decision.
   c. he escaped from prison.
   d. the mayor's daughter pleaded for lenience for him.

_____ 2. Tom Simson was devoted to Oakhurst because
  a. Oakhurst had not kept the money he had won from Simson.
  b. Simson was Oakhurst's nephew.
  c. Oakhurst was his father.
  d. Simson wanted to be a gambler just like Oakhurst.

_____ 3. Tom Simson is often referred to as the
  a. stupid boy.
  b. handsome young man.
  c. unlucky kid.
  d. innocent.

_____ 4. Piney and Simson were
  a. already secretly married.
  b. on their way to getting married.
  c. planning to live together unmarried.
  d. brother and sister.

_____ 5. The group could not leave the cabin because
  a. Uncle Billy had stolen the mules.
  b. Piney became very ill.
  c. a posse had been sent out to track them down.
  d. Oakhurst would not let them.

_____ 6. Mother Shipton died from
  a. a fall from a cliff.
  b. pneumonia.
  c. self-inflicted starvation.
  d. old age.

_____ 7. Simson
  a. died.
  b. left to find help.
  c. was killed by Uncle Billy.
  d. ran off to save himself.

_____ 8. Oakhurst
  a. ran off to save himself.
  b. left to find help.
  c. was killed by a bear.
  d. committed suicide.

_____ 9. Piney and the Duchess
  a. froze to death.
  b. were rescued by villagers.
  c. found their way back to Poker Flat.
  d. lived on at the cabin alone.

_____ 10. In the end,
  a. no one ever discovered what happened to the outcasts.
  b. Oakhurst returned to Poker Flat and told their story.
  c. Poker Flat residents found the outcasts.
  d. Piney's father, Jake Woods, found them.

Allow 10 points per correct answer.   Your score _____ %
Number of words: 4100   Your rate _____
Answer key is on page 272.
Record rate and comprehension score on Course Data Sheet in Good Comprehension columns.

POSTVIEW QUESTIONS

_____ 1. From what Oakhurst said and did and from what the author said about him, we know that Oakhurst
   a. hated and was disappointed with life.
   b. regarded life as an uncertain game.
   c. accepted whatever life had to offer.
   d. had a plan to get rich and settle down.

_____ 2. We can say that one of the author's purposes for introducing Piney and Simson to the group of outcasts probably was to show how
   a. the sins of the outcasts' crimes appeared worse next to the purity of the innocent.
   b. the innocent are influenced by the wicked.
   c. the wicked outcasts responded to friendly and accepting treatment.
   d. wickedness begins with youth.

_____ 3. From the way Poker Flat was described, we can conclude that it was
   a. as bad as the outcasts themselves.
   b. a virtuous place wanting to stay that way.
   c. an evil place wanting to reform.
   d. no better or worse than Sandy Bar.

_____ 4. Oakhurst's weakness mentioned at the end probably referred to his
   a. manner of treating the women courteously.
   b. overindulgence in alcohol.
   c. frail, weak body.
   d. inability to accept losing the game.

_____ 5. The ending underlined the idea that the outcasts' trip over the mountain to Sandy Bar was probably a symbolic trip
   a. returning to a previous state of innocence.
   b. to hell.
   c. to heaven.
   d. to an imaginary magical place.

Allow 20 points per correct answer.   _Your score_ _____ %
Number of words: 4100   _Your rate_ _____
Answer key is on page 272.
Record rate and comprehension score on Course Data Sheet in Postview columns.

FAHRENHEIT 451
PREVIEW QUESTIONS

_____ 1. _Fahrenheit 451_ is considered to be
   a. a romantic novel.
   b. a historical novel.
   c. a science fiction classic.
   d. a nonfiction mystery.

_____ 2. Clarisse was
   a. Montag's wife.
   b. a neighbor.
   c. Beatty's wife.
   d. Mrs. Montag's friend.

_____ 3. The mechanical Hound
    a. hunted people through smell.
    b. was a robot servant.
    c. started fires.
    d. supplied computerized information.

_____ 4. Firemen usually did one of the following:
    a. put out fires.
    b. started fires.
    c. fireproofed homes.
    d. instructed people on how to start fires.

_____ 5. Beatty was a
    a. former English professor.
    b. leader of the Underground.
    c. doctor.
    d. fire chief.

_____ 6. In this society, the primary goal of most people was to
    a. be happy.
    b. be educated.
    c. end wars.
    d. be informed.

_____ 7. Faber was a
    a. former English professor.
    b. leader of the Underground.
    c. doctor.
    d. fire chief.

_____ 8. Mildred was
    a. Montag's wife.
    b. a neighbor.
    c. Montag's girlfriend.
    d. Beatty's wife.

_____ 9. In this society, the taking of drugs was
    a. forbidden.
    b. neither encouraged nor forbidden.
    c. rarely done.
    d. encouraged as a way of life.

_____ 10. In Montag's society, it was not considered acceptable to
    a. talk about modern inventions.
    b. discuss personal problems.
    c. describe the Mechanical Hound.
    d. talk about the past.

Allow 10 points per correct answer.   *Your score* _____ %
Number of words: 47,950   *Your rate* _____
Answer key is on page 272.
Record rate and comprehension score on Course Data Sheet in Preview columns.

FAHRENHEIT 451
GOOD COMPREHENSION QUESTIONS

_____ 1. The effect that Clarisse had upon Montag was to make him
  a. suspect that she had hidden books.
  b. realize how happy his life was.
  c. aware that he was really unhappy.
  d. afraid of people who were different.

_____ 2. The incident that first caused Montag to reconsider his work as a fireman was when
  a. he watched a woman burn with her books.
  b. Mildred left him.
  c. Mildred's friend cried at his poetry reading.
  d. Mildred took an overdose of sleeping pills.

_____ 3. Montag first visited Faber because he wanted Faber to
  a. turn in friends with books.
  b. tell him what happened to Clarisse.
  c. teach him what was in books and how to understand them.
  d. confess that he was hiding books.

_____ 4. One fire that Montag started was in
  a. Clarisse's house.
  b. his own house.
  c. Beatty's house.
  d. a school.

_____ 5. Montag's plan to save humanity was to
  a. start a revolution.
  b. take over television stations.
  c. get a new president elected.
  d. "plant" books in firemen's houses.

_____ 6. When Montag escaped, he went to
  a. another country.
  b. a group of hobos with college degrees.
  c. Mildred's family's house.
  d. an underground hiding place.

_____ 7. The police
  a. finally found Montag.
  b. knowingly killed another man and said he was Montag.
  c. gave up the search.
  d. were still searching at the end.

_____ 8. In the end
  a. the city was destroyed by an atomic bomb.
  b. the people realized what was happening to them and they rebelled.
  c. Beatty, Faber, and Montag began to educate the people.
  d. the enemy in the war surrendered.

_____ 9. The ideal home in the city had
  a. wall-to-wall television.
  b. open ceilings.
  c. garden views.
  d. radios in every room.

_____ 10. Captain Beatty believed all but one of the following:
   a. Everyone is made equal.
   b. Everyone is born equal and free.
   c. Everyone must be alike.
   d. Each man must be the image of every other man so all may be happy.

_____ 11. Clarisse was afraid of children her own age because they
   a. killed each other.
   b. were always playing in the park and would not let her play with them.
   c. were better students than she in school.
   d. were jealous of her car and her ability to drive fast.

_____ 12. One of the problems that greatly bothered Montag was that
   a. his job as a fireman was physically difficult.
   b. he couldn't afford a fourth television wall.
   c. he didn't know how to read.
   d. people didn't talk anymore.

_____ 13. The symbolic number 451 on the fireman's helmet stood for the temperature
   a. on the sun.
   b. of a bonfire.
   c. at which man goes on fire.
   d. at which paper burns.

_____ 14. To get rid of frustrations, people often would
   a. get into fights.
   b. drive fast and kill animals and people.
   c. take long walks.
   d. go to a football game.

_____ 15. The purpose of four-walled television, attention getters on buses, and community loudspeakers was to keep people from learning that
   a. the world was at war.
   b. life in other parts of the world was peaceful.
   c. most of the world was democratic.
   d. other people were free.

_____ 16. In this society, people had all of the following *except*
   a. wall incinerators.
   b. fireproof houses.
   c. psychiatrists.
   d. porches.

_____ 17. Faber described three things missing from Montag's life that kept him from being happy. Which of the following is *not* one of these things?
   a. The quality or texture of information recorded in books.
   b. Leisure to digest it.
   c. A selected course of study.
   d. The right to carry out actions based on what we learn from the interaction of the other two.

_____ 18. One *major* conflict in this story was that of Montag against the
   a. society.
   b. war.
   c. use of drugs.
   d. firemen.

_____ 19. Another *major* conflict was that of
   a. Montag against Beatty.
   b. Montag as a member of this society and his inner feelings of wanting something more.
   c. Montag against the Hound.
   d. Montag against Mildred.

_____ 20. The real reason for the public creation of book burning was because
   a. of the laws.
   b. people had stopped reading.
   c. it created jobs.
   d. of the crowds that enjoyed each burning.

Allow 5 points per correct answer.   Your score _____ %
Number of words: 47,950   Your rate _____
Answer key is on page 272.
Record rate and comprehension score on Course Data Sheet in Good Comprehension columns.

FAHRENHEIT 451
POSTVIEW QUESTIONS

_____ 1. The significance of the conflict between Montag and his society was to show that
   a. society is always wrong.
   b. society will always contain some misfits.
   c. laws cannot change people's basic desire to have a meaningful life.
   d. happiness can never be achieved no matter how hard society may try.

_____ 2. The significance of the conflict between Montag and his inner feelings was to show that
   a. destruction and emptiness as a way of life cannot bring happiness.
   b. people will always have inner conflicts.
   c. books are necessary for happiness.
   d. people don't really want happiness.

_____ 3. Books are used as a symbol to represent all of the following *except*
   a. a tie to the past.
   b. knowledge.
   c. thinking as an individual.
   d. inner emptiness.

_____ 4. The theme could be stated as follows:
   a. The world is headed for destruction no matter what we do.
   b. It is better to die happy than to live miserably.
   c. A society that only stresses happiness and forgets the past and individuality will lead to the inner destruction of people and the outer destruction of civilization; only those who maintain ties with the past and think for themselves will survive.
   d. It is the obligation of the government to see that its people are happy by educating them; supplying them with the necessities of food, clothing, housing, and employment; and keeping a peaceful world.

_____ 5. The significance of the relationship between Montag and Mildred was to show
    a. lack of love and the deterioration of the marital bond.
    b. increased dependence of women.
    c. effects of excessive television on a relationship.
    d. that the divorce rate will continue to increase in the future.

Allow 20 points per correct answer.   *Your score* _____ %
Number of words: 47,950   *Your rate* _____
Answer key is on page 272.
Record rate and comprehension score on Course Data Sheet in Postview columns.

ADVANCED NOVEL
GENERAL PREVIEW QUESTIONS

1. Name the main character. _____

2. Name two other characters. (1) _____

    (2) _____

3. Where does this story take place? _____

_____

4. Approximately when does this story take place? _____

5. What type of story is it? _____

6. Name the relationships between the various characters (husband and wife,

    father and son, friends, enemies, etc.). _____

_____

_____

7. Who is telling the story? Author? _____ A character? _____

_____

8. Write one sentence stating what this story is about. _____

_____

Correct your general preview answers after completing the postview.
Allow 12½ points per correct answer.   *Your score* _____ %
Figure out the total number of words in   *Your rate* _____
your novel; then figure out your rate.
Total number of words _____

ADVANCED NOVEL
GENERAL GOOD COMPREHENSION QUESTIONS

1. Write one sentence summarizing how the story begins. _____

_____

2. Write two or three sentences summarizing the central part of the story. ___

_____

_____

_____

3. Write one sentence summarizing how the story ends. _____

_____

4. Who is telling the story: (1) the author, as a god, who knows what is in the minds of the characters? _____ (2) the author, as an observer, who tells only what he can see and hear? _____ (3) a narrator who is a character in the story? _____ Name the narrator-character. _____

5. Is the story told in an orderly time sequence, or does it jump around in time? _____

6. Around what major conflict or problem does the story revolve: (1) a character vs. a character? _____ (2) a character vs. society? _____ (3) a character vs. some natural force? _____ (4) a character vs. some aspect of himself? _____

7. How is this problem or conflict solved? _____

_____

8. Is the main character a good person (hero) or a bad person (antihero)? ___

9. What does the whole story illustrate; that is, what is the author's message?

_____

_____

10. Are there any obvious symbols in this story? If so, name at least one symbol and tell what it means. symbol: _____

meaning: _____

Correct after the postview.
Allow 10 points per correct answer.   Your score _____ %
Total number of words _____   Your rate _____

ADVANCED NOVEL GENERAL POSTVIEW

Postview to find out if you answered the preview and good comprehension questions correctly. Score these tests. Record rates and comprehension scores on Course Data Sheet in the appropriate columns.

15

Studying History

Materials:
- Reading:
  "Social Themes"
- Drill book

Objectives:
- To become aware of the special characteristics of history
- To learn how to apply the speed-study method to history
- To learn how to organize the important information obtained from history for easier studying and remembering

DRILL PRACTICE

For this drill use a book that you have previously read (*Fahrenheit 451* is a good choice.) Because you already know the story, you will have the experience of going at a fast drill rate and still get some meaning from the story.

Start at the beginning of the story. Try to go faster than any previous week. Ready? Begin (1 minute). Stop. Begin a recall sheet.

Count the number of pages you went over; add an equal number so that you will go over the story twice as fast. Start out as fast as you can, and keep up the pace. Back to the beginning. Ready? Begin (10 seconds . . . 1 minute). Stop. Add to your recall.

This time you will go over the same amount of material in half the time. Back to the beginning. Ready? Begin. (10 seconds . . . 30 seconds). Stop. Add to your recall.

Begin at the top of a page in new material in the same book for a drill rate. Ready? Begin (1 minute). Stop. Figure your rate and record it on your Course Data Sheet 2.

CHARACTERISTICS OF HISTORY

History is a subject with which many people frequently have difficulty, mainly because they try to read history in the same manner as they read general materials. When you recognize the specific characteristics of histories and the manner in which they are written, reading history becomes easier and more enjoyable.

All histories have certain common limiting characteristics. Each historical article or book covers a particular segment of time. It does not cover all history, because to do so would require numerous volumes. It is also limited to a geographical area and a particular culture. For example, a history book may be limited to the history of the United States, which will then be limited to a particular geographical area in North America and a specific culture, which is a portion of the Western as opposed to the Eastern culture. The scope of the history may be restricted to an area as small as one home or expanded to include the entire universe. It may be confined to one family or to all living creatures. Recognizing the range of a particular history provides a framework within which you can organize the information supplied by the author.

The manner in which a history is written is another important consideration. Although histories may be written in many different ways, they are most frequently arranged or organized according to time sequence and/or themes or ideas. When organized so as to emphasize chronology or time, the most important aspects of that history will

asylums and jails would be emptied. In a time when people and notably intellectuals believed naively in "science," the eugenicists announced that banning alcohol would improve the race. Doctors no longer raised the spectre—seriously advanced in the nineteenth century—of spontaneous combustion, but they did confuse morals and medicine in their professional opinions. In addition, taxes would fall, husbands would leave the dirty saloons and return to their families. Prohibitionists promised a "sort of millenial Kansas afloat on a nirvana of pure water."

Instead America got poisoned whiskey and a growing problem of organized crime. But the fanatical prohibitionists had perhaps gotten what they wanted: first, a way of exercising control over the immigrant by closing his saloons, and second, the kind of gratification a deeply felt cause can give—a sense of personal purification and moral glory. Many of the more honest "drys" eventually admitted that the "noble experiment" had failed, and when the Depression brought a compelling need for liquor tax revenues, prohibition was repealed in 1933.

THE KU KLUX KLAN

The white-sheeted fraternal order of the Ku Klux Klan flourished and then disintegrated during the course of the decade. Founded in 1915 in Georgia as an imitation of the Reconstruction Klan, the new organization gathered its 2 million members chiefly during the early twenties. It was anti-Negro in the South but mainly anti-Catholic both there and in the rest of the country. The Klan's popularity came from the lure of secrecy and from association with religious and patriotic institutions. One of the Klan's most popular songs, sung to the tune of "The Battle Hymn of the Republic," combined symbols of both:

> We rally round Old Glory in our robes of spotless white,
> While the Fiery Cross is burning in the silent, silv'ry night,
> Come join our glorious army in the cause of God and Right,
> The Klan is marching on.

The Klan lost face when financial and sexual scandals struck some of its leaders in the mid-twenties. Decline also resulted from success. One of the Klan's triumphs came in helping to insure that Governor Al Smith of New York would not win the Democratic presidential nomination in 1924. The Klan did its part to spread anti-Catholic rumors that the pope, crowded in the Vatican, aspired to new headquarters in the Mississippi Valley and that his minions were tunneling their way under the Atlantic Ocean to give orders to Smith in New York. Wily Jesuits had killed President Harding with "hypnotic-telepathic thought waves," and even the dollar bill bore a rosary cleverly inscribed in the background.

The Klan—which could with some justification claim to have "elected" a number of congressmen and senators in the South and West—also contributed some small part, along with organized labor and most social workers, to ending the decades of immigration that had contributed so much to variety and mobility in American life. In 1921 Congress passed a law setting immigration quotas based on the proportion of each ethnic group to the general population in 1920. When the formula proved too generous to southern and eastern Europeans, quotas were reduced and the date of computation was set back, by the Johnson Act of 1924, to the census of 1890, when fewer aliens had infected the "pure" American culture. In the following quarter-century fewer European immigrants came to the United States than in the single year of 1907.

RURAL-URBAN TENSIONS

The antiforeign and antiradical sentiments of the postwar years found near-perfect expression in the Sacco-Vanzetti case. Nicola Sacco and Bartolomeo Vanzetti had been found guilty in 1921 of murdering a factory paymaster and a guard during a robbery in South Braintree, Massachusetts. Recent evidence suggests that Sacco alone was guilty of the crime, but it is plain from the court transcript that Judge Webster Thayer permitted the prosecuting attorney to exploit the defendants' draft evasion and anarchist beliefs in order to secure a conviction. Numerous appeals and finally a special investigatory commission headed by the president of Harvard University merely postponed their execution until 1927. In the meantime, Vanzetti's touching letters from prison, along with publicity given the case by radicals, made it a *cause célèbre* throughout Europe as well as among American intellectuals.

The Scopes trial in Dayton, Tennessee, became a symbol of the decline of the old ways. In 1925 John T. Scopes, a high school biology teacher, challenged the Tennessee law that forbade the teaching of Darwinian evolution in public schools as contrary to biblical literalism. When Scopes was indicted, the ruralists' great champion William Jennings Bryan volunteered to help the prosecution. Now increasingly given to the defense of prohibition and to religious fundamentalism, Bryan was confronted in Dayton by the famous criminal lawyer and agnostic Clarence Darrow. During one sultry day Judge Raulston of Gizzard's Cove moved the proceedings out onto the courthouse lawn, and there Darrow exposed Bryan's simplistic religious beliefs. Actually, Darrow displayed an equally childlike faith in science, and Bryan's rural provincialism had its counterpart in the lawyer's urban narrowness. Bryan died ten days after the trial, and with his passing much of the heart went out of the rural crusades.

In the long view, the new urban culture was winning out. The census of 1920 was premature in declaring that more people lived in the cities than in the country; it took as its definition of "urban" a population of twenty-five hundred or more, which included many a hinterland village. By 1930, however, metropolitan areas had increased greatly in size at the expense of rural America. Young people left the farms to seek excitement and their fortunes in the city, and economic needs drove whole families to a city factory life. The cities' victory over the countryside went deeper even than population figures suggest. The countryside's moral victories such as antievolution laws and prohibition were short-lived. Urban culture had all the big weapons: advertising, the new mass media of radio and the movies, and the products—such as the automobile—that tied the countryside to urban styles, markets, and values. *Variety*, a show business newspaper, conducted a survey of popular taste in motion pictures and discovered that even country people did not want movies on country subjects: "Stix Nix Hix Pix" read the famous headline.

Above all, the needs of a mass-production economy forced the old ways aside. The rural values of thrift and restraint fell before the need for consumer credit as a device to extend consumption. The film, broadcasting, and advertising industries increased the expectations of the masses and turned them toward the leisure and pleasure patterns of modern urban America. With the values of rural America increasingly flouted and its economic health in jeopardy, bigotry and intolerance predictably resulted. Ironically, the Catholic, Jew, and Negro had less to do with destroying the old values than the mass-production and mass-consumption needs of the new corporations.

WOMEN AND THE FAMILY

By the 1920s many of the institutional functions of the family had declined. Recreation moved outside the home to the movie house and the automobile. The family itself was becoming smaller—particularly in urban areas, where an increase in apartment living also substantially reduced the time traditionally used in maintaining a home. Concurrent with changes in family size came a more subtle but equally important change on the domestic scene. The family was beginning to turn inward toward a greater preoccupation with the proper upbringing of children, the growth of their personalities, and their education. Such a concern brought with it a new emphasis on the role of the woman, her place as mother, household manager, and consumer tending to supersede that of household worker.

At the same time, while young unmarried women tended to predominate in the female work force, the percentage of working married women increased steadily, as did the number endeavoring to remain at their jobs after marriage. Between 1900 and 1930 the total number of employed women doubled, but the number of employed married women increased fourfold. In the same years their work shifted away from domestic services and manufacturing and more toward clerical, professional, and trade-oriented work. Some clerical occupations have ever since been considered "women's work."

The early twenties appear to have been a peak period for professional gains among women, most of which had been accomplished before World War I. While there has been an absolute gain in the number of professional women since that time, women's position relative to men has steadily declined since the twenties. One Ph.D. in seven went to a woman in 1920; this dropped to one in ten by 1956. The percentage of women on college faculties fell from 30 percent in the mid-twenties to 24 percent in the mid-sixties.

With increased employment came an increasing variety in female dress and a greater sexual freedom. Yet in today's view the short-skirted "flapper" was not really free but a frivolous object in a masculine world. Nor did the vogue of Freudian psychology contribute to the liberation of women. Freud and other psychoanalysts, each in his own way, stressed the uniqueness of feminine sexuality and inadvertently made women relatively ineffectual as professional and social beings.

Granting women the vote was really not such

a great stride forward. For after the Nineteenth Amendment took effect in 1920 the threat of a women's political coalition dissolved: women simply voted as their husbands did, and even the League of Women Voters took a position of political neutrality. Once again it was shown that there is no conspiracy against women in which they themselves are not co-conspirators.

The women's rights movement, so prominent in the activity of suffragettes fighting for their vote during the progressive era, became divided in the twenties. After gaining the vote their first goal was to fight against discriminatory practices and legislation; a state and national campaign began for the passage of equal employment laws. But to those women who had desperately fought for social welfare legislation to protect their hours and conditions of labor, the new campaign threatened to jeopardize hard-won victories. In short, by the twenties the accomplishments of women were paradoxical: they went to work but did "women's work"; they consolidated some of their sexual freedom, but a new view of women emphasizing their feminine roles seriously minimized chances for fruitful social careers.

LITERARY ACHIEVEMENT

The 1920s was no aesthetic wasteland. America's most culturally productive period since the 1850s, the decade produced a great quantity of fine writers and artists. The novels of Sinclair Lewis, F. Scott Fitzgerald, and Ernest Hemingway are of particular importance for an understanding of the period. Lewis's characters are sometimes burlesques, but he is often brilliant in observing the small things that contain the culture of a people. Lewis possessed a phonographic, as well as a photographic, memory. In *Main Street* (1920), which satirized the dullness of a small midwestern town, and in *Babbitt* (1922), which parodied the materialistic businessman, he studied the surfaces of life and mined the native American vein of self-criticism. Both bestsellers, their success illustrates our profound attachment for didactic literature and especially for criticism of ourselves. Lewis's popularity suggests that many Americans stirred restlessly in the twenties.

F. Scott Fitzgerald treated the wealthy, whose glamour and vitality tantalized and disturbed him. *The Great Gatsby* (1925) studies a powerful and vulnerable figure—Jay Gatsby, authentic American, self-made man 1920s style—a bootlegger who aspired to success and love through sheer will and determination. In Gatsby the American genius attempted to force reality itself to bend and be shaped anew. This arrogance was a deep-seated trait in the American psyche and a powerful force in a nation that so far had conquered all before it.

Ernest Hemingway, the master of short, crisp dialogue, revealed in *The Sun Also Rises* (1926) and *A Farewell to Arms* (1929) the capacity for both heroism and disillusionment that war could produce. Hemingway wrote about a generation of American young men and women born around the turn of the century and brought to maturity during the war. The phrase "lost generation" was usually applied to the American writers who lived in Paris after the war. They had lost not only their own sense of country but also the restricting past; found was the revelation through art of new concepts that the older generation could not accept.

Intellectuals generally were critical of American life in the twenties. H. L. Mencken attracted many with snide remarks about the "puritanism" of the American "booboisie." Asked why he stayed in America if he despised it so much, he replied: "Why do people go to the zoo?" Some writers cited the newly popular cult of Freudian psychoanalysis in attacking what they saw as America's repressive small-town morality. They turned to European culture protesting America's hostility to new ideas and to the worship of art protesting its smug materialism. A few, such as Joseph Wood Krutch in *The Modern Temper*, went beyond criticisms of American culture to a bleak view of all industrial society, civilized out of all belief and in need of some rejuvenating force.

A number of intellectuals saw this hoped-for rebirth in the very social changes that frightened other Americans. The city with its strange new peoples could offer the diversity that American writers found lacking in the villages. Some, like Randolph Bourne, envisioned America as a salad bowl of races and groups rather than a melting pot, a variegated world in which each exotic group preserved its own life and culture for the enrichment of all. This cultural pluralism would become increasingly important in the twentieth century.

BEHAVIOR

The twenties digested startling changes in American manners and morals, as standard notions of propriety disintegrated. The world war played a major role in this process through the disruption of social patterns which had been based on Victorian ideals, but it did not create the ideas and movements of the twenties. The new thought and behavior blossomed from prewar seedlings and often employed or reflected the advancing technology of the period.

In the cultural development of the twenties, few events were of more significance than the arrival of the "new psychology." This movement received impetus as early as 1909 from the American tour of its greatest prophet, Sigmund Freud, but came to fruition in the professional and popular mind only during the postwar decade. In its variously distorted forms, Freudianism quickly became an apparent influence in most literature and entertainment, affecting thousands who had never heard of Freud.

The influence of sex and repression in human behavior dominated the national understanding of the new psychology. Sexual restraint preached by late nineteenth-century social guardians seemed now positively counterproductive; social problems stemmed from an unhealthy containment of sexual urges. To be unrestrained, to release inner desires and tensions, became a worthy goal. Such conclusions in general psychological theory provided a ready rationalization for ignoring custom and violating taboos.

The general currency of Freud's ideas and his intellectual respectability were important in making sex a fit subject for mixed-group discussion among the sophisticated. Men and women at the modish cocktail parties of the twenties talked about sex under the guise of science, spicing their remarks with choice selections from tempting psychoanalytic vocabulary. The desire to be shocking encouraged daring rather than caution; with this accelerator, the subject of sex moved in a few years from nonentity to notoriety. The new psychology was not alone in its support of the revolution in manners and morals. Other more tangible influences, affecting the young in particular, shaped innovative social patterns.

Automobile ownership spread rapidly in the twenties and provided a mobility previously unknown. Yet the family car could be used for more than commuting to work or driving about on a Sunday. As closed cars increasingly dominated the market, the automobile became in effect a room on wheels, a room which could be moved and stopped where prying eyes and interruptions were unlikely. Soon automobiles were being held directly responsible for a portion of the birth statistics. Sexual experimentation was not, of course, limited to parked cars. Petting parties were in vogue before the war and magazines discussed the "petting question" throughout the twenties. Yet the automobile provided a uniquely available vehicle for the passionate and the curious.

The subtle social infiltrations of sex were by no means confined to covert couplings. Wary guardians of morality were shocked to find sex barely disguised in brazen forms of popular culture, such as jazz—immediately suspect for its Negro origins. Beyond that, defenders of hymnal and hearth quickly saw insidious sensuality within the music itself. Jazz often featured the "passionate crooning and wailing" of the saxophone—a far cry from the parlor piano—and no one could doubt the corruption and disarray evidenced in the threatening evil of syncopation. Dancing in the twenties passed from fad to fad in a fury of exuberant creativity, including early dances like the Horse Trot, the Grizzly Bear, and the often berated Bunny Hug, while the famous Charleston came later in the decade. One religious newspaper tied together music, sex, and the new dances in one broad condemnation: "The music is sensuous, the embracing of partners—the female only half dressed—is absolutely indecent; and the motions—they are such as may not be described, with any respect for propriety, in a family newspaper."

The growing mass culture industries of the twenties may have heard the critics, but they listened to the demands of their audience. During the day radio stations aired a variety of programs including inspirational and educational material; but in the evening, during "prime time," most stations concentrated on popular music, especially jazz. Similarly, the motion picture industry churned out a mixed product, but the movies which drew the largest audiences relied heavily on sex as a theme, some of the earliest pictures being the most explicit. Yet even after luring Postmaster General Will Hays from the Harding Cabinet to maintain moral standards the industry, in many pictures, conforming on the surface to the old morality and the happy ending, nevertheless depended for their appeal on plots permeated with sexual innuendo.

On the newsstands the evidence of a new kind of popular literature glared: the confession and sex magazines. *True Story*, founded in 1919, achieved the most spectacular success in this genre, by 1926 reaching a circulation of nearly 2 million on the strength of such stories as "What I Told My Daughter the Night Before Her Marriage" and "The Primitive Lover." Frequently, as in the movies, these provided a moral ending or gratuitous preaching of trite homilies, but the subject was clearly the same. Interestingly, remarkable similarities appeared between the "confessions" in pulp magazines and the case studies of popular psychoanalysts, revealing perhaps one more unintended influence of Freudian theory.

Many of the cultural clashes of the twenties stood clearly revealed on the battlefield of women's fashion. Social conservatives idealized the nineteenth-century woman, her skirts reaching the ground, a face plain and scrubbed, with her long hair in a bun. Any change in such an appearance represented obvious sexual impurity. Nonetheless, fashion trends in the twenties embraced the same freedom from old forms implied by the changes in music, dancing, and entertainment; and in doing so, they came into direct conflict with the older image of woman. Skirts rose from ankle to knee in the first half of the decade; bobbed hair became stylish, first among the young but soon for women of all ages; cosmetics came to be not only permissible but also essential—the beauty industry expanded astonishingly during the twenties. In her early exaggeration of these trends, the "Flapper" symbolized the

tide of sexuality and experimentation that so disturbed those who were not busy participating.

Not everything in the twenties revolved around explicit sexuality or the rejection of older values. Feeding on increasing leisure and prosperity, various sports claimed far greater public attention than ever before. Some encouraged participation; golf, for instance, aided by the developing role of the country club as a social center, became especially popular. But the era showed a tendency to watching professional athletes. Golf itself boasted Bobby Jones and Walter Hagen; tennis proclaimed Bill Tilden; in football Red Grange should perhaps top any list; the boorish Babe Ruth gave a lift to baseball; boxing fans thrilled to two Dempsey—Tunney fights. Huge crowds attended college football games and millions heard the first professional sportscasters on their radios. Spectatorship emerged as an art.

The cultural turmoil of the twenties was inescapable. By the end of the decade, even a religiously and socially conservative family in some obscure hamlet might well have owned or at least listened to a radio. Such slight exposure still changed their world. No earlier decade had so stirred American society.

Directions: *Before answering the preview questions, begin to organize the information by adding the beginning and ending dates to the time line below (refer to Figure 15-1 on page 171 to see how to do this), and by listing the primary issues covered in this selection. Use additional paper if needed.*

TIME LINE

Beginning Date _____ Ending Date

LIST OF ISSUES

1. _____
2. _____
3. _____
etc.

PREVIEW QUESTIONS

_____ 1. This segment of American history in "Social Themes" covers the
    a. 1850s.
    b. years 1900–1919.
    c. post-Civil War period.
    d. 1920s.
    e. 1930s.
    f. 1940s.
    g. 1950s.

_____ 2. The social themes discussed in this section include all of the following *except*
    a. prohibition.
    b. the Klu Klux Klan.
    c. the Depression.
    d. rural-urban tensions.
    e. women's issues.

_____ 3. The literary achievements during this era were
    a. extremely productive culturally.
    b. insignificant.
    c. not a reflection of life of the times.
    d. primarily in the field of science fiction.

_____ 4. According to the authors, the behavior of Americans during this period was
    a. a return to excessively high moral values.
    b. a continuation of social patterns based on the Victorian ideals.
    c. a lack of interest in sexual issues.
    d. highlighted by a disintegration of previous standards of propriety.

_____ 5. The authors sum up the era in the phrase
    a. cultural turmoil.
    b. cultural integration.
    c. social wasteland.
    d. status quo.

Allow 20 points per correct answer.   *Your score* _____ %
Number of words: 5,400   *Your rate* _____
Answer key is on page 272.
Record rate and comprehension score on Course Data Sheet in Preview columns.

    Before answering the good comprehension questions, go back to your time line and list of issues. Fill in as much additional information as you can at this time.

GOOD COMPREHENSION QUESTIONS

_____ 1. The Prohibition Amendment was repealed because
    a. the Depression brought a compelling need for liquor revenues.
    b. many people died from poisonous "bootlegged" liquor.
    c. the immigrants suffered severely by the closing of the saloons.
    d. it had emptied the jails and asylums.

_____ 2. One area of important tensions that influenced the social issues greatly was between
    a. men and women.
    b. rich and poor.
    c. city and country dwellers.
    d. Republicans and Democrats.

_____ 3. One reason for the decline of the Klu Klux Klan is stated as
    a. financial and sexual scandals involving their leaders.
    b. education of the American public.
    c. increase in the Negro population.
    d. increase in the number of immigrants.

_____ 4. A sentiment that was popular at this time was that
   a. mass production should be restricted.
   b. immigration should be drastically restricted.
   c. automobiles polluted the air.
   d. education should be free for all.

_____ 5. During this period, women gained all of the following *except*
   a. the right to vote.
   b. increased employment.
   c. professional gains.
   d. increased family influence on their children.

_____ 6. The technological advances that most influenced Americans' lives during this era were (was) the
   a. automatic washer and dryer.
   b. radio and automobile.
   c. automatic cloth-weaving machine.
   d. airplane and teletype.

_____ 7. A person who had a profound influence on the cultural development of Americans during this time was
   a. John Kenneth Galbraith.
   b. John Steinbeck.
   c. Sigmund Freud.
   d. Walt Whitman.
   e. Martin Luther King, Jr.

_____ 8. During this period, the women's rights movement
   a. began to achieve much important legislation in favor of women
   b. became the nucleus for a strong, influential women's political coalition.
   c. was influential in passing equal employment laws.
   d. accomplished very little.

_____ 9. Which of the names below was *not* one of the literary giants of this era?
   a. Ernest Hemingway.
   b. F. Scott Fitzgerald.
   c. Harriet Beecher Stowe.
   d. Sinclair Lewis.

_____ 10. The authors state that the sexual social pattern at this time
   a. was to refrain from discussing sex in mixed company.
   b. tended toward the sexually shocking and unrestrained.
   c. reverted to earlier strict moral codes of behavior.
   d. was to show a lack of interest in sex.

Allow 10 points per correct answer. *Your score* _____ %
Number of words: 5,400 *Your rate* _____
Answer key is on page 272.
Record your rate and comprehension score on Course Data Sheet in Good Comprehension columns.

   To complete your concise personal organization of the significant information from this selection, return to your time line and list of issues and add any missing data. You may postview the selection if necessary.

16

Studying a Text with a Specialized Vocabulary

Materials: • Readings:
"That Filing System Inside Your Head"
Body Language, or a book on a subject requiring a specialized vocabulary

Objective: • To learn how to speed study materials that contain a specialized vocabulary

DRILL PRACTICE

Repeat the drills given at the beginning of Chapter 15 on page 169. Take your drill rate for this week and record it on your Course Data Sheet.

SPECIALIZED VOCABULARY

In reading materials for academic subjects such as math, psychology, biology, or philosophy, you will come across words that are specifically used in that subject. These words are the specialized vocabulary having to do particularly with that subject. If you have great familiarity with the subject, these words may not be new to you; however, if you are unfamiliar with the subject, you may not know their meanings. Although it is not always necessary to look up the definition of each new word that you meet in your regular reading, because the way in which it is used will usually enable you to understand what it means as used in that particular context, technical or specialized words are different. These specialized words are basic to the understanding of the material and may even be its central idea. When this is so, none of the material will make sense unless you understand the meanings of the technical terms. Since rapid reading depends on instantaneous recognition of the vocabulary, it is important

to know the meanings of these technical words before you attempt to read the material for good comprehension.

Method

To the basic speed-study method presented in Chapter 13, you must add two more steps:

Step One Mark any words with which you are unfamiliar and which appear to be important to the central topic of the work. Do this during the preview (other text markings are done during the good comprehension reading), and place the mark in the margin closer to the word being marked. Although you may use any mark you wish, I suggest a small dash (—), since it is a sign not being used to designate anything else if you are using the marking system presented in Chapter 10. Do not look too hard for the specialized words or you will miss the general meaning of the work, your primary reason for previewing. The specialized terms will usually "jump out at you." In textbooks they are often in boldface or italics the first time they are used.

Step Two Learn the meanings of the marked words. After the preview and before the good comprehension reading, go through the text to find each of the words you marked. On a piece of paper, write the word; then read the sentence in which it appears to see if a definition has been provided by the author or if you can figure out the meaning from the context. If the text provides no help, you should look in the back of the book to see if there is a glossary (a small dictionary of certain words used in the book). If you are fortunate enough to have a glossary, copy down the definition. If you own the book, you might want to write the word and its definition in the margin at the top of the page on which it appears so that you will have it for reference whenever you read this material. However, if no definition can be found in the book, you must use a good dictionary. Be sure to read all the meanings given for that word because it may have both an ordinary meaning and a specialized one. It is your job to select the meaning that applies to the way the word is being used in this subject. When you have noted the definitions of all the marked words, go over the list until you feel that you will understand these words correctly when you meet them in your reading. You are now ready to read the material for good comprehension.

Note: This method of speed studying may be used when you are reading any material that has an unusually difficult vocabulary.

Practice Reading: An Article

For this exercise use the article, "That Filing System Inside Your Head," at the end of this chapter. Study this article by using the four-step speed-study techniques you have learned (Chapter 13), including the additional two steps presented in this chapter.

Preview the article, marking the difficult specialized words that you don't know. Make a list of these words with their definitions. (A starter list is given at the end of the article.) Study the list. Then take the vocabulary test that accompanies this article. If your test score is very low, study the words again before doing the good comprehension read-ing. Answer the preview questions. Remember to pay special attention to the subtitle and the begin-ning of each section as you preview.

In the good comprehension reading, mark the text for the important ideas. Then take the test for this reading.

Postview to find the correct answers to ques-tions you missed on the preview and good compre-hension readings. You may scan for the answers or use any postview method (page 138) you feel will accomplish your purpose.

Record your preview and good comprehen-sion rates and scores on your Course Data Sheet.

Practice Reading: A Book

Use *Body Language* or any book on a subject with a specialized vocabulary. Survey. Preview, marking the specialized terms. Make your own list of the terms and their definitions on the sheet provided (page 191). Study the list. Take the test on page 192. Answer the preview questions.

Read for good comprehension, marking the important ideas. Answer the good comprehension questions.

Postview. If you have not tried the postview method of rereading by skimming the difficult chapters only, try it on this book. Or you may wish to reread only the parts marked as important. Another alternative is to read the questions first and scan for the answers. Answer the postview questions.

Record all rates and scores on the Course Data Sheet.

SUMMARY

When reading materials that contain key words unknown to you, you should mark these words during the preview and find and learn their mean-ings before attempting a good comprehension reading.

THAT FILING SYSTEM INSIDE YOUR HEAD*

Roy Rowan

Memory remains a mysterious function. But one thing is known for sure: there are things you can do to improve it.

Within milliseconds his facile brain can summon forth the whole summer production schedule, review unit costs under the new union contract, and match this information against the seasonally adjusted fall sales projections. This same steel-trap mind can put first and last names on a thousand faces over at the plant, or revive with uncanny clarity a directors meeting that took place ten years ago—right down to the timbre of the voices, the comptroller's cryptic comments, even the fragrant cigar aroma that permeated the pile-carpeted boardroom after it was all over. "J.B.'s like an elephant. He never forgets a thing," his awed subordinates say. "We don't know how he does it."

FADING AT THE PEAK

Most chief executives credit highly developed analytical powers, rather than a sharply honed memory, for their climb to the top. Nevertheless, many of them recognize memory as a great business asset, synonymous with efficiency. Sometimes, to their horror, they detect telltale signs that it's beginning to fade, often as they reach the peak of their career. Yet they do not always realize that, just as with a weak forehand in tennis or a stunted backswing in golf, memory can be trained to perform more effectively. A few corporations have even rung in pros to iron out the problems, not that the pros themselves fully understand how memory works.

And for that matter, neither do the scientists who have spent a lifetime studying man's information-retrieval process. They still don't know whether human memory is chemical or electrical, highly structured or random, and whether it has unlimited storage space or, like the file cabinets in an office, must be continuously culled to make room for new information. In fact, they don't know exactly where in the brain memories are filed.

This is not to say that the scientists have been sitting idle. To be sure, they have constructed elaborate computer models to simulate both "episodic memory" (used to recall a single event such as a name, face, or date), and "semantic memory" (used to recall entire information systems such as language, mathematics, or how to drive a car). They have also diagrammed the theoretical distinctions between "short term" and "long-term" memory, made microscopic comparisons between new prenatal and old senile brains, even ground up the brain tissue of trained mice and injected the particles into their untrained brothers, to determine if memory is transferable from one living creature to another. (In mice it appears to be.) While nothing definitive has come from all these experiments, a number of new insights have been gleaned that should prove encouraging to business executives.

• Biologically there is much less memory loss accompanying advancing age than was previously suspected. However, as more knowledge is acquired, there occurs what psychologists call "proactive interference" between competing new and old memories. (Ever reach for the emergency brake where it was in your previous car?) Also, you tend not to remember how much you used to forget. (Just ask your children.)

• Memory impotence, like male sexual impotence, feeds on the fear of failure. Don't panic. Frequently a less direct attack on the elusive name or number will produce the answer.

• A certain amount of stress can actually improve memory by forcing the body to produce chemical brain stimulants. Individuals usually have their own optimum levels of stress. Too much stress—"George, this $10-million contract hangs on your presentation"—may produce "final-exam syndrome," a disruption of the cognitive process resulting from high anxiety.

• What is assumed to be a memory loss may simply be the effect of an environmental change. Psychologists refer to "summer" and "winter" memories, which become confused when triggered out of season. This same out-of-context bewilderment can cause you not to recognize your own secretary when you unexpectedly run into her at the airport. Similarly, transferred executives sometimes complain about memory slippage, when the problem is that they are in new surroundings.

FROM PLATO'S BED OF WAX

Ever since the Golden Age of Greece, man has been trying to solve the mystery of memory. The problem always was, he had only vague notions of what he was looking for. Plato, in *Thaetetus*, described memory as a "bed of modeling wax," receiving the impressions of thoughts and sensations as if they had been imprinted by a signet. Descartes pictured memories as "traces and vestiges that are just like the creases in a piece of paper that make it easier to fold again."

Today, most scientists subscribe to one form or another of the so-called "switchboard theory" of memory. They believe ten billion neurons composing man's brain arrange themselves into interconnected electrochemical circuits called engrams. According to this view, the engram is memory's pathway. Like the light bulbs in those moving signs that spell out late-news headlines across the front of a building, each neuron may be turning on and off in an infinite number of engrams. The problem is, nobody has ever seen an engram.

A radically different view of memory is offered by Dr. E. Roy John, director of the brain-research laboratories at New York University Medical Center. Dr. John does not envision memory as interconnected circuitry, but as "coherent temporal patterns" of resonating neurons. According to his theory, the neurons act in "ensembles," not as individual units. "The brain is a big democracy," he says. "It doesn't listen to a single voice." As for his frustrated fellow scientists searching for an engram, he thinks they're looking for the wrong thing. "Instead of a groove, they should be looking for a wave. The engram is like a radio signal. You can't see it. But you can pick it up on your receiver."

Although nobody's seen an engram, the brain's myriad neurons have been seen and studied for years. Each neuron consists of a nucleus, an axon that serves as the cell's transmitter, and a number of receiving antennae called dendrites. The gaps between the neurons are known as synapses. And it is the molecular action at the synapse, when one neuron fires and its chemical signal is picked up by neighboring neurons on the other side of the gap, that intrigues scientists. They see this action at the synapse gap as holding the secret to memory storage and transmission.

A MEMORABLE CHAT

Dr. James McGaugh, a noted psychobiologist and the executive vice chancellor of the University of California at Irvine, has experimented extensively with memory-enhancement drugs (caffeine is one) that amplify the signals between one neuron and another, presumably strengthening the synaptic connections. He offers laboratory confirmation of something everybody already suspects: fright or extreme elation can produce the same stimulus—provided, just as with the drugs, they immediately follow the experience. As an example, he cites a man called into the boss's office for a chat. "Nothing memorable about that," says McGaugh.

"I'm delighted to have this opportunity to talk to you," says the boss, still not making the encounter memorable. Then he adds: "Because YOU'RE FIRED."

"Wham!" says McGaugh. "Those two words, 'you're fired'—or they just as well could have been 'you're promoted'—suddenly modify the encounter." According to McGaugh's hypothesis (developed in collaboration with Dr. Paul Gold, currently at the University of Virginia), escalating the emotional level of an experience can trigger the release of certain hormones that strengthen the synaptic connections, thus etching a sharp and lasting memory. McGaugh has found that rats will remember a mild electrical shock as a severe shock if they are immediately given an amphetamine injection, which serves as a memory stimulant. But the memory process can also be reversed. Scopolamine, a drug that blocks signal reception at the synapse, is frequently given to women to make them forget the pain of childbirth.

At M.I.T., Dr. Richard Wurtman is similarly studying nerve action at the synapse, but his experiments are with diet as a means of enhancing memory. Choline, found in such foods as eggs, soybeans, and liver, he discovered, is absorbed directly from the bloodstream by the brain, where it is converted into acetylcholine, a chemical transmitter that carries nerve impulses across the synapse. Dr. Wurtman is not ready to recommend that anybody who wants to sharpen his memory should begin each day with a hefty four-egg omelette. Yet he is optimistic that diet will someday play an important role in memory improvement.

A NEW BRAIN EVERY MONTH

The idea that there may indeed be food for thought is new, but it has long been known that chronic and heavy drinking obliterates memory. Alocholics are subject to Korsakoff's syndrome, a permanent impairment that causes them to create memories from fantasy, but prevents them from recognizing people they have daily contact with. Even social drinking weakens memory, probably because the brain tends to shrink under the influence of alcohol. Alcohol is known to interfere with the brain's ability to make proteins, the building blocks of the neurons, and possibly the real storehouse of memory. Although the neurons cannot reproduce themselves (a loss of brain tissue through illness or injury is permanent), their protein content is constantly forming and disappearing so that man in effect grows a new brain every month, but with the same neurons and engrams—just as the remake of an LP record has the same grooves and squiggles and plays the same old song.

While brain researchers are wrestling with the mysteries of the memory mechanism, and striving to improve its efficiency with drugs or diet, another group, the behaviorists, are looking for new ways to maximize its use. They, too, have their own picturesque analogies. "Memory is like a muscle," they maintain. It must be exercised to retain its tone. Overreliance on a superefficient assistant or secretary can cause the mechanism to atrophy.

"Memory is like a library," they also say. "But there is no use in having books if you can't find them." However, they point out that memories can in effect be xeroxed and cross-filed in the mind under different headings for easier retrieval.

Studying a Text with a Specialized Vocabulary   **183**

Some behaviorists, however, view memory as a more haphazard process, resembling the action of a pinball machine. We players, they indicate, can usually shoot the memory ball in the right direction, and nudge it along the desired path, though it may bounce out of control, lighting up unexpected names and numbers. They have an expression, "TOT (tip-of-the-tongue) syndrome," for this problem of being able to retrieve only memory fragments, but not the whole thing.

Behaviorists break down the memory process into three phases: registration, consolidation, and retrieval. In phase No. 1, paying attention is obviously essential for acquiring new information. "But usually you have to do more than just experience an event to remember it," says Thomas Landauer, a psychologist in the Human Information Processing Department at Bell Laboratories in Murray Hill, New Jersey. "You have to do some kind of work on it." But rapidly repeating the same fact over and over immediately upon its receipt, he believes, is futile, except for short periods; repetition will help one to remember a telephone number long enough to dial it, but that's about it.

For permanent retention, Landauer recommends what he calls "spacing of practice" (allowing an interval between rehearsals). With each practice, he claims, you are in fact creating a new memory, which may be stored in a different place. It has also been established that when memories are updated, as happens in periodic encounters with people over their lifetimes, your memory of them after they die tends to strike an average between a youthful and an older image.

Forming an "integrated image" with all the information concisely placed in a single mental picture also helps to preserve a memory. So does the use of verbal structure or cadence such as is found in poetry ("Thirty days hath September . . ."). Categorizing, or "chunking," in the lexicon of the behaviorists, helps in the recall of lists (housewives out shopping should think of vegetables, meats, and dairy products separately). Landauer disdains reliance on the subconscious to abet memory. As an extreme example, he cites the use of under-the-pillow tape players by students to learn a foreign language while they sleep. "The amount they remember," he says, "is determined by how poorly they sleep."

"RELAX TO REMEMBER"

Other theorists do put reliance on the subconscious. Jerome Wahlman, a New York hypnotherapist and the only expert who advertises "Memory Improvement Training" in the Manhattan Yellow Pages, predicates his teaching on the belief that all memories are stored in the subconscious mind. "I try to make the subconscious perform in a predictable and controlled manner," he says.

Wahlman urges his students to switch into a relaxed "alpha state" (characterized by the slow alpha waves preceding sleep) when they are receiving new information. The alpha state is induced by what he calls "sense-imagery exercises," involving the recall of pleasurable experiences. "Learn passively," he advises. "Also, relax to remember, or your mind will set up a block." Dr. Arthur Hastings, director of the Holistic Medicine Project at the Institute of Noetic Sciences in San Francisco, gives scientific backing to this approach. He recommends meditation (a deep alpha state) to make stored ideas and facts become more accessible.

Memory systems such as Wahlman's are as old as civilization. Early Roman orators used *loci* (places)—e.g., the floor plan of their own homes—to help them recall long speeches. The opening thought would be associated with the front door, the next thought with the vestibule. In recent years numerous new memory systems have been devised that, depending on the jargon of their inventors, provide "hooks," "pegs," "chains," "links," or "locks" to help forgetful individuals dredge up the names, numbers, phrases, and faces that lie buried in their brains.

THE YELLOW-PIMPLED MOOSE

All of these systems rely on association—linking the thing you are trying to remember to something you already know. (The reason children can always draw a map of Italy.) Harry Lorayne, who frequently proves on the Johnny Carson and Merv Griffin shows that he can master the name of everybody in the audience within twenty minutes, is the most celebrated salesman of memory association.

Lorayne has been called to lecture executives of I.B.M., G.E., Borg-Warner, Westinghouse, and U.S. Steel on memory improvement. He was flown to England to do the same thing for F.W. Woolworth's British suppliers. And Bear Stearns Co. in New York hired him to teach a hundred brokers how to memorize the name, face, and telephone number of every customer. "Businessmen think they have bad memories," he claims, "but they have fantastic memories. I become their motivator."

In Harry Lorayne's case this involves teaching them to make absurd associations. "It is essential to convert the verbal into the visual," he explains. "But it's weird pictures that you remember." If you want to remember the French word for grapefruit, *pamplemousse*, he suggests thinking of a moose covered with grapefruit-sized yellow pimples. Minnesota is easily remembered as a mini-soda, Nebraska as a new brass car. "Using the imagination this way," he adds, "further assists memory."

Lorayne also advocates "original awareness," which simply means making the initial encounter meaningful. Businessmen at conventions, he insists, spend too much time studying name tags instead of faces. Pick the most pronounced facial feature (pug nose, mole, cleft chin), he advises, and then merge it with a ridiculous word picture of the person's name. If you're introduced to someone with bushy eyebrows, named Miesterman, visualized yourself stirring the man's eyebrows (Me stir man's eyebrows) with a spoon.

Lorayne has written ten books, the last one a best-seller (*The Memory Book*, Ballantine, 1975), in collaboration with former Knick basketball star Jerry Lucas. Lucas, whose own mind-boggling memory system involves putting the letters of a name in alphabetical order the instant he hears it (Jerry Lucas becomes Ejrry Aclsu), once memorized 500 columns of the Manhattan phone book as a stunt.

For those who fear loss of memory almost more than death, researchers are coming up with some good news. Gerontology specialists are discovering that the human brain remains quite plastic and capable of learning until relatively late in life—into the seventies, and even the eighties and nineties—provided the person remains sufficiently challenged. This discovery, of course, had already been signaled by such late bloomers as Thomas Edison, Henry Ford, Pablo Casals, and Grandma Moses. But now the biological evidence has been gathered, too.

Dr. Arnold Scheibel of the Brain Research Institute of U.C.L.A. has spent five years performing microscopic studies of the brains of aged people within a few hours following their deaths. He can indeed pinpoint the deterioration of those synaptic connections, believed to be so crucial for memory transmission and storage. However, only in cases of severe senility (Alzheimer's disease) did he find the deterioration to be acute.

At the same time, experimenting with rats, he has discovered that those living in what he calls an "enriched environment" with wheels to run on and toys to play with, suffer noticeably less synaptic deterioration than rats who live in boredom. These two concurrent studies have led Dr. Scheibel, who is also a practicing psychiatrist, to make some observations about the memory of the aging executive.

"High-powered executives," he says, "suffer a narcissistic insult when their perks and responsibilities are taken away. After all, they have been nursed to the top by their companies in an enriched environment. Then suddenly they must adapt themselves to big losses." Scheibel is convinced that learning new skills, such as a foreign language or a musical instrument, or accepting new community responsibilities, will slow the retired executive's memory deterioration. "We sabotage ourselves," he says. "One has to be trained to age meaningfully. To retire *to* something, not *from* something."

PROGRAMMED OBSOLESCENCE

Drs. Lissy Jarvik and Aseneth LaRue, a noted team of research psychologists at the Brentwood Veterans Hospital in Los Angeles, confirm Dr. Scheibel's findings. Their studies of people between sixty and ninety lead them to believe that depression and the lack of vocational and intellectual stimulation accounts for more memory erosion than does age.

According to Dr. Robert Butler, director of the National Institute on Aging in Bethesda, Maryland, only 4 to 6 percent of the population suffers from acute senility. And about a third of these individuals are actually suffering from such curable ailments as depression or nutritional deficiencies. Butler believes that most executives who complain of memory loss are in fact victims of "programmed obsolescence." "Businessmen get bored to death doing the same thing day after day," he says. "There are relatively few who wouldn't like to change careers after twenty-five years." Portable pensions, transferable from one company to another, he thinks, would keep executives from feeling locked in and would stave off memory deterioration.

But then, forgetting may help ease the pain of growing old in a youth-oriented society. Or it may simply keep the human memory bank from getting overloaded. Nobody knows. In any case, even the sharpest-etched memories can prove to be mercurial. Sometimes they just vanish into thin air.

Name _____

VOCABULARY LIST

Directions: *You should have checked the following and other difficult words in your preview reading. Some of the definitions are provided. Write in the definitions* not *provided. Refer to the article; read the sentence in which the word appears (if you checked the word, you should be able to find it). If the meaning is not given in the text, use a dictionary.*

Add other words you checked to this list. Supply their definitions.

Study this list. Then take the vocabulary test on the next page before *doing the good comprehension reading.*

Episodic memory: _____

_____

Semantic memory: _____

_____

Proactive interference: old memory interfering with and competing with a new memory.

Cognitive process: the mental and sensory steps in gaining information; the process of knowing or perceiving.

Vestiges: _____

_____

Neuron: _____

_____

Engrams: interconnected electrochemical circuits or pathways in the brain.

Axon: _____

_____

Dendrite: _____

_____

Synapses: _____

_____

Lexicon: _____

_____

Gerontology: _____

_____

Narcissistic: _____

_____

Mercurial: _____

_____

ADD YOUR   ADD DEFINITIONS:
OWN WORDS
BELOW:

_____   _____

                     _____

_____   _____

                     _____

VOCABULARY TEST

Directions: *From memory, match the words with their definitions.*

_____ 1. Episodic memory

_____ 2. Semantic memory

_____ 3. Proactive interference

_____ 4. Cognitive process

_____ 5. Vestiges

_____ 6. Neuron

_____ 7. Engrams

_____ 8. Axon

_____ 9. Dendrite

_____10. Synapses

_____11. Lexicon

_____12. Gerontology

_____13. Narcissistic

_____14. Mercurial

a. the unit of the nervous system
b. special vocabulary of particular field of study
c. changeable, fickle
d. recalling entire information systems
e. transmitter of nerve impulses
f. gaps between the neurons
g. excessive interest in one's image
h. recalling a single event
i. to waste away or fail to develop
j. mental and sensory steps involved in gaining information
k. electrochemical circuits in the brain
l. receiver of nerve impulses
m. scientific study of aging process
n. marks of something that once existed
o. old memory competing with new memory

Add your words and definitions from memory:

_____   _____

                 _____

_____   _____

                 _____

Correct the test with the answer key on page 272.
For each incorrect answer, subtract 7 points from 100.

Your score: _____ %

PREVIEW QUESTIONS

_____ 1. The main topic of "That Filing System Inside Your Head" is
   a. functions of various parts of the brain.
   b. creative thinking.
   c. memory.
   d. using language effectively.

_____ 2. The major portion of this article deals with the presentation of
   a. various theories of authorities on the subject.
   b. only one tested and proven method for improvement, given step by step.
   c. a highly scientific explanation describing each area of the brain.
   d. the evolution of the human brain.

_____ 3. One important subject discussed is
   a. teaching young children language abilities.
   b. aging and memory.
   c. brain surgery.
   d. how to enjoy the retirement years.

_____ 4. Another subject discussed is
   a. substances and circumstances that strengthen and those that interfere with certain brain functions.
   b. how ancient theories of brain functions are still accepted by modern scientists.
   c. the importance of dreams.
   d. ways to recall childhood memories.

_____ 5. This article contains
   a. general references to various types of scientists without naming them specifically.
   b. specific names of scientists.
   c. many footnotes with important information.
   d. no subheadings or divisions of the information.

Allows 20 points per correct answer.   _Your score _____ %_
Number of words: 3,500   _Your rate _____
Answer key is on page 272.
Record rate and comprehension score on Course Data Sheet in Preview columns. Be sure that you have made a list of the specialized words, studied the list, and taken the vocabulary test before you do a good comprehension reading.

GOOD COMPREHENSION QUESTIONS

_____ 1. Regarding memory, scientists
   a. know exactly how it works and which parts of the brain store memory information.
   b. don't know how it works but do know with certainty where in the brain memory information is stored.
   c. don't know where memory information is stored but do know exactly how memory works.
   d. don't know how memory works or where memory information is stored.

_____ 2. The basic structural and functional unit of the brain is called a(n)
   a. neuron.
   b. synapse.
   c. dendrite.
   d. axon.

_____ 3. One theory by Jerome Wahlman on improving memory recommends
   a. strenuous physical activity just before receiving the information.
   b. soft background music at the time of receiving the information.
   c. being in a very relaxed state while receiving and recalling the information.
   d. increasing the body's temperature by wearing warm clothing while receiving and recalling information.

_____ 4. Another theory by Thomas Landauer proposes that memory retention can be improved by
   a. rapidly repeating the same fact over and over immediately after receiving the information.
   b. spacing the rehearsals of the information so that there is an interval of time between practices.
   c. just experiencing the event to be remembered.
   d. listening to the information played on a tape recorder while sleeping.

_____ 5. One theory by Dr. Richard Wurtman proposes that memory can be improved by
   a. diet.
   b. exercise.
   c. alcohol.
   d. scopolamine drug.

_____ 6. Regarding memory loss with aging, this article says that
   a. severe memory loss is an inevitable part of the aging process.
   b. memory loss can be lessened if the person remains sufficiently mentally challenged.
   c. excessive use of the memory mechanism during a long life causes deterioration of the brain cells involved in the memory process.
   d. there is little memory loss of past events, but learning new things and forming new memories are almost impossible.

_____ 7. One popular system by Harry Lorayne for memory improvement relies on
   a. association, linking the thing you want to remember to something you already know.
   b. writing down the fact to be remembered.
   c. looking intently at the fact in print.
   d. relaxation and not worrying about remembering.

_____ 8. Memory deterioration occurs under all the following circumstances *except*
   a. heavy drinking of alcohol.
   b. Alzheimer's disease.
   c. boredom in old age.
   d. eating more than two eggs a week.

_____ 9. According to Dr. James McGaugh, a memory can be enhanced or strengthened when the incident is immediately followed by all of the following *except*
   a. caffeine.
   b. fright.
   c. alcohol.
   d. elation or joy.

———— 10. Some insights on memory mentioned in this article include all of the following *except* that

    a. memory failure can be caused by panic and the fear of failure.

    b. the more stress involved, the easier it is to remember.

    c. new surroundings can cause certain types of memory loss.

    d. a certain amount of stress can improve memory.

Allow 10 points per correct answer.   *Your score* ———————— %

Number of words: 3,500   *Your rate* ————————

Answer key is on page 272.

Record rate and comprehension score on Course Data Sheet in Good Comprehension columns. Postview to find the answers to the questions you missed on the preview and good comprehension readings.

Name _____

SPECIALIZED VOCABULARY LIST (for Book)

Directions: *This list is to be used with* Body Language *or another book.*
  List ten specialized words you marked in the preview. Find their definitions in the book itself or in a dictionary. Use brief descriptions and synonyms wherever possible.

VOCABULARY   DEFINITIONS

1. _____   _____

2. _____   _____

3. _____   _____

4. _____   _____

5. _____   _____

6. _____   _____

7. _____   _____

8. _____   _____

9. _____   _____

10. _____   _____

Go over this list and the definitions several times, until you feel you will understand the words when you see them in the good comprehension reading. Take the test on the next page.

SPECIALIZED VOCABULARY TEST

Directions: *This test is to be used with* Body Language *or another general book.*

Copy your list of words in the space below. Without looking at the definitions, see how many definitions you can supply from memory. Correct by comparing the definitions here with the ones you looked up.

VOCABULARY   DEFINITIONS

1. _____   _____

                    _____

2. _____   _____

                    _____

3. _____   _____

                    _____

4. _____   _____

                    _____

5. _____   _____

                    _____

6. _____   _____

                    _____

7. _____   _____

                    _____

8. _____   _____

                    _____

9. _____   _____

                    _____

10. _____   _____

                    _____

Allow 10 points per correct answer.   *Your score* _____ %.

If you read a book other than Body Language, *answer the questions beginning on page 197.*

BODY LANGUAGE
PREVIEW QUESTIONS

_____ 1. Body language is
  a. to hit first, then ask questions.
  b. nonverbal but physical and emotional communication.
  c. talking with your hands.

_____ 2. The swiftest and most obvious type of body language is the
  a. smile.
  b. wink.
  c. touch.

_____ 3. Nonverbal language is
  a. partly instinctive.
  b. partly taught.
  c. partly imitative.
  d. all of the above.
  e. a and c only.

_____ 4. Territorial zones are
  a. an inviolate area around us that each of us keeps for our own.
  b. boundaries drawn between properties.
  c. psychological "wins" we achieve over each other.

_____ 5. Proxemics is the
  a. theories and observations about zones of territory and how we use them.
  b. written and scientific study of body language.
  c. the smallest recordable movement.

_____ 6. Masking is
  a. hiding our feelings by sitting off in the corner of an area.
  b. the outer face we show the world regardless of how we feel.
  c. disguising our physical discomforts by taking aspirins at will.

_____ 7. Kinesics is the
  a. science that deals with motion of masses.
  b. written form and scientific study of body language.
  c. theories and observations about zones of territory and how we use them.

_____ 8. We are using our understanding of body language in the best way if we use it to
  a. help us understand ourselves.
  b. psychoanalyze other people.
  c. develop our behavior patterns.

_____ 9. When body language is combined with self-confrontation it can
  a. cause self-deception.
  b. make a person do things contrary to his own wishes.
  c. make a person know when what he is doing with his body contradicts what he is saying with his mouth.

_____ 10. One thing you can do to test the validity of body language is to
  a. follow all the accepted rules.
  b. break a few rules and see what happens.
  c. speak to your friends about using body language.

Allow 10 points per correct answer.   Your score _____ %
Number of words: 61,500   Your rate _____

Answer key is on page 272.
Record rate and comprehension score on Course Data Sheet in Preview columns. Be sure that you have made a list of the specialized words, studied the list, and taken the vocabulary test before you do a good comprehension reading.

BODY LANGUAGE
GOOD COMPREHENSION QUESTIONS

_____ 1. There are two main elements to body language,
   a. the reflexive and nonreflexive actions.
   b. the delivery of the message and the reception of the message.
   c. the physical and the mental.

_____ 2. The struggle for superiority between animals
   a. is often only symbolic.
   b. usually ends in fierce death.
   c. requires intervention, whenever possible, to prevent death.

_____ 3. Close intimate distance is reserved for
   a. subways.
   b. very close friendships.
   c. boss-employee relationships.

_____ 4. The zones of man's space or territory are
   a. intimate distance.
   b. personal distance.
   c. social distance.
   d. all of these.
   e. none of these.

_____ 5. A distance of seven to twelve feet, as between a boss's desk and an employee, is the
   a. far phase of personal distance.
   b. close phase of public distance.
   c. far phase of social distance.
   d. close phase of social distance.

_____ 6. The reason the Arab may push his way into line in a public place is because
   a. he is rude.
   b. he is from the Middle East.
   c. Arabs have too much space in their own houses and by contrast tend to be pushy in public.
   d. he feels within his rights to do so, as he has no concept of privacy in a public place.

_____ 7. When an employee rushes into his executive's office, he
   a. probably has a great deal of status himself.
   b. will probably be reprimanded for his rudeness.
   c. is acting out of line and violating status.

_____ 8. Nonpersons are
   a. subhumans.
   b. people in a crowded place, such as a subway, whom one does not recognize as individuals in order to protect one's privacy.
   c. people who try to introduce themselves to strangers in crowded places.

_____ 9. Physical masking, such as the use of a veil by Middle Eastern women, is primarily used to
   a. create the image of a nonperson.
   b. create the freedom of anonymity in sexual encounters.
   c. conceal the woman's true emotions, thereby protecting her from male aggression.

_____ 10. The link of posture to emotions can be seen in the relationship between
   a. the sway back and an insecure ego.
   b. the double chin and an aggressive person.
   c. bowed shoulders and an angry person.

_____ 11. When one acts out one's deepest hidden emotions, such as beating a pillow to act out hostility toward a loved one, the result is often
   a. a release of other, positive emotions toward that person which were repressed by that hostile emotion.
   b. the unleashing of a psychotic person who will then beat things whenever he or she feels hostile.
   c. an exchange of apathy for hostility toward that person thereafter.

_____ 12. A presentation is
   a. a speech that is prepared carefully.
   b. all the positions a person goes through during the course of a conversation.
   c. a network of body language used to show rejection of a subject.

_____ 13. Eye management in our society means that
   a. there are accepted rules of how and how not to look at someone.
   b. eye levels are controlled by heights and positions.
   c. people who want respect require that others look at them in certain ways.

_____ 14. Crossed legs can be
   a. a sign of a person's personality.
   b. a clue to what a person is feeling at the moment.
   c. an indication of someone's mental health.

_____ 15. The following is generally true (choose one):
   a. If while you are speaking you look away, you are saying, "I agree with you."
   b. If while you are speaking you look at the listener, you are signaling, "I am certain of what I am saying."
   c. If while you are listening you look at the speaker, you mean, "I don't want you to know what I feel."

_____ 16. Sideways glances are
   a. a look from someone to the side of you.
   b. looks that involve turning quickly to the side to see what a person looks like.
   c. looks that want to see but not be seen.

_____ 17. We generally cross our arms in the same way all the time because
   a. arm crossing is a genetic, inborn trait.
   b. our personalities are fixed by the time we learn to cross our arms.
   c. we copy our parents.

_____ 18. Kinesic pictographs are
      a. tests of body language reactions.
      b. a notational system for body language.
      c. programmed therapy for body language.

_____ 19. A person's ethnic background
      a. probably creates differences in body language.
      b. is of no concern in body language.
      c. is the most important factor in body language.

_____ 20. The smallest measurement of body language is a
      a. presentation.
      b. dynamic.
      c. kine.

Allow 5 points per correct answer.   *Your score* _____ %
Number of words: 61,500   *Your rate* _____
Answer key is on page 272.
Record rate and comprehension score on Course Data Sheet in Good Comprehension columns.

BODY LANGUAGE
POSTVIEW QUESTIONS

_____ 1. Body language covers
      a. the collective unconscious.
      b. a mixture of conscious and unconscious body movements.
      c. gestures, nuance of language, and social patterns.

_____ 2. One form of nonverbal communication is guarding our territorial zones, which if violated
      a. will always be defended and retaliated for.
      b. causes individual reactions from uneasiness to aggression.
      c. changes the basic character and quality of any relationship.

_____ 3. When people remove the possibility of verbal communication and communicate only with body language
      a. the mask of language is gone and the truth somehow finds a way of expressing itself.
      b. people will not be able to communicate true feelings.
      c. everyone relaxes and has a good time.

_____ 4. Which of the following statements is true?
      a. Body language is a language all of its own and people can be interpreted through it exclusively.
      b. Spoken language is the clearest language of all.
      c. Both body language and spoken language are needed to grasp the full meaning of what a person is communicating.

_____ 5. The future of body language is
      a. our own development of it.
      b. in the development of more and more scientific analysis of its importance.
      c. in the use of body language for political gains and pleasing the crowd.

Allow 20 points per correct answer.   *Your score* _____ %
Number of words: 61,500   *Your rate* _____
Answer key is on page 272.
Record rate and comprehension score on Course Data Sheet in Postview columns.

BOOK WITH A SPECIALIZED VOCABULARY
GENERAL PREVIEW QUESTIONS

(To be used with a book other than *Body Language*.)

Title of Book _____

Author _____

1. What is the subject of this book? _____
   _____ (20 points)

2. For whom is this book intended (general population, law students, biology students, scientists, teachers, etc.)? _____
   _____ (20 points)

3. Name two topics mentioned in this book.

   (1) _____ (10 points)

   (2) _____ (10 points)

4. What was the writer's purpose in writing this book (usually stated in Preface or Introduction)? Check one:

   _____ a.   to explain the facts on the subject in detail.

   _____ b.   to report what happened.

   _____ c.   to give you *his* or *her* ideas on the subject.

   _____ d.   to persuade you to take some action.   (20 points)

5. Which of the following are included in this book (write "yes" or "no")? (2½ points each)

   _____ a.   introduction   _____ e.   index

   _____ b.   preface   _____ f.   graphs or charts

   _____ c.   glossary   _____ g.   illustrations, other than photographs

   _____ d.   chapter summaries _____ h.   bibliography

Directions: *To correct, find the answers in the book and check the accuracy of your answers. The point value of each answer is given after each question. Count up the points for each correct answer to find your score.*   Your score _____ %

Figure out the number of words in the book.   Your rate _____

Record title, rate, and comprehension score on Course Data Sheet in Preview columns. Using the form on page 191, be sure that you have made a list of the specialized words, studied the list and taken the vocabulary test before *you do the good comprehension reading.*

BOOK WITH A SPECIALIZED VOCABULARY
GENERAL GOOD COMPREHENSION QUESTIONS

1. What is the most important thing the author says about the subject of this book (write a brief sentence)?

   _____

   _____

2. Write two sentences stating two other important things said about the subject of this book.

    (1) _____

    (2) _____

3. At the end, does the author state a conclusion? _____

    What is the conclusion? _____

    _____

4. Of the specialized words you checked in the preview, which word appears to be the most important and is used the most often in this book? _____

5. Without looking at your list of definitions, write the meaning of the word you wrote in question 4.

    _____

    _____

6. Name another important specialized word you checked. _____

7. What is the definition of the word you named in question 6?

    _____

8. What is the most interesting thing you learned from this book (in one sentence)? _____

    _____

9. What is the most useful thing you learned from this book (in one sentence)?

    _____

    _____

10. From the information given in this book, what conclusion can *you* come to?

    _____

Postview to correct your answers.   *Your score* _____ %
Allow 10 points per correct answer.
Number of words _____   *Your rate* _____
Record rate and comprehension score on Course Data Sheet in Good Comprehension columns.

17

Critical Reading

Materials:
- Readings:
  Fahrenheit 451, or another previously read novel as a drill book
  "A Modest Proposal"
  "Paul's Case"

Objectives:
- To gain familiarity with critical thinking vocabulary
- To understand the sequence of literal, interpretive, critical reading
- To use critical thinking skills to evaluate fiction and nonfiction
- To learn how to apply the speed-study method for critical reading

DRILL PRACTICE

Using the book *Fahrenheit 451,* or another novel that you have previously read, do eye-pacing drills following the directions in Chapter 15, page 169. Take a drill rate and record it on your Course Data Sheet.

CRITICAL THINKING VOCABULARY

Since having familiarity with the terminology used to discuss critical reading and thinking will greatly improve comprehension of the concepts that will be presented in this chapter, begin by spending some time going over the vocabulary now, and later, refer back to it frequently, especially as you answer the questions on the practice readings.

These terms are grouped, as much as possible, according to their relationships to each other:

Critical Thinking Vocabulary

Critical Thinking–a logical thought process that questions, analyzes, and interprets for the purpose of evaluating and judging

Analysis–a breaking up of the whole into its parts and an examination of these parts to find out their nature, function, and interrelationships

Evaluation–the determination of the worth or quality

Judgment–an opinion or estimate

Interpretation–a recognition and understanding of the meaning author intended; one's own understanding of the work

Literal–based on the actual words in their ordinary meaning, not symbolic

Figurative Language–writing that uses figures of speech

Simile–a figure of speech in which a similarity between two objects is directly expressed using "like" or "as"

Metaphor–a figure of speech in which a similarity between two objects is suggested without being directly stated

Symbol–something which is itself and at the same time evokes other levels of meaning

Imagery–mental pictures or impressions evoked by the literal or figurative meanings

Irony–a form of expression in which the intended meaning is opposite to the usual sense

Sarcasm–a sneering, hurtful remark stated as opposite to its intended meaning

Satire—a literary writing attitude that blends a critical attitude with humor and wit for the purpose of exposing and improving a wrongful situation

Connotation—suggested meaning(s) of a word

Denotation—the dictionary meaning of a word

Generalization—overall principles usually derived from particular instances or details

Fact—a thing that has actually happened or is really true

Opinion—a conclusion or judgement based on one's feelings, attitude, or beliefs that seem true or probable to one's own mind, but have not been proven and are open to dispute

Evidence—something that tends to prove something else

Inference—the act of arriving at a decision or opinion by reasoning from known evidence

Conclusion—the final logical step in a reasoning process

Assumption—the taking for granted something to be a fact that has not been proven

Hypothesis—a tentative, unproven theory or idea

Valid—something that conforms to laws, logic, and fact and therefore cannot be disputed.

Tone—a manner of writing that shows the author's attitude toward the work; the predominant feeling of the work

CRITICAL THINKING AND READING

Basic to critical reading is critical thinking, thinking that carefully analyzes and evaluates every aspect of the work for the purpose of making a judgment about the value of the various aspects and the work as a whole. With this knowledge you come to a conclusion as to the intention of the author; and then, you decide if the author succeeded. This process, however, is complex, and you must avoid jumping to conclusions before you have uncovered all the pertinent information. Keep an open mind, but a questioning one that is not easily swayed.

Critical thinking is actually an advanced step in a series of steps. The first and most fundamental step is understanding the literal meaning of the work. The literal meaning is based on the actual written words used according to their ordinary dictionary meaning. When you comprehend what the words, sentences, and paragraphs actually mean without adding any thoughts or meanings not specifically stated, you are understanding the literal meaning.

The next step is understanding the interpretative meaning, which is based on a discriminating comprehension of the nature, function and interrelationships of the various parts of the work (analysis). Here you look for the suggested (connotative) meanings of words, phrases, and ideas. Recognize if the author is serious, joking, or sarcastic (tone). Conjure up the mental pictures the writing suggests (imagery). Recognize the way in which idea comparisons (similes, metaphors) clarify and affect the meaning. Use all the skills and techniques you possess to bring to light all the underlying (interpretive) meanings, those the author intended and your own understanding of the work.

Finally, now that you have set the ground work through understanding the literal and interpretive meanings, critical thinking and reading can occur. You have the necessary information to make a value judgment (critical thinking). Some general judgments about the effectiveness and success of the work apply to both fiction and nonfiction, but each form also has its unique aspects upon which judgments are made. These are discussed individually in the following sections.

Evaluating Nonfiction

In nonfiction the interpretive step also consists of examining and understanding additional areas such as recognizing facts, opinions, cause-effect relationships, and conclusions stated.

The critical thinking step evaluates each of these and other items. Are the facts actually true, or has the author taken for granted that which has not been proven (assumption)? When opinions are given, are they backed up with sufficient reliable proof (evidence) to make them acceptable? Do the causes and effects truly relate, or are they falsely related? Are the conclusions a logical result of the proof given in the body of the work?

From your evaluation of each part of the nonfiction work, you are prepared to accept or reject the ideas presented or to accept them with some reservations. You have come to your own conclusions regarding the value of the work.

Evaluating Fiction

In fiction, the interpretive step is a lengthy process because it consists of examining and completely understanding all the elements of fiction:

characters, plot, conflict, point-of-view, setting, style, symbol, and theme. (See page 153 for their definitions.)

The critical thinking step evaluates the author's choices and uses of the elements of fiction. Are the characters believable, drawn fully enough to accomplish the author's purposes for them? Does the action (plot) flow from what these characters would do, or has the author manipulated the story through coincidence? Is the problem around which the story revolves (conflict) justified and motivated by the characteristics and actions of the characters, leading to an inevitable resolution? Are the symbols necessary to complete the story, or are they superficially added to give the appearance of depth of meaning? Is the story revealed in the best possible way (point-of-view)? Is the author's style natural, and does the language both interest the reader and express the author's ideas well? And finally, is the author's message (theme) worthwhile?

The Reading Method

Use the four-step speed-study method (page 136) as the basic framework and do all the things for each step as previously instructed, but to the basic method (Chapter 13) add an additional step, a serious recall and thinking interlude that begins after the good comprehension reading and before the postview and continues through the postview.

These are the steps used for critical reading:

1. *Survey.* Determine if the work is fiction or nonfiction so that you will know whether to apply the speed-study method described in Chapter 13 (nonfiction) or in Chapter 14 (fiction).
2. *Preview-skim.* If the work is nonfiction, try to get a general idea of what the work covers, a sense of the organizational pattern, the difficulty level, and the main idea. If the work is fiction, recognize the main characters, the setting, point-of-view, and general sequence of events.
3. *Good Comprehension Reading.* In both nonfiction and fiction, try to understand the literal meaning and begin to unravel the interpretative meaning by recognizing the tone, connotative meanings, and imagery. Marking the text here is important.

In nonfiction, watch for facts, opinions, assumptions, evidence, cause-effect relationships, and conclusions.

In fiction, pay attention to all the elements of fiction as shown on the fiction chart, page 154, and allow yourself to pick up any thoughts that go beyond the literal meaning.

3A. *Recall and Think Interlude.* This step is first done alone, and then in conjunction with postviewing. At first spend time just remembering the literal and interpretative meanings and asking yourself the questions discussed previously either under "Evaluating Fiction" or "Evaluating Non-Fiction." Jot down your ideas. After you have evaluated and judged all the areas covered by the questions and are satisfied that you can do no more, begin the postviewing step.

4. *Postview.* Think of what possible information you have not been able to recall that would help you improve your evaluation. Postview, looking for the needed information. The best way to do this is to try to figure out where in the work the sought-for information is most likely to be found. Go directly to that spot. If you have no idea where to look, begin at the beginning. Skim a few pages; if the ideas are on the subject for which you are looking, continue until you find the exact information. If the ideas are not pertinent, skip several pages or go directly to the next chapter and continue skimming. Once you possess the additional information, resume evaluating and judging.

Think of what else you need; postview more to obtain it; evaluate and judge. Continue this think/postview/evaluation process until you are satisfied that your evaluations and judgments are thorough and valid.

Practice in Critical Reading

Following the modified speed-study method described, critically read the essay (nonfiction) "A Modest Proposal," on page 202 and the short story (fiction) "Paul's Case," on page 208.

SUMMARY

Critical reading is reading for the purpose of evaluating and judging the merits of a work. It is the final step in an analytical process that first recognizes the literal meaning, discovers the interpretive meaning, and finally judges the success of the work.

The method for reading critically uses the speed-study reading method to which a recall and think segment is added after the good comprehension reading and is continued through the postview step.

A MODEST PROPOSAL

Jonathan Swift

(Written in 1729, during a time when Ireland was experiencing a great famine, poverty, and English oppression.)

For Preventing the Children of Poor People in Ireland From Being a Burden to Their Parents or Country, and for Making Them Beneficial to the Public

It is a sad object to those who walk through this great town of Dublin or travel in the country, when they see the streets, the roads, and cabin doors, crowded with beggars of the female-sex, followed by three, four, or six children, all in rags and asking every passenger for money. These mothers, instead of being able to work for their honest livelihood, are forced to employ all their time in strolling to beg sustenance for their helpless infants, who, as they grow up, either turn thieves for want of work, or leave their dear native country to fight for Spain or sell themselves to the Barbadoes as mercenaries.

I think it is agreed by all parties that this enormous number of children in the arms, or on the backs, or at the heels of their mothers, and frequently of their fathers, is in the present deplorable state of the kingdom a very great additional grievance; and therefore whoever could find out a fair, cheap, and easy method of making these children sound, useful members of the commonwealth would deserve so well of the public as to have his statue set up for a preserver of the nation.

But my intention is very far from being confined to provide only for the children of professed beggars; it is of a much greater extent, and shall take in the whole number of infants at a certain age who are born of parents in effect as little able to support them as those who demand our charity in the streets.

As to my own part, having turned my thoughts for many years upon this important subject, and maturely weighed the several schemes of other projectors, I have always found them grossly mistaken in their computation. It is true, a child just dropped from its mother may be supported by her milk for a year, with little other nourishment; at most not above the value of two shillings, which the mother may certainly get, or the value in scraps, by her lawful occupation of begging; and it is exactly at one year old that I propose to provide for them in such a manner as instead of being a charge upon

This story has been adapted by the author for use in this book.

their parents or the parish, or wanting food and clothing for the rest of their lives, they shall on the contrary contribute to the feeding, and partly to the clothing, of many thousands.

There is likewise another great advantage in my scheme, that it will prevent those voluntary abortions, and that horrid practice of women murdering their bastard children, alas, too frequent among us, sacrificing the poor innocent babes, I doubt, more to avoid the expense than the shame, which would move tears and pity in the most savage and inhuman breast.

The number of souls in this kingdom being usually reckoned one million and a half, of these I calculate there may be about two hundred thousand couple whose wives are breeders; from which number I subtract thirty thousand couples who are able to maintain their own children, although I understand there cannot be so many under the present distresses of the kingdom; but this being granted, there will remain an hundred and seventy thousand breeders. I again subtract fifty thousand for those women who miscarry, or whose children die by accident or disease within the year. There only remain a hundred and twenty thousand children of poor parents annually born. The question therefore is, how this number shall be reared and provided for, which, as I have already said, under the present situation of affairs, is utterly impossible by all the methods hitherto proposed. For we can neither employ them in handicraft or agriculture; we neither build houses (I mean in the country) nor cultivate land. They can very seldom pick up a livelihood by stealing till they arrive at six years old; although I confess they learn the rudiments much earlier, during which time they can however be looked upon only as probationers, as I have been informed by a principal gentleman in the county of Cavan, who protested to me that he never knew above one or two instances under the age of six, even in a part of the kingdom so renowned for the quickest proficiency in that art.

I am assured by our merchants that a boy or a girl before twelve years old is no salable commodity; and even when they come to this age they will not yield above three pounds, or three pounds and half a crown at most on the Exchange; which cannot turn to account either the parents or the kingdom, the charge of food and clothing having been at least four times that value.

I shall now therefore humbly propose my own thoughts, which I hope will not be liable to the least objection.

I have been assured by a very knowing American of my acquaintance in London, that a young healthy child well nursed is at a year old a most delicious, nourishing, and wholesome food, whether stewed, roasted, baked, or boiled; and I make no doubt that it will equally serve in a fricasse or a ragout.

I do therefore humbly offer it to public consideration that of the hundred and twenty thousand children, already computed, twenty thousand may be reserved for breed, whereof only one fourth part to be males, which is more than we allow to sheep, cattle, or swine; and my reason is that these children are seldom the fruits of marriage, a circumstance not much regarded by our savages, therefore one male will be sufficient to serve four females. That the remaining hundred thousand may at a year old be offered in sale to the persons of quality and fortune through the kingdom, always advising the mother to let them suck plentifully in the last month, so as to render them plump and fat for a good table. A child will make two dishes at an entertainment for friends; and when the family dines alone, the fore or hind quarter will make a reasonable dish, and seasoned with a little pepper or salt will be very good boiled on the fourth day, especially in winter.

I have reckoned upon a medium that a child just born will weigh twelve pounds, and in a solar year if tolerably nursed increaseth to twenty-eight pounds.

I grant this food will be somewhat dear, and therefore very proper for landlords, who, as they have already devoured most of the parents, seem to have the best title to the children.

Infant's flesh will be in season throughout the year, but more plentiful in March, and a little before and after. For we are told by a grave author, an eminent French physician, that fish being a prolific diet, there are more children born in Roman Catholic countries about nine months after Lent than at any other season; therefore, reckoning a year after Lent, the markets will be more glutted than usual, because the number of popish infants is at least three to one in this kingdom; and therefore it will have one other collateral advantage, by lessening the number of Papists among us.

I have already computed the charge of nursing a beggar's child (in which list I reckon all cottagers, laborers, and four fifths of the farmers) to be about two shillings per annum, rags included; and I believe no gentleman would complain to give ten shillings for the carcass of a good fat child, which, as I have said, will make four dishes of excellent nutritive meat, when he hath only some particular friend or his own family to dine with him. Thus the squire will learn to be a good landlord, and grow popular among the tenants; the mother will have eight shillings net profit, and be fit for work till she produces another child.

Those who are more thrifty (as I must confess the times require) may strip the carcass; the skin of which artificially dressed will make admirable gloves for ladies, and summer boots for fine gentlemen.

As to our city of Dublin, shops may be appointed for this purpose in the most convenient parts of it, and butchers we may be assured will not be wanting; although I rather recommend buying the children alive, and dressing them hot from the knife as we do roasting pigs.

A very worthy person, a true lover of his country, and whose virtues I highly esteem, was lately pleased in discoursing on this matter to offer a refinement upon my scheme. He said that many gentlemen of this kingdom, having of late destroyed their deer, he conceived that the want of venison might be well supplied by the bodies of young lads and maidens, not exceeding fourteen years of age nor under twelve, so great a number of both sexes in every county being now ready to starve for want of work and service; and these to be disposed of by their parents, if alive, or otherwise by their nearest relations. But with due deference to so excellent a friend and so deserving a patriot, I cannot be altogether in his sentiments; for as to the males, my American acquaintance assured me from frequent experience that their flesh was generally tough and lean, like that of our schoolboys, by continual exercise, and their taste disagreeable; and to fatten them would not answer the charge. Then as to the females, it would, I think with humble submission, be a loss to the public, because they soon would become breeders themselves: and besides, it is not improbable that some scrupulous people might be apt to censure such a practice (although indeed very unjustly) as a little bordering upon cruelty; which, I confess, hath always been with me the strongest objection against any project, how well soever intended.

But in order to justify my friend, he confessed that this expedient was put into his head by the famous Psalmanazar, a native of the island Formosa, who came from thence to London about twenty years ago, and in conversation told my friend that in his country when any young person happened to be put to death, the executioner sold the carcass to persons of quality as a prime dainty; and that in his time the body of a plump girl of fifteen, who was crucified for an attempt to poison the emperor, was sold to his Imperial Majesty's prime minister of state, and other great mandarins of the court, in joints from the gibbet, at four hundred crowns. Neither indeed can I deny that if the same use were made of several plump young girls in this town, who without one

204   *Critical Reading*

single groat to their fortunes cannot stir abroad without a chair, and appear at the playhouse and assemblies in foreign fineries which they never will pay for, the kingdom would not be the worse.

Some persons of a desponding spirit are in great concern about that vast number of poor people who are aged, diseased, or maimed, and I have been desired to employ my thoughts what course may be taken to ease the nation of so grievous an encumbrance. But I am not in the least pain upon that matter, because it is very well known that they are every day dying and rotting by cold and famine, and filth and vermin, as fast as can be reasonably expected. And as to the younger laborers, they are now in almost as hopeful a condition. They cannot get work, and consequently pine away for want of nourishment to a degree that if at any time they are accidentally hired to common labor, they have not strength to perform it; and thus the country and themselves are happily delivered from the evils to come.

I have too long digressed, and therefore shall return to my subject. I think the advantages by the proposal which I have made are obvious and many, as well as of the highest importance.

For first, as I have already observed, it would greatly lessen the number of Papists, with whom we are yearly overrun, being the principal breeders of the nation as well as our most dangerous enemies; and who stay at home on purpose to deliver the kingdom to the Pretender, hoping to take their advantage by the absence of so many good Protestants, who have chosen rather to leave their country than to stay at home and pay tithes against their conscience to an Episcopal curate.

Secondly, the poorer tenants will have something valuable of their own, which by law may be made liable to distress, and help to pay their landlord's rent, their corn and cattle being already seized and money a thing unknown.

Thirdly, whereas the maintenance of an hundred thousand children, from two years old and upwards, cannot be computed at less than ten shillings a piece per annum, the nation's stock will be thereby increased fifty thousand pounds per annum, besides the profit of a new dish introduced to the tables of all gentlemen of fortune in the kingdom who have any refinement in taste. And the money will circulate among ourselves, the goods being entirely of our own growth and manufacture.

Fourthly, the constant breeders, besides the gain of eight shillings sterling per annum by the sale of their children, will be rid of the charge of maintaining them after the first year.

Fifthly, this food would likewise bring great custom to taverns, where the vintners will certainly be so prudent as to procure the best receipts for dressing it to perfection, and consequently have their houses frequented by all the fine gentlemen, who justly value themselves upon their knowledge in good eating; and a skillful cook, who understands how to oblige his guests, will contrive to make it as expensive as they please.

Sixthly, this would be a great inducement to marriage, which all wise nations have either encouraged by rewards or enforced by laws and penalties. It would increase the care and tenderness of mothers toward their children, when they were sure of a settlement for life to the poor babes, provided in some sort by the public, to their annual profit instead of expense. We should see an honest emulation among the married women, which of them could bring the fattest child to the market. Men would become as fond of their wives during the time of their pregnancy as they are now of their mares in foal, their cows in calf, or sows when they are ready to farrow; nor offer to beat or kick them (as is too frequent a practice) for fear of miscarriage.

Many other advantages might be enumerated. For instance, the addition of some thousand carcasses in our exportation of barreled beef, the propagation of swine's flesh, and improvement in the art of making good bacon, so much wanted among us by the great destruction of pigs, too frequent at our tables, which are no way comparable in taste or magnificence to a well-grown, fat, yearling child, which roasted whole will make a considerable figure at a lord mayor's feast or any other public entertainment. But this and many others I omit, being studious of brevity.

Supposing that one thousand families in this city would be constant customers for infants' flesh, besides others who might have it at merry meetings, particularly weddings and christenings, I compute that Dublin would take off annually about twenty thousand carcasses, and the rest of the kingdom (where probably they will be sold somewhat cheaper) the remaining eighty thousand.

I can think of no one objection that will possibly be raised against this proposal, unless it should be urged that the number of people will be thereby much lessened in the kingdom. This I freely own, and it was indeed one principal design in offering it to the world. I desire the reader will observe, that I calculate my remedy for this one individual kingdom of Ireland and for no other that ever was, is, or I think ever can be upon earth. Therefore let no man talk to me of other expedients: of taxing our absentees at five shillings a pound: of using neither clothes nor household furniture except what is of our own growth and manufacture: of utterly rejecting the materials and instruments that promote foreign luxury: of curing the expensiveness of pride, vanity, idleness, and gaming in our women: of introducing a vein of economy, prudence, and temperance: of learning to love our country, in the want of which we differ even from Laplanders and the inhabitants of Topinamboo: of quitting our animosities and factions: of being a little cautious not to sell our country and conscience for nothing: of teaching landlords to have at least one degree of mercy toward their tenants: lastly, of putting a spirit of honesty, industry, and skill into our shopkeepers; who, if a resolution could now be taken to buy only our native goods, would immediately unite to cheat and exact upon us in the price, the measure, and the goodness, nor could ever yet be brought to make one fair proposal of just dealing, though often and earnestly invited to it.

Therefore I repeat, let no man talk to me of these and the like expedients, till he has at least some glimpse of hope that there will ever be some hearty and sincere attempt to put them in practice.

But as to myself, having been wearied out for many years with offering vain, idle, visionary thoughts, and at length utterly despairing of success, I fortunately fell upon this proposal, which, as it is wholly new, so it hath something solid and real, of no expense and little trouble, full in our own power, and whereby we can incur no danger in disobliging England. For this kind of commodity will not bear exportation, the flesh being of too tender a consistence to admit a long continuance in salt, although perhaps I could name a country which would be glad to eat up our whole nation without it.

After all, I am not so violently bent upon my own opinion as to reject any offer proposed by wise men, which shall be found equally innocent, cheap, easy, and effectual. But before something of that kind shall be advanced in contradiction to my scheme, and offering a better, I desire the author or authors will be pleased maturely to consider two points. First, as things now stand, how they will be able to find food and clothing for an hundred thousand useless mouths and backs. And secondly, there being a round million of creatures in human figure throughout this kingdom, whose sole subsistence put into a common stock would leave them in debt two millions of pounds sterling, adding those who are beggars by profession to the bulk of farmers, cottagers, and laborers, with their wives and children who are beggars in effect; I desire those politicians who dislike my overture, and may perhaps be so bold to attempt an answer, that they will first ask the parents of these mortals whether they would not at this day think it a great happiness to have been sold for food at a year old in the manner I prescribe, and thereby have avoided such a perpetual scene of misfortunes as they have since gone through by the oppression of landlords, the impossibility of paying rent without money or trade, the want of common sustenance, with neither house nor clothes to cover them from the inclemencies of the weather, and the most inevitable prospect of entailing the like or greater miseries upon their breed forever.

I profess, in the sincerity of my heart, that I have not the least personal interest in endeavoring to promote this necessary work, having no other motive than the public good of my country, by advancing our trade, providing for infants, relieving the poor, and giving some pleasure to the rich. I have no children by which I can propose to get a single penny; the youngest being nine years old, and my wife past childbearing.

PREVIEW QUESTIONS

(You may need to refer to the "Critical Thinking Vocabulary" to understand the questions.)

_____ 1. The problem addressed in this proposal is
    a. the war between Ireland and England.
    b. what to do with the large number of poor children.
    c. the shortage of meat.
    d. the laziness of the poor.

_____ 2. The proposal primarily
    a. presents a solution.
    b. requests others to offer a solution.
    c. admits there is no solution.
    d. argues in favor of accepting the situation as it is.

_____ 3. The proposal appears to have
    a. only one main argument to influence the reader.
    b. two main arguments.
    c. three arguments.
    d. many arguments.

_____ 4. The tone *appears* to be
    a. serious.
    b. comic.
    c. sad.
    d. angry.

_____ 5. The organization appears to consist of the following parts
a. problem, comparison-contrast, solution.
b. questions, cause-effect, answers.
c. problem, solution, arguments, alternatives.
d. accusations, possible penalties.

Allow 20 points per correct answer.   *Your score* _____ %
Number of words: 4000   *Your rate* _____
Answer key is on page 272.
Record rate and comprehension score on Course Data Sheet in Preview columns.

GOOD COMPREHENSION QUESTIONS

_____ 1. A precise term for the tone is
a. sarcasm.
b. tragedy.
c. comedy.
d. satire.

_____ 2. The problem, as *literally* stated, regarding the poor is that
a. parents refuse to take care of their children.
b. the children are a burden on parents and society.
c. the children are evil.
d. the rich take unfair advantage of the poor.

_____ 3. The major solution presented suggests that children of the poor be
a. educated.
b. aborted before birth.
c. sold for food and clothing to the rich.
d. transported to another country.

_____ 4. One stated advantage to this proposal would be to
a. improve the poor mothers' lot.
b. equalize the wealth of the country.
c. deprive the rich of delicacies.
d. make the country a democracy.

_____ 5. The author frequently states that his proposal would be
a. universally acceptable.
b. easy, cheap, and fair.
c. difficult but profitable.
d. the only possible solution.

_____ 6. It is written in the
a. first person, using "I," "our," and "we."
b. second person, using "you," and "your."
c. third person, referring only to "he," "him," and "they."

_____ 7. Frequently the author refers to poor people using words generally used for
a. livestock.
b. objects.
c. rich people.
d. foreigners.

_____ 8. One type of evidence frequently used is
   a. comparisons and contrasts.
   b. cause-effect relationships.
   c. examples of specific people.
   d. specific numbers and figures.

_____ 9. Toward the end, Jonathan Swift offers a list of several alternative solutions we could interpret as being
   a. totally without merit.
   b. proposals he truly endorses.
   c. good ones, but ones that would not work.
   d. ones that would ruin the country.

_____ 10. We could classify the proposal aspect of this work as being based on
   a. fact.
   b. opinion.

Allow 10 points per each correct answer.   *Your score* _____ %
Number of words: 4000   *Your rate* _____
Answer key is on page 272.
Record rate and comprehension score on Course Data Sheet in Good Comprehension columns.

RECALL/THINK (Write the answers on a separate sheet.)

1. Summarize the literal meaning of the proposal.
2. Name the known facts of the situation discussed.
3. Interpret the author's opinion by writing what you think it actually is.

After the following postview, compare your answers to the preceding questions with the sugested answers on page 272. This score is *not* recorded on Course Data Sheet.

POSTVIEW QUESTIONS

_____ 1. The intention of the author is to
   a. ridicule England's handling of Ireland's poverty situation.
   b. ridicule cannibalism practiced in many countries.
   c. entertain the reader through shock.
   d. improve his literary reputation.

_____ 2. One reason we can most probably attribute his succeeding in his intention is
   a. his use of authoratative, educated words.
   b. the immediate recognition by the reader that he doesn't mean it.
   c. his serious, detailed descriptions of his plan.
   d. his making fun of important, but unpopular dignitaries.

_____ 3. Another reason for his great success is probably his
   a. stating that he, personally, would not profit from the plan.
   b. creating suspense by keeping the plan a secret until the end.
   c. obvious humor.
   d. depicting the problem in detail right at the beginning.

_____ 4. Another reason for his success is probably his stated
   a. support of a revolution to help the poor.
   b. attitude of wanting to help the poor, as well as the country and the rich.
   c. condemnation of England's actions toward the poor.
   d. revulsion against the poor begging for food.

_____ 5. The extreme revulsion the reader may feel upon recognition of the literal interpretation is
   a. not justified by the result.
   b. beyond the bounds of human decency.
   c. indicative of the weakness of the work.
   d. a technique that adds to the work's success.

Allow 20 points per correct answer.   Your score _____ %
Number of words: 4000   Your rate _____
Answer key is on page 273.
Record rate and comprehension score on Course Data Sheet in Postview columns.

PAUL'S CASE
A Study in Temperament

Willa Cather

It was Paul's afternoon to appear before the faculty of the Pittsburgh High School to account for his various misdemeanours. He had been suspended a week ago, and his father had called at the Principal's office and confessed his perplexity about his son. Paul entered the faculty room suave and smiling. His clothes were a trifle outgrown and the tan velvet on the collar of his open overcoat was frayed and worn; but for all that there was something of the dandy about him, and he wore an opal pin in his neatly knotted black four-in-hand, and a red carnation in his buttonhole. This latter adornment the faculty somehow felt was not properly significant of the contrite spirit befitting a boy under the ban of suspension.

Paul was tall for his age and very thin, with high, cramped shoulders and a narrow chest. His eyes were remarkable for a certain hysterical brilliancy and he continually used them in a conscious, theatrical sort of way, peculiarly offensive in a boy. The pupils were abnormally large, as though he were addicted to belladonna, but there was a glassy glitter about them which that drug does not produce.

When questioned by the Principal as to why he was there, Paul stated, politely enough, that he wanted to come back to school. This was a lie, but Paul was quite accustomed to lying; found it, indeed, indispensable for overcoming friction, His teachers were asked to state their respective charges against him, which they did with such a rancour and aggrievedness as evinced that this was not a usual case. Disorder and impertinence were among the offenses named, yet each of his instructors felt that it was scarcely possible to put into words the real cause of the trouble, which lay in a sort of hysterically defiant manner of the boy's; in the contempt which they all knew he felt for them, and which he seemingly made not the least effort to conceal. Once, when he had been making a synopsis of a paragraph at the blackboard, his English teacher had stepped to his side and attempted to guide his hand. Paul had started back with a shudder and thrust his hands violently behind him. The astonished woman could scarcely have been more hurt and embarrassed had he struck at her. The insult was so involuntary and definitely personal as to be unforgettable. In

one way and another, he had made all his teachers, men and women alike, conscious of the same feeling of physical aversion. In one class he habitually sat with his hand shading his eyes; in another he always looked out of the window during the recitation; in another he made a running commentary on the lecture, with humorous intention.

His teachers felt this afternoon that his whole attitude was symbolized by his shrug and his flippantly red carnation flower, and they fell upon him without mercy, his English teacher leading the pack. He stood through it smiling, his pale lips parted over his white teeth. (His lips were continually twitching, and he had a habit of raising his eyebrows that was contemptuous and irritating to the last degree.) Older boys than Paul had broken down and shed tears under that baptism of fire, but his set smile did not once desert him, and his only sign of discomfort was the nervous trembling of the fingers that toyed with the buttons of his overcoat and an occasional jerking of the other hand that held his hat. Paul was always smiling, always glancing about him, seeming to feel that people might be watching him and trying to detect something. This conscious expression, since it was as far as possible from boyish mirthfulness, was usually attributed to insolence or "smartness."

As the inquisition proceeded, one of his instructors repeated an impertinent remark of the boy's, and the Principal asked him whether he thought that a courteous speech to have made a woman. Paul shrugged his shoulders slightly and his eyebrows twitched.

"I don't know," he replied. "I didn't mean to be polite or impolite, either. I guess it's a sort of way I have of saying things regardless."

The Principal, who was a sympathetic man, asked him whether he didn't think that a way it would be well to get rid of. Paul grinned and said he guessed so. When he was told that he could go, he bowed gracefully and went out. His bow was but a repetition of the scandalous red carnation.

His teachers were in despair, and his drawing master voiced the feeling of them all when he declared there was something about the boy which none of them understood. He added: "I don't really believe that smile of his comes altogether from insolence; there's something sort of haunted about it. The boy is not strong, for one thing. I happen to know that he was born in Colorado, only a few months before his mother died out there of a long illness. There is something wrong about the fellow."

The drawing master had come to realize that, in looking at Paul, one saw only his white teeth and the forced animation of his eyes. One warm afternoon the boy had gone to sleep at his drawing-board, and his master had noted with amazement what a white, blue-veined face it was; drawn and wrinkled like an old man's about the eyes, the lips twitching even in his sleep, and stiff with a nervous tension that drew them back from his teeth.

His teachers left the building dissatisfied and unhappy; humiliated to have felt so vindictive toward a mere boy, to have uttered this feeling in cutting terms, and to have set each other on, as it were, in the gruesome game of intemperate reproach. Some of them remembered having seen a miserable street cat set at bay by a ring of tormentors.

As for Paul, he ran down the hill whistling the Solders' Chorus from *Faust* looking wildly behind him now and then to see whether some of his teachers were not there to writhe under his lightheartedness. As it was now late in the afternoon and Paul was on duty that evening as usher at Carnegie Hall, he decided that he would not go home to supper. When he reached the concert hall the doors were not yet open and, as it was chilly outside, he decided to go up into the picture gallery—always deserted at this hour—where there were some of Raffelli's gay studies of Paris streets and an airy blue Venetian scene or two that always exhilarated him. He was delighted to find no one in the gallery but the old guard, who sat in one corner, a newspaper on his knee, a black patch over one eye and the other closed. Paul possessed himself of the place and walked confidently up and down, whistling under his breath. After a while he sat down before a blue Rico and lost himself. When he bethought him to look at his watch, it was after seven o'clock, and he rose with a start and ran downstairs, making a face at Augustus, peering out from the cast-room, and an evil gesture at the Venus of Milo as he passed her on the stairway.

When Paul reached the ushers' dressing-room half-a-dozen boys were there already, and he began excitedly to tumble into his uniform. It was one of the few that at all approached fitting, and Paul thought it very becoming—though he knew that the tight, straight coat accentuated his narrow chest, about which he was exceedingly sensitive. He was always considerably excited while he dressed, twanging all over to the tuning of the strings and the preliminary flourishes of the horns in the music-room; but to-night he seemed quite beside himself, and he teased and plagued the boys until, telling him that he was crazy, they put him down on the floor and sat on him.

Somewhat calmed by his suppression, Paul dashed out to the front of the house to seat the early comers. He was a model usher; gracious and smiling he ran up and down the aisles; nothing was too much trouble for him; he carried messages and brought programmes as though it were his greatest pleasure in life, and all the people in his section thought him a charming boy, feeling that he remembered and admired them. As the house filled, he grew more and more vivacious and animated, and the colour came to his cheeks and lips. It was very much as though this were a great reception and Paul were the host. Just as the musicians came out to take their places, his English teacher arrived with checks for the seats which a prominent manufacturer had taken for the season. She betrayed some embarrassment when she handed Paul the tickets, and a *hauteur* which subsequently made her feel very foolish. Paul was startled for a moment, and had the feeling of wanting to put her out; what business had she here among all these fine people and gay colours? He looked her over and decided that she was not appropriately dressed and must be a fool to sit downstairs in such togs. The tickets had probably been sent her out of kindness, he reflected as he put down a seat for her, and she had about as much right to sit there as he had.

When the symphony began Paul sank into one of the rear seats with a long sigh of relief, and lost himself as he had done before the Rico. It was not that symphonies, as such, meant anything in particular to Paul, but the first sigh of the instruments seemed to free some hilarious and potent spirit within him; something that struggled there like the Genius in the bottle found by the Arab fisherman. He felt a sudden zest of life; the lights danced before his eyes and the concert hall blazed into unimaginable splendour. When the soprano soloist came on, Paul forgot even the nastiness of his teacher's being there and gave himself up to the peculiar stimulus such personages always had for him. The soloist chanced to be a German woman, by no means in her first youth, and the mother of many children; but she wore an elaborate gown and a tiara, and above all she had that indefinable air of achievement, that world-shine upon her, which, in Paul's eyes, made her a veritable queen of Romance.

After a concert was over Paul was always irritable and wretched until he got to sleep, and tonight he was even more than usually restless. He had the feeling of not being able to let down, of its being impossible to give up this delicious excitement which was the only thing that could be called living at all. During the last number he withdrew and, after hastily changing his clothes in the dressing-room, slipped out to the side door where the soprano's carriage stood. Here he began pacing rapidly up and down the walk, waiting to see her come out.

Over yonder the Schenley, in its vacant stretch, loomed big and square through the fine rain, the windows of its twelve stories glowing like those of a lighted cardboard house under a Christmas tree. All the actors and singers of the better class stayed there when they were in the city, and a number of the big manufacturers of the place lived there in the winter. Paul had often hung about the hotel, watching the people go in and out, longing to enter and leave schoolmasters and dull care behind him forever.

At last the singer came out, accompanied by the conductor, who helped her into her carriage and closed the door with a cordial *auf wiedersehen* which set Paul to wondering whether she were not an old sweetheart of his. Paul followed the carriage over to the hotel, walking so rapidly as not to be far from the entrance when the singer alighted and disappeared behind the swinging glass doors that were opened by a negro in a tall hat and a long coat. In the moment that the door was ajar it seemed to Paul that he, too, entered. He seemed to feel himself go after her up the steps, into the warm, lighted building, into an exotic, a tropical world of shiny, glistening surfaces and basking ease. He reflected upon the mysterious dishes that were brought into the dining-room, the green bottles in buckets of ice, as he had seen them in the supper party pictures of the *Sunday World* supplement. A quick gust of wind brought the rain down with sudden vehemence, and Paul was startled to find that he was

still outside in the slush of the gravel driveway; that his boots were letting in the water and his scanty overcoat was clinging wet about him; that the lights in front of the concert hall were out, and that the rain was driving in sheets between him and the orange glow of the windows above him. There it was, what he wanted—tangibly before him, like the fairy world of a Christmas pantomime, but mocking spirits stood guard at the doors, and, as the rain beat in his face, Paul wondered whether he were destined always to shiver in the black night outside, looking up at it.

He turned and walked reluctantly toward the car tracks. The end had to come sometime; his father in his night-clothes at the top of the stairs, explanations that did not explain, hastily improvised fictions that were forever tripping him up, his upstairs room and its horrible yellow wall-paper, the creaking bureau with the greasy plush collar-box, and over his painted wooden bed the pictures of George Washington and John Calvin, and the framed motto, "Feed my Lambs," which had been worked in red worsted by his mother.

Half an hour later, Paul alighted from his car and went slowly down one of the side streets off the main thoroughfare. It was a highly respectable street, where all the houses were exactly alike, and where business men of moderate means begot and reared large families of children, all of whom went to Sabbath-school and learned the shorter catechism, and were interested in arithmetic; all of whom were as exactly alike as their homes, and of a piece with the monotony in which they lived. Paul never went up Cordelia Street without a shudder of loathing. His home was next to the house of the Cumberland minister. He approached it to-night with the nerveless sense of defeat, the hopeless feeling of sinking back forever into ugliness and commonness that he had always had when he came home. The moment he turned into Cordelia Street he felt the waters close above his head. After each of these orgies of living, he experienced all the physical depression which follows a debauch; the loathing of respectable beds, of common food, of a house pene-

trated by kitchen odours; a shuddering repulsion for the flavourless, colourless mass of every-day existence; a morbid desire for cool things and soft lights and fresh flowers.

The nearer he approached the house, the more absolutely unequal Paul felt to the sight of it all; his ugly sleeping chamber; the cold bathroom with the grimy zinc tub, the cracked mirror, the dripping spiggots; his father, at the top of the stairs, his hairy legs sticking out from his night-shirt, his feet thrust into carpet slippers. He was so much later than usual that there would certainly be inquiries and reproaches. Paul stopped short before the door. He felt that he could not be accosted by his father to-night; that he could not toss again on that miserable bed. He would not go in. He would tell his father that he had no car fare, and it was raining so hard he had gone home with one of the boys and stayed all night.

Meanwhile, he was wet and cold. He went around to the back of the house and tried one of the basement windows, found it open, raised it cautiously, and scrambled down the cellar wall to the floor. There he stood, holding his breath, terrified by the noise he had made, but the floor above him was silent, and there was no creak on the stairs. He found a soap-box, and carried it over to the soft ring of light that streamed from the furnace door, and sat down. He was horribly afraid of rats, so he did not try to sleep, but sat looking distrustfully at the dark, still terrified lest he might have awakened his father. In such reactions, after one of the experiences which made days and nights out of the dreary blanks of the calendar, when his senses were deadened, Paul's head was always singularly clear. Suppose his father had heard him getting in at the window and had come down and shot him for a burglar? Then, again, suppose his father had come down, pistol in hand, and he had cried out in time to save himself, and his father had been horrified to think how nearly he had killed him? Then, again, suppose a day should come when his father would remember that night, and wish there had been no warning cry to stay his hand? With this last supposition Paul entertained himself until daybreak.

The following Sunday was fine; the sodden November chill was broken by the last flash of autumnal summer. In the morning Paul had to go to church and Sabbath-school, as always. On seasonable Sunday afternoons the burghers of Cordelia Street always sat out on their front "stoops," and talked to their neighbors on the next stoop, or called to those across the street in neighbourly fashion. The men usually sat on gay cushions placed upon the steps that led down to the sidewalk, while the women, in their Sunday "waists," sat in rockers on the cramped porches, pretending to be greatly at their ease. The children played in the streets; there were so many of them that the place resembled the recreation grounds of a kindergarten. The men on the steps—all in their shirt sleeves, their vests unbuttoned—sat with their legs well apart, their stomachs comfortably protruding, and talked of the prices of things, or told anecdotes of the sagacity of their various chiefs and overlords. They occasionally looked over the multitude of squabbling children, listened affectionately to their high-pitched, nasal voices, smiling to see their own proclivities reproduced in their offspring, and interspersed their legends of the iron kings with remarks about their sons' progress at school, their grades in arithmetic, and the amounts they had saved in their toy banks.

On this last Sunday of November, Paul sat all the afternoon on the lowest step of his "stoop," staring into the street, while his sisters, in their rockers, were talking to the minister's daughters next door about how many shirt-waists they had made in the last week, and how many waffles some one had eaten at the last church supper. When the weather was warm, and his father was in a particularly jovial frame of mind, the girls made lemonade, which was always brought out in a red-glass pitcher, ornamented with forget-me-nots in blue enamel. This the girls thought very fine, and the neighbours always joked about the suspicious colour of the pitcher.

To-day Paul's father sat on the top step, talking to a young man who shifted a restless baby from knee to knee. He happened to be the young man who was daily held up to Paul as a model, and after whom it was his father's dearest hope that he would pattern. This young man was of a ruddy complexion, with a compressed, red mouth, and faded, near-sighted eyes, over which he wore thick spectacles, with gold bows that curved about his ears. He was clerk to one of the magnates of a great steel corporation, and was looked upon in Cordelia Street as a young man with a future. There was a story that, some five years ago—he was now barely twenty-six—he had been a trifle dissipated but in order to curb his appetites and save the loss of time and strength that a sowing of wild oats might have entailed, he had taken his chief's advice, oft reiterated to his employees, and at twenty-one had married the first woman whom he could persuade to share his fortunes. She happened to be an angular schoolmistress, much older than he, who also wore thick glasses, and who had now borne him four children, all near-sighted, like herself.

The young man was relating how his chief, now cruising in the Mediterranean, kept in touch with all the details of the business, arranging his office hours on his yacht just as though he were at home, and "knocking off work enough to keep two stenographers busy." His father told, in turn, the plan his corporation was considering, of putting in an electric railway plant at Cairo. Paul snapped his teeth; he had an awful apprehension that they might spoil it all before he got there. Yet he rather liked to hear these legends of the iron kings, that were told and retold on Sundays and holidays; these stories of palaces in Venice, yachts on the Mediterranean, and high play at Monte Carlo appealed to his fancy, and he was interested in the triumphs of these cash boys who had become famous, though he had no mind for the cash-boy stage.

After supper was over, and he had helped to dry the dishes, Paul nervously asked his father whether he could go to George's to get some help in his geometry, and still more nervously asked for car fare. This latter request he had to repeat, as his father, on principle, did not like to hear requests for money, whether much or little. He asked Paul whether he could not go to some boy who lived nearer, and told him that he ought not to leave his school work until Sunday; but he gave him the dime. He was not a poor man, but he had a worthy ambition to come up in the world. His only reason for allowing Paul to usher was, that he thought a boy ought to be earning a little.

Paul bounded upstairs, scrubbed the greasy odour of the dish-water from his hands with the ill-smelling soap he hated, and then shook over his fingers a few drops of violet water from the bottle he kept hidden in his drawer. He left the house with his geometry conspicuously under his arm, and the moment he got out of Cordelia Street and boarded a downtown car, he shook off the lethargy of two deadening days, and began to live again.

The leading juvenile of the permanent stock company which played at one of the downtown theatres was an acquaintance of Paul's, and the boy had been invited to drop in at the Sunday-night rehearsals whenever he could. For more than a year Paul had spent every available moment loitering about Charley Edwards's dressing-room. He had won a place among Edwards's following not only because the young actor, who could not afford to employ a dresser, often found him useful, but because he recognized in Paul something akin to what churchmen term "vocation."

It was at the theatre and at Carnegie Hall that Paul really lived; the rest was but a sleep and a forgetting. This was Paul's fairy tale, and it had for him all the allurement of a secret love. The moment he inhaled the gassy, painty, dusty odour behind the scenes, he breathed like a prisoner set free, and felt within him the possibility of doing or saying splendid, brilliant, poetic things. The moment the cracked orchestra beat out the overture from *Martha*, or jerked at the serenade from *Rigoletto*, all stupid and ugly things slid from him, and his senses were deliciously, yet delicately fired.

Perhaps it was because, in Paul's world, the natural nearly always wore the guise of ugliness, that a certain element of artificiality seemed to him necessary in beauty. Perhaps it was because his experience of life elsewhere was so full of Sabbath-school picnics, petty economics, wholesome advice as to how to succeed in life, and the unescapable odours of cooking, that he found this existence so alluring, these smartly-clad men and women so attractive, that he was moved by these starry apple orchards that bloomed perennially under the limelight.

It would be difficult to put it strongly enough how convincingly the stage entrance of that theatre was for Paul the actual portal of Romance. Certainly none of the company ever suspected it, least of all Charley Edwards. It was very like the old stories that used to float about London of fabulously rich Jews, who had subterranean halls there, with palms, and fountains, and soft lamps and richly apparelled women who never saw the disenchanting light of London day. So, in the midst of that smoke-palled city, enamoured of figures and grimy toil, Paul had his secret temple, his wishing carpet, his bit of blue-and-white Mediterranean shore bathed in perpetual sunshine.

Several of Paul's teachers had a theory that his imagination had been perverted by garish fiction, but the truth was that he scarcely ever read at all. The books at home were not such as would either tempt or currupt a youthful mind, and as for reading the novels that some of his friends urged upon him—well, he got what he wanted much more quickly from music; any sort of music, from an orchestra to a barrel organ. He needed only the spark, the indescribable thrill that made his imagination master of his senses, and he could make plots and pictures enough of his own. It was equally true that he was not stage struck—not, at any rate, in the usual acceptation of that expression. He had no desire to become an actor, any more than he had to become a musician. He felt no necessity to do any of these things; what he wanted was to see, to be in the atmosphere, float on the wave of it, to be carried out, blue league after blue league, away from everything.

After a night behind the scenes, Paul found the school-room more than ever repulsive; the bare floors and naked walls; the prosy men who never wore frock coats, or violets in their buttonholes; the women with their dull gowns, shrill voices, and pitiful seriousness about prepositions that govern the dative. He could not bear to have the other pupils think, for a moment, that he took these people seriously; he must convey to them that he considered it all trivial, and was there only by way of a jest, anyway. He had autographed pictures of all the members of the stock company which he showed his classmates, telling them the most incredible stories of his familiarity with these people, of his acquaintance with the soloists who came to Carnegie Hall, his suppers with them and the flowers he sent them. When these stories lost their effect, and his audience grew listless, he became desperate and would bid all the boys good-bye, announcing that he was going to travel for a while; going to Naples, to Venice, to Egypt. Then, next Monday, he would slip back, conscious and nervously smiling; his sister was ill, and he should have to defer his voyage until spring.

Matters went steadily worse with Paul at school. In the itch to let his instructors know how heartily he despised them and their homilies, and how thoroughly he was appreciated elsewhere, he mentioned once or twice that he had no time to fool with theorems; adding—with a twitch of the eyebrows and a touch of that nervous bravado which so perplexed them—that he was helping the people down at the stock company; they were old friends of his.

The upshot of the matter was, that the Principal went to Paul's father, and Paul was taken out of school and put to work. The manager at Carnegie Hall was told to get another usher in his stead; the door-keeper at the theatre was warned not to admit him to the house; and Charley Edwards remorsefully promised the boy's father not to see him again.

The members of the stock company were vastly amused when some of Paul's stories reached them—especially the women. They were hard-working women, most of them supporting indigent husbands or brothers, and they laughed rather bitterly at having stirred the boy to such fervid and florid inventions. They agreed with the faculty and with his father that Paul's was a bad case.

The east-bound train was ploughing through a January snowstorm; the dull dawn was beginning to show grey when the engine whistled a mile out of Newark. Paul started up from the seat where he had lain curled in uneasy slumber, rubbed the breath-misted window glass with his hand, and peered out. The snow was whirling in curling eddies above the white bottom lands, and the drifts lay already deep in the fields and along the fences, while here and there the long dead grass and dried weed stalks protruded black above it. Lights shone from the scattered houses, and a gang of labourers who stood beside the track waved their lanterns.

Paul had slept very little, and he felt grimy and uncomfortable. He had made the all-night journey in a day coach, partly because he was ashamed, dressed as he was, to go into a Pullman, and partly because he was afraid of being seen there by some Pittsburgh business man, who might have noticed him in Denny & Carson's office. When the whistle awoke him, he clutched quickly at his breast pocket, glancing about him with an uncertain smile. But the little, clay-bespattered Italians were still sleeping, the slatternly women across the aisle were in open-mouthed oblivion, and even the crumby, crying babies were for the nonce stilled. Paul settled back to struggle with his impatience as best he could.

When he arrived at the Jersey City station, he hurried through his breakfast, manifestly ill at ease and keeping a sharp eye about him. After he reached the Twenty-third Street station, he consulted a cabman, and had himself driven to a men's furnishing establishment that was just opening for the day. He spent upward of two hours there, buying with endless reconsidering and great care. His new street suit he put on in the fitting-room; the frock coat and dress clothes he had bundled into the cab with his linen. Then he drove to a hatter's and a shoe house. His next errand was at Tiffany's, where he selected his silver and a new scarf-pin. He would not wait to have his silver marked, he said. Lastly, he stopped at a trunk shop on Broadway, and had his purchases packed into various travelling bags.

It was a little after one o'clock when he drove up to the Waldorf, and after settling with the cabman, went into the office. He registered from Washington; said his mother and father had been abroad, and that he had come down to await the arrival of their steamer. He told his story plausibly and had no trouble, since he volunteered to pay for them in advance, in engaging his rooms; a sleeping-room, sitting-room and bath.

Not once, but a hundred times Paul had planned his entry into New York. He had gone over every detail of it with Charley Edwards, and in his scrap book at home there were pages of description about New York hotels, cut from the Sunday papers. When he was shown to his sitting-room on the eighth floor, he saw at a glance that everything was as it should be; there was but one detail in his mental picture that the place did not realize, so he rang for the bell boy and sent him down for flowers. He moved about nervously until the boy returned, putting away his new linen and fingering it delightedly as he did so. When the flowers came, he put them hastily into water, and then tumbled into a hot bath. Presently he came out of his white bath-room, resplendent in his new silk underwear, and playing with the tassels of his red robe. The snow was whirling so fiercely outside his windows that he could scarcely see across the street, but within the air was deliciously soft and fragrant. He put the violets and jonquils on the taboret beside the couch, and threw himself down, with a long sigh, covering himself with a Roman blanket. He was thoroughly tired; he had been in such haste, he had stood up to such a strain, covered so much ground in the last twenty-four hours, that he wanted to think how it had all come about. Lulled by the sound of the wind, the warm air, and the cool fragrance of the flowers, he sank into deep, drowsy retrospection.

It had been wonderfully simple; when they had shut him out of the theatre and concert hall, when they had taken away his bone, the whole thing was virtually determined. The rest was a mere matter of opportunity. The only thing that at all surprised him was his own courage—for he realized well enough that he had always been tormented by fear, a sort of apprehensive dread that, of late years, as the meshes of the lies he had told closed about him, had been pulling the muscles of his body tighter and tighter. Until now, he could not remember the time when he had not been dreading something. Even when he was a little boy, it was always there—behind him, or before, or on either side. There had always been the shadowed corner, the dark place into which he dared not look, but from which something seemed always to be watching him—and Paul had done things that were not pretty to watch, he knew.

But now he had a curious sense of relief, as though he had at last thrown down the gauntlet to the thing in the corner.

Yet it was but a day since he had been sulking in the traces; but yesterday afternoon that he had been sent to the bank with Denny & Carson's deposit, as usual—but this time he was instructed to leave the book to be balanced. There was above two thousand dollars in checks, and nearly a thousand in the bank notes which he had taken from the book and quietly transferred to his pocket. At the bank he had made out a new deposit slip. His nerves had been steady enough to permit of his returning to the office, where he had finished his work and asked for a full day's holiday to-morrow, Saturday, giving a perfectly reasonable pretext. The bank book, he knew, would not be returned before Monday or Tuesday, and his father would be out of town for the next week. From the time he slipped the bank notes into his pocket until he boarded the train for New York, he had not known a moment's hesitation. It was not the first time Paul had steered through treacherous waters.

How astonishingly easy it had all been; here he was, the thing done; and this time there would be no awakening, no figure at the top of the stairs. He watched the snow flakes whirling by his window until he fell asleep.

When he awoke, it was three o'clock in the afternoon. He bounded up with a start; half of one of his precious days gone already! He spent more than an hour in dressing, watching every stage of his toilet carefully in the mirror. Everything was quite perfect; he was exactly the kind of boy he had always wanted to be.

When he went downstairs, Paul took a carriage and drove up Fifth Avenue toward the Park. The snow had somewhat abated; carriages and tradesmen's wagons were hurrying soundlessly to and fro in the winter twilight; boys in woollen mufflers were shovelling off the doorsteps; the avenue stages made fine spots of colour against the white street. Here and there on the corners were stands, with whole flower gardens blooming under glass cases, against the sides of which the snow flakes stuck and melted; violets, roses, carnations, lilies of the valley—somehow vastly more lovely and alluring that they blossomed thus unnaturally in the snow. The Park itself was a wonderful stage winterpiece.

When he returned, the pause of the twilight had ceased, and the tune of the streets had changed. The snow was falling faster, lights streamed from the hotels that reared their dozen stories fearlessly up into the storm, defying the raging Atlantic winds. A long, black stream of carriages poured down the avenue, intersected here and there by other streams, tending horizontally. There were a score of cabs about the entrance of his hotel, and his driver had to wait. Boys in livery were running in and out of the awning stretched across the sidewalk, up and down the red velvet carpet laid from the door to the street. Above, about, within it all was the rumble and roar, the hurry and toss of thousands of human beings as hot for pleasure as himself, and on every side of him towered the glaring affirmation of the omnipotence of wealth.

The boy set his teeth and drew his shoulders together in a spasm of realization; the plot of all dramas, the text of all romances, the nerve-stuff of all sensations was whirling about him like the snow flakes. He burnt like a faggot in a tempest.

When Paul went down to dinner, the music of the orchestra came floating up the elevator shaft to greet him. His head whirled as he stepped into the thronged corridor, and he sank back into one of the chairs against the wall to get his breath. The lights, the chatter, the perfumes, the bewildering medley of colour—he had, for a moment, the feeling of not being able to stand it. But only for a moment; these were his own people, he told himself. He went slowly about the corridors, through the writing-rooms, smoking-rooms, reception-rooms, as though he were exploring the chambers of an enchanted palace, built and peopled for him alone.

When he reached the dining-room he sat down at a table near a window. The flowers, the white linen, the many-coloured wine glasses, the gay toilettes of the women, the low popping of corks, the undulating repetitions of the *Blue Danube* from the orchestra, all flooded Paul's dream of bewildering radiance. When the roseate tinge of his champagne was added—that cold, precious, bubbling stuff that creamed and foamed in his glass—Paul wondered that there were honest men in the world at all. This was what all the world was fighting for, he reflected; this was what all the struggle was about. He doubted the reality of his past. Had he ever known a place called Cordelia Street, a place where fagged-looking businessmen got on the early car; mere rivets in a machine they seemed to Paul,—sickening men, with combings of children's hair always hanging to their coats, and the smell of cooking in their clothes. Cordelia Street—Ah! that belonged to another time and country; had he not always been thus, had he not sat here night after night, from as far back as he could remember, looking pensively over just such shimmering textures, and slowly twirling the stem of a glass like this one between his thumb and middle finger? He rather thought he had.

He was not in the least abashed or lonely. He had no especial desire to meet or to know any of these people; all he demanded was the right to look on and conjecture, to watch the pageant. The mere stage properties were all he contended for. Nor was he lonely later in the evening, in his lodge at the Metropolitan. He was now entirely rid of his nervous misgivings, of his forced aggressiveness, of the imperative desire to show himself different from his surroundings. He felt now that his surroundings explained him. Nobody questioned the purple; he had only to wear it passively. He had only to glance down at his attire to reassure himself that here it would be impossible for anyone to humiliate him.

He found it hard to leave his beautiful sitting-room to go to bed that night, and sat long watching the raging storm from his turret window. When he went to sleep it was with the lights turned on in his bedroom; partly because of his old timidity, and partly so that, if he should wake in the night, there would be no wretched moment of doubt, no horrible suspicion of yellow wall-paper, or of Washington and Calvin above his bed.

Sunday morning the city was practically snow-bound. Paul breakfasted late, and in the afternoon he fell in with a wild San Francisco boy, a freshman at Yale, who said he had run down for a "little flyer" over Sunday. The young man offered to show Paul the night side of the town, and the two boys went out together after dinner, not returning to the hotel until seven o'clock the next morning. They had started out in the confiding warmth of a champagne friendship, but their parting in the elevator was singularly cool. The freshman pulled himself together to make his train, and Paul went to bed. He awoke at two o'clock in the afternoon, very thirsty and dizzy, and rang for ice-water coffee, and the Pittsburgh papers.

On the part of the hotel management, Paul excited no suspicion. There was this to be said for him, that he wore his spoils with dignity and in no way made himself conspicuous. Even under the glow of his wine he was never boisterous, though he found the stuff like a magician's wand for wonder-building. His chief greediness lay in his ears and eyes, and his excesses were not offencive ones. His dearest pleasures were the grey winter twilights in his sitting-room; his quiet enjoyment of his flowers, his clothes, his wide divan, his cigarette and his sense of power. He could not remember a time when he had felt so at peace with himself. The mere release from the necessity of petty lying, lying every day and every day, restored his self-respect. He had never lied for pleasure, even at school; but to be noticed and admired, to assert his difference from other Cordelia Street boys; and he felt a good deal more manly, more honest, even, now that he had no need for boastful pretensions, now that he could, as his actor friends used to say, "dress the part." It was characteristic that remorse did not occur to him. His golden days went by without a shadow, and he made each as perfect as he could.

On the eighth day after his arrival in New York, he found the whole affair exploited in the Pittsburgh papers, exploited with a wealth of detail which indicated that local news of a sensational nature was at a low ebb. The firm of Denny & Carson announced that the boy's father had refunded the full amount of the theft, and that they had no intention of prosecuting. The Cumberland minister had been interviewed, and expressed his hope of yet reclaiming the motherless lad, and his Sabbath-school teacher declared that she would spare no effort to that end. The rumour had reached Pittsburgh that the boy had been seen in a New York hotel, and his father had gone East to find him and bring him home.

Paul had just come in to dress for dinner; he sank into a chair, weak to the knees, and clasped his head in his hands. It was to be worse than jail, even; the tepid waters of Cordelia Street were to close over him finally and forever. The grey monotony stretched before him in hopeless, unrelieved years; Sabbath-school, Young People's Meeting, the yellow-papered room, the damp dish-towels; it all rushed back upon him with a sickening vividness. He had the old feeling that the orchestra had suddenly stopped, the sinking sensation that the play was over. The sweat broke out on his face, and he sprang to his feet, looked about him with his white, conscious smile, and winked at himself in the mirror. With something of the old childish belief in miracles with which he had so often gone to class, all his lessons unlearned, Paul dressed and dashed whistling down the corridor to the elevator.

He had no sooner entered the dining-room and caught the measure of the music than his remembrance was lightened by his old elastic power of claiming the moment, mounting with it, and finding it all sufficient. The glare and glitter about him, the mere scenic accessories had again, and for the last time, their old potency. He would show himself that he was game, he would finish the thing splendidly. He doubted, more than ever, the existence of Cordelia Street, and for the first time he drank his wine recklessly. Was he not, after all, one of those fortunate beings born to the purple, was he not still himself and in his own place? He drummed a nervous accompaniment to the Pagliacci music and looked about him, telling himself over and over that it had paid.

He reflected drowsily, to the swell of the music and the chill sweetness of his wine, that he might have done it more wisely. He might have caught an outbound steamer and been well out of their clutches before now. But the other side of the world had seemed too far away and too uncertain then; he could not have waited for it; his need had been too sharp. If he had to choose over again, he would do the same thing to-morrow. He looked affectionately about the dining-room, now gilded with a soft mist. Ah, it had paid indeed!

Paul was awakened next morning by a painful throbbing in his head and feet. He had thrown himself across the bed without undressing, and had slept with his shoes on. His limbs and hands were lead heavy, and his tongue and throat were parched and burnt. There came upon him one of those fateful attacks of clear-headedness that never occurred except when he was physically exhausted and his nerves hung loose. He lay still and

closed his eyes and let the tide of things wash over him.

His father was in New York; "stopping at some joint or other," he told himself. The memory of successive summers on the front stoop fell upon him like a weight of black water. He had not a hundred dollars left; and he knew now, more than ever, that money was everything, the wall that stood between all he loathed and all he wanted. The thing was winding itself up; he had thought of that on his first glorious day in New York, and had even provided a way to snap the thread. It lay on his dressing table now; he had got it out last night when he came blindly up from dinner, but the shiny metal hurt his eyes, and he disliked the looks of it.

He rose and moved about with a painful effort, succumbing now and again to attacks of nausea. It was the old depression exaggerated; all the world had become Cordelia Street. Yet somehow he was not afraid of anything, was absolutely calm; perhaps because he had looked into the dark corner at last and knew. It was bad enough, what he saw there, but somehow not so bad as his long fear of it had been. He saw everything clearly now. He had a feeling that he had made the best of it, that he had lived the sort of life he was meant to live, and for half an hour he sat staring at the revolver. But he told himself that was not the way, so he went downstairs and took a cab to the ferry.

When Paul arrived at Newark, he got off the train and took another cab, directing the driver to follow the Pennsylvania tracks out of the town. The snow lay heavy on the roadways and had drifted deep in the open fields. Only here and there the dead grass or dried weed stalks projected, singularly black, above it. Once well into the country, Paul dismissed the carriage and walked, floundering along the tracks, his mind a medley of irrelevant things. He seemed to hold in his brain an actual picture of everything he had seen that morning. He remembered every feature of both his drivers, of the toothless old woman from whom he had bought the red flowers in his coat, the agent from whom he had got his ticket, and all of his fellow-

passengers on the ferry. His mind, unable to cope with vital matters near at hand, worked feverishly and deftly at sorting and grouping these images. They made for him a part of the ugliness of the world, of the ache in his head, and the bitter burning on his tongue. He stooped and put a handful of snow into his mouth as he walked, but that, too, seemed hot. When he reached a little hillside, where the tracks ran through a cut some twenty feet below him, he stopped and sat down.

The carnations in his coat were drooping with the cold, he noticed; their red glory all over. It occurred to him that all the flowers he had seen in the glass cases that first night must have gone the same way, long before this. It was only one splendid breath they had, in spite of their brave mockery at the winter outside the glass; and it was a losing game in the end, it seemed, this revolt against the homilies by which the world is run. Paul took one of the blossoms carefully from his coat and scooped a little hole in the snow, where he covered it up. Then he dozed a while, from his weak condition, seemingly insensible to the cold.

The sound of an approaching train awoke him, and he started to his feet, remembering only his resolution, and afraid least he should be too late. He stood watching the approaching locomotive, his teeth chattering, his lips drawn away from them in a frightened smile; once or twice he glanced nervously sidewise, as though he were being watched. When the right moment came, he jumped. As he fell, the folly of his haste occurred to him with merciless clearness, the vastness of what he had left undone. There flashed through his brain, clearer than ever before, the blue of Adriatic water, the yellow of Algerian sands.

He felt something strike his chest, and that his body was being thrown swiftly through the air, on and on, immeasurably far and fast, while his limbs were gently relaxed. Then, because the picture making mechanism was crushed, the disturbing visions flashed into black, and Paul dropped back into the immense design of things.

PREVIEW QUESTIONS

_____ 1. One of the settings central to the story is the
  a. friend's house.
  b. store.
  c. club.
  d. theater.

_____ 2. Paul is
  a. a high school student.
  b. a young man about 25.
  c. an older man about 50.
  d. a very old man.

_____ 3. Regarding the point-of-view, the story is told by
  a. the author.
  b. the character Paul.
  c. a teacher.
  d. Paul's father.

_____ 4. The story relates the actions of
  a. four main characters.
  b. two main characters.
  c. one main character.
  d. a group of people.

_____ 5. This story could be classified as a
  a. love story.
  b. psychological case study.
  c. science fiction.
  d. comedy.

Allow 20 points per correct answer.   Your score _____ %
Number of words: 8400   Your rate _____
Answer key is on page 273.
Record rate and comprehension score on Course Data Sheet in Preview columns.

GOOD COMPREHENSION QUESTIONS

_____ 1. To his teachers, Paul appeared to be
  a. an ordinary schoolboy.
  b. a strange, haunted, defiant boy.
  c. unnaturally and excessively polite and obedient.
  d. a "sissy" and "cry-baby."

_____ 2. Paul worked as an usher at Carnegie Hall because he
  a. was required to pay room and board to his father.
  b. was being punished for his misdemeanors.
  c. enjoyed the romance and unreality of the theatre.
  d. was unable to find any other job.

_____ 3. Paul's life at home with his father was
   a. depressing, hateful, and intolerable to him.
   b. unpleasant but acceptable.
   c. friendly but without understanding.
   d. wonderful, with home as a refuge from the intolerable outside world.

_____ 4. Paul took a trip to New York to
   a. live out his fantasy.
   b. go to school.
   c. become an actor.
   d. find a better paying job.

_____ 5. In New York, he felt
   a. disappointment; things were not as he had expected.
   b. guilt over spending so much money on the trip.
   c. a new appreciation for his life back home.
   d. exhilaration and joy with the expensive surroundings into which he fit easily.

_____ 6. Paul obtained the money for his New York trip
   a. from his father.
   b. by saving his wages from his job as an usher.
   c. by stealing the money from his employer.
   d. by borrowing the money from a friend.

_____ 7. Paul's New York adventure threatened to come to an end when
   a. his father arrived in New York.
   b. the police came to arrest him.
   c. his savings were spent.
   d. his friend needed the borrowed money returned.

_____ 8. In the end Paul
   a. returned home.
   b. escaped to Europe.
   c. stayed in New York.
   d. committed suicide.

_____ 9. In this story, Paul is shown as a character who
   a. recognizes that reality is drab and dull but must be accepted.
   b. does not even notice the ugliness of reality because he turns the ugly to beautiful in his mind.
   c. is acutely aware of the differences between the ugly reality and the beauty in his fantasies, which are more real to him than reality.
   d. is totally insensitive to beauty or ugliness.

_____ 10. The author has written this story in such a way that it primarily shows the reader how
   a. Paul sees the world—his inner world.
   b. Paul's teachers, father, and friends see the world.
   c. the world sees Paul.
   d. an uninvolved stranger sees Paul.

Allow 10 points per correct answer.   *Your score _____ %*
Number of words: 8,400   *Your rate _____*
Answer key is on page 273.
Record rate and comprehension score on Course Data Sheet in Good Comprehension columns.

RECALL/THINK (Write the answers on a separate sheet.)

Answer these questions as best you can, first from memory and thinking, and then, as you postview later, add to your answers.

1. List as many of Paul's characteristics as you can.
2. Given Paul, as he is drawn, is there some other believable ending possible, perhaps a happier one? What would it be?
3. If Paul had narrated the story, how would it have changed the story? Would it be an improvement?
4. How many references in the language, actions, or descriptions can you find that refer to plays, the past, places, pageants, and other references to earlier eras?

After the following Postview, compare your answers to the above questions with the suggested answers on page 273. This score is *not* recorded on Course Data Sheet.

POSTVIEW QUESTIONS

_____ 1. Paul acts as he does because he
   a. fears his teachers and his father.
   b. possesses a temperament that requires beauty and elegance.
   c. is a spoiled, selfish child.
   d. lost his mother at an early age.

_____ 2. The reader could interpret the whole story symbolically as a
   a. journey to heaven.
   b. journey to hell.
   c. theatrical performance.
   d. travel through the subconscious of each person.

_____ 3. Since the author's genuine love for Paul is apparent, we can expect that Paul's actions reflect some of her beliefs. Logically, one such belief is that she
   a. upheld parental discipline.
   b. rebelled against the conventional.
   c. was in favor of suicide.
   d. disliked people.

_____ 4. Regarding the language, we notice that it
   a. is packed with precise details.
   b. leaves much open to various interpretations.
   c. leaves out important details.
   d. sounds as if it was written hundreds of years ago.

_____ 5. One statement of the probable theme would be:
   a. Strict fathers and teachers may lead a sensitive person to suicide.
   b. The only solution for an emotionally disturbed person is suicide.
   c. Some sensitive souls cannot live in today's ordinary world.
   d. It is better to be dead than poor.

Allow 20 points per correct answer.   Your score _____ %
Number of words: 8400   Your rate _____
Answer key is on page 273.
Record rate and comprehension score on Course Data Sheet in Postview columns.

18

Choosing the Appropriate Reading Method, and Reading Footnotes

Materials:
- Readings:
  "The Will to Win: How to Get It and Uie It"
  "You Know More Than You Think"
  The Population Bomb, or another nonfiction book
- Nonfiction drill book (*Body Language,* or another book)

Objectives:
- To learn some guidelines for determining how any particular work should be read
- To gain experience in applying the guidelines
- To learn how to read footnotes

DRILL PRACTICE

Today, do eye-pacing drills in a nonfiction book that you have already read. I suggest *Body Language.* Follow the directions given in Chapter 15, page 169. Take a drill rate and record it on your Course Data Sheet.

CHOICE OF READING METHOD

Oh, the variety we find in print! So many kinds of short stories and novels: mysteries, science fiction, love stories, adventures, horror tales, humorous stories, and on and on. Nonfictional books and articles also exhibit an impressive array of types: biographies, histories, "how to's" for almost anything, textbooks, presentations on one major theme, writings to persuade you to take action, works that are purely informational—these are just a few.

With such an assortment, how do you, as the reader, determine your approach to a particular work? There are no set rules that you can apply to give you the exact reading method to be used for each and every work. There are only guidelines to help you determine for yourself the probable method of reading that will accomplish your purpose.

Your purpose for reading may not always be to study the material, as you have been doing in the last few chapters. Therefore, the four-step speed-study method may not always be appropriate. The following choices are available to you:

1. Survey; one or more good comprehension readings.
2. Survey; one or more good comprehension readings; one or more postviews.
3. Survey; preview; one or more good comprehension readings.
4. Survey; preview; one or more good comprehension readings; one or more postviews.

GUIDELINES FOR DETERMINING METHOD

The reading method you choose will depend on (1) your purpose for reading, (2) the type of material to be read, and (3) the difficulty of the material.

Step One   Consciously determine your purposes for reading this material. Do you need to study it so that you know it thoroughly, perhaps for a test? Do you want to understand it well but will not be tested on it? Do you only want to know what it's about and are not concerned with the minor details? Will just getting the general idea be sufficient?

Step Two   Survey the work to determine its type and how difficult you can expect it to be. The survey should consist of careful attention to

1. the title
2. the front and back covers
3. the introductory portions and preface
4. the contents (this will generally tell you the type of work it is)
5. skimming the first chapter of a book or the first few paragraphs of an article

In the skimming, be alert to signs that indicate whether this work will be difficult or easy to read: Are most of the words familiar or unfamiliar? Are the sentences generally short or long and complicated? Are you able to read the chapter rapidly with ease, or do you have to slow down with excessive frequency? Are you able to understand the main idea of this portion of the work? Is it on a subject about which you know little or nothing?

Step Three   Make a tentative decision on which reading method will best enable you to fulfill your purpose, dealing effectively with the type of material and its level of difficulty.

Step Four   Begin to read, using the method you have chosen. If all proceeds as planned, fine. However, if you find that your choice was not the best one, you can make adjustments and changes in the following manner:

1. You thought it was easy and chose only to do a good comprehension reading. You now find the material more difficult than expected. *Speed up* and make this reading a preview; then do a good comprehension reading, and perhaps also a postview if you find you need it.

2. You thought it was difficult and chose to do a preview reading first, but in the preview you find that you understand the material better than you expected. *Slow down* slightly and make this reading a good comprehension reading instead of a preview.

3. You expected the material to be very difficult and you need to know it thoroughly. You have done a preview, a good comprehension reading, and even a postview, and still you don't feel you obtained enough information. Postview as many times as necessary to get what you need from the material, or do another good comprehension reading and another postview.

Some Considerations

1. If your purpose is to know the material thoroughly, unless it is very easy, the four-step speed-study method should be used.
2. If it is a theme work, a work that presents only one major idea and goes on to explain that idea or to give supporting evidence, one reading is all that is usually required. You need to remember the main idea and the major supporting points.
3. If it is a "how to" work, one that tries to teach you how to do something in a better manner, you need to follow the sequence of steps (perhaps mark them). If you plan to go back later and reread the steps, one reading should be enough. A brief list of the steps is helpful.
4. If it is a purely informational work and the topic is nontechnical, one reading will do. However, if the topic is highly technical, use the techniques described in Chapter 16. Naturally, the most important points of information must be remembered.
5. If the author's purpose is to persuade you to take some action, do one reading; but you must be able to recognize the arguments presented and the action sought by the author.
6. If it is a history and your purpose is to know the ideas thoroughly, read it as instructed in Chapter 15.

Practice: Articles

Survey the article, "The Will to Win: How to Get It and Use It," on page 222. Skim the first few paragraphs. In this case your purpose for reading is to be able to answer all the questions on the article. Determine its type. Decide on the method you think will accomplish your purpose considering the level of difficulty you anticipate. Go through the steps of the reading process you decided are appropriate but be prepared to change if you find you chose poorly.

If you previewed, answer the preview questions after the preview reading and answer the good comprehension questions after that reading. However, no matter which method you chose, answer both sets of questions. If you chose appropriately, you should be able to do so with no difficulty. If you can't answer most of the questions, you need to postview one or more times.

Read the footnotes according to the instructions given in this chapter on this page. Compute rates and comprehension scores and record them on the Course Data Sheet.

Now, survey "You Know More Than You Think," on page 227. Your purpose is to be able to answer all three sets of questions on this article. Determine its type and anticipated level of difficulty; decide on the appropriate method. During the reading process, adjust your method as necessary to accomplish your purpose.

Practice: Book

Survey *The Population Bomb* or a nonfiction book of your choice and skim the first chapter. Decide on your reading method. Change the method if you find it not suited to your purpose, which is to be able to answer the questions on this book. Answer the appropriate questions after each reading (questions begin on page 234); but all the questions must be answered even if you chose to do only one reading. Read the footnotes as instructed on this page. Compute rates and scores and record them on the Course Data Sheet.

Since the questions cover material from the book's prologue, forward, appendix, letters and update, include these in your readings.

READING FOOTNOTES

Basically there are three types of footnotes, and each has its own use: documentation, explanation or commentary, and additional supportive evidence or illustration. The documentation footnote gives credit to the source from which an idea or quote was taken; it contains the name of the author, title of the work, name of the publisher, date and place of publication, and the number of the page on which the idea or quote appeared. The explanatory footnote adds information or comments which, though related to the subject, would interrupt the flow of the text; it is an "extra" that the author thinks will interest you. The supportive evidence footnote usually cites other writers who agree with the idea presented in the text; it often begins with "see also" and proceeds to give the same data as the documentation footnote and/or to quote or paraphrase portions of the cited author's work to show the agreement.

The way you read the footnote will depend primarily on its placement—at the bottom of the page, at the end of the chapter, or at the end of the entire work—and secondarily on its typeface. When the footnote is placed at the bottom of the page, you wait until you reach that portion of the page to read it; you do not interrupt your hand movement to jump to the footnote. When it is placed at the end of the chapter or the work, as you complete each chapter, you skim through the ones that apply to that chapter. Since the footnote is in smaller print than the text, you must use a smaller, tighter version of your hand movement to read it. While reading the text, you may wish to skip the documentation footnote. Later, if you want to look up the source, you can go back to it (you would, no doubt, have forgotten the exact data anyway). The explanatory and supportive evidence footnotes should always be read; they may help your comprehension.

SUMMARY

For each work you intend to read, you should determine the most appropriate method of reading. You do this by surveying the total work and skimming the first chapter of a book or the first couple of paragraphs of an article. Decide on the best method according to your purpose and the type and difficulty of the material. Change the method of reading in process if you find you have not chosen the appropriate method. The method may include a preview, one or more good comprehension readings, one or more postviews, either all these steps, only one step, or any combination of steps.

Read footnotes as you reach them at the bottom of the page or after you have finished each chapter if they are at the end of the chapter or in the back of the book. Use a smaller, tighter hand movement. Documentation footnotes may be skipped entirely.

THE WILL TO WIN: HOW TO GET IT AND USE IT*

Michael Korda

It may seem paradoxical to talk of the fear of success. But it is in fact an enormous obstacle, because success implies change, and change is frightening. People build comfortable, predictable lives around failure. They are reluctant to give up its assurance and familiarity, in much the same way as people with a physical complaint are often unwilling to have it cured. How many people do we know who use illness as a lever to get what they want? Pain and suffering, whether real or self-created, give them a reliable excuse for not doing the things they do not want to do. . . . But to build a life around suffering is a distortion of reality, and so it is to build a life around the security of failure.

THE WILL TO FAIL

[Theodore] Reik has described masochism in modern man as "victory through defeat." Life being what it is, we can assert ourselves in two ways. One is to succeed, to justify or even exceed other people's expectations of us. The other way to assert ourselves is to fail. By failing we demonstrate our own power, even at the cost of total self-defeat. In the words of one psychiatrist, "Many of the shortcomings and inadequacies we ordinarily attribute to someone's being 'shiftless' or 'lazy' are in reality expressions of a driving and urgent hunger for power. . . . In doing 'nothing' [these people] are indeed doing a very important 'something,' and that is maintaining a sense of power by balking, by not doing what people expect them to do." It is vitally important to realize that failure can be a mechanism, that it constitutes a productive and satisfying way of life for a large number of people, of whom you may be one.

Children are often impelled to show their power by proving that they can't or won't do something; infants, in fact, have no other way of asserting themselves. It is an easy habit to fall into, and the rewards can be substantial to the ego. As a child, you can punish your parents by not eating, by not succeeding at school, by not making the most of yourself. As an adult, you can punish your wife, your children and yourself by failing. Yes, yourself! For guilt, too, is part of the mechanism of failure, perhaps its strongest part. And guilt is an addictive drug as strong and destructive as heroin, and far more widespread.

Freud commented that "people occasionally fall ill precisely because a deeply rooted and long-cherished wish has come to fulfillment." [Otto] Fenichel,[1] too,

noted that the fear of success was strong in some patients, in whom "a success may not only mean something that must bring immediate punishment, but also something that stimulates ambition and thus mobilizes fear concerning future failure and future punishment.". . .

THE ICARUS COMPLEX[2]

It is almost worth inventing an "Icarus complex," named after the unfortunate youth who fell to his death after flying too high and too close to the sun. And it is not insignificant that Icarus died, not only because he flew too high (i.e. overachieved), but also because he disobeyed his father, and soared higher than his parent.

Many of us feel, profoundly and unconsciously, that "the higher you climb, the harder you fall," and solve the problem by not climbing at all. Dr. Daniel B. Schuster has commented on the common phenomenon among most people of "the inability to enjoy good fortune, even though passively acquired." It is common enough to talk about "paying the price" for some piece of good fortune or "paying one's dues," as if it were somehow necessary to suffer in a measurable quantity for every gain or achievement. We fear that other people will resent our success, that our every advancement will create hostility and envy, that our every step upward will provoke some form of punishment. In many people, success is a country full of ill-defined but potent dangers, and the closer they come to their goals, the greater their fears. Failure thus becomes a kind of security blanket, a warm, enveloping familiar comfort that answers a deep, yearning need for punishment, and protects against the uncertain, but dreaded, consequences that success might entail. By failing, we satisfy the inner need for suffering and expiation, while at the same time avoiding the pain that other people might impose on us if we took the risk of offending them by succeeding.

Hubris, or pride, was the one sin the Greek gods never forgave and always punished, and half the Greek legends involve the elaborate and ruthless stratagems by which the Olympians clipped mortals' wings and taught them the futility of human ambition and achievement—poor, blind Oedipus was punished as much for being a successful king as for inadvertently killing his father and marrying his mother. The fear that success will bring down on our heads the revenge of the gods, that by failing we are protecting ourselves against a dreadful Olympian vengeance, still holds us back, even in an age

Glamour, December, 1977. Reprinted by permission of the author.

[1]Otto Fenichel (1897–1946), psychoanalyst, author of the classic book *The Psychoanalytic Theory of Neurosis* (1945). *Note:* All footnotes are by Lillian P. Wenick.

[2]Icarus: son of Daedalus in Greek mythology. Both escaped from prison in Crete by using wings made of feathers and wax. Icarus flew too close to the sun, which melted the wax, and he fell into the Icarian Sea.

when material success is supposed to be the common denominator of human behavior.

The epic tragedy of the Kennedys has been taken by many people as a moral lesson, and seen as a naturally fitting end to overwhelming ambition and success. Joseph Kennedy, according to popular legend, acquired great wealth with singular ruthlessness and drove his sons hard to achieve greatness, which they did with equal ruthlessness. They were also handsome, popular, energetic, courageous and sexually successful to an extraordinary degree. Joseph Kennedy, Jr., was killed in the war [World War II]; Robert and John Kennedy were assassinated; Edward Kennedy's political career was destroyed by the Chappaquiddick scandal. . . . When a great many people answered a national poll by arguing that the Kennedys "deserved what they got," they were not talking out of right-wing fanaticism so much as out of a basic, moral feeling that the consequences of success are always tragic. Hubris must be punished. Pride goeth before a fall. The price of ambition is death. These are popular fallacies.

STOP PUNISHING YOURSELF

Before you can be successful, you have to rid yourself of these fears and learn to stop punishing yourself. The methods by which people assure their own failure are subtle, devious and complex, so much so that you may be unable to see just how you have done it. People consistently choose the wrong job for themselves, submit themselves to masochistic relationships with employers who hate and use them, behave in ways that are guaranteed to ensure they will not get a raise or a promotion, ignore their strengths and follow their weaknesses. The instinct toward self-defeat is strong and insidious.[3] Like all rationalizations, it disguises itself as common sense most of the time. Except in rare individuals, the instinct to do nothing, to stay put, to accept the second-rate, is far stronger than the urge to succeed and has been built into the personality so solidly and purposefully that it is, in any case, hard to overcome.

The fear of success is not necessarily fanciful or unrealistic. Success does imply risks—the risk of new responsibilities, the risk of living up to new and greater expectations, the risk of losing what one has in the pursuit of what one wants. It is, however, important to recognize these fears as realistic, and to confront them in a sensible and organized way:

• Ask yourself how much responsibility you are prepared to take.
• Don't set your expectations so high that you are bound to fail.
• Assess just how willing you are to lose what you have in order to rise up the next step.

[3]Insidious: operating in a way not readily seen or understood.

What you must do is separate the rational fears from the irrational and neurotic ones. It is sensible to wonder if your attempt to win a vice-presidency may cost you your present job if you're unsuccessful in the promotion race. If the odds seem heavily weighted against you, wait for another try, or change jobs and try somewhere else. On the other hand, if you feel that you won't get the vice-presidency because you have always been "unlucky," or if you feel, like so many people, that the promotion can only bring you trouble, grief and possible retaliation, then you're holding yourself back out of unnecessary guilt and fear.

One telling sign of this is the attempt to placate hostility in advance or to exorcise disaster before it has even happened. Do you preface a remark or an opinion by saying, for example, "I may be wrong about this, but . . .," or "You may disagree with me, but . . .," or any variation of these rather common disclaimers? This kind of self-minimalization can become an ingrained habit. If you do this in conversation, you are almost certainly doing it unconsciously on a larger scale.

The first step to success is to accept the consequences of knowing that you're right, when that is the case. It is not so much a matter of being assertive, as of giving up the comfortable cocoon of apologies and guilt in which most of us have chosen to live.

TURNING FAILURE INTO SUCCESS

The freedom to fail is vital if you're going to succeed. Most successful men fail time and time again, and it is a measure of their strength that failure merely propels them into some new attempt at success.

We all know the clichés: the branch that bends does not break, the building that sways in the wind does not collapse in the storm, the ship that creaks and moves in every timber withstands the heavy seas. Yet, obstinately, most of us are unable to apply these rules to our lives. We are determined to be inflexible, to maintain a straight course, to find some way to anchor ourselves in a secure system of beliefs. We are comfortable with the predictable and the familiar, and will go to incredible lengths to manufacture make-believe worlds in which we can pretend that everything is normal and under control. This is a dangerous illusion, and a deep-seated impediment to success.

Some of our best-known folk heroes have, in fact, been experts at failing big until, as it were, they fall downward to success, fame and a place in the grateful nation's memory. . . .

George Washington, the Father of our Country, was, in the words of Neil Hickey, an early practitioner of "upward failure." So notorious was his reputation for ineptly losing battles that John Adams called him "an old muttonhead" and Thomas Jefferson commented, with great and polite understatement, that Washington was "not a great tactician."

To be a successful failure, one must master the art

of escape. This requires a precise feel for the exact moment at which it is necessary to abandon the sinking ship and its crew to fate, and a ruthless lack of sentiment about getting off in time. . . . These failures do not waste energy, emotion and time in attempting to justify their own role in a disaster. They get out as quickly as they can and move on to something else. . . . They know better than to identify themselves with a losing cause: They may have been the captain of the ship, but not its owner. . . . Remember: projects fail, plans fail, companies fail—you need not.

Furthermore, failure has its positive points:

• Failure provides you with a pause in which to reassess your motives, your abilities and your opportunities. A career of uninterrupted success would not only be dull, but would probably peak early, for want of any real opportunity for self-examination or self-criticism.

• Failure can sometimes be made to seem more dramatic and exciting in some ways than success. Very often, the best way of drawing attention to our abilities is to fail on a major scale.

• Failure teaches you far more than success ever can, if only because failure sharpens the survival instincts, and forces you to learn your business or profession in depth and detail. It is on the way down that we learn how things work. On the way up, we are enjoying the ride too much to pay attention.

• Failure is the best school for success. There is nothing like it for hardening the will and maturing the personality.

Therefore, do not be afraid to fail. You are joining a distinguished fellowship! . . . Einstein was a backward student and an unsuccessful mathematics teacher. Franklin Delano Roosevelt was judged a mediocrity and "a lightweight" by almost everybody who knew him, even after he was elected governor of New York State, and his own mother not only shared this disparaging opinion of her son's abilities but vocally expressed it to anyone who would listen. Napoleon languished for many years as an artillery officer of little promise. . . . Howard Hughes was a conspicuous failure at every school he was sent to, and was thought not worth sending to college.

Remember: Early promise seldom blooms, and success without the tempering effect of failure is seldom long-lasting.

"HE TRAVELS THE FASTEST WHO TRAVELS ALONE . . ."

One of the paradoxical things about failure is that those who love you may unconsciously want you to fail. Failure is sometimes more comfortable and easier to live with for your wife, mother, husband or children.

Most marriages can withstand failure, but success has a dangerous tendency to destroy the relationship

quickly. In the case of a woman, failure in the business or professional world is not only less threatening to her husband and children, but may even be expected and rewarded. In the case of a man, he often finds that his wife will accept far more easily a pattern of failure, despite the financial disadvantages, than the changes that inevitably accompany success. We have all known marriages that endured years of poverty and broke up the moment the man succeeded: A woman spends years supporting her husband, but is often unprepared for the strain and tension that develop when he unexpectedly succeeds.

As one successful executive told me, discussing the collapse of his marriage, "Everything went fine so long as I was a failure. Jane never complained that we couldn't move to a larger apartment or buy a lot of things we wanted. She felt safe because we formed, I guess, a small enclosed world. Then suddenly I was making a lot of money, and I began to look outward and gain self-confidence. I needed her less, it's as simple as that, and every step up I took was against her pulling me back down. As a failure, she had control of me. As a success, she felt her control slipping, and it scared her. I was scared to stop, and she was scared to watch me go on, and finally I couldn't stand it anymore and I left. Success gave me a new life, but it didn't improve the old one, and I could see it wasn't going to. Success in Jane's eyes was a kind of betrayal. I think if I gave up my job and went back to her, she'd be perfectly happy because she'd have me 100 percent again. But no way." . . .

The lesson is that we must be careful to avoid settling into those comfortable roles of risk-free failure which the people who love us may well find convenient for us to adopt, or may honestly think are best for us.

In some cases, married people share a *symbiotic*[4] failure. A husband or wife who fears success for himself or herself will deliberately prevent the spouse from succeeding, as though failure were more bearable when shared equally. The operative sentiment in such cases is, "Never mind what other people think, you're good enough for me." . . .

There is psychological truth here which must be taken into account: The more you allow yourself to be thought of by other people as a failure, the more likely you are in the end to regard yourself as one. Therefore, all the disparagements that are the small change of life are to be guarded against strongly. Do not let yourself be criticized, diminished, made fun of or "put down" by anyone near to you, however much you may love them. In order to succeed you must first persuade yourself that you are a success, and in order to do that, you need the support and backing of other people's belief in the possibility of your success.

It is, of course, possible to overcome other people's view of you as a failure, and as we have seen, many great men have done just that. But it requires a lot of will-

---

[4]Symbiotic: pertaining to a relationship based on mutual dependence.

power to succeed against everyone's preconceived view of you as a natural failure. In most cases, their opinion (particularly if "they" are close to you) tends to become your opinion of yourself and holds you back. It is hard enough to succeed in the first place, without having to fight your family to do so. You must begin by convincing those around you that you can succeed, you must encourage them at every opportunity to share your own belief and determination, and you must teach them to take a positive attitude toward each step you take on the road to success.

The popular notion that the family that fails together stays together is not necessarily true. It is important to talk about your work and your ambitions, and equally important not to complain and ask for sympathy because you work hard or have problems. Create a positive environment for yourself in which your success is shared, understood and enjoyed.

Many people—men especially—go out into the world every day to be dazzling, charming and successful, and return home every night to take out their fatigue, their irritations, their fears and their bad temper on their family. Under the circumstances, it is hardly surprising that they fail to find in their family any kind of real support for their future ambitions. There is nothing wrong with shoptalk—indeed, for many of us it is the only subject on which we are likely to be interesting, knowledgeable and enthusiastic—but it should be positive and informative, not simply an account of the terrible things that happened to you during the course of the day.

As women [of the middle class] are forever saying to their husbands—and not a few husbands are learning to say to their wives—"If you hate it so much, why do it?" It is a question bound to enrage, and in fact designed to, because if the point were pushed to its logical conclusion, the answer would normally have to be, "I'm doing it because I want to," in which case the complaints and demands for sympathy are unjustified and irrational. Do not become a martyr to success; nobody ever succeeded who didn't want to, and if it weren't worth the effort and the troubles, you wouldn't reach for it in the first place. Enjoy it!

And do not be afraid of failure, or ashamed of it. The road to success is a long one, and day-to-day judgments may be very deceptive. You have to be strong enough to believe in your own goal, whatever other people think of it, and to bear in mind that success lies in the final accomplishment of your hopes and dreams, and cannot be measured at any single point in a lifetime, but only at the end.

PREVIEW QUESTIONS

_____ 1. "The Will to Win" states that people fail because they
   a. are sometimes unlucky.
   b. have the will to fail.
   c. were born into poor circumstances and can't get out.
   d. don't use enough common sense.

_____ 2. The first step toward acquiring the will to win is to
   a. become more educated.
   b. be willing to hurt others to get what you want.
   c. change jobs.
   d. stop punishing yourself.

_____ 3. Vital to success is that
   a. you must allow yourself the freedom to fail.
   b. you succeed in everything you do.
   c. you "stick to it" in everything until the end, never giving up.
   d. you try only those things at which you excel.

_____ 4. According to this article, those who love you
   a. always want you to succeed.
   b. may unconsciously want you to fail.
   c. can usually be counted on to help you succeed.
   d. can usually accept either your success or your failure.

_____ 5. We learn the most from
   a. success.
   b. failure.
   c. watching other people.
   d. going to school.

Allow 20 points per correct answer.   Your score _____ %
Number of words: 2,500   Your rate _____
Answer key is on page 273.
Record rate and comprehension score on Course Data Sheet in Preview columns.

GOOD COMPREHENSION QUESTIONS

_____ 1. Failure is often an expression of
   a. power and assertion.
   b. laziness.
   c. lack of power.
   d. an inferior personality.

_____ 2. Most people who fail really
   a. want to succeed.
   b. feel that success or good fortune has a price that is punishing.
   c. are those who take risks easily.
   d. fear failure.

_____ 3. The Icarus complex is
   a. the desire to be rid of one's father and to marry one's mother.
   b. the ability to enjoy good fortune.
   c. the fear of achieving more than a parent and thereby disobeying the parent and deserving punishment.
   d. the willingness to take risks to succeed.

_____ 4. In the process of achieving success, you should do all of the following *except*
   a. ask yourself how much responsibility you are willing to take.
   b. not set your expectations too high.
   c. disregard the realistic odds against your succeeding and go ahead anyway.
   d. assess just how willing you are to lose what you have in order to rise to the next step.

_____ 5. Regarding the concept others have of you as a success or failure, you should
   a. accept their concept of you since they see you realistically.
   b. ignore their criticisms since they will have no effect on you.
   c. not allow others to criticize you since you need their support and their belief in the possibility of your success.
   d. complain about your work until others feel sorry for you and want you to change.

_____ 6. Many of the successful men in history
   a. showed promise of success early in life.
   b. were really failures who became lucky.
   c. knew when to abandon a losing cause.
   d. never achieved success; history lied.

_____ 7. Failure may do all of the following *except*
   a. provide a familiar and comfortable way of life.
   b. be the wish-fulfillment mentioned by Freud.
   c. lead to success.
   d. assure the breakup of a marriage.

_____ 8. What do you consider yourself:
   a. a success?
   b. a failure?
   c. don't know?
   d. a person who is taking the risks of failure that will eventually lead to success?

_____ 9. You will succeed when you
   a. become lucky.
   b. become more educated and suited to success.
   c. want to succeed.
   d. have failed over and over again.

_____ 10. True success is measured
   a. at the end of each venture.
   b. at the end of a lifetime.
   c. according to others' view of you.
   d. according to the standard of the culture in which you live.

Allow 10 points per correct answer   *Your score* _____ %
Number of words: 2,500   *Your rate* _____
Answer key is on page 273.
Record rate and comprehension score on Course Date Sheet in Good Comprehension columns.
   Regarding the reading method you chose, did you choose to preview _____, *do a good comprehension reading* _____, *postview* _____? *Did you find it necessary to change your method after you started?* _____

YOU KNOW MORE THAN YOU THINK*

Kenneth L. Woodward

Our minds, scientists believe, are storehouses of information we don't even know we possess. With their techniques, we can learn to use these hidden assets to accomplish things we never dreamed possible.

Like most teachers these days whose students have been raised on television, Micaela Kelly had been having a great deal of difficulty getting her fifth- and sixth-grade pupils in Middletown, New York, to write imaginative English compositions. So last fall Ms. Kelly tried an unusual technique designed to empty the youngsters' minds of artificial fantasies borrowed from TV and to stimulate their own creative imaginations.

"We had just finished reading tall tales, like those about Paul Bunyon,"[1] she reported, "when I told them to put their heads down on their desks, and in five minutes they were all in a state of deep and dreamy relaxation." In this state of subdued consciousness, the children heard the teacher tell them to imagine themselves alone in a foggy forest. There they would meet a very special person who can do things no one else in the world had ever done. Ms. Kelly told them to talk to this extraordinary person and watch closely what he or she does.

McCall's, January 1977, pp. 101, 131–134. Reprinted by permission of the author.

[1] A giant lumberjack of American folklore who, with the help of his blue ox, Babe, performed various superhuman feats.

Afterward, the children wrote down what they had experienced. "The results were astonishing," Ms. Kelly reports. "Kids who had never written more than three sentences for me filled three pages. Every paper was more vivid in content and expression and about five times longer than previous assignments." The reason, as Ms. Kelly explained to her equally astonished colleagues on the faculty, was deceptively simple: The children had created their own experiences to write about, dramas they had literally experienced for themselves within the rich inner environment of their own creative consciousness.

In psychological terms, what Ms. Kelly had done was open up her pupils to the natural power and resources of their own unconscious minds.

Ever since Freud used dreams to explore the hidden recesses of the mind, the idea of the "unconscious" has taken on sinister connotations. We tend to imagine it as a dark cave where untamed instincts and childhood traumas lurk, producing neuroses and psychoses that—left unchecked—can literally drive us crazy.

In recent years, however, many psychologists, neurologists and behavioral scientists have taken a broader, more positive view of the mind's unconscious realm. They tend to see it as a storehouse of accumulated ideas, emotions, images, and sensory information that the conscious mind can draw upon, like some private trust fund. These researchers point out that most highly creative people are able to tap the hidden resources of their minds to solve problems, and make new breakthroughs—in science and business as well as in the arts and religion. All of us, they feel, could benefit by using this reservoir of "human potentials"—if only we knew how.

Among the most exciting investigators in the burgeoning human-potentials movement are behavioral scientists Robert Masters and Jean Houston, a husband-and-wife team who together make up the Foundation for Mind Research in Pomona, New York. In their pioneering work, Masters and Houston have experimented with a number of ways by which we can break through what they call "the surface crust" of mental and physical habits that prevent us from utilizing our full human potential. The techniques that they have developed have been taught to hundreds of people like Micaela Kelly who work with others—teachers, social workers, doctors, government officials, priests—and who in turn are helping the people they work with to accomplish things they had never before imagined possible.

"We've found that thinking, sensing and feeling are all interrelated," says Bob Masters, a soft-spoken Midwesterner, "so that by improving one of these capacities you improve all the others."

The foundation is located on a rural estate fifty miles north of New York City, in a spacious house built by actor Burgess Meredith. James Thurber[2] drew many of his celebrated cartoons there, and the music of *My Fair Lady* was composed on the piano that still commands an area off the living room. What Masters and Houston are doing there, however, may give Meredith House—and its current occupants—more than celebrity status.

A few years ago, for instance, shortly after his flight to the moon, astronaut Edgar Mitchell visited the foundation. Mitchell said that throughout his lunar exploration he was so busy manipulating machinery and responding to minute-by-minute instructions from earth that what his mind and senses actually experienced on the moon never really registered on his conscious mind.

Bob and Jean took him up to their second-floor laboratory and placed him in one of several devices they use for inducing a trancelike state in which the usual patterns of mental activity are temporarily suppressed. Mitchell stretched out on a metal swing that is suspended so that the subject rotates like a human pendulum. Gradually, the astronaut slipped into an altered state of consciousness, losing all sense of normal time and space. In this state, the "doors" to deeper consciousness are opened and the mind is flooded with images and impressions stored up in the cells of the brain. With verbal suggestions from Bob Masters, Mitchell was guided back to the moon and was able to experience, consciously, many of the sights and sensations that had previously lain dormant in his unconscious. "The tapes we made of this second lunar voyage," says Masters, "indicate that he had an absolutely wonderful time."

In other experiments at the foundation Masters and Houston have discovered that they can:

• accelerate mental processes, so that a concert pianist can, during a trance state, achieve in one minute the equivalent of an hour's practice.
• stimulate a novelist's blocked imagination so that he will actually see, as if watching a film, the unfolding final chapter of a novel that he had previously been unable to finish for over a year.
• increase the learning rate among students—both normal and learning-disabled—by teaching them how to think in images as well as words.

After almost twenty years of research, Masters and Houston are bringing the results of their investigations to lecture audiences at Harvard, Columbia and dozens of other major universities. More important, they are training hundreds of educators, psychotherapists, clergy and others in the helping professions through workshops at the foundation.

In essence, Masters and Houston are convinced that all of us have many mental capacities that have been distorted, inhibited or altogether blocked. "Very early in life," Jean Houston argues, "children are taught to repress and ignore their natural capacities to wonder, dream, fantasize and imagine—some of the richest ways we have of understanding and interpreting reality." The key to healthier minds and bodies, they believe, is the ability to break up our conditioned ways of thinking, feeling and acting. We all do this—if only briefly—when we sleep, meditate, do yoga or take drugs—including that relaxing martini before dinner. "Boredom is the mind's

---

[2]James Thurber (1894–1961) was an American comic writer and cartoonist associated with *The New Yorker* magazine. He is most famous for his story, "The Secret Life of Walter Mitty."

greatest enemy," says Jean, which is why we all seek escape from time to time. But, she insists, there are better ways of enriching our lives.

At the foundation Bob and Jean employ a variety of techniques, both ancient and modern, to evoke the hidden contents and processes of the mind. What I found most intriguing is their huge collection of ancient art and artifacts from dozens of different cultures. On one wall is a large painting used by Mazatec Indians in Mexico to effect healings in those who meditate on it. Other walls are hung with sacred symbols, called mandalas, used in Buddhist, Hindu and other Oriental religions. But the real jewels of the collection are numerous small statues—one of them over 3,000 years old—of the ancient Egyptian goddess, Sekhmet, with the body of a woman and the head of a lioness.

"We've found in working with artists," Jean reports, "that one ancient Egyptian statue can do more than anything else to stimulate the unconscious. The ancient Eygptians understood the unconscious perhaps better than any other people who ever lived. They could create hypnotic art objects that still evoke archetypal images in those who meditate on them. We've found that when particularly sensitive people meditate on these statues, images readily come up from the depths of the unconscious." At my request, Bob demonstrated some of the practical results of their research. "If you want to improve the way you use your body," he explained, "you literally have to put your mind to it. Most of us have become so unaware of our own bodies that we have to learn to experience them all over again. But once we understand how mental awareness affects our bodies—and vice versa—there is no end to the ways in which we can improve how we feel, move and act."

The unconscious, of course, is not just a warehouse of images. Rather, it is like a computer in which information is coded in symbols, images and archetypes that form various patterns. Often, these patterns contain creative solutions to problems that the conscious mind alone cannot solve. Indeed, Bob and Jean have conducted numerous experiments with artists that lead them to believe that moments of creative breakthroughs—when solutions seem to arrive from nowhere—actually result from tapping these deeper patterns of information.

In one experiment, for example, Bob and Jean put a young novelist suffering from writer's block in a device similar to the one astronaut Edgar Mitchell used. As soon as the writer had gone into a trance state, he was told that he would see the final chapter of his book appear before him. He would be able to watch his characters and hear them speak; afterwards, he would remember what they said and did. Four times the author went into trance and each time he experienced a different scenario for his final chapter. After the last one, Jean reports, he went home in great excitement and in two days finished his book.

Masters and Houston have also discovered that thinking images can also be used to practice almost any art or sport. Just as we can experience in a minute of sleep dreams that seem to last for an hour, so they have found that in an altered state of consciousness any mental process can be speeded up. Since playing the piano or a game of tennis involves the mind as well as the body, these activities can be rehearsed in a minute of trance, and the benefits are similar to an hour's practice.

In practice, learning through the imagination involves what Masters and Houston call the "master-teacher" technique, which has proved useful in helping everyone from painters and poets to golfers and tennis buffs. For instance, tennis instructor Bob Massie, a former collegiate star at Rollins College in Florida, uses it to help students improve their strokes. As he explains it, Bob plays a set with a student to see where he or she needs help. Then he has his student lie down in a quiet place until his consciousness is in a state of relaxation.

Next, Bob tells the student that he will receive in fifteen minutes of clock time a three-hour lesson from his favorite tennis star, who will show him how to hit the ball properly. "One of my students is an intermediate player whose favorite pro is Chris Evert," Bob explained to me. "This young woman needed help in developing her forehand ground stroke. So I had her imagine a talk, in an altered state of consciousness, with Chris. Afterward, we went back out on the court and she found that her stroke had become smoother and more efficient.

"I find the exercise works every time," Bob reports. "What happens, I think, is that the conscious mind is held at bay so that it can't cause the player to choke up. Meanwhile, in the personification of the master teacher, the body is able to teach the student what it already knows how to do—execute a fluid stroke. It's a way of screening out interference from the mind."

As tools for psychotherapists, many of the symbolizing techniques developed by Masters and Houston have proved to be of immense practical benefit. Dr. Joseph Spear, a psychotherapist in Tulsa, reports that after working with 51 Oklahoma prison inmates who were classified as borderline recidivists—that is, prisoners rated likely to return to a life of crime—ninety percent of them have remained crime-free four years after undergoing therapy that included symbolizing exercises.

It is one thing to unblock the mind in a laboratory setting, quite another to design workshops in which others can achieve similar results for themselves. At Jean's invitation, I joined a group of thirty teachers, psychotherapists and counselors, for a ten-day intensive program. Gone were the machines, the ancient statues and other elaborate devices to alter mind and body.

Beginning with light yoga exercises at 7:30 in the morning, Jean worked with her class for seventeen hours a day, closing with deep meditation. Despite this demanding schedule, Elsa A. Porter, chief of the Analysis and Development Division for the U.S. Civil Service Commission, discovered that she could get up an hour earlier than her classmates each morning to finish writing a report that had boggled her mind for months. "I feel my mind has been loosened and activated," she told me, "although I can't point to one specific exercise that has done it."

Indeed, Jean's method is rather like a theater director who teaches basic movements, yet improvises according to the mood and interests of her students. "Think of your entire body as a grid on which the whole surface of your skin, your fingers, the back of your head, your solar plexus are all picking up information," she instructed us. After "priming" each of these information centers through various exercises, she taught us to call on these centers to feed back the information they were receiving. Basically, this required us to pay more attention to how these various parts of our bodies felt while Jean read aloud from a newspaper than to what our brains were receiving through our ears.

"Let the mind go," Jean urged. "Your body will pick up the information." Gradually we found that we could recall information by remembering how our fingers, for instance, had felt while Jean was reading a dull article on business economics from *The New York Times*.

"The mind," Jean continued, "works several thousand times faster than the spoken word. And so with practice we can turn even the dullest classroom lecture into an adventure by throwing the senses and the imagination into the act." As a practical demonstration, Jean told us to let our minds wander where they would for 90 seconds. Thus, for the next minute and a half, my own mind raced across the years, visited four continents, relived perhaps fifty different experiences. And when Jean signaled that time was up, I—like everyone else in the room—admitted that it had seemed as if twenty minutes or more had passed.

The trick, she explained, is to listen to what is said and let the imagination form pleasant images to go along with what is heard. Then, by recalling these images, the verbal content of the lecture can also be retrieved.

In response to several questions from teachers in the group, Jean drew our attention to the possibilities such exercises hold for enhancing classroom techniques. "Young children are feisty, multidi-mensional human beings who need to be addressed on more than one level of learning," she says. "Besides learning how to spell C-A-T, they should be taught to feel the word, to smell it, to visualize it—and then they'll never forget it. Even if their minds wander, their senses will be hooked into the spelling lesson."

Jean's approach to writing is equally iconoclastic. One of the major ways in which every culture imposes limits on creative expression, she argues, is through language, which locks the mind into rigid grammatical patterns. As a result, she believes, fresh insights often fail to surface and writers frequently suffer from unnecessary blocks. To help break those blocks when they occur, Jean taught us a technique that had everyone talking in nonsense syllables, much as fundamentalist Christians do when they pray in tongues during Pentacostal church services. In this exercise, we were trying to let impulses from our conscious break up conventional patterns of expression.

Soon the whole room was a babble of animated gibberish. Then we divided into conversational pairs and carried on dialogues in this manner, emphasizing points with our hands, bodies and voice inflections.

Once we began to get the hang of what our partners were trying to say, Jean directed each of us to write a poem using only nonsense syllables. After that, we were to translate our poems into English. I let my mind go blank, so that the sounds alone would flow through it like a stream:

Hosh-ka miska mowaway
Sa shan lagua nonaway
Klam alam ma-paninquay.

Just as mysteriously, the "translation" came to me:

The fire that burns is healing
The water that flows is cleansing
And I am dry as bone.

Jean listened to several of us recite what we had written, then drew our attention to certain decidedly unmysterious features. Many of the poetic images, she noted, bore resemblances to Nordic or German myths; in some cases, students reported, the exercise had taken them back to nursery rhymes and fairy tales their mothers had told them. Still other poems, such as mine, contained imagery and emotions associated with traditional religious themes.

"A Freudian or Jungian psychoanalyst would probably relate these images to early childhood experiences or to embedded human archetypes," Jean explained. "But you don't need an analyst to make practical use of this exercise."

Whenever we can't find the words for what we want to say, she suggested that we try to say it first in nonsense syllables as a way of breaking through writer's block. Indeed, she pointed out that the British author J.R.R. Tolkien wrote his multivolume epic, *The Lord of the Rings,* in precisely this fashion. First he invented a nonsense language for his mythological characters, then wrote each book in that language and finally translated his manuscript into English.

Many of the technqiues taught by Masters and Houston, such as Micaela Kelly's teaching of creative writing, have been put to practical use by their students. Jean has also been especially helpful in revising the entire curriculum of Mead School, in Greenwich, Connecticut. There, her emphasis on visualizing numbers as well as words has been incorporated into the regular program. This emphasis, says Elaine de Beauport, founder of the experimental school, has been particularly helpful to dyslectic children who have difficulty distinguishing numbers and letters visually on a blackboard. By visualizing them first in their minds—without the aid of paper and pencil—they find they can overcome their learning disability. "It also helps to build up their self-confidence by emphasizing what they can do, not what they can't," says Ms. de Beauport. As a result, the school now grades students on their ability to think visually as well as logically.

Through other workshop students, Masters and Houston are generating new programs for the aged throughout the greater New York area. In one typical program at the Ethical Culture School of

Adult Education in New York City, gerontologist Ruth Hersh has organized a "journey of self-discovery." "We use Masters and Houston's mind exercises to call up a whole flood of images from the past," she says. "The elderly are able to reexperience childhood memories and share them with each other. They also learn to summon up long-buried sensations in writing short stories and poems. Sometimes we have them dance out answers to personal problems that the mind alone can't resolve, or use their kinesthetic imagination to relearn how to play a sport."

"They helped me finish the unfinished business of my life," said one 72-year-old woman who recently decided, after taking the course, that she could continue to maintain her own apartment in New York City rather than move in with her children. Another man, in his late 60's, found that he could recapture his old sense of self-confidence—so much so that he was recently elected head of the board of directors in his apartment house after months of keeping disconsolately to himself.

"We're not doing this just to keep the elderly busy," Ms. Hersh concludes. "We're actually giving them back their bodies and their minds." Bob and Jean could not have put it any better.

PREVIEW QUESTIONS

_____ 1. The primary researchers mentioned in this article are
   a. Freud and Jung.
   b. Woodward and Kelly.
   c. Masters and Houston.
   d. Thurber and Meredith.

_____ 2. The title refers to
   a. things you know but lack confidence to tell anyone.
   b. facts you have read about but have forgotten.
   c. multisensory information you have gained from varied sources that you have stored in your unconscious mind.
   d. your ability to use more of your brain power by consciously spending more time thinking with problem-solving techniques.

_____ 3. This article originally appeared in
   a. *Psychology Today.*
   b. *McCall's.*
   c. *Scientific American.*
   d. *Primer in Psychology.*

_____ 4. The main idea of this article could be stated as follows:
   a. Researchers have discovered techniques to help release the hidden deeper patterns of information stored in the unconscious so that they may be used in everyday life.
   b. Some people have the unusual ability to use the information stored in the unconscious to solve problems creatively.
   c. In the future, we may discover how to unlock the vast storage of information in the unconscious and put it to use in solving problems.
   d. There are a few exceptional teachers who know how to use scientific research to teach students to be more creative.

_____ 5. The author organized this entire article so that he
   a. contrasted the newest techniques in psychology with older, more traditional ones.
   b. defined the limits of the unconscious mind.
   c. revealed the causes of some observable effects of the unconscious.
   d. described some techniques that tap the unconscious and gave some illustrations of how these techniques have been used.

Allow 20 points per correct answer.   Your score _____ %
Number of words: 4,440   Your rate _____
Answer key is on page 273.
Record rate and comprehension score on Course Data Sheet in Preview columns.

GOOD COMPREHENSION QUESTIONS

_____ 1. The astonishing results of Ms. Kelly's experiment with her students can be explained in psychological terms as children
  a. responding to any novel teaching method.
  b. using their natural power and resources of their own unconscious minds.
  c. trying to please a teacher whom they liked.
  d. expending more effort to do a good job because they were allowed to choose their own topics about which to write.

_____ 2. This article states that the unconscious is
  a. just a warehouse of images.
  b. a computer where information is coded in symbols, images, and archetypes that form various patterns.
  c. a dark cave where untamed instincts and childhood traumas lurk.
  d. that part of one's mind which comprises repressed thoughts, feelings, memories, impulses, and desires.

_____ 3. In experiments by investigators of the human-potential movement, behavioral scientists have discovered that one of the things that can be done is to
  a. increase one's learning rate by thinking in images as well as words.
  b. increase one's reading comprehension by learning to pay more attention to each word.
  c. eliminate neurotic behavior by reading articles on psychology.
  d. slow down the mental processes to achieve better mastery over a particular skill.

_____ 4. Through experimentation, Masters and Houston have discovered that
  a. their techniques do not work on older people.
  b. words must be used to unblock the mind for creative language expression.
  c. to help those with learning disabilities distinguish between numbers and letters, writing the symbols on paper several times works best.
  d. thinking in images can also be used to practice almost any art or sport.

_____ 5. According to this article
  a. when following the spoken word, as in a lecture, the mind becomes unaware of the other senses.
  b. the mind works several thousand times faster than the spoken word.
  c. letting the mind go into the imagination process hinders the recall of information.
  d. when the mind is allowed to wander, the passage of time seems to be faster than it actually is.

_____ 6. This article states that information is picked up
  a. by the mind through the spoken and written word primarily.
  b. through the mind and all portions of the body.
  c. only when we pay attention to what is going on.
  d. primarily through sight.

_____ 7. From the article, we know that Mr. Woodward, the author, obtained much of his information for this article from
  a. reading about what psychotherapists are currently doing all over the country.
  b. setting up his own workshop and experimenting with new techniques.
  c. interviewing children who were involved in the research using these new techniques.
  d. participating in a workshop conducted by Masters and Houston.

_____ 8. Masters and Houston are convinced that
   a. the childhood abilities to wonder, dream, fantasize, and imagine cannot be recaptured in adult life.
   b. the key to healthier minds and bodies is to learn to use our conditioned ways of thinking, feeling, and acting.
   c. all of us have many mental capacities that have been distorted, inhibited, or altogether blocked.
   d. meditation and yoga may relax the body but do nothing to unblock unconscious information.

_____ 9. Masters and Houston have been doing research in their techniques for almost
   a. 10 years.
   b. 15 years.
   c. 20 years.
   d. 30 years.

_____ 10. One way Masters and Houston use to open the "doors" to a state of deeper consciousness is by means of
   a. a device similar to a rotating metal swing.
   b. hypnosis.
   c. truth serum.
   d. a closed room that simulates the weightlessness of outer space.

Allow 10 points per correct answer.   *Your score _____ %*
Number of words: 4,440   *Your rate _____*
Answer key is on page 273.
Record rate and comprehension score on Course Date Sheet in the Good Comprehension *columns.*

POSTVIEW QUESTIONS

_____ 1. Regarding Edgar Mitchell's voyage to the moon, Masters and Houston helped him to
   a. respond rapidly to instructions on his voyage.
   b. consciously remember the sights and sensations he experienced.
   c. recover from the exhausting ordeal.
   d. prepare to be alert on the trip.

_____ 2. We could infer from the information given in this article that memory can be improved by
   a. consciously paying attention to what is said and blocking out any other sensations.
   b. taking a memory course.
   c. reexperiencing the physical sensations that occurred at the time the information to be recalled was originally received.
   d. consciously trying harder to remember.

_____ 3. This article states that memory images and impressions are
   a. stored in the cells of the brain.
   b. unimportant for remembering factual information.
   c. stored in an unknown place somewhere in the body.
   d. impossible to retrieve from the memory once they are forgotten.

_____ 4. Art objects are sometimes used to
   a. stimulate the unconscious.
   b. evoke archetypal images.
   c. aid in meditation.
   d. all of the above.

———— 5. One way of breaking through writer's block used here is to
   a. force the writer to write according to a preplanned schedule.
   b. have the writer read other works until he gets ideas.
   c. have the writer write first in nonsense syllables and then translate what he has written.
   d. bolster the writer's ego by telling him good things about himself.

Allow 20 points per correct answer.   *Your score* ———————— %
Number of words: 4,440   *Your rate* ————————
Answer key is on page 273.
Record rate and comprehension score on Course Date Sheet in Postview columns.
Regarding the reading method you chose, did you choose to preview ————, do a good comprehension reading ————, postview ————? Did you find it necessary to change your method after you started? ————

THE POPULATION BOMB
PREVIEW QUESTIONS

Note that these questions cover material from the book's prologue, foreword, appendix, letters, and update.

———— 1. Population control is
   a. birth control as practiced by whoever desires it.
   b. a conscious regulation of the number of human beings to meet the needs of society as a whole.
   c. zero population growth.
   d. an appeal to cut population.

———— 2. Whereas in underdeveloped countries, the problem of overpopulation produces mass starvation, in developed countries the present problems are
   a. too many cars.
   b. too few schools to educate the mass of population.
   c. overcrowded living environments with one person per every one hundred feet.
   d. environmental deterioration and difficulty in obtaining resources to support the people's affluence.

———— 3. A scenario is
   a. a song, including words and music.
   b. an outline for a series of events, real or imagined.
   c. newspaper articles.
   d. a logical argument presented to influence the reader to take action.

———— 4. At the end of this book are letters that
   a. the author received from friends.
   b. people wrote to tell how this book helped them.
   c. people wrote to others urging them to action regarding the population problem.
   d. the author received from people with opposing points of view

———— 5. The author updated this book in
   a. 1978.
   b. 1970.
   c. 1980.
   d. 1972.

Allow 20 points per correct answer.   *Your score* ———————— %
Number of words: 79,550   *Your rate* ————————
Answer key is on page 273.
Record rate and comprehension score on Course Data Sheet in Preview columns.

THE POPULATION BOMB
GOOD COMPREHENSION QUESTIONS

Note that these questions cover material from the book's prologue, foreword, appendix, letters, and update.

_____ 1. The main problem of malnutrition, a lack of one or more essential elements in the diet, is lack of
a. minerals.
b. calories.
c. protein.
d. all of the above.

_____ 2. The present rate at which the population *doubles* is estimated at once every
a. 35 years.
b. 200 years.
c. 17 years.
d. 100 years.

_____ 3. A population continues to grow if
a. the birthrate exceeds the death rate.
b. every family produces two or more children.
c. people continue to have as many children as they want.

_____ 4. The only solution(s) to the population problem is (are)
a. the birthrate solution (cut it down).
b. the death-rate solution (raise it).
c. both of the above.
d. neither of the above.

_____ 5. The agricultural revolution resulted in
a. a reduction of life-threats and an increase in population.
b. a centralization of population and an increase in disease and large-scale warfare.
c. neither of the above.
d. both of the above.

_____ 6. Major world-killing diseases such as bubonic plague and cholera are
a. not likely to rise above their present status.
b. more possible with an increase in malnutrition, more crowded population, a resurgence of certain disease-carrying insects, and global transportation systems.
c. forever squelched by the miracles of modern medicine.

_____ 7. One reason that statistics on death and starvation are hard to count is because
a. undernourished people do not usually starve to death.
b. people often die of some disease they contract as they weaken from starvation.
c. death-rate statistics do not list deaths by starvation alone.

_____ 8. The Green Revolution is
a. the birth of the ecologically concerned.
b. scientific advances in new wheat and rice varieties.
c. the development of new fruits and vegetables for the future.

_____ 9. Scenario I occurred because the
a. people were suffering from malnutrition.
b. government was trying to improve the food supply of the nation.
c. government valued economics and politics above ecology.

_____ 10. In Scenario II, although one-half of the world's children and one and one-half billion people were lost, due to LASSA fever, the hope for the future was that
   a. the United Nations would sign a world treaty against biological warfare.
   b. the U.N. agencies would regulate population and environment.
   c. in the future the United Nations would supply serum to all affected countries.

_____ 11. Scenario III provides a solution to the food population imbalance through
   a. the opening of China's borders.
   b. the International Survival Tax on overdeveloped countries.
   c. the moral fibre of the American leadership and populace.
   d. major worldwide population control, food rationing, and equitable protein distribution.

_____ 12. The following are some sound solutions to population control:
   a. abortion.
   b. male vasectomy.
   c. income-tax deductions for smaller families.
   d. all of the above.
   e. a and c only.

_____ 13. The unfarmed lands are not farmed because
   a. there is some combination of bad soil, lack of water, or suitable climate in that area.
   b. man needs to develop better technology for farming these lands.
   c. we have no need for these lands and just haven't started farming them yet.

_____ 14. Population control is
   a. practiced widely in underdeveloped countries.
   b. regarded as unnecessary at this time by most governments.
   c. not popular with most governments.
   d. actively being researched and developed in most countries.

_____ 15. Family planning is ineffective for population control because
   a. most people want families of a size that will keep the population growing.
   b. usually people consider it after they have already had too many children.
   c. people "space" their children while they continue to have too many.

_____ 16. Mankind's inalienable rights include the right to
   a. enjoy natural beauty.
   b. go wherever we want.
   c. have limitless families.

_____ 17. Some things *you* can do to help the food-population problem are
   a. eat less.
   b. have two or fewer children.
   c. send your extra food to UDC's.

_____ 18. To the people who already have large families, we should
   a. emphasize that the need for family limitation was not as obvious before.
   b. reprimand them and socially outcast them.
   c. explain that everyone is entitled to make a mistake.

_____ 19. It is advocated in the book that the Catholic Church
   a. reeducate its followers on the rhythm method so that it can work better.
   b. favor abortion.
   c. widen its views on birth control.

_____ 20. On the question of eugenics (certain people breed and others are sterilized), it is stated that
   a. the average I.Q. will drop if we don't use eugenics.
   b. intelligence in man has both genetic and environmental components.
   c. diet is far more important than genetics.

Allow 5 points per correct answer. Your score _____ %
Number of words: 79,550 Your rate _____
Answer key is on page 273.
Record rate and comprehension score on Course Data Sheet in Good Comprehension columns.

THE POPULATION BOMB
POSTVIEW QUESTIONS

Note that these questions cover material from the book's prologue, foreword, appendix, letters, and update.

_____ 1. Dr. Paul Ehrlich, author of *The Population Bomb,* is
   a. a responsible layperson.
   b. a successful novelist.
   c. an eminent professor of biology.

_____ 2. This book is organized as
   a. a nonfiction argument with scientific and statistical facts.
   b. a scientific case study.
   c. a novel of a future time.

_____ 3. According to this book, the possibility that the United States will face a mass starvation similar to that of the underdeveloped countries is
   a. a sure possibility.
   b. a far-fetched possibility.
   c. an unlikely possibility.
   d. an immediate possibility.

_____ 4. Facing the possibility of famine, underdeveloped countries probably will
   a. cooperate with overdeveloped countries' demands for their resources in the hopes that they will help with their food problem.
   b. try to develop their own resources for food.
   c. starve to death while they continue to supply ODC's with the resources they need.
   d. suspend their cooperative attitude about exporting to the ODC's whatever resources they normally export.

_____ 5. It can be inferred from this book that the author advocates any workable solution to the overpopulation problem.
   a. true.
   b. false.

Allow 20 points per correct answer. Your score _____ %
Number of words: 79,550 Your rate _____
Answer key is on page 273.
Record rate and comprehension score on Course Data Sheet in Postview columns.
Regarding the reading method you chose, did you choose to preview _____, do a good comprehension reading _____, postview _____? Did you find it necessary to change your method after starting? _____

GENERAL NONFICTION PREVIEW QUESTIONS

Title _____ Author _____

1. Which of the following does this book contain ("yes" or "no," 2½ points each)?

   _____ a. preface   _____ e. index

   _____ b. introduction   _____ f. bibliography

   _____ c. contents   _____ g. data on the author

   _____ d. glossary   _____ h. maps, charts, graphs

2. Explain the meaning of the title. _____
   _____

3. What type of book is it (history, scientific, "how to," biography, textbook, etc.)? _____

4. What is the subject of this book? _____
   _____

5. What does the writer's purpose appear to be (check one)?

   _____ a. to explain factual information on the subject

   _____ b. to report what happened

   _____ c. to give *his* or *her* ideas on the subject

   _____ d. to persuade you to take some action

   _____ e. to teach you how to perform some act

To correct, find the answers in the book.
Allow 20 points per correct answer. (Each part of question one is worth 2½ points.)

Figure out the number of words in the   Your score _____ %
book. _____   Your rate _____
Record title, rate, and comprehension score on Course Data Sheet in Preview columns.

GENERAL NONFICTION
GOOD COMPREHENSION QUESTIONS

1. Write one sentence stating the most important thing the author says about the subject of this book (the main idea). _____
   _____

2. Write two short sentences stating two other important things brought out in this book.

   (1) _____

   (2) _____

3. At the end, does the author state a conclusion? _____

   What is it? _____
   _____

4. What is the most interesting thing you learned from this book? _____

_____

5. What is the most useful thing you learned from this book? _____

_____

6. Write a short summary of the information this book covers. _____

_____

_____

_____

7. List three important details the author gives to support the main idea.

(1) _____

(2) _____

(3) _____

8. Is this book written according to a logical, sequential time order (what happened first, second, third, etc.), or does it jump around in time? _____

9. Does the author refer to or quote authorities or sources in this field of knowledge, or is the information presented as all his or her ideas? _____

10. From the information given in this book, what conclusion can *you* come to?

_____

Correct by finding the answers in the book.
Allow 10 points per correct answer.   *Your score* _____ %
Number of words _____   *Your rate* _____
Record rate and comprehension score on Course Data Sheet in Good Comprehension columns.
Did the method you chose include a preview _____, *good comprehension reading* _____, *postview* _____? *After making your initial choice on which method to use, did you change during the reading?* _____

19

Reading for Enjoyment

Materials: • Any book of your choice that you can finish in one hour

Objective: • To have pleasurable reading by using speed-reading techniques

Now that you have learned how to tackle the difficult type of reading that studying requires, reading for enjoyment will seem easy. Perhaps you have not had much time for this kind of reading in the past because you could never find the time to finish a book in a reasonable length of time, and reading only a few pages a day bored you. You may even be one of those people who has a long list of books that you really want to read "someday." By spending only one hour a week you can now finally read all those books that you've been planning to get to "someday."

CHOOSING READING FOR ENJOYMENT

Although getting involved in the adventures of the imaginary people of a story as a means of escaping one's own life for a brief time is a healthy and acceptable purpose for reading, good books have more to offer. Thoughtful, well-written stories enrich and supplement life's experiences. Informational books supply knowledge that can be useful in coping with life. Fulfilling these purposes can add to your pleasure in reading.

Through good literature you learn about yourself and others and experience new situations and places often impossible to experience in real life. The number of people you can really get to

"know" in life is greatly limited, and you can never know what really goes on inside another person, even if he or she chooses to confide in you. Through literature you can get inside other people and totally understand them—people like yourself and people you might never meet in real life, people from other countries and in different circumstances. You can know what the characters are thinking, what motivates them, how they react, what they do when alone; in fact, you can obtain information never available to you in life. Through identification with the characters in a story, you are able to try out new situations and respond emotionally. By being aware of your feelings as you respond, you learn about yourself—how you might react and feel in these untried experiences. You have the chance to feel the total spectrum of emotions without paying any of the consequences. You can travel to foreign lands, earlier times in history, even future times, and all without leaving your comfortable chair or spending one cent.

If you choose to spend your reading time with the great minds of the past or present, you will meet these real people and ideas that have shaped the world and may, in some way, shape your life. Books have left us marvelous records of the thoughts of a Freud, a Plato, and a vast array of divergent, innovative thinkers. You have only to choose to share their thoughts, and the result is

240

often the opening of new doors to your own thoughts, a delightful kind of pleasure!

If you choose to read informational books on any particular subject, you can become an expert in that field by learning what the authorities in that field already know. As you read in any one area, each successive book becomes easier because your knowledge in the field grows, and the more you know about a topic, the easier it is to understand and remember as you read rapidly.

Reading for enjoyment does not mean only light, frivolous reading. It emcompasses all reading you do for your own pleasure; and if you gain self-insight, provocative ideas, and extended knowledge, you will find these extra benefits can add immeasurably to the pleasure and accomplishment of reading.

METHOD

Since you are reading only for yourself and not for a test or a research paper, the process of reading for enjoyment is more comfortable and may be done at a leisurely pace. It is still important to survey the book first to get an idea of what it is going to be about so that you don't begin reading completely "cold." This survey need only involve looking at the front and back covers. Then you begin. (A preview reading is not necessary). Your pace should be one with which you feel at ease. The first chapter should be read more slowly so that you can learn the names of the characters, the time and place, and the general setting. After the first chapter, you will find that you can speed up and still feel as if you are going slowly enough to understand the entire story. I do not recommend that you slow down to your old very slow reading, because you want to keep your newly acquired rapid-reading skill and not slip back into your old habits. Besides, it isn't necessary. If you continue to use your hand as instructed, you may feel as if you are reading almost word by word; but you will actually be going at a rapid rate. Take a reading rate for a chapter, and you will verify that it is true. Continue to slow down and speed up according to the difficulty of the material, and before you realize it, you will have finished the book.

At this point you may be thinking, "What about those wonderfully written passages that I want to savor and enjoy? Can I still enjoy them going rapidly?" The speed-reading techniques that you have been learning have not taken anything away from you. You can still read at one word a minute, if you wish. You have been learning additional skills so that you now have choices about which speed best serves your purpose. Before you could only read slowly. Now you can still read slowly, but you can also read at various rapid rates when you choose to do so. However, you will find that even at your slowest rate, when you are able to savor the literature, you will still be reading faster than you were before you learned this rapid-reading method.

However, all portions of any book are not of equal interest to you or worthy of your equal attention. On the parts that interest you, the parts you want to "experience" thoroughly, slow down as much as you need to and enjoy them. On the parts of lesser interest, speed up to a very rapid rate. In this way, you can both enjoy and finish the book rapidly. The secret is to use a wide range of flexibility.

Reading Practice

For practice, choose a book that you have been wanting to read. Survey the front and back covers. Write down your starting time. Begin to read. Read the first chapter more slowly. Speed up with the second chapter, but use lots of flexibility so that you slow down on the most enjoyable parts and speed up greatly on the other parts. Record you finish time. Compute the approximate number of words in the book and figure your rate. (When reading at home purely for enjoyment, this step is not necessary.) This rate will probably be lower than your rates for materials on which you were tested in previous chapters; but I think you will be surprised to find that it is higher than you thought it would be, considering how slowly you thought you were reading. Record the title of the book, your rate, and an estimate of your comprehension on the Course Data Sheet. Complete the Novel or Nonfiction Reading For Enjoyment Report at the end of this chapter.

You can read a book a day if you want to. Get started on that list you've been keeping for years!

SUMMARY

Reading for enjoyment requires only a brief survey. Use a wide range of flexibility: Slow down slightly on the first chapter, slow down as much as you like on the interesting parts, and speed up greatly on the less interesting parts.

Add to your pleasure by choosing books that have more than just a good story to offer.

NOVEL READING FOR ENJOYMENT REPORT

Your Name _____ Date _____

Title _____ Author _____

Number of words _____

Finishing time _____

Starting time _____

Your time to read _____

1. Survey: Look at the covers; glance through the book.

   a. What type of book is it (mystery, love story, science fiction, historical novel, etc.)? _____

   b. Have you read anything by this author before? _____

   c. Why did you choose this book? _____

2. Read (use your speed-reading skills).

   a. How does the story begin? _____
   _____

   b. Write a *very* brief summary of what the story is about.
   _____
   _____

   c. How does it end? _____

3. Comments.

   a. If you like the story, what did you like about it? _____
   _____

   b. If you didn't like the story, what didn't you like about it?
   _____
   _____

   c. Did you identify with any particular character? _____
   Which one? _____

   d. Did you learn something about yourself? _____ About other people?
   _____
   What? _____

   e. Do you feel that you really read the story? _____

   f. What rating would you give for your comprehension of this story (100%, 90%, 80%, etc.)? _____

Record title, rate and estimation of your comprehension on Course Data Sheet in the Good Comprehension columns. Your reading rate _____

NONFICTION READING FOR ENJOYMENT REPORT

Your Name _____ Date _____

Title _____ Author _____

Number of words _____

Finishing time _____

Starting time _____

Your time to read _____

1. Survey: Look at covers, contents; glance through the book.

   a. What type of book is it (history, philosophy, psychology, science, how-to,

      etc.)? _____

   b. Have you read anything by this author before? _____

   c. Why did you choose this book? _____

2. Read (use your speed-reading skills).

   a. What is the subject of this book? _____

      _____

   b. Is this book written by or about a recognized authority on this subject? _

   c. What did you find the most interesting in this book? _____

      _____

   d. What did you find the most useful to you? _____

      _____

   e. Write a very brief summary of the main idea the author is trying to get

      across to you. _____

      _____

      _____

3. Comments.

   a. Do you expect this book to spur you on to think more on this subject?

      _____

   b. Will you want to read other books on this subject? _____

      By this author? _____

   c. Was this book worth the time you spent on it? _____

      Did you really enjoy it? _____

   d. Do you feel you really read it? _____

   e. Did you slow down on beginnings and especially interesting or impor-

      tant parts? _____

   f. What comprehension rating would you give yourself (100%, 90%, 80%,

      etc.)? _____

                                        Your reading rate _____

Record title, rate, and estimation of your comprehension on Course Data Sheet in Good Comprehension columns.

Conclusion

What will happen when you are on your own, after these exercises are completed? That will, of course, depend on you! As long as you continue to use the speed-reading techniques regularly, you will retain your present level of competency. However, if you should go through long periods of time without using these newly acquired skills, your reading rate will decrease. When this happens, you can do two things that will immediately improve your rate: one, conscientiously drill for several days (various drills are given in the Appendix), and two, push yourself to go faster when you are reading.

Will you have to use your hand as a pacer forever? Not necessarily, but I would recommend that you do continue to use it. Before learning these speed-reading techniques, you had paced your eyes for many years to move slowly. In a few months the work of so many years cannot be completely eradicated; it will take a few years of consistent rapid reading before your mind has acquired the habit of automatically pacing your eyes rapidly without an external pacer such as your hand.

Learning this new skill has given you a new dimension of yourself, a sense of the hidden powers within you. You now know that you can read faster than you have ever read before. Of what other feats are you capable? I hope that your success in speed reading has given you the courage to try other new experiences in order to find out. *You do know more than you think!*

RATE AND COMPREHENSION POSTTEST

Directions: *In the space provided, record the times that you start and finish reading this article in hours, minutes, and seconds. Subtract your starting time from the finishing time to find your total.*

	Hours	Minutes	Seconds
Your finishing time:			
Your starting time:			*(subtract)*
Your total time:			

THE DUAL NATURE OF STRESS

Lillian P. Wenick

In recent years an enormous amount of attention has centered on stress, what it is, what it does, and how to cope with it. Magazine articles abound in explanations of stress and remedies for avoiding it. Doctors prescribe far more antistress drugs such as Valium or Lithium than antibiotics. Stress is blamed for heart attacks and high blood pressure and is said to be a factor in almost all diseases, even cancer.

This view that stress is a villain to be totally avoided is not unanimous, however. There are those who believe that stress is a positive, necessary ingredient to learning and to enjoying life, that without it life would be dull and creativity would be greatly diminished. There is evidence to back up both views, indicating that stress has a dual nature; it is both good and bad.

Stress is the term first applied by Hans Selye about 40 years ago to the physical symptoms that accompany the state "arousal." These symptoms include the speeding up of bodily processes: faster heart beats, increased blood pressure, more than normal hormonal output. The body becomes prepared for unusual physical activity. As a result of the physical changes, mental reactions occur which are not always predictable. They can range from elation and good feelings to fright and terror.

Any kind of excitement can trigger the symptoms of stress. While walking in the street the sound of screeching brakes will make our hearts race, but our hearts also race during a passionate kiss with a lover. Being called in unexpectedly to the boss's office will speed up the bodily processes. It makes no difference if the boss is going to fire you or promote you: the physical reactions will be the same. Almost any unexpected happening, or an unexpected one full of threat or excitement, causes the bodily processes to speed up.

Those who view stress as harmful propose that any new situation is stressful, even if it is a pleasurable one. Thomas Holmes and Richard Rahe developed the Holmes-Rahe Stress Scale, which attempts to determine the total stress on a person at any given time. The Holmes-Rahe Stress Scale gives stress points to each situation that causes speeding up of bodily functions. According to this scale, a certain number of points is assigned to each situation that causes a change in the routine of life. The greater the change, the more points it carries, and as the number of points increases the possibility of illness due to stress becomes more real. Good changes such as a move to a nicer home or a better job as well as bad changes such as being fired increase the number of points on the scale. It's the total number of changes and stress points that count, not whether they are pleasure stresses or panic stresses.

According to the Holmes-Rahe Stress Scale, the life changes of getting married, moving out of your present home to a new home, buying new furniture, taking a better new job, going on a honeymoon, becoming pregnant with a wanted child, all add up to a dangerous number of stress points even though the life changes are considered good. The unpleasant life changes of divorce, moving to a less expensive smaller home, and supporting a family for the first time may not be more stressful than the pleasant changes.

On the other hand, those who believe that stress plays a positive role in our lives propose that a certain amount of stress is essential. They state that stress produces energy and is essential to creativity. Stress motivates us to seek new ways of solving problems, and the speeding up of bodily functions produces the energy to create the solutions. They also believe that pleasurable stresses actually decrease the effects of unpleasant stress on a type of "uplift scale" that balances the downlift events. These believers go so far as to propose that lack of stress decreases motivation and makes life uninteresting and unexciting, which may lead to apathy, depression and poor functioning. They even suggest that some people suffer from too little stress, that they need more external stimuli, more activity and less "quiet" time which can act as sensory deprivation.

The proponents of stress as necessary point to certain known facts. Mild stress is known to improve learning. A totally relaxed child will not be as receptive to new information as a child experiencing mild stress. It is also known that when the stress of working at a job is removed when elderly people retire they age more quickly unless new activities are substituted in their lives. It is thought that senility occurs more frequently with inactivity than with continued activity. Much of the great art, inventions and discoveries has resulted from the stress of the creators. Would we have the Sistine Chapel if Michaelangelo had lived a quiet stressless life?

We must also admit that the bodily changes that occur under stress often lead to activities that could not be performed under normal circumstances. The 110-pound woman who lifts a one-ton automobile to release her child caught under the wheels could not ordinarily perform this feat; the bodily changes produced by the stress of the situation enable her to do this superhuman act. An athlete relies on the changes that occur under stress to help him run faster, tackle harder, and win the game.

It appears that the amount of harmful stress any particular individual experiences depends upon how he views the stressful experience. If he sees it as threatening, it is a bad stress; but if he views it as a challenge, it can be a beneficial stress. Also, his personality type plays a significant role in the determination of whether the stress is good or bad. Certain types of people appear to need stress to make their lives exciting and meaningful—it keeps them young, alive, and functioning. Other types seem to need routine, quiet, and a peaceful environment.

Should you avoid stress or encourage it? The experts don't have the answer. Since stress has always been part of the human condition and life is not static—unexpected things do happen—complete avoidance is impossible. In fact, worrying about stress is a stress itself. Some authorities suggest that everyone use meditation and relaxation techniques to lessen the effects of stress. They favor changing our busy life-styles to slower-paced living, striving less, and staying put more. Other authorities state that these methods may erase the beneficial effects of stress and that if you receive gratifications from a hectic life-style, adopting a more relaxed routine may deprive you of needed stimuli and lower the quality of your life.

All do agree that attitude is one of the most important factors. A positive attitude can make stress your ally. A negative attitude will make stress your enemy. Since we may never know whose advice to follow, perhaps the best course is to accept stress as inevitable, both good and bad, and to keep the stress that feels good and try to eliminate the stress that feels bad. You be your own expert!

COMPREHENSION QUESTIONS

_____ 1. The term *stress* was first applied to certain physical symptoms
     a. 10 years ago.
     b. 40 years ago.
     c. 100 years ago.
     d. 500 years ago.

_____ 2. In stress the body
     a. slows bodily processes.
     b. speeds up bodily processes.
     c. slows some bodily processes and speeds up others.
     d. maintains the normal rate of bodily processes but changes psychological reactions.

_____ 3. The Holmes-Rahe Stress Scale measures the stress of
     a. pleasant situations only.
     b. unpleasant situations only.
     c. all changes in life situations.
     d. sickness.

_____ 4. This article states that
     a. all authorities agree that all stress is harmful.
     b. all authorities agree that certain stresses are beneficial.
     c. some authorities propose that there is really no such state as stress.
     d. some authorities believe that stress can be beneficial.

_____ 5. Which of the following situations would be considered stressful?
     a. getting married.
     b. losing a job.
     c. a passionate kiss.
     d. moving to a beautiful home.
     e. all of the above.

_____ 6. One belief mentioned is that stress
     a. may be a factor in all illness.
     b. has nothing to do with illness and disease.
     c. is only a factor in heart disease and high blood pressure.
     d. causes senility.

_____ 7. Another belief mentioned is that stress
     a. decreases motivation.
     b. increases motivation.
     c. always decreases creativity.
     d. decreases energy.

_____ 8. Learning occurs best when
     a. there is no stress.
     b. the person is experiencing maximum stress.
     c. the person is experiencing mild stress.
     d. the teacher is under extreme stress.

_____ 9. The attitude of a person
     a. definitely does not influence the effects of stress.
     b. may influence the effects of stress.
     c. is always one of depression when stress is present.
     d. is always one of panic when stress is present.

_____ 10. This article concludes with the idea that
    a. to play it safe all stress should be eliminated.
    b. stress should be increased to make life more exciting.
    c. you judge for yourself which stresses to increase and which to decrease.
    d. if you are an athlete you should increase stress; if you are not an athlete you should decrease stress.

Allow 10 points per correct answer.   *Your score* _____ %
Number of words: 1100   *Your rate* _____
Answer key is on page 273.
Record rate and comprehension score on Course Data Sheet.

Appendix

DRILLS

Drill 1

Read as fast as you can for one minute. Count the number of pages read. Add an equal number of pages to the material you read. Read it all in the same amount of time, one minute. You will need to go twice as fast as before in order to reach your new goal. Repeat.

Drill 2

Read as fast as you can for one minute. Add one page. Reread the same material plus the extra page in the same amount of time, one minute. Add two additional pages (in addition to the page added last time). Read all the material in one minute. Add three additional pages. Read it all in one minute. Add four pages, five pages, and so on until you can no longer reach your goal or come close to it in the one minute's time.

Drill 3

Read as fast as you can for two minutes. Reread the same material in one and one-half minutes. Reread the same material in one minute. Reread the same material in one-half minute.

Drill 4

Read as fast as you can for one minute. Set a new goal for yourself by adding as many pages as you wish. Try to reach this new goal in one minute. Set another new goal. Repeat as many times as you wish.

Drill 5

Read as fast as you can for one minute. Choose a partner and tell your partner how many more pages you will read at the next try. Read for one minute, trying to reach your goal. Report to your partner how close you came to your goal. Repeat.

Drill 6 (warm-up)

Read as fast as you can for thirty seconds. Read the same amount of material in fifteen seconds.

Drill 7 (warm-up)

Read five pages. Reread, going faster. Reread, going still faster. Repeat.

Drill 8

Use textbook material. Preview an entire chapter. Mark off a short boldface section. Preview and recall. Read and recall. Postview and recall. Reread and recall.

Drill 9

Read as rapidly as you can for ten minutes in an easy junior high school book. Do this several days in a row.

Drill 10

In a book that you have read before, read very rapidly (drill rate), trying to follow the ideas. Try to finish the whole book.

Drill 11 (to lessen subvocalization)

In a story that you have read before, read and say *aloud* a condensed version of what is happening in the story.

Drill 12

In a story you have read before, read and at the same time repeat 1, 2, 3, over and over again *aloud.*

SUPPLEMENTARY BOOK LIST

Chapter 8:
> *Lilies of the Field*, Barrett (Popular Library), 19,800 words

Chapter 9:
> *The Old Man and the Sea*, Hemingway (Scribner's), 29,000 words

Chapter 10:
> *The Incredible Journey*, Burnford (Bantam), 33,500 words

Chapter 11:
> *Dr. Jekyll and Mr. Hyde*, Stevenson (Bantam) 33,000 words

Chapter 12:
> *The Call of the Wild*, London (Bantam), 25,000 words

Chapter 13:
> *What to Say When You Talk to Your Self*, Helmstetter (Pocket), 74,000 words

Chapter 14:
> *Fahrenheit 451*, Bradbury (Ballantine), 47,950 words

Chapter 16;
> *Body Language*, Fast (Pocket), 61,500 words

Chapter 18:
> *The Population Bomb*, Ehrlich (Ballantine), 79,550 words

ADDITIONAL READING REPORT:
Assignment #1

Name _____ Date _____

I. Choose a novel that you have read previously, or a simple one with large print. Read for fifteen minutes, three times a week, *going as fast as you can*, at a drill rate and using the latest hand movement. Figure your rate.

Title	**Rate**	**Time Spent**
_____	_____	_____
_____	_____	_____
_____	_____	_____

II. Read any two articles of your choice (1,200 words or more in length). Preview each article before reading. Use the latest hand movements. If your comprehension is very low, do *not* slow down, but instead read the article several times before answering the questions. Time your first reading; figure your rate; answer the following questions for each article.

   1. Title of article _____

      Name of magazine, book, etc. _____

      Date of publication _____ Number of words _____

     a. What is the main idea presented? (Answer in one or two short sentences.) _____

       _____

       _____

     b. List and describe briefly three important details.

       1. _____

         _____

       2. _____

         _____

       3. _____

         _____

     c. What is the author's conclusion? _____

       _____

       _____

     d. How would you evaluate your comprehension for this article (excellent, good, fair, poor, understood nothing)? _____

       _____

     e. Your rate _____

2. Title of article _____

   Name of magazine, book, etc. _____

   Date of publication _____ Number of words _____

   a. What is the main idea presented? (Answer in one or two short sentences.) _____

   _____

   _____

   b. List and describe briefly three important details.

      1. _____

         _____

      2. _____

         _____

      3. _____

         _____

   c. What is the author's conclusion? _____

      _____

      _____

   d. How would you evaluate your comprehension for this article (excellent, good, fair, poor, understood nothing)? _____

   e. Your rate _____

III. (Optional) Record anything you read by using this method.

Title	Time Spent
_____	_____
_____	_____
_____	_____
_____	_____
_____	_____
_____	_____
_____	_____
_____	_____

ADDITIONAL READING REPORT:
Assignment #2

Name _____ Date _____

I. Choose a novel that you have read previously, or a simple one with large print. Read for fifteen minutes, three times a week, *going as fast as you can,* at a drill rate and using the latest hand movement. Figure your drill rate.

Title	**Rate**	**Time Spent**
_____	_____	_____
_____	_____	_____
_____	_____	_____

II. Read any two articles of your choice (1,200 words or more in length). Preview each article before reading. Use the latest hand movements. If your comprehension is very low, do *not* slow down, but instead read the article several times before answering the questions. Time your first reading; figure your rate; answer the following questions for each article.

1. Title of article _____

   Name of magazine, book, etc. _____

   Date of publication _____ Number of words _____

   a. What is the main idea presented? (Answer in one or two short sentences.) _____

   _____

   _____

   b. List and describe briefly three important details.

   1. _____

   _____

   2. _____

   _____

   3. _____

   _____

   c. What is the author's conclusion? _____

   _____

   _____

   d. How would you evaluate your comprehension for this article (excellent, good, fair, poor, understood nothing)? _____

   _____

   e. Your rate _____

2. Title of article _____

   Name of magazine, book, etc. _____

   Date of publication _____ Number of words _____

   a. What is the main idea presented? (Answer in one or two short sentences.) _____   _____

   _____

   _____

   b. List and describe briefly three important details.

      1. _____

      _____

      2. _____

      _____

      3. _____

      _____

   c. What is the author's conclusion? _____

   _____

   _____

   d. How would you evaluate your comprehension for this article (excellent, good, fair, poor, understood nothing)? _____

   e. Your rate _____

III. (Optional) Record anything you read by using this method.

Title	**Time Spent**
_____	_____
_____	_____
_____	_____
_____	_____
_____	_____
_____	_____
_____	_____
_____	_____
_____	_____

ADDITIONAL READING REPORT:
Assignment #3

Name _____ Date _____

I. Choose a novel that you have read previously, or a simple one with large print. Read for fifteen minutes, three times a week, *going as fast as you can,* at a drill rate and using the latest hand movement. Figure your rate.

Title   **Rate**   **Time Spent**

_____   _____   _____

_____   _____   _____

_____   _____   _____

II. Read any two articles of your choice (1,200 words or more in length). Preview each article before reading. Use the latest hand movements. If your comprehension is very low, do *not* slow down, but instead read the article several times before answering the questions. Time your first reading; figure your rate; answer the following questions for each article.

1. Title of article _____

   Name of magazine, book, etc. _____

   Date of publication _____ Number of words _____

   a. What is the main idea presented? (Answer in one or two short sentences.) _____

   _____

   _____

   b. List and describe briefly three important details.

      1. _____

      _____

      2. _____

      _____

      3. _____

      _____

   c. What is the author's conclusion? _____

   _____

   _____

   d. How would you evaluate your comprehension for this article (excellent, good, fair, poor, understood nothing)? _____

   _____

   e. Your rate _____

2. Title of article _____

   Name of magazine, book, etc. _____

   Date of publication _____ Number of words _____

   a. What is the main idea presented? (Answer in one or two short sentences.) _____

   _____

   _____

   b. List and describe briefly three important details.

      1. _____

      _____

      2. _____

      _____

      3. _____

      _____

   c. What is the author's conclusion? _____

   _____

   _____

   d. How would you evaluate your comprehension for this article (excellent, good, fair, poor, understood nothing)? _____

   e. Your rate _____

III. (Optional) Record anything you read by using this method.

Title	**Time Spent**

ADDITIONAL READING REPORT:
Assignment #4

Name _____ Date _____

I. Choose a novel that you have read previously, or a simple one with large print. Read for fifteen minutes, three times a week, *going as fast as you can,* at a drill rate and using the latest hand movement. Figure your rate.

Title	Rate	Time Spent
_____	_____	_____
_____	_____	_____
_____	_____	_____

II. Read any two articles of your choice (1,200 words or more in length). Preview each article before reading. Use the latest hand movements. If your comprehension is very low, do *not* slow down, but instead read the article several times before answering the questions. Time your first reading; figure your rate; answer the questions below for each article.

1. Title of article _____

   Name of magazine, book, etc. _____

   Date of publication _____ Number of words _____

   a. What is the main idea presented? (Answer in one or two short sentences.) _____

   _____

   _____

   b. List and describe briefly three important details.

      1. _____

      _____

      2. _____

      _____

      3. _____

      _____

   c. What is the author's conclusion? _____

   _____

   _____

   d. How would you evaluate your comprehension for this article (excellent, good, fair, poor, understood nothing)? _____

   _____

   e. Your rate _____

2. Title of article _____

   Name of magazine, book, etc. _____

   Date of publication _____ Number of words _____

   a. What is the main idea presented? (Answer in one or two short sentences.) _____

      _____

      _____

   b. List and describe briefly three important details.

      1. _____

         _____

      2. _____

         _____

      3. _____

         _____

   c. What is the author's conclusion? _____

      _____

      _____

   d. How would you evaluate your comprehension for this article (excellent, good, fair, poor, understood nothing)? _____

   e. Your rate _____

III. (Optional) Record anything you read by using this method.

Title   Time Spent

_____   _____

_____   _____

_____   _____

_____   _____

_____   _____

_____   _____

_____   _____

_____   _____

_____   _____

ADDITIONAL READING REPORT:
Assignment #5

Name _____ Date _____

I. Choose a novel that you have read previously, or a simple one with large print. Read for fifteen minutes, three times a week, *going as fast as you can,* at a drill rate and using the latest hand movement. Figure your rate.

Title   Rate   Time Spent

_____   _____   _____

_____   _____   _____

_____   _____   _____

II. Read any two articles of your choice (1,200 words or more in length). Preview each article before reading. Use the latest hand movements. If your comprehension is very low, do *not* slow down, but instead read the article several times before answering the questions. Time your first reading; figure your rate; answer the questions below for each article.

1. Title of article _____

   Name of magazine, book, etc. _____

   Date of publication _____ Number of words _____

   a. What is the main idea presented? (Answer in one or two short sentences.) _____

   _____

   _____

   b. List and describe briefly three important details.

      1. _____

      _____

      2. _____

      _____

      3. _____

      _____

   c. What is the author's conclusion? _____

   _____

   _____

   d. How would you evaluate your comprehension for this article (excellent, good, fair, poor, understood nothing)? _____

   _____

   e. Your rate _____

2. Title of article _____

   Name of magazine, book, etc. _____

   Date of publication _____ Number of words _____

   a. What is the main idea presented? (Answer in one or two short sentences.) _____

   _____

   _____

   b. List and describe briefly three important details.

      1. _____

      _____

      2. _____

      _____

      3. _____

      _____

   c. What is the author's conclusion? _____

   _____

   _____

   d. How would you evaluate your comprehension for this article (excellent, good, fair, poor, understood nothing)? _____

   e. Your rate _____

III. (Optional) Record anything you read by using this method.

Title	Time Spent
_____	_____
_____	_____
_____	_____
_____	_____
_____	_____
_____	_____
_____	_____
_____	_____

ADVANCED ADDITIONAL READING REPORT: FICTION BOOK

Your name _____ Date _____

Title of book _____ Number of words _____

Author _____ Number of pages _____

1. *Survey.* Study front and back covers. Read contents, preface, and introduction.

   Book will be about _____

   Type of book (mystery, love story, adventure, science fiction): _____

2. *Preview-skim* the *entire book.* Rate _____

   Main characters: _____

   Setting: _____

3. *Do a good comprehension reading.* Rate _____

   Identify the problem or conflict around which the story revolves.

   _____

   _____

   Who is telling the story (point of view)? _____

4. *Postview.* Rate _____

   Name the major symbols and tell their meanings. _____

   _____

   _____

   What does the whole story illustrate (theme)? _____

   _____

   _____

5. *Comments.*

   Did you like the book? Why? Why not? _____

   _____

   _____

   Did you understand the book? _____

   Were you able to follow the ideas? _____

   Estimate your comprehension (excellent, good, fair, poor). _____

   _____

ADVANCED ADDITIONAL READING REPORT: NONFICTION BOOK

Your name _____ Date _____

Title of book _____ Number of words _____

Author _____ Number of pages _____

1. *Survey.* Study the front and back covers. Read the contents, preface, and introduction.

    Book will be about _____

    Type of book (history, science, etc.): _____

2. *Preview-skim* the *entire book*. Rate _____

    What is the author's main idea? _____

3. *Do a good comprehension reading.* Rate _____

    List the important ideas. _____

    _____

    List the important details. _____

    _____

4. *Postview.* Rate _____

    What is the author's conclusion? _____

    What is your conclusion? _____

5. *Comments.*

    Did you like the book? Why? Why not? _____

    _____

    Did you understand the book? _____

    Were you able to follow the ideas? _____

    Estimate your comprehension (excellent, good, fair, poor). _____

ADVANCED ADDITIONAL READING REPORT: ARTICLE

Your name _____ Date _____

Title of article _____ Number of pages _____

Author _____ Total word count _____

Magazine or book title _____

Date of publication _____

1. *Survey.* Read the title, first paragraph, subtitles, last paragraph.

   What is the article about? _____

2. *Preview-skim* the *entire article.* Rate _____

   What is the author's main idea? _____

3. Good comprehension reading. Rate _____

   List the important ideas. _____

   _____

   List important details that support the main idea. _____

   _____

4. *Postview.* Rate _____

   What is the author's conclusion? _____

   _____

   Do you agree or disagree with the author? Why? _____

   _____

5. *Comments.*

   Did you like the article? Why? Why not? _____

   _____

   Were you able to follow the ideas? _____

   Estimate your comprehension of this article (excellent, good, fair, poor, etc.). _____

ADVANCED ADDITIONAL READING REPORT: ARTICLE

Your name _____ Date _____

Title of article _____ Number of pages _____

Author _____ Total word count _____

Magazine or book title _____

Date of publication _____

1. *Survey.* Read the title, first paragraph, subtitles, last paragraph.

   What is the article about? _____

2. *Preview-skim* the *entire article.* Rate. _____

   State the main idea. _____

3. *Good comprehension reading.* Rate _____

   List other important ideas. _____

   _____

   Add details to main ideas. _____

   _____

4. *Postview.* Rate _____

   What is the author's conclusion? _____

   _____

   Do you agree or disagree with the author? Why? _____

   _____

5. *Comments.* Did you like the article? Why? Why not? _____

   _____

   Were you able to follow the ideas? _____

   How would you rate your comprehension of this article (excellent, good,

   fair, poor, etc.). _____

COURSE DATA SHEET #1

Name _____ Phone Number _____ Date _____

Pretest Rate _____ Pretest Score _____% Goal _____

Directions: *Record all drill rates and all rates and scores for all readings. Use the blank spaces to record titles of alternate works read for which you answered the general questions.*
Note: The longer titles are given in an abbreviated form.

Drill Rate	Date	Title of Reading	Rate	Score	Comments
		"The Anniversary"			
		"To Build a Fire"			
		"Dream Your Way to a Better You"			
		"The Lady, or the Tiger?"			
		"Going for the Goal"			
		"Superman—An Immigrant"			
		"Mysterious Powers of Body and Mind"			
		"The Tell-Tale Heart"			
		Lilies of the Field			
		"Visions to Boost Immunity"			
		"Adventure of the Speckled Band"			
		The Old Man and the Sea			
		"The Ph.D. Degree"			
		The Incredible Journey			
		Dr. Jekyll and Mr. Hyde			
		"Career Charisma"			
		"Money: Our Intimate Relationship"			
		The Call of the Wild			

Table for Converting Seconds to
Tenths of a Minute

Seconds	*Rounded Tenths*
5	.1
10	.2
15	.2
20	.3
25	.4
30	.5
35	.6
40	.7
45	.7
50	.8
55	.9
60	1.0

Note: If the number of seconds in
your time falls between any of the
numbers listed above, use the clos-
est listed number. For example, if
your number is 21, use the number
20.

COURSE DATA SHEET #2

Drill Rate	Date	Title of Reading	Preview rate	Preview score	Good rate	Comprehension score	Postview rate	Postview score	Comments
		"Robots and Beyond"							
		What to Say When You Talk to Your Self							
		"The Outcasts of Poker Flat"							
		Fahrenheit 451							
		"Social Themes"							
		"That Filing System Inside Your Head"							
		Body Language							
		"A Modest Proposal"							
		"Paul's Case"							
		"The Will to Win: How to Get It and Use It"							
		"You Know More Than You Think"							
		The Population Bomb							
		"The Dual Nature of Stress"							

Table for Converting Seconds to
Tenths of a Minute

Seconds	Rounded Tenths
5	.1
10	.2
15	.2
20	.3
25	.4
30	.5
35	.6
40	.7
45	.7
50	.8
55	.9
60	1.0

Note: If the number of seconds in
your time falls between any of the
numbers listed above, use the clos-
est listed number. For example, if
your number is 21, use the number
20.

Answer Keys

Pretest: "Getting Your Head Together"
1.d 2.c 3.a 4.c 5.d 6.d 7.a 8.b 9.c 10.a.

Chapter 2: "The Anniversary"
1.b 2.c 3.a 4.a 5.b 6.d 7.c 8.b 9.c 10.b.
"To Build a Fire"
1.a 2.b 3.d 4.a 5.b 6.a 7.b 8.d 9.d 10.b.

Chapter 3: "Dream Your Way to a Better You"
Preview Responses(p. 31):

The organizational pattern is a list of the states of dreaming and sublists of the purposes for each state.

The information you need to remember when you read this article is 1) the names of the states of dreaming and 2) the purposes for each state.
1.c 2.a 3.c 4.b 5.d 6.b 7.b 8.a 9.a 10.d.
Here is the completed outline you filled in on page 35.
States of dreaming:

1. Daydreaming
   Purposes
   1. Trying out situations
   2. Accepting social and moral values
   3. Dissipating aggressive feelings
   4. Developing the imagination
   5. Enriching the environment
2. "Twilight dreaming"
   Purposes
   1. Getting in touch with creative insights
   2. Eliminating mental blocks
   3. Learning new modes of behavior and information
3. Sleep dreaming
   Purposes
   1. Preserving efficiency of brain
   2. Keeping inner and outer realities separate
   3. Keeping us sane

Chapter 4: "The Lady, or the Tiger?"
1.c 2.b 3.d 4.a 5.a 6.c 7.a 8.c 9.a 10.c.
"Going for the Goal"
1.a 2.d 3.b 4.a 5.c 6.a 7.d 8.b 9.a 10.d.

Chapter 5: "Superman—An Immigrant Who Really Made It"
1.b 2.b 3.a 4.c 5.b 6.c 7.d 8.b 9.d 10.b.

Chapter 7: "The Mysterious Powers of Body and Mind"
1.c 2.b 3.a 4.c 5.a 6.d 7.b 8.c 9.a 10.b.
"The Tell-Tale Heart"
1.b 2.a 3.d 4.c 5.b 6.c 7.d 8.a 9.b 10.d.

Chapter 8: *Lilies of the Field*
1.c 2.a 3.a 4.c 5.b 6.c 7.c 8.a 9.b 10.d.

Chapter 9: "Visions to Boost Immunity"
1.b 2.c 3.a 4.d 5.a 6.b 7.d 8.a 9.b 10.c.
"The Adventure of the Speckled Band"
1.c 2.d 3.b 4.a 5.a 6.a 7.d 8.b 9.c 10.a.
The Old Man and the Sea
1.b 2.c 3.a 4.b 5.a 6.c 7.d 8.c 9.b 10.b.

Chapter 10: Skimming
Main Idea: Provides information on the Ph.D. Degree: what it is, how to get it, what jobs Ph.Ds can get, and the employment outlook.

Chapter 10: Scanning
Ph.D.: 55 times. Doctor of Philosophy: 2 times. Total: 57 times.
"The Ph.D. Degree: What It Is and Where It Takes You"
1.c 2.a 3.a 4.d 5.c 6.d 7.a 8.a 9.c 10.d.
The Incredible Journey
1.c 2.a 3.b 4.d 5.a 6.d 7.a 8.c 9.c 10.a.

Chapter 11: *Dr. Jekyll and Mr. Hyde*
1.b 2.c 3.d 4.d 5.a 6.a 7.c 8.d 9.a 10.b.

Chapter 12: "Career Charisma"
1.b 2.d 3.a 4.c 5.b 6.b. 7.c 8.d 9.a 10.c.
"Money: Our Most Intimate Relationship"
1.d 2.b 3.a 4.a 5.c 6.a 7.b 8.d 9.c 10.d.
The Call of the Wild
1.d 2.c 3.c 4.a 5.c 6.a 7.d 8.b 9.c 10.c.

Chapter 13: "Robots and Beyond: The Age of Intelligent Machines"
Preview: 1.d 2.c 3.b 4.a 5.b.
Good Comprehension:
1.a 2.d 3.d 4.b 5.b 6.c 7.a 8.a 9.c 10.c.
Postview: 1.c 2.d 3.b 4.a 5.c.
What to Say When You Talk to Your Self
Preview: 1.c 2.a 3.b 4.d 5.a.
Good Comprehension:
1.b 2.c 3.b 4.d 5.d 6.b 7.c 8.c 9.b 10.d.
Postview: 1.b 2.a 3.d 4.d 5.a.

Chapter 14: "The Outcasts of Poker Flat"
Preview: 1.d 2.b 3.c 4.c 5.a.
Good Comprehension:
1.b 2.a 3.d 4.b 5.a 6.c 7.b 8.d 9.a 10.c.
Postview: 1.b 2.c 3.a 4.d 5.a.
Fahrenheit 451
Preview:
1.c 2.b 3.a 4.b 5.d 6.a 7.a 8.a 9.d 10.d.

Good Comprehension:
1.c 2.a 3.c 4.b 5.d 6.b 7.b 8.a 9.a 10.b
11.a 12.d 13.d 14.b 15.a 16.d 17.c 18.a
19.b 20.b.
Postview: 1.c 2.a 3.d 4.c 5.a.

Chapter 15: "Social Themes"
Preview: 1.d 2.c 3.a 4.d 5.a.
Good Comprehension:
1.a 2.c 3.a 4.b 5.d 6.b 7.c 8.d 9.c 10.b.

Chapter 16: "That Filing System Inside Your Head"
Vocabulary Test:
1.h 2.d 3.o 4.j 5.n 6.a 7.k 8.e 9.l
10.f 11.b 12.m 13.g 14.c.
Preview: 1.c 2.a 3.b 4.a 5.b.
Good Comprehension:
1.d 2.a 3.c 4.b 5.a 6.b 7.a 8.d 9.c 10.b.
Body Language
Preview:
1.b 2.c 3.d 4.a 5.a 6.b 7.b 8.a 9.c 10.b.
Good Comprehension:
1.b 2.a 3.b 4.d 5.c 6.d 7.a 8.b 9.c
10.a 11.a 12.b 13.a 14.b 15.b 16.c 17.a
18.b 19.a 20.c.
Postview: 1.b 2.b 3.a 4.c 5.b.

Chapter 17: "A Modest Proposal"
Preview: 1.b 2.a 3.d 4.a 5.c.
Good Comprehension:
1.d 2.b 3.c 4.a 5.b 6.a 7.a 8.d 9.b 10.b.
Recall/Think:
1. Jonathan Swift, an Irishman, proposes a fair, cheap, and easy solution to the problem of what to do with the overwhelming number of poor children for whom their parents cannot provide. He proposes to reserve one-fourth of the poor children for breeding and to sell the rest for food and the production of leather goods. This solution would provide money for the parents, delicacies for the rich, cost the government nothing, relieve everyone of bothersome beggars, and provide additional benefits such as preventing abortions and encouraging marriage.
2. The facts are:
   1)Ireland has a serious problem; there are too many starving people.
   2) There are 120,000 children born annually to parents too poor to provide them with the necessities of life.
   3) There are no jobs for the poor.
   4) The author is not satisfied with any current means being used to handle these problems.

3. The author actually deplores the way the poor are being treated. He wants changes made that would create jobs, tax the rich, improve the economy, show compassion and mercy toward the unfortunate poor, and most of all would treat the poor as worthwhile humans instead of as objectionable animals.

Postview: 1.a 2.c 3.d 4.b 5.d.

"Paul's Case"
Preview: 1.d 2.a 3.a 4.c 5.b.
Good Comprehension:
1.b 2.c 3.a 4.a 5.d 6.c 7.a 8.d 9.c 10.a.
Recall/Think:
1. Paul's characteristics:
Misbehaves in school; doesn't like to read
Strange eyes: have hysterical brilliance, used in theatrical way
Lies; tells incredible stories
Impertinent, defiant, haunted, nervous, restless, fearful
False exterior; a thief
Teases others; feels superior to ordinary people
Daydreams frequently; vivid imagination
Hates reality; acts out fantasies; leads a double life
Likes artificiality; materialistic; hates to economize
2. Possible endings: Paul could have
a. escaped to a more distant land and never have been found (But his money would have run out.)
b. continued his dual life between reality and fantasy (But the case study would not have been complete.)
c. totally retreated into fantasy without going anywhere (This would have lost the excitement of the climax and the ironic ending of his becoming one with the "immense design of things" when, in life, he had always felt very separated from others.)
Given Paul's temperament, no happy ending is possible.
3. If Paul had narrated the story:
    The story is a case study of a character who rejects reality and embraces fantasy. It is shown as a progression from rejection of reality to an actual escape from it into fantasy and finally death. Had Paul been the narrator, the action of the story would not have changed, but the experience of the reader would have changed to seeing the world through Paul's eyes instead of studying Paul from the outside.
4. Reference to plays, the past, places, pageants, and earlier times:
    London, Naples, Egypt, the Adriatic Sea, Algeria, Newark, Pittsburgh, Jersey City, Washington, New York, San Francisco, Pennsylvania, the Mediterranean Sea, Monte Carlo, Fifth Avenue, Paris, Venice, Carnegie Hall, a concert hall.
    Paul's clothes seen as costumes; the theater as a reception; whistling from *Faust* (a play), *Rigoletto*, and *Martha* (operas); "Queen of Romance;" "a fairy world of Christmas Pantomime;" Cordelia Street (Cordelia is a Shakespearean character); "legends of iron kings;" the park as a "stage winterpiece," "magician's wand," "dress the part," and "the play was over." "Bowed as in earlier times;" "thrown down the gauntlet."
Postview:
1.b 2.c 3.b 4.a 5.c.

Chapter 18: "The Will to Win: How to Get It and Use It"
Preview: 1.b 2.d 3.a 4.b 5.b.
Good Comprehension:
1.a 2.b 3.c 4.c 5.c 6.c 7.d 8.a,b,c,d 9.c 10.b.
"You Know More Than You Think"
Preview: 1.c 2.c 3.b 4.a 5.d.
Good Comprehension:
1.b 2.b 3.a 4.d 5.b 6.b 7.d 8.c 9.c 10.a.
Postview: 1.b 2.c 3.a 4.d 5.c.
The Population Bomb
Preview: 1.b 2.d 3.b 4.c 5.a.
Good Comprehension:
1.c 2.a 3.a 4.c 5.d 6.b 7.b 8.b 9.c
10.b 11.d 12.d 13.a 14.c 15.a 16.a 17.b
18.a 19.c 20.b.
Postview: 1.c 2.a 3.d 4.d 5.a.

Posttest: "The Dual Nature of Stress"
1.b 2.b 3.c 4.d 5.e 6.a 7.b 8.c 9.b 10.c.

Suggested Study Plans

CONDENSED STUDY PLAN: 10 WEEKS, 3 HOURS PER WEEK

	First Session	*Second Session*

Week 1	Introduction
	    Pretest, p. 4
		Chapter 1: The Start Toward a New Reading Method, p.9
		    Drill rate

Week 2	Chapter 2:More Rapid-Reading Techniques,p.13
	    "The Anniversary,"p.17
	    "To Build a Fire,"p.20
	    Drill rate
		Chapter 3: Using Rapid-Reading skills on Informational Material, p.29
		    "Dream Your Way to a Better You,"p.32
		    Additional Reading Assignment

Week 3	Chapter 4: A New Way of Thinking and Focus, p.38
	    "The Lady, Or the Tiger?"p.42
	    "Going for the Goal,"p.48
	    Drill rate
		Chapter 5: New Reading Patterns, p.53
		    "Superman—An Immigrant Who Really Made It," p.56

Week 4	Chapter 7: Flexibility, p.66
	Chapter 12: Finding Your Level of Best Comprehension, p.118
	    "Money: Our Most Intimate Relationship," p.127
	    "Career Charisma,"p.120
	    Drill rate
		Chapter 6: Using Rapid-Reading Skills on the Newspaper, p.62
		    "The Mysterious Powers of Body and Mind,"p.69

Week 5	Chapter 9: Using Key Words, p.81
	    "The Adventure of the Speckled Band," p.87
	    "Visions to Boost Immunity,"p.83
	    Drill rate
		Chapter 8: Speed Reading an Easy Novel, p.76
		The Old Man and the Sea, p.93

Week 6	Chapter 10: Skimming, Scanning, and Marking a Text, p.96
	   "The Ph.D. Degree: What It Is and Where It Takes You," p.99
	   Drill rate
		Chapter 11: Speed Research Reading, p.109

Week 7	Chapter 13: The Basic Speed-Study Method, p.135
	   "Robots and Beyond: The Age of Intelligent Machines," p.140
	   Drill rate
		Chapter 14: Speed Studying Fiction, p.152
		   "The Outcasts of Poker Flat," p.156

Week 8	Chapter 15: Studying History, p.169
	   "Social Themes," p.171
	   Drill rate
		Chapter 16: Studying a Text with a Specialized Vocabulary, p.179
		   "That Filing System Inside Your Head," p.181

Week 9	Chapter 17: Critical Reading, p.199
	   "A Modest Proposal," p.202
	   Drill rate
		Chapter 18: Choosing the Appropriate Reading Method and Reading Footnotes, p.219
		   "The Will to Win, How to Get It and Use It," p.222
		   "You Know More Than You Think," p.227

Week 10	Chapter 19: Reading for Enjoyment, p.240
	   A book of your choice
		Conclusion, p.245
		   Posttest, p.245

STUDY PLAN: 18 WEEKS, 3 HOURS PER WEEK

	First Session	*Second Session*
Week 1	Introduction	Pretest, p.4

Week 2	Chapter 1: The Start Toward a New Reading Method, p.9
	    Drill rate
		Chapter 2: More Rapid Reading Techniques, p.13
		    "The Anniversary," p.17
		    "To Build a Fire," p.20

Week 3	Chapter 3: "Using Rapid-Reading Skills on Informational Material," p.29
	    "Dream Your Way to a Better You," p.32
	    Drill rate
	    Additional Reading
	    Assignment
		Chapter 4: "A New Way of Thinking and a Shift in Focus," p.38
		    "The Lady, or the Tiger," p.42
		    "Going for the Goal," p.48

Week 4	Chapter 5: New Reading Patterns, p.53
	    "Superman—An Immigrant Who Really Made It," p.56
	    Drill rate
		Chapter 6: Using Rapid-Reading Skills on the Newspaper, p.62

Week 5	Chapter 7: Flexibility, p.66
	    "The Mysterious Powers of Body and Mind," p.69
	    "The Tell-Tale Heart," p.72
	    Drill rate
		Chapter 8: Speed Reading an Easy Novel, p.76
		Lilies of the Field, p.78 or another general novel, p.79

Week 6	Chapter 9: Using Key Words, p.81
	    "Visions to Boost Immunity," p.83
	    "The Adventure of the Speckled Band," p.87
	    Drill rate
		The Old Man and the Sea, p.93, or another general novel, p.95

Week 7	Chapter 10: Skimming,Scanning, and Marking a Text, p.96
	  "The Ph.D. Degree: What It Is and Where It
	    Takes You," p.99
	  Drill rate
		The Incredible Journey, p.106, or another general novel,p.107

Week 8	Chapter 11: Speed Research Reading, p.109 Drill rate	*Dr. Jekyll and Mr. Hyde,* p.115, or another general novel, p.116

Week 9	Chapter 12: Finding Your Level of Best Comprehension, p.118
	  "Career Charisma,"p.120
	  "Money: Our Most Intimate Relationship," p.127
	  Drill rate
		The Call of the Wild, p. 132, or another general novel,p.134

Week 10	Chapter 13: The Basic Speed-Study Method, p.135
	  "Robots and Beyond: The Age of Intelligent Machines,"p.140
	  Drill rate
	  Additional Reading Assignment
		*What to Say When You Talk to Your Self,*p.147, or another general nonfiction book, p.149, survey and preview

Week 11	*What To Say When You Talk to Your Self,*p.147, or another general nonfiction book, p. 150, good comprehension, and postview	Chapter 14:Speed Studying Fiction, p.152
		  "The Outcasts of Poker Flat," p.156
		  Drill rate

Week 12	*Fahrenheit 451,* p. 162, or another general novel,p.167, survey and preview	*Fahrenheit 451,* p.164, or another general novel, p.167, good comprehension and postview.

Week 13	Chapter 15: Studying History, p.169
	  "Social Themes,"p.171
	  Drill rate
		Chapter 16: Studying a Text with a Specialized Vocabulary, p.179
		  "That Filing System Inside Your Head,"p.181
		  Drill rate

Week 14	*Body Language,*p.193, or another book with specialized vocabulary,p.191, survey, preview, vocabulary	*Body Language,*p.194, or another book with a specialized vocabulary, p. 197, good comprehension and postview

Week 15	Chapter 17: Critical Reading, p.199
	  "A Modest Proposal,"p.202
	  Drill rate
		"Paul's Case," p.208

Week 16	Chapter 18: Choosing the Appropriate Reading Method, and Reading Footnotes, p.219
	  "The Will to Win: How to Get It and Use It"
	    p.222
	  "You Know More Than You Think,"p.227
	  Drill rate
		The Population Bomb, p.234 or another general book(fiction or nonfiction), p.238

Week 17	*The Population Bomb,* p.234 or another general book,p.238	Chapter 19: Reading for Enjoyment, p.240 A book of your choice
Week 18	Conclusion, p. 245 Review	Posttest, p. 245